Before the End of the Age
Signs of the Coming Chastisement

Paul F. Caranci

Paul F. Caranci

To Karen:
Though we may be headed for some difficult
times we know with prayer, fasting and penance we
can survive until Jesus comes again.

Paul

Publisher's Cataloging-In-Publication Data
(Prepared by The Donohue Group, Inc.)

Names: Caranci, Paul F., author.
Title: Before the end of the Age : signs of the coming chastise-
    ment / Paul F. Caranci.
Description: First Stillwater River Publications edition. | Paw-
    tucket, RI, USA : Stillwater River Publications, [2020]
Identifiers: ISBN 9781952521652
Subjects: LCSH: End of the world. | Prophecy--Christianity. |
    Natural disasters--Religious aspects--Christianity. | God
    (Christianity)--Will. | Repentance--Christianity.
Classification: LCC BT877 .C37 2020 | DDC 236.9--dc23

About the Cover

The cover art is taken from a triptych painting called The Last Judgment painted by sixteenth century artist Hieronymus Bosch. While only the interior middle panel is reflected on the cover, the full artwork has five panels. The two outside panels depict St. Bavo on the left and St. James on the right. Each painted in grisaille (tones of gray) meant to mimic the exterior stones of a church.

As these panels are opened, a vivid colorful story unfolds on three panels. The top of the left panel, shown on the back cover, depicts a majestic God in heaven. There are hundreds of angels engaged in battle in a scene depicting the fall of the rebel angels, a rebellion led by Lucifer and ending with the rebel's expulsion from heaven only to be forced to spend eternity in hell. The panel also reflects scenes from the creation of Eve and the temptation of Adam and Eve. The entire panel draws a parallel between the devil's defiance of God and expulsion from heaven to Adam and Eve's defiance of God and their expulsion from paradise.

The bottom of the panel on the right shows Lucifer sitting in a type of mock judgment of the souls that have been found to have been sinful. He is meting out to them the terrible punishments according to their crimes in life. In the doorway behind him are images of toads, which are figures often used as implements of torture in images of the Last Judgment. Above that, on the roof, are all the damned in hell, wailing, crying and flailing their arms as they find they will, for all of eternity, be in this place of fire, brimstone, and torture.

The central panel of this triptych, the largest of the panels and the one depicted on the front cover, shows Christ functioning as judge. There are angels with long golden trumpets who are announcing the end of time. Below it, taking up most of the central panel, is an image of the edges of hell. This scene is combined with images of the seven deadly sins, the sins that cause mankind to spend eternity in hell. The bottom two-thirds is filled with torture and the terrible crimes that people inflict upon each other, but here are enacted by the devils and composite creatures.

The punishments depicted in the painting are for specific crimes, and the punishments are related to the crimes. On the left side is something that resembles an inn. On the roof, a figure, who seems remarkably oblivious to everything that is happening, walks as if on a fashion runway, but surrounding and biting her is a hideous insect. She is led by an equally hideous dragon to a type of hellish brothel. They are accompanied by two demons, one playing the lute and the other following close behind blowing a horn which appears as an extension of the demon's nose. Here, Bosch uses music as one vehicle for sinfulness, an indication of the evils of indulgence in pleasure.

Below the representation of pride, or vanity, is the sin of gluttony. Here is depicted an overweight man who is having liquid forcibly poured down his throat as he is restrained by devils. A closer look above the barrel shows that the liquid being poured into the barrel via a siphon, and subsequently being forced into the man, is actually the excrement of another devil, whose backside is seen through the bars of a window. Below that is a large demonic fish devouring another; a reference to a northern proverb that the big fish eats the smaller fish, showing that people take advantage of those smaller, weaker, and less powerful.

To the right of that, one can see inside the inn where there are a series of hanging figures. Below that, a large cauldron with a series of figures that seem to be boiling. It is understood that they are being boiled in molten metal that had been melted from their money. This represents the sin of avarice and greed.

There are endless representations of pain and suffering in the painting. There are men being roasted or fried by demonic frogs. In one case, there is a frying pan in which lay pieces of a human body. This frog-like figure appears ready to crack two of her eggs into the pan as well, making a type of human omelet.

The implied theme throughout the painting is the everydayness of the devilish figures who torture human beings. They are simply going through their day; that includes cooking and torturing, as though it were normal everyday activity. It is a reminder that hell is for eternity.

In the middle of the central panel is the sin of anger, represented by three knights who are particularly awful. The knight in the middle wears a helmet with a severed and blindfolded head atop. Below that are images of corruption, and scattered throughout the foreground are images of bodies that have been mutilated. They have been shot with arrows, cut, wounded, and devoured in various ways.

Taken in its entirety, the triptych is an apocalyptic scene of the horrors of hell that encourages one to live a virtuous life meant to avoid the eternity of hell.

Top: The outer shutters of the triptych; Bottom: The three interior panels.

Table of Contents

Part IV – Hell is Real, and it Matters!

Part V – What Does It All Mean?

Dedication

This book is dedicated, first and foremost, to my family: My father and mother who began my faith formation back in the days of my earliest memory and continued their lessons in devotion up to the moment of their passing; my wife Margie with whom I have had the opportunity and pleasure to grow in the faith as a family for over fifty-two years, the bedrock who keeps me grounded and, to the extent that her supplications have taken hold, humble; my children Heather and Matthew who, like their parents, have not yet attained the fulfillment of their faith, but whose characters have strengthened exponentially; my grandchildren, Matthew Jr., Jacob, Vincent, and Casey, whose obedience to the precepts of the faith inspires an ongoing exercise of prayer and patience, an exercise that may well exceed all expectation; and my sister Linda, brother-in-law Dennis, and their family who, it seems, think my enthusiasm for the faith might sometimes be a bit over the edge, but who nevertheless provide encouragement and quiet example.

This work is also dedicated to Doris Brissette, who shares my understanding of the significance of the events described herein. She, along with Nick Gizzarelli and John Marcello, to whom this book is also dedicated, provide recurrent inspiration by their serene faith example. Finally, to Fr. Joseph Brice who speaks to me, it seems, even in his silence. Though I may not readily admit it to him, I do listen!

Acknowledgments

Writing this book during the Covid-19 pandemic that kept many libraries, museums, and other research facilities closed while much of my research was taking place, certainly created a challenge, but didn't dampen my enthusiasm. In fact, the shelter-in-place orders of the early part of 2020 helped keep me focused even if the availability of research material was sometimes difficult to obtain. I was forced to rely on internet material sources to a greater extent than I am normally accustomed. Consequently, I want to acknowledge former Vice President Al Gore for inventing the internet.

I would also like to acknowledge Doris Brissette, who is continually willing to lend a hand regardless of the project. In this case she provided some very helpful research material from which I was able to formulate key chapters of the book.

Finally, a salute to Steve and Dawn Porter of Stillwater River Publications, who, despite my procrastination, always manage to put the published work in my hands at the most opportune time.

While still more people gathered in the crowd, Jesus said to them,
"This generation is an evil generation;
it seeks a sign, but no sign will be given it,
except the sign of Jonah.
Just as Jonah became a sign to the Ninevites,
so will the Son of Man be to this generation.
At the judgment
the queen of the south will rise with the men of this generation
and she will condemn them,
because she came from the ends of the earth
to hear the wisdom of Solomon,
and there is something greater than Solomon here.
At the judgment the men of Nineveh will arise with this generation
and condemn it,
because at the preaching of Jonah they repented,
and there is something greater than Jonah here."

~Luke 11:29-32

Preface

Thomas M. Bolin, a professor of Theology and Religious Studies at St. Norbert College, who has published extensively on the biblical books of Jonah and Ecclesiastes, recounts the tagline from *Dragnet*, a popular television crime drama of the 1960s. Each episode of the show began with the words, *"This is the city."* The program took place on the streets of Los Angeles, California, a place that *"embodied the best and worst of human life: the mundane, dramatic, and tragic."[1]* Bolin notes that it has always been this way because cities are *"morally ambivalent places that hold out the promise of excitement and the threat of danger, at once sites of corruption and of great human achievements."[2]*

Former U.S. Congressman, Thomas P. "Tip" O'Neill, who served over thirty-four years in the House of Representative, ten of them as Speaker of the House, once quipped, *"all politics is local."* The same, it seems, can be said of moral ambivalence. It begins with a single person and is spread like a cancer, throughout an entire village, city, state, and eventually the world. When the subject is a corrupt political practice, the offender, if caught, may be prosecuted and punished with imprisonment or death. When, however, the subject of corruption is embedded in the moral fiber of a person or society who is in violation of the laws of God, the chastisement may be more universal in nature and of much greater consequence. War, sickness, plagues, and natural disasters are all within God's control and all have been used by Him to punish morally bankrupt societies throughout time.

While the historical aspects of some of the stories of the Bible have been well documented and therefore verified in the writings of contemporary historians, the veracity of other stories is simply left to faith. Webster's Dictionary defines faith as *"a firm belief in something for which there is no proof."[3]* By definition then, faith-based occurrences can't be explained by science, at least not based on the scientific advances of today. However, over the course of time, with modern advances in science coupled with new archeological discoveries, we find that many of the Biblical stories that were once accepted as a simple matter of faith actually have a historic and/or scientific foundation. Moreover, post-biblical stories, such as the apparitions of Our Lady of Guadalupe to Juan Diego in 1531, once thought to be something accepted only as a matter of faith, have become verifiable through scientific discovery.

Throughout the pages of the Bible, God warns his people to turn away from sin in favor of repentance, prayer, and sacrifice. The failure of man to forgo their acts of moral depravity results in radical displays of God's anger in the form of small or great chastisements. Several times throughout history, such events have been witnessed by humankind. Some of the earliest examples, stories taken from the Pentateuch, are taken as a matter of faith, even though some of the stories are verified through historic writings. For some others, more recent scientific and archeological discoveries lend some credence to the stories. Regardless of the enormity of proof offered, however, there are those in modern society who still refuse to believe.

History shows that man has had several warnings of a great chastisement that is coming to earth. Prophets of old, as well as modern-day mystics and visionaries, have given very specific warnings of a terrible punishment to come. They have identified precursors to that chastisement and those signs are all around us today. Refusing to heed the warnings, or to recognize the signs for what they are, in no way mitigates the reality of what is to come.

It is said that for a person of faith, no miracle is needed, while for those of no faith, no miracle is believed. To this latter point, while this book may be more meaningful to those of great faith, it has a far greater relevance to those of little to no faith. The contents of this book should serve as a warning to all of mankind. While some may choose to not read it, and others to read but ignore the message, the wise will heed the warning and prepare.

Foreword

In 1976 the forty-first International Eucharistic Congress was convened in the City of Brotherly Love: Philadelphia, Pennsylvania. The history of the Eucharistic Congress dates to 1881 when the first Congress, a one-day event, was held in Lille, France and was attended by some eight hundred people. The Philadelphia Congress, which coincided with the two hundredth anniversary of the signing of the United States Declaration of Independence from England, lasted for a week and drew over 1.5 million people, including forty-four cardinals and four hundred seventeen bishops from around the world.

Cardinal Karol Wojtyla, later known as Pope John Paul II, rocked the conference with a homily that included this prophetic pronouncement:

> *"We are now standing in the face of the greatest historical confrontation humanity has ever experienced. I do not think that the wide circle of the American Society, or the whole wide circle of the Christian Community realize this fully. We are now facing the final confrontation between the Church and the anti-church, between the gospel and the anti-gospel, between Christ and the Antichrist. The confrontation lies within the plans of Divine Providence. It is, therefore, in God's Plan, and it must be a trial which the Church must take up, and face courageously."[4]*

The full dimension of this statement has gone unrealized even to this day. Pope John Paul II was making a frantic appeal to the faithful and to the world because an anti-church requires an earthly leader, and that leader may well be the Antichrist himself. This futuristic analysis was supported by Archbishop Carlo Maria Vigano who called Wojtyla's words *"profoundly Prophetic,"[5]* and by Blessed Bishop Fulton J. Sheen, who affirmed:

> *"There will be a Mystical Body of the Antichrist, which will resemble in all its externals the Mystical Body of Christ."[6]*

The 1976 thinking of Pope Saint John Paul II regarding the evils of the twentieth century is not a unique viewpoint in history, though it is now almost a half century old. In 2015, the Most Reverend Thomas J.

Olmsted, Bishop of Phoenix, penned a series for the Knights of Columbus called *The Veritas Series: Proclaiming the Faith in the Third Millennium*. The series is an exhortation to men of the Knights to engage in the battle that rages around everyone. In the book, Bishop Olmsted wrote:

> *The world is under attack by Satan, as our Lord said it would be (1 Peter 5:8-14). This battle is occurring in the Church herself, and the devastation is all too evident. Since AD 2000, 14 million Catholics have left the faith, parish religious education of children has dropped by 24%, Catholic school attendance has dropped by 19%, infant baptism has dropped by 28%, adult baptism has dropped by 31%, and sacramental Catholic marriages have dropped by 41%. This is a serious breach, a gaping hole in Christ's battle lines...The losses are staggering.*[7]

A similar warning was given to three young Portuguese shepherd children in 1917 by Our Lady of Fatima. The Blessed Virgin presented the children with a secret prophetic vision in which the Church was attacked, its leaders killed, and a destructive government force known as Communism was spread throughout the world. The Third Secret of Fatima, as the vision has come to be known, was revealed to the Pope in 1960 and to the world, at least in part, sometime later.

During a visit to Fulda, Germany in 1980, Pope John Paul II was asked how things were going with the Church relative to the Third Secret of Fatima. The Pope replied,

> *"We must prepare ourselves for the great trials in the near future. Yes, they may even require giving our lives, and total dedication to Christ and for Christ! It can be softened by your and our prayer, but it cannot be averted. Only in this way can the true renewal of the Church arrive. How often has the renewal of the Church been born from blood. It will not be any different this time. Let us be strong and let us prepare and trust in Christ and His Holy Mother. Let us pray the Rosary very much and often."*[8]

A direct reference to the Third Secret of Fatima and the trials referenced by Pope John Paul II can also be found in the Catechism of the Catholic Church.

> *"Before Christ's second coming the Church must pass through a final trial that will shake the faith of many believers. The persecution that accompanies her pilgrimage on earth will unveil the*

mystery of iniquity in the form of a religious deception offering men an apparent solution to their problems at the price of apostasy (a falling away from the faith) *from the Truth. The supreme religious deception is that of the Antichrist, a pseudo-messianism by which man glorifies himself in the place of God and his Messiah who has come in the flesh.*

The Antichrist's deception already begins to take shape in the world every time the claim is made to realize within history that messianic hope that can only be realized beyond history through the eschatological judgment. The Church has rejected even modified forms of this falsification of the kingdom to come under the name of millenarianism, especially the 'intrinsically perverse' political form of a secular messianism.

The Church will enter the glory of the kingdom only through this final Passover, when she will follow her Lord in his death and Resurrection. The kingdom will be fulfilled, then, not by a historic triumph of the Church through a progressive ascendancy, but only by God's victory over the final unleashing of evil, which will cause his bride to come down from heaven. God's triumph over the revolt of evil will take the form of the Last Judgment after the final cosmic upheaval of this passing world."[9]

The words of Pope John Paul II, underwritten by the Catechism of the Catholic Church, are ominous indeed, but to what trials does the holy pontiff refer, and why can they not be avoided? For centuries, saints, venerables, blesseds, monks, priests, nuns, and other holy people have prophesied about a great chastisement to be sent by God in retribution for the many sins of mankind. The punishment will be preceded by great signs. Many of those signs are unfolding today. They are a last call to prayer and repentance as the only means of delaying God's correction. Survival itself depends on our ability to recognize the signs and to take the prescribed measures. But what are the signs and how can we recognize them? And once we do, what do we need to do to prepare for, and survive, the Great Chastisement?

Introduction

The Apocalypse. For centuries, people have had a fascination with the last days. The end of the age has been the subject of numerous books, movies, discussions, and debates. Many have tried, without success, to imagine what the end will be like. Now, based upon extensive research into both public and private prophesy, a relatively detailed story can be told of those last days.

Beginning in the mid-nineteenth century and continuing throughout the twentieth century, there will *"be an almost total corruption of customs within the Catholic Church and Satan would rule almost completely by means of the Masonic sects. In the Church the Sacraments will be profaned and abused, and the light of Faith would be almost completely extinguished in souls. Truly religious souls would be reduced to a small number and many [religious] vocations would perish. Great impurity would reign, and people would be without any care for spiritual matters."*[10]

At some point in the twenty-first century, civil wars will envelop Western Europe. Western democracies will begin to crumble as Arab forces, with the help of the Russian military, will invade Portugal, Spain, France, Belgium, the Netherlands, the United Kingdom, Ireland, Luxembourg, Liechtenstein, Monaco, Vatican City, Italy, Switzerland, Germany, Greece, and Austria. The United States will engage China and virtually the entire world will be engulfed in war. Christians will be persecuted, churches will be closed, and the Pope will be forced from Rome. He will die while in exile and the Catholic Church will fall into complete disarray. An anti-pope will be installed, taking up residence at the Vatican, and the Catholic Church will be left without a true leader. Communism will take hold throughout Western Europe and will appear to be victorious. The followers of Muhammad, the prophet of Islam, will invade all of Europe and will be responsible for inestimable atrocities.

Christians living in the various nations of North and South America, however, will be unified in their support of an unexpected leader, a great prince who has served as an officer in the army and who is of a royal bloodline. Despite a great deal of determination and virtuous intentions, it will appear that their efforts will bear no fruit, but eventually, the Christian leader from the West will develop his army and soundly defeat the Germano-Russian Army. He will accumulate victory upon victory until Communism falls everywhere. The Muslims will be deposed as the war is carried to Africa and the Middle East, where the Arabs are crushed in battle. Around this time, the United States will send troops to Western Europe.

While this is happening, and afterward, earth will experience a significant increase in scope, intensity, and frequency of natural disasters. These will bring about droughts, floods, famines, earthquakes, and other calamities around the globe. At around the same time, two things will happen almost simultaneously. First, a red cross will appear in the sky. It will be visible the world over. Second, a comet will enter earth's atmosphere on a collision course with the planet. It will crash to earth or pass by at so close a distance that it will cause mountains to split open. Tsunamis will wash over low lying lands and fiery stones will fall from the sky. A poisonous gas will spread through the atmosphere and three days of darkness will cover the entire earth for seventy-two hours. The cold will be intense. During these days of darkness, people must remain in their homes and cover all their locked windows carefully. Reminiscent of a scene from the Passover described in the Book of Exodus, all the doors and windows must remain locked, and everyone must be vigilant about not leaving the house or even looking outside, as God does not want His creation to witness His wrath. Those who disobey will be struck down instantly.

During the darkness, electricity and batteries will be ineffective, and the only source of light will be from holy candles blessed on Candlemas and possibly from blessed religious statues. People should have on hand water and food sufficient for three days. The gates of hell will be opened, and all the demons will freely roam the earth, searching for souls to ensnare. Demons will try to trick their way into the home by disguising their voices as those of loved ones, but make no mistake, the voice will belong to Satan and his minions who will be standing outside the door. Everyone in the home must be completely engaged in prayer during these three days. Praying the Rosary and reading from the Bible or other religious books will become the only means of survival during these days. People will tremble with fear at the events taking place outside and many, even the righteous, will die of fright. The righteous who die in this way will be considered martyrs and will go directly to heaven. Hurricanes of fire will pour forth from clouds. Violent thunderbolts and prolonged earthquakes will occur, and an uninterrupted rain of fire will fall from the sky. Only through hoping in Jesus, believing in His words, and seeking His Mother's protection, will anyone be saved from God's just wrath.

Following these days, people will emerge from their homes to find between one third and three quarters of the world's population dead. At that time, the devastation, death, and loss of virtually everything of former significance will cause the living to envy the dead, but this sorrow will be short lived.

With a greatly reduced population, the people of the world will begin to establish new governments and religious structure will be restored. A new Pope, one showing great firmness, will be elected in Rome. He will restore all the former disciplines to the Catholic Church. All the nations of Western Europe will unite in support of the great Christian Prince, a Great Monarch, chosen by God, to lead the new Roman Empire. The Great Monarch and the Pope will work together harmoniously, and the triumph of the Catholic Church will be universal. The former Communist nations of Russia and China will convert to Catholicism as will the Muslims. All non-Catholics, in fact, will convert. This new period of complete peace and unprecedented prosperity throughout the world will also last only a short time, however, before mankind is again seduced by the power of Satan. At that point, the Antichrist will arise, and this will be followed in short-order by the Second Coming of Christ, the resurrection of the dead and the final judgment of God.

While these events sound like something out of a science fiction movie, God's chastisement is not without precedent in history. Part one of this book will review some of the more significant historical chastisements brought about by the hand of God.

Part I

Chastisements of the Bible

Chapter 1

The First Chastisement
The Story of Adam and Eve

Those who know and love God understand that He is both merciful and just. While His mercy is never ending, His judgments are quick and His punishments harsh. The very first chapter of the very first book of the Bible, the Book of Genesis, tells the story of creation. The second chapter describes how the creation of the first man and woman, Adam and Eve, came about. In the third chapter, God inflicts His very first punishment on Adam and Eve for their sin of disobedience, and the chastisement was severe. Some might even argue that the punishment did not fit the crime, but we know the wisdom of a just and merciful judge must not be questioned.

For listening to the serpent who tricked the woman into eating of the fruit of the forbidden tree, God said to Eve:

> *I will intensify your toil in childbearing; in pain you shall bring forth children. Yet your urge shall be for your husband and he shall rule over you.*[11]

Then, turning to Adam, God said:

> *Because you listened to your wife and ate from the tree about which I commanded you, you shall not eat from it, cursed is the ground because of you. In toil you shall eat its yield all the days of your life. Thorns and thistles it shall bear for you, and you shall eat the grass of the field. By the sweat of your brow you shall eat bread, until you return to the ground, from which you were taken; for you are dust, and to dust you shall return.*[12]

One might think that this punishment was severe enough, but God was not yet done.

> *The Lord God therefore banished him from the Garden of Eden, to till the ground from which he had been taken. He expelled the man, stationing the cherubim and the fiery revolving sword east of the garden of Eden, to guard the way to the tree of life.*[13]

Despite the severity of the punishment, the lesson was not learned. The very next chapter of the Book of Genesis tells about the continued evil perpetrated by Adam and Eve's firstborn son, Cain, on his brother Abel, resulting in the ultimate murder of Abel at the hands of Cain. For this and many other acts of disobedience, a future punishment would be inflicted on the people of the earth.

Chapter 2

The Second Chastisement
Noah and the Story of the Great Flood

T he story of Noah and his Ark is perhaps one of the most recognizable stories of the Old Testament. Contained in the Book of Genesis, the very first book of the Bible, the story recounts God's disappointment with the evil and wickedness that accompanied the expansion of the human race, provoking Him to eliminate virtually every living thing and begin again.

Among all the wickedness, God recognized that Noah and his family were different. Noah was a righteous man and blameless in his generation. He walked with God and found favor with Him. So, God elected to save Noah, his family, and a variety of all the birds of the sky and animals that walked the planet. These He chose to repopulate the earth after His chastisement.

God instructed Noah on the construction of a great ark. Made of gopherwood, the ark was to contain several compartments and was to be covered with pitch. His instructions were very specific. The ark was to be three hundred cubits in length and fifty cubits wide. The height needed to be thirty cubits with an opening of one cubit at the top for daylight. The entrance was to be on the side and there were to be three decks.

God said to Noah,

> *"I, on My part, am about to bring the flood waters on the earth, to destroy all creatures under the sky in which there is the breath of life; everything on earth shall perish. I will establish my covenant with you. You shall go into the ark, you and your sons, your wife and your sons' wives with you. Of all living creatures you shall bring two of every kind into the ark, one male and one female, to keep them*

alive along with you. Of every kind of bird, of every kind of animal, and of every kind of thing that crawls on the ground, two of each will come to you, that you may keep them alive. Moreover, you are to provide yourself with all the food that is to be eaten, and store it away, that it may serve as provisions for you and for them."[14]

Noah complied with God's command.

Then the Lord said to Noah: "Go into the ark, you and all your household, for you alone in this generation have I found to be righteous before me. Of every clean animal, take with you seven pairs, a male and its mate; and of the unclean animals, one pair, a male and its mate; likewise, of every bird of the air, seven pairs, a male and a female, to keep their progeny alive over all the earth. For seven days from now I will bring rain down on the earth for forty days and forty nights, and so I will wipe out from the face of the earth every being that I have made."[15]

Again, Noah complied.

On the seventeenth day of the second month, torrential rains came and flooded the earth just as God had said. For forty days the floods continued until all the highest mountains under the heavens were submerged, and then rose another fifteen cubits. Every creature and all of humankind was destroyed except for those on the ark. The waters would not subside for one hundred and fifty days until, on the seventeenth day of the seventh month, *"the ark came to rest on the mountains of Ararat."[16]*

It wasn't until the first day of the tenth month that mountaintops appeared. Forty-seven days later, a dove that was released by Noah returned with an olive leaf, indicating that the waters had diminished on the earth. Seven days hence another dove was released, but this one did not return. And so, on the first day of the first month of the six hundred and first year of his life, *"Noah removed the covering of the ark and saw that the surface of the ground had dried. In the second month, on the twenty-seventh day of the month, the earth was dry."[17]*

Noah and his family left the ark and released all the animals. Immediately, Noah constructed an altar,

and choosing from every clean animal and every clean bird, he offered burnt offerings on the altar. When the Lord smelled the sweet odor, the Lord said to Himself: "Never again will I curse the ground because of human beings, since the desires of the human heart are evil from youth; nor will I ever again strike down every living being, as I have done."[18]

Many consider this story to be allegorical myth. Others, however, believe it to be a true recounting of an historic event. Scientific explorers had searched for years without success to find some scientific evidence that might prove the story true. In 2010, however, a six-member team of Turkish and Chinese evangelical Christian explorers claim to have found the remains of Noah's ark within a glacier near the summit of Mt. Ararat and actually entered into some of the ark's chambers. Filmmaker Yeung Wing-cheung, who accompanied the explorers, said the team is about 99.9 percent certain that the remains are part of Noah's Ark.

The team made the initial discovery in 2007 and 2008 when they located "seven large wooden compartments buried at 13,000 feet above sea level, near the peak of Mount Ararat. They returned to the site with a film crew in October 2009"[19] and are now so convinced their claim is authentic that on April 25, 2010, they held a press conference in Hong Kong to present their findings.

Geologists insist that geologic studies "show no evidence of a world-wide flood that would have wiped out all plants, animals, and most traces of human civilization... But members of the Chinese-Turkish team stood by their finding. 'How [else] can a ship be on a mountain?' Wing-cheung, said in defense of his claim."[20]

Despite the photographic evidence of the claim that the exploration team has provided, as well as the lack of absolute proof that the evidence has been manufactured, many, even those who identify as Christians remain skeptical.

Chapter 3

The Third Chastisement
Abraham and the Story of
Sodom & Gomorrah

The story of Sodom and Gomorrah is another biblical warning of the damaging consequences of sin. Sodom was one of the most ancient cities of Syria, and though most commonly associated with Gomorrah, it was also close to Admah, Zeboim, and Zoar. The outcry against Sodom and Gomorrah was so great, and the sin of the people so mortal, that God decided to descend to the earth to determine if the sins of the inhabitants of Sodom and Gomorrah were as bad as the outcry. After witnessing the debauchery, God decided the destruction of the cities was warranted and confided the fact to Abraham.

The book of Genesis records God's appearance to Abraham as follows:

> *"The Lord appeared to Abraham by the oak of Mamre, as he sat at the entrance of his tent while the day was growing hot. Looking up, [Abraham] saw three men standing near him."*

The "men," the story continues, were the Lord God and two of his angels. During the ensuing conversation, the Lord revealed that this time next year, Abraham and his wife would have a son despite their advanced age.

The three men stayed with Abraham that night and on the following day, Abraham walked with them as they set out toward Sodom. Along the way, the Lord revealed to Abraham His plan to destroy Sodom and Gomorrah because of the wickedness that was found there. But as the other two men walked on, Abraham stopped with the Lord and pleaded, saying:

> *"'Will you really sweep away the righteous with the wicked? Suppose there were fifty righteous people in the city; would you really sweep away and not spare the place for the sake of the fifty righteous people within it? Far be it from you to do such a thing, to kill the righteous with the wicked, so that the righteous and the wicked are treated alike! Far be it from you! Should not the judge of all the world do what is just?' The Lord replied: 'If I find fifty righteous people in the city of Sodom, I will spare the whole place for their sake.' Abraham spoke up again: 'See how I am presuming to speak to my Lord, though I am only dust and ashes! What if there are five less than fifty righteous people? Will you destroy the whole city because of those five?' 'I will not destroy it,' he answered, 'if I find forty-five there.' But Abraham persisted, saying, 'what if only forty are found there?' He replied: 'I will refrain from doing it for the sake of the forty.' Then he said, 'do not let my Lord be angry if I go on. What if only thirty are found there?' He replied: 'I will refrain from doing it if I can find thirty there.' Abraham went on, 'Since I have thus presumed to speak to my Lord, what if there are no more than twenty?' 'I will not destroy it,' he answered, 'for the sake of the twenty.' But he persisted: 'Please, do not let my Lord be angry if I speak up this last time. What if ten are found there?' 'For the sake of the ten,' he replied, 'I will not destroy it.'"[21]*

With their conversation complete, God departed from the site and Abraham returned home. The two men, the angels of God, continued on their journey to Sodom and Gomorrah, where they were met at the entrance of the city by the gatekeeper, Lot, who greeted them by bowing down with his face to the ground and inviting them to his home for the night. Though *"Lot was a foreigner to the realm of Sodom and [had] not succumbed to the lustful, degenerate sins rampant in the city,"*[22] the men rejected the invitation, saying instead that they would pass the night in the town square. Lot's urging was so compelling, however, that the angels eventually relented and agreed to dine and stay with Lot and his family for the night.

When the townspeople caught wind of the news that there were two strangers in town, they approached Lot's door insisting that he send the two men out.

"Where are the men who came to your house tonight? Bring them out to us that we may have sexual relations with them."

Lot went out to meet the townspeople, offering instead his two virgin daughters for their purpose. The townsmen would hear none of it, however, and threatened to break down the door and storm the house in search of the two visitors. The angels pulled Lot back into the house and caused a flash of light so blinding that the thugs were struck sightless and unable to even find the doorway.

Although a focus of attention in Genesis, sins of a sexual nature are not the only sins of the inhabitants of Sodom. Ezekiel tells us that *"they were guilty of sinful pride. In addition, they were selfish; they had an overabundance of food and wealth but would not take care of the poor and needy."[23]* The book of Isaiah 3:9 tells us *"that not only were Sodom and Gomorrah guilty of all these sins against God, but they were arrogant about it, not thinking that sin against God was something shameful."[24]*

Vowing to destroy the city, the angels urged Lot and his wife, their two daughters, and their daughters' betrotheds, to leave the city before it was destroyed. Unable to convince his two sons-in-law to heed the warning, Lot left the city with his wife Sarah and their two daughters at the break of dawn. The angels accompanied Lot and his family to the city gate and warned them to head for the mountains. Lot requested that his family be allowed instead to go to the nearby city of Zoar. The angels granted his request but warned the family to do so without looking back, for if they looked upon God's wrath, they would be killed. Lot and his daughters did as instructed, but his wife, Sarah, identifying with the people of Sodom to some extent, disobeyed the angels' instruction and looked back. Instantly she was turned to a pillar of salt.

"The next morning, Abraham hurried to the place where he had stood before the Lord. As he looked down toward Sodom and Gomorrah and the whole region of the Plain, he saw smoke over the land rising like the smoke from a kiln."[25]

The story of Sodom and Gomorrah imparts many lessons. The obvious one is that God will judge those who reject Him. Perhaps less obvious is the appearance that Lot, rather than serving as an inspiration to the inhabitants of Sodom, allowed himself to be influenced by them, a concept that St. Paul would warn Christians against thousands of years later in his writings to the Corinthians (1 Corinthians 15:33). Finally, despite Lot having knowledge of the corrupt and sinful nature of the Sodomites, he chose to live among them anyway, repudiating the concept that the best way to avoid sin is to stay far from its tempting influence.

The biblical description of Sodom and Gomorrah may be one of the darkest stories in the Bible. It demonstrates the utterly corrosive nature and the power of sin, as well as the lengths that God will go to inflict punishment for such sinfulness. The story also shows, however, the mercy and grace of God in that He made a way of escape for those who trusted in Him. God still offers that remedy today for those who place their trust in Him. From the letter of St. Paul's to the Romans *"we know that all things work for the good for those who love God."*[26]

Chapter 4
A Fourth Chastisement Averted -
Jonah and the Story of Nineveh

Nineveh may have been one of the greatest of all the ancient cities of the Old Testament, and the Bible portrays it as *"a complex blend of historical reality, symbolic force, and legendary embellishment."*[27] The city lay on the eastern bank of the Tigris River and stretched back toward the eastern hills. Historically, Nineveh was the capital of the savagely cruel Assyrian Empire, at a time when relations between the Israelites and Nineveh were strained. The many prior Assyrian conquests that left *"mounds of heads, impaled bodies, enslaved citizens and avaricious looters testified to the ruthlessness of the Assyrians"*[28] and prompted the Prophet Nahum to describe Nineveh as a *"city of bloodshed."*[29] The destruction of Nineveh was something that all Israelites longed for. The book of the Prophet Nahum is, in fact, consumed with prophesies of Nineveh's destruction during the fall of the Assyrian empire.

The stories of Nineveh are more than just Biblical tales as *"the Assyrians' ruthless military tactics are also pictured in reliefs from the king's palace in Nineveh, now in the British Museum,"*[30] confirming the historical reality of the stories. Lost for some two thousand years, the city was disentombed by Austin Henry Layard in 1846 and 1847 when he began to search the vast mounds that lay along the opposite bank of the river. One of the buildings discovered was the palace of Assyrian King Sargon and it yielded some of the most amazing sculptures and relics of the ancient city.

The ancient city of Nineveh, in all its wickedness, is the subject of a potentially significant biblical chastisement. It is, however, a chastisement that never materialized because of the sincere repentance by King Assur-dan III and his subjects. The Book of Jonah describes it this way:

Then the word of the Lord came to Jonah a second time. "Go to the great city of Nineveh and proclaim to it the message I give you." Jonah obeyed the word of the Lord and went to Nineveh. Now Nineveh was a very large city; it took three days to go through it. Jonah began by going a day's journey into the city, proclaiming, "Forty more days and Nineveh will be overthrown." The Ninevites believed God. A fast was proclaimed, and all of them, from the greatest to the least, put on sackcloth.

When Jonah's warning reached the king of Nineveh, he rose from his throne, took off his royal robes, covered himself with sackcloth and sat down in the dust. This is the proclamation he issued in Nineveh: "By the decree of the king and his nobles: Do not let people or animals, herds or flocks, taste anything; do not let them eat or drink. But let people and animals be covered with sackcloth. Let everyone call urgently on God. Let them give up their evil ways and their violence. Who knows? God may yet relent and with compassion turn from his fierce anger so that we will not perish."

When God saw what they did and how they turned from their evil ways, he relented and did not bring on them the destruction he had threatened.[31]

Historical references to Nineveh support the Bible's assessment of the city as great, lawless, and eventually ruined according to Thomas Bolin, a professor at St. Norbert College. Historians whose writings support Biblical accounts of Nineveh include Herodotus (485 – 426 B.C.E) and Aristotle (385 – 323 B.C.E), two Greek literary giants, and Diodorus of Sicily, a first century B.C.E. Greek historian.

Like the story of Sodom and Gomorrah, the story of Jonah and his prophetic warning to the Ninevites imparts several lessons for the world today. First, it tells of God's control over all things, including the destiny of nations. Second, it speaks to mankind's accountability to the Lord. Third, it demonstrates that people, regardless of how ruthless and horrific their behavior, can change. Fourth, the story proves that repentance requires work. It was not enough for the Ninevites to pray that God might relent of His planned chastisement of the city; they had to sacrifice and fast in order to validate the sincerity of their commitment to change. Finally, the story of Nineveh clearly establishes the mercy of God and the conditional nature of prophesy. *"The prophet declared that the great city would be destroyed in forty days. But it survived for a century and a half beyond that time. Clearly, therefore, the prediction of doom was conditioned upon Nineveh's response to the prophetic message."[32]* This final point is a lesson that the people of the world today would be well advised to learn.

Chapter 5

The Fifth Chastisement
Moses and the Ten Plagues of Egypt

The fifth major chastisement mentioned in the Bible is, in at least two ways, different from the others. First, God appears to have intentionally hardened Pharaoh's heart in order to demonstrate His almighty power. The free will that was so prevalent in the hearts of men who fell victim to the previously mentioned chastisements, seems to have been suspended in this instance. Second, this chastisement was, in reality, a series of ten punishments or plagues that God inflicted on Egypt because of the Pharaoh's refusal to release from bondage the Israelites who he had enslaved.

While there is no historical record of the Israelite captivity outside of the Bible, it is widely believed that Ramses the Great (aka Ramses II) was the Pharaoh at the time of the ten disasters that befell Egypt. Ramses II was the third king of nineteenth dynasty of Egypt and reigned from 1279 B.C.E to 1213 B.C.E. He was the longest serving pharaoh in Egyptian history.

As revealed in the book of Exodus, Moses was tending his father-in-law's sheep when he came to Horeb, the mountain of God. *"There the angel of the Lord appeared to him as fire flaming out of a bush."*[33] When Moses saw that the bush, though on fire, was not being consumed, he turned aside to look closer. Seeing this, God called to him. Moses responded and was told to remove his sandals and remain at a distance as this was holy ground. God then commissioned Moses to approach Pharaoh and demand the release of God's chosen people, the Israelites.

Moses initially resisted, thinking himself incapable of pulling off such an amazing feat, but God reassured Moses, giving him precise instructions on what to say to Ramses. God appointed Moses's brother

Aaron to accompany him and the pair reluctantly set out. Upon reaching Pharaoh, Moses and Aaron found him to be with hardened heart, not only refusing to release the enslaved Israelites, but, rather, increasing their workload instead.

God, in response, made it appear to Pharaoh that Moses was as a god, and Aaron like a prophet as He instructed them what to say and do before Pharaoh. The two told Pharaoh of the impending plagues that God would send if Pharaoh didn't relent. When Pharaoh again refused to release the Israelites from their bondage, Moses threw his staff at Pharaoh's feet, where it was turned into a serpent. Despite the miracle, Pharaoh's heart was not softened. As promised, God unleashed the first plague upon Egypt.

The First Plague

God instructed Moses to go to the bank of the Nile with his staff, the same staff that had been temporarily turned into a serpent, in hand. Reaching the staff out toward the water, Moses was told to say to Pharaoh:

> "The Lord, the God of the Hebrews, sent me to you with the message: Let my people go to serve me in the wilderness. But as yet you have not listened. Thus, says the Lord: This is how you will know that I am the Lord. With the staff here in my hand, I will strike the water in the Nile and it will be changed into blood. The fish in the Nile will die, and the Nile itself will stink so that the Egyptians will be unable to drink water from the Nile."[34]

Moses did exactly as God commanded and, in full view of the Pharaoh and his servants, all the waters of the Nile, even the water that had been drawn and contained in wooden pails and stone jars, was turned to blood.

The Second Plague

After seven days had passed with Pharaoh remaining obstinate to God's demands, God instructed Moses to once again reach out to Pharaoh with a new threat.

> "If you refuse to let [my people] go, then I will send a plague of frogs over all the territory. The Nile will teem with frogs. They will come up and enter into your palace and into your bedroom and onto your bed, into the houses of your servants, too, and among your

people, even into your ovens and your kneading bowls. The frogs
will come up over you and your people and all your servants. "[35]

When Pharaoh remained unmoved, God instructed Moses to have
Aaron stretch out his hand and staff over the streams, the canals, and the
ponds. Aaron did as he was instructed, and immediately frogs came from
the water to overrun the land. Pharaoh summoned Moses and Aaron saying that if, on the following day, Moses prayed that the frogs might return
to the sea, he would release the Hebrew slaves to Moses. Moses did as
Pharaoh requested of him and immediately all the frogs that had come
ashore died, leaving a terrible stench upon the land. Pharaoh, for his part,
reneged on his offer to release the slaves from their bondage.

The Third Plague
God then instructed Moses to tell Aaron to stretch out his staff, striking with it the dust of the earth, thereby turning the dust into gnats. The
two men did as God had told them, immediately turning the dust into
gnats which,

> *"came upon human being and beast alike. All the dust of the*
> *earth turned into gnats throughout the land of Egypt."* [36]

In response, Pharaoh hardened his heart further.

The Fourth Plague
The following morning, Moses, obeying God's instructions, inter-
cepted Pharaoh as he set out toward the water, warning that if Pharaoh
did not release the captives, the Lord God would send swarms of flies
upon Pharaoh and his servants, the people and their houses – everywhere
except the land of Goshen, where the Israelites were being held. In this
way God would make a clear distinction between the Egyptians and the
Israelites. Still Pharaoh did not relent and the following day,

> *"thick swarms of flies entered the house of Pharaoh and the*
> *houses of his servants; throughout Egypt the land was devastated on*
> *account of the swarms of flies."* [37]

Pharaoh summoned Moses and told him that he would allow Moses
to journey with his people for three days in order to make sacrifice to
their God if he would pray for an end to the plague. Moses did so, insisting that Pharaoh not act deceitfully again. With the agreement secured,

"the swarms of flies left from Pharaoh, his servants, and his people. Not one remained. But once more Pharaoh became obstinate and would not let the people go."[38]

The Fifth Plague

God again instructed Moses, who went to Pharaoh and said,

"Let my people go to serve me. For if you refuse to let them go and persist in holding them, the hand of the Lord will strike your livestock in the field – your horses, donkey, camels, herds and flocks – with a very severe pestilence."[39]

Once again God promised to spare the animals of Israel. When Pharaoh was still unmoved, the Lord God acted, killing all the livestock of the Egyptians. Still Pharaoh would not relent.

The Sixth Plague

God again told Moses and Aaron what to do, so they took soot from a kiln. Appearing before Pharaoh with a new warning, Moses scattered the soot toward the sky as God had told him to do. The dust *"caused festering boils on human being and beast alike."[40]* As God had foretold Moses, Pharaoh's heart remained hardened.

The Seventh Plague

Then God told Moses to meet with Pharaoh early the following morning and tell him:

"Thus says the Lord, the God of the Hebrews: Let my people go to serve me, for this time I will unleash all my blows upon you and your servants and your people, so that you may know that there is none like me anywhere on earth. For by now I should have stretched out my hand and struck you and your people with such pestilence that you could have vanished from the earth. But this is why I have let you survive: to show you my power and to make my name resound throughout the earth."[41]

For his continued arrogance, Moses promised that on the following day, God would cause fierce hail to rain down on Egypt, killing everything that remained unsheltered.

Moses stretched out his staff to the sky in the presence of the unrelenting Pharaoh and immediately there came from heaven, *thunder and hail. Lightning flashed toward the earth, and the Lord rained down hail upon the land of Egypt. There was hail and lightning flashing here and there through the hail, and the hail was so fierce that nothing like it had been seen in Egypt since it became a nation. Throughout the land of Egypt, the hail struck down every-thing in the fields, human being and beast alike; it struck down all the vegetation of the fields and splintered every tree in the fields. Only in the land of Goshen, where the Israelites were, was there no hail.*[42]

Once again, Pharaoh agreed to let the Israelites go, but as soon as Moses asked God to calm the sky, Pharaoh again reneged.

The Eighth Plague

Moses and Aaron once again approached Pharaoh, bringing God's ad-monition for Pharaoh's constantly hardened heart and promising to bring locusts into the territory so that they would cover the surface of the earth, making the surface invisible and consuming anything not destroyed by the hail, filling the houses of Pharaoh, his servants, and his people.

Under unrelenting pressure from the Egyptians who recognized that the plagues of God were destroying them and their land, Pharaoh told Moses and his brother that he would allow the male slaves to leave, but with the women, children, and livestock remaining. With that, Pharaoh dismissed them.

Clearly, this did not meet God's demand. Consequently, and in accord with God's instructions, Moses raised his hand and staff to the sky and,

the Lord drove an east wind over the land all that day and all night. When it was morning, the east wind brought locusts. The locusts came up over the whole land of Egypt and settled down over all its territory. Never before had there been such a fierce swarm of locusts, nor will there ever be again. They covered the surface of the whole land, so that it became black. They ate up all the vegetation in the land and all the fruit of the trees the hail had spared. Nothing green was left on any tree or plant in the fields throughout the land of Egypt.[43]

Once more, Pharaoh summoned Moses and, acknowledging his sin before Moses and God, begged him to intercede with God to *"take this death from me."*[44] Moses did so and God caused the wind to shift to a very strong west wind which took up the locusts and hurled them into the Red Sea. Still, though seemingly fearful of the God of Moses, Phar-aoh refused to let the Israelites go.

The Ninth Plague

God then instructed Moses to stretch out his hand toward the sky so that darkness would come over the land. Moses complied and,

> there was a dense darkness throughout the land of Egypt for three days. People could not see one another, nor could they get up from where they were for three days. But all the Israelites had light where they lived.[45]

Again, Pharaoh summoned Moses and Aaron, telling them the enslaved men, women, and children could go serve the Lord, but the flocks and herds would be detained. Moses insisted that not only must the livestock be released as well, but Pharaoh himself must provide sacrifices and burnt offerings that the Israelites could make to the Lord. Pharaoh was indignant. *"Leave me and see to it that you do not see my face again,"* he said to Moses and Aaron. *"For if you do see my face you will die."* [46]

The Tenth Plague

The Lord promised Moses that he would bring a final plague upon Pharaoh and the land of Egypt before Moses could depart the land with his people. After this plague, Pharaoh would drive Moses and his people out, God told him. As God instructed, Moses did, saying to the enslaved Israelites:

> *"Instruct the people that every man is to ask his neighbor and every woman her neighbor, for silver and gold articles and for clothing."*[47]

To Pharaoh Moses said:

> *"Thus says the Lord: 'About midnight I will go forth through Egypt. Every firstborn in the land of Egypt will die, from the firstborn of Pharaoh who sits on his throne to the firstborn of the slave-girl who is at the hand-mill, as well as all the firstborn animals. Then there will be loud wailing throughout the land of Egypt, such as has never been, nor will ever be again. But among all the Israelites, among human beings and animals alike, not even a dog will growl, so that you may know that the Lord distinguishes between Egypt and Israel. All these servants of yours will then come down to me and bow down before me, saying: "Leave, you and all your followers!" Then I will depart.'" With that he left Pharaoh's presence in hot anger.*[48]

Because Pharaoh still refused to allow the enslaved people to leave, God provided very specific instructions to Moses and Aaron so that the Israelites would be saved from this final plight. The chosen people marked doors with the blood of a lamb as a sign to the angel of death to pass over that house, sparing all the inhabitants. They all did as Moses and his brother instructed,

> *and so at midnight the Lord struck down every firstborn in the land of Egypt, from the firstborn of Pharaoh sitting on his throne to the firstborn of the prisoner in the dungeon, as well as the firstborn of the animals. Pharaoh arose in the night, he and all his servants and all the Egyptians; and there was loud wailing throughout Egypt, for there was not a house without its dead.*[49]

The houses marked as God had instructed, however, were passed over as God had promised.

With this final admonition, Pharaoh's heart was softened, and the Israelites were released, *"indeed, the Lord had made the Egyptians so well disposed toward the people that they let them have whatever they asked for. And so, they despoiled the Egyptians."*[50]

Several times throughout this story, Pharaoh was going to allow the Israelites to leave, but each time, his heart was hardened by God in order that God might show to all of Egypt His mighty Power.

God shows his wrath in the Old Testament some 499 times, and 448 of those came after God issued the Ten Commandments to Moses on Mt. Sinai, indicating:

> *law and justice are tied to covenant in the Old Testament. Two parties voluntarily enter into an agreement. The powerful partner (God) promised to keep them safe and bless their agricultural life, their resources. He also instituted the priesthood to teach them how to keep the law, and he set up the sacrificial system administered by the priests for when the people sinned. The righteous party (God) forgave their sins over and over, for centuries. He sent prophets to warn them and remind them of their agreement.*
>
> *But sometimes the human party to the covenant went so far in their bad faith, they broke the law so egregiously for centuries, the aggrieved party (God) finally took action. He judged and punished them, but not in his full wrath and not to destroy them. He was merciful to his chosen lawbreakers. This is the perfect blend of mercy and justice. This is the story of God's wrath in the Old Testament, in a nutshell – and we*

haven't discussed what kind of lawbreaking they did, acting like the un-wholesome (to say the least) nations around them.[51]

Without question, willful violations of the Law of Moses, that is, sin, brings about the wrath of God. From the first moments after creation it was man's failure to abide by God's laws and commands, original sin, that brought suffering and death into the world. *"Poverty, pain, sickness, death and all the torments of the mind, all are the result of sin."*[52] The birth and death of Jesus, the promised Messiah, did not change that. Christ did not introduce the cross to the world. It was already here as a result of sin. Christ did, however, change *"man's suffering into His Passion. Man's suffering became redemptive."*[53] The cross offered hope. No mere man alone could have atoned for sin, not by combining all the sufferings of the world. Brother Craig Driscoll, founder of The Monks of Adoration and author of the book *The Coming Chastisement*, noted:

> *"because sin is against God, only God can atone for sin. But because Christ is God and He has given His own life to be man's life, man's sorrow has become Christ's sorrow, and everything is reversed. Now the cross [formerly dead weight] bears flower...and now, one small suffering of the most insignificant human creature can atone for sin."*[54]

Jesus transformed man's suffering into His own Passion and through His cross suffering has become redemptive. Had Jesus never become man, suffering would still be with us, but it would have been in vain. Suffering's futility would have been destructive and useless. The cross of Jesus changed all that. Our own sin brought about suffering, but as Brother Driscoll points out, God did not force us to sin. That was brought about by our exercise of the free will God gave us. It was given to us, not to sin, but to love. But God loves us too much to take away our free will and thereby forcing us to love Him. Our redemption comes only by freely *choosing* to love Him. The consequence of choosing sin over the love of God is chastisement.

Part II

Warnings of the New Chastisement
A Chronological History

Chapter 6

The Coming Chastisement
Biblical Information

For centuries, prophets, visionaries, holy people of God and sinners alike have warned of a coming chastisement. These warnings were received through visions, locutions, and inner feelings and were imparted to them by Jesus, the Blessed Virgin Mary, St. Joseph, and/or the Arch Angels. The warnings have been communicated to them in a single message or in multiple apparitions spanning decades. Regardless of the century in which the warning was issued, or the source and style of the delivery, the message is universal and relatively consistent: God is angry at the sinfulness of man and will bring about a great chastisement upon the earth if man does not repent of his own sins, sacrifice for the conversion of sinners, and pray, pray, pray.

Vincent T. Bemowski, author of *The Wrath of God in the New Testament*, writes, *"God's wrath is part and parcel of his judgment against wrongdoing, injustice and evil."* That God punishes evil is evident in the several Old Testament chastisements discussed previously. Generally, the Bible tells us that *"God is slow to anger."* [55] These words are written in no less than seven verses and are contained in at least six different books of the Old Testament. The story of Nineveh, furthermore, demonstrates that God will not only provide time for people to change their hearts, but will even relent of his punishment if there is a departure from the sinful ways of man and a turning to Him in prayer and sacrifice.

Though God, as presented in the Old Testament, is slow to anger, he does indeed get angry, and that anger is enough to bring about chastisements, both great and small, to the earth. But, did the chastisements sent by God the Father in the Old Testament cease with the birth of Jesus?

There is no question that the life, death, and resurrection of Jesus, while providing new hope through His conquering of the effects of sin and death, did not put an end to God's standing as the merciful judge. Notwithstanding God's mercy, however, stories of chastisement do abound in the New Testament as well. Here are a few examples where God's wrath is swift and certain even after the crucifixion of Jesus.

The Book of Acts 5:1-11 tells how Ananias and Sapphira sold their house and kept some of the proceeds for themselves. This, in and of itself, is not a problem. However, Ananias then lied, telling Peter that he had turned over all the proceeds to the community. Peter exposed Ananias's deceit, telling him, *"You have lied, not to human beings, but to God. When Ananias heard these words, he fell down and breathed his last."*[56]

Likewise, the Book of Acts 13:8-12, exposes a Jewish false prophet by the name of Bar-Jesus who attempted to

> *"turn the proconsul away from the faith. But Saul, also known as Paul, filled with the Holy Spirit, looked intently at him and said, 'You son of the devil, you enemy of all that is right, full of every sort of deceit and fraud. Will you not stop twisting the straight paths of [the] Lord? Even now the hand of the Lord is upon you. You will be blind, and unable to see the sun for a time.' Immediately a dark mist fell upon him, and he went about seeking people to lead him by the hand."*[57]

In these instances, God's anger was evident and his judgment immediate. Clearly, according to the Bible, God is not only slow to anger, plenteous in mercy, and full of compassion, but is *"great in power and will not acquit the wicked."*[58]

All the chastisements mentioned to this point, however, describe past events that occurred around or before the time of their recording. What, if anything, does the Bible tell us about the chastisements that will befall mankind in the future? St. Peter the Apostle writes in fairly plain language about these futuristic events:

> *"But false prophets also arose among the people, just as there will be false teachers among you, who will secretly bring in destructive heresies, even denying the Master who brought them, bringing upon themselves swift destruction. And many will follow their sensuality, and because of them the way of truth will be blasphemed. And in their greed, they will exploit you with false words. Their condemnation from long ago is not idle, and their destruction is not asleep. For if God did not spare angels when they sinned, but cast them into*

hell and committed them to chains of gloomy darkness to be kept until the judgment; if he did not spare the ancient world, but preserved Noah, a herald of righteousness, with seven others, when he brought a flood upon the world of the ungodly; and turning the cities of Sodom and Gomorrah into ashes, condemned them with an overthrow, making them an example unto those that after should live ungodly; and delivered just Lot, vexed with the filthy conversation of the wicked...The Lord knoweth how to deliver the godly out of temptations, and to reserve the unjust unto the day of judgment to be punished...But it happened unto them according to the true proverb, The dog is turned to his own vomit again; and the sow that was washed to her wallowing in the mire."[59]

The New Testament provides many warnings of the consequences of the sinful and unrepentant nature of man. Jesus spoke of the end times to some of His Apostles, and the Book of Revelation, written by St. John the Evangelist, provides great detail about the second coming of Christ. Jesus himself, however, gave a prophetic warning of the events that will precede His second coming. Jesus's words describe the signs that will foretell of the last days. These are the events of the great chastisement that will occur prior to the last day. The Gospels of Mark (13:1-27) and Luke (21:5-28) use very similar language when recollecting the words of Jesus as He told some of His apostles of His second coming and the events leading up to it.

As he was sitting on the Mount of Olives opposite the temple area, Peter, James, John and Andrew asked him privately, Tell us, when will this happen, and what sign will there be when all these things are about to come to an end? Jesus began to say to them, "See that no one deceives you. Many will come in my name saying, 'I am he,' and they will deceive many. When you hear of wars and reports of wars do not be alarmed; such things must happen, but it will not yet be the end. Nation will rise against nation and kingdom against kingdom. There will be {powerful} earthquakes and there will be famines and {plagues} from place to place {and awesome sights and mighty signs will come from the sky}. These are the beginnings of the labor pains. Watch out for yourselves. {Before all this happens, however,} they will hand you over to the courts. You will be beaten in synagogues. You will be arraigned before governors and kings because of me, as a witness before them. But the gospel must first be preached to all nations. When they lead you away and hand you over, do not worry beforehand about what you are to say. But say whatever will be given to you at that hour. For it will not *be you who are speaking but the Holy Spirit. Brother will hand over brother to death, and the father his child; children will rise up against parents and have them put to death. You will be hated by all because of my name. But the one who perseveres to the end will be saved. When you see the desolating abomination standing where he should, then those in Judea must flee to the mountains, [and] a person on a housetop must not go down or enter to get anything out of his house, and a person in a field must not return to get his cloak. {For these days are the time of punishment when all the scriptures are fulfilled.} Woe to pregnant women and nursing mothers in those days {for a terrible calamity will come upon the earth and a wrathful judgment upon this people.} Pray that this does not happen in winter. For those times will have tribulation such as has not been since the beginning of God's creation until now, nor ever will be. If the Lord had not shortened those days, no one would be saved; but for the sake of the elect whom he chose, he did shorten the days. If anyone says to you then, 'Look, here is the Messiah! Look, there he is!' do not believe it. False messiahs and false prophets will arise and will perform signs and wonders in order to mislead, if that were possible, the elect. Be watchful! I have told it all to you beforehand. But in those days after the tribulation the sun will be darkened, and the moon will not give its light, and the stars will be falling from the sky, and the powers in the heavens will be shaken. {People will die of fright in anticipation of what is coming upon the world, for the powers of heaven will be shaken.} And then they will see 'the Son of Man coming in the clouds' with great power and glory, and then he will send out the angels and gather [his] elect from the four winds, from the end of the earth to the end of the sky. {But when these signs begin to happen, stand erect and raise your heads because your redemption is at hand.}* [60]*

While the biblical references to the great chastisement and the last day are numerous, the information provided is relatively vague. There are warnings of wars, famines, and natural disasters, but events such as these have occurred throughout history in isolated corners of the world. None of those events have yet signaled the end of times and the second coming of Jesus. If more information isn't needed for mankind to heed the call, it is certainly desired to better describe what those days will be like and when they might occur. Fortunately, we have been given that information, though one might be hard-pressed to find it as easily as one finds the public revelations provided us by God in His Bible.

Chapter 7

The Coming Chastisement
Private Revelations

The revelations that have been discussed to this point are called public, biblical, or scriptural revelations because they have been given to us by God and are contained in Sacred Scripture.

> *The supreme revelation of God to the world is Jesus Christ, His Son, His Word made flesh, who lived among us (Jn 1:14). In Him, the Church received, through His words and deeds, a Divine Revelation, a deposit of faith (1 Tm 6:20; 2 Tm 1:12-14) that is unique, complete, definitive, intended for all people of all generations, and confirmed by God Himself as worthy of faith.[61]*

The public revelations were preserved and transmitted to everyone in Sacred Scripture and Tradition. They are considered to be preached with authenticity and interpreted by the teaching office of the Church, known as the Sacred Magisterium. All Catholics are required to accept them as divine faith. Public revelation is now complete even though its *"meaning, mysteries, and implications continue to be understood more fully and deeply through the Holy Spirit's enlightening work in the Church."[62]*

Other revelations given to us since the time of Christ, whether received through apparitions, visions, dreams, and/or locutions (words heard interiorly) with or without prophecies, are referred to as private revelations.

> *Private revelations do not belong to the deposit of faith and, as such, are not binding upon our faith. Nevertheless, it is an*

indisputable fact that Almighty God often speaks to His servants in an unmistakable manner.[63]

Regardless, of the "unofficial" status of private revelations, many Catholic devotions, such as the Rosary, given by Our Lady to St. Dominic, and the Scapula received of the Blessed Virgin Mary by St. Simon Stock, even the Chaplet of Divine Mercy given by Jesus to St. Faustina, are based in their entirety upon private revelations.

Over the years, many individuals, and groups of individuals, have claimed to have received private revelations from Jesus, His Blessed Mother, or from angels. The Church is very careful in its discernment of these revelations and generally undergoes a very intricate evaluation and investigation into them before informing the faithful regarding their authenticity and proclaiming them worthy of belief. Catholics may then choose to believe or not believe them. Belief in private revelations, unlike public revelations, is not required of the faithful. A great many of the private revelations disclosed have not been found to be worthy of belief by the Church and therefore, with very limited exception, are not presented in this book.

The importance of prophesy within the faith is also of great consequence and was established by St. Paul who said,

> *"Pursue love, but strive eagerly for the spiritual gifts, above all that you may prophesy. For one who speaks in tongues does not speak to human beings but to God, for no one listens; he utters mysteries of the spirit. On the other hand, one who prophesies does speak to human beings, for their building up, encouragement, and solace. Whoever speaks in a tongue builds himself up, but whoever prophesies builds up the church. Now I should like all of you to speak in tongues, but even more to prophesy. One who prophesies is greater than he who speaks in tongues unless he interprets, so that the church may be built up."*[64]

Yves Dupont, author of *Catholic Prophecy: The Coming Chastisement,* notes that prophesy warns against errors, casting a light on problems and preparing us for dangers to come. They are, Dupont says, "manifestations of the power of God."[65] Hundreds, if not thousands, of prophetic pronouncements have been made over the past nineteen and a half centuries, and several of those speak to the great chastisement that mankind will experience before the end of time.

Details of the great chastisement that will lead to the second coming of Christ, what precedes it and what follows it, have been revealed through private revelations for centuries. These revelations continue to the present day and many new details have been provided about what these days will entail. Jesus, the Blessed Virgin Mary, St. Joseph and the Arch Angels have given warnings to many saints, members of the clergy, and laypeople, including men, women, and children. Many of these revelations have been reviewed by the Catholic Church and many have been deemed reliable. The details that were presented in the introduction of this book are based on these prophecies. The next chapters will examine the prophetic words more closely.

It should be noted that there are hundreds of prophecies provided by hundreds of prophets. Many of the prophecies have been studied by the Catholic Church and have been deemed worthy of belief. Many other prophecies were examined by the Church and, while a formal finding of their worthiness was not issued, neither was there a condemnation of the prophecy. Still others were deemed by the Church to be unworthy of belief. This book focuses only on those prophecies that have not been found by the Church to be heretic and unworthy of belief. In fact, with only a very few exceptions, all prophecies used within are approved or not disapproved by the Catholic Church. Some of the prophecies might appear dull as compared to others, but are included because they contribute to the entirety of events that will constitute the end times and are, therefore, most relevant to this story.

Part III

The Prophecies

Chapter 8

The Early Prophecies
Pre-Nineteenth Century

4ᵗʰ Century – 251 – 356 A.D: St. Anthony the Abbot (A.K.A Anthony the Great, Antony the Great, Anthony of Egypt, Anthony of the Desert, Anthony the Anchorite, Anthony of Thebes, Abba Antonius and Father of all Monks) *(Prophecy Detail – Faith becomes complex, People lose their faith, Church is modernized and becomes one with the world)*

His parents were of nobility and had considerable wealth when Anthony was born in Egypt in the year 251. As the Christian child was reared among his kinfolk, he remained ignorant of his familial ancestry or the history of his own people. He did not learn to read or write, preferring a simple and modest life. He was taught to fear the Lord and clung heavily to his parents until they died when Anthony was only about eighteen years of age, leaving him to run the house and care for his younger sister. His inheritance also left him very wealthy.

Anthony spent a great deal of his time in church in meditation and it was there that he was overcome with a strong inspiration to meditate on how the apostles, and those who came after them, forsook everything to follow Jesus. Shortly following his meditation, and during the Gospel reading of St. Matthew (Mt 19:21), Anthony heard the words of Jesus, who said to the rich man, *"If thou wishest to be perfect, go and sell everything which thou hast, and give to the poor, and take thy cross, and come after Me, and there shall be unto thee treasure in heaven."*[66] Anthony took this coincidence to be a sign, believing that the reading and his own private meditation did not coincide as a matter of chance, but in order that this righteous idea be confirmed through his own actions.

He left church immediately to place his own house in order. Some of his inheritance, including three hundred fields and a large estate that produced an abundance of crops, were handed over to the people of his village, enabling them to provide for themselves and for his sister. The house and everything in it were sold for a considerable amount of money, which was then given to the poor, keeping just a little for his sister's wants. Within a short time, however, he was able to convince his sister to be of like mind and she was delivered to an order of chaste nuns who lived in the area.

With that, he set out for a life of solitude as a monk, initially living in a tomb in a cemetery near Koman. Anthony worried about nothing but his soul and undertook the habits of strict abstinence and self-denial. He found a small house at the edge of the village so that he might be set apart from all others. He fasted constantly and prayed fervently, with no pretext of envy toward those who lived in monasteries. Rather, he wished that other like-minded monks might be drawn together with him to progress in their careers. The others saw in him all good qualities and were drawn to him, giving him the name "Theophilus," which means, "God-loving." The others loved him as a brother or son.

Before long, Anthony's reputation had grown among all the monks in Egypt and large numbers of them began to come to him so they might imitate his life and deeds. The laity came as well that Anthony might pray over them and heal their sicknesses. Those who saw him realized that his deprived lifestyle of fasting and penance had not made his appearance feeble, but rather found that his appearance, stature, and countenance were as they had always been in the days before he began his solitude. Anthony feared that those who came to him for healing were placing too much confidence in his own abilities. He would, however, speak to them, sometimes with prophetic words. Among his prophecies, St. Anthony said:

> *"Men will surrender to the spirit of the age. They will say that if they had lived in our day, Faith would be simple and easy. But in their day, they will say, things are complex; the Church must be brought up to date and made meaningful to the day's problems. When the Church and the World are one, then those days are at hand. Because our Divine Master placed a barrier between His things and the things of the world."[67]*

While he performed many healings, Anthony feared that his popularity and healings might become a source of pride. He decided to take action to prevent that and, shortly thereafter, he set out to live in the desert where he remained for twenty years. He struggled with constant temptations where the evil one made him question his actions in selling all his possessions and giving the money to the poor. He also missed his sister and relatives and longed for company, attributing all these thoughts to Satan. Through it all, he prayed and fasted to overcome the temptations of the devil.

Throughout these years, many people still came to him for advice and healing. He refused to see them until, one day, they broke down his door. Anthony emerged and spoke with them, healing some and comforting others. Many remained with him and those who did formed a Christian monastery where each lived separately, emerging only to listen to Anthony speak.

Anthony lived to the age of one hundred and five, remaining so humble that he refused to die in Egypt where, according to custom, they might embalm him and place his body in a house. He chose, rather, to be placed in an undisclosed hole in the earth to remain until the resurrection of the dead, when he would once again receive his body without corruption.

Saint Anthony the Abbot's insightful and prophetic words are quite descriptive of the "me" generation that has gained momentum in the early part of the twenty-first century and are prescient of today's use of words such as "up to date," and "meaningful" to justify selfish and reckless innovations.

4th Century - 291 – 371 A.D: St. Hilarion the Great *(Prophecy Detail – World wars, The Holy Man, The era of peace, The comet, The chastisements)*

Hilarion led a life of extreme poverty, shunning the pleasures of the day and choosing instead to live in the desert at an early age. Only after the death of his parents did he return to the home of his birth in Thabatha, Palestine. He stayed, however, only long enough to give his share of his inheritance to his siblings and to the poor, quickly returning to the desert to pray and fast unencumbered by the interruptions of material possessions. Some consider him the founder of Palestinian monasticism, but he was also a prophet of some notoriety. His biography was recorded by St. Jerome shortly after Hilarion's death in 371. These are among his prophecies:

> *After the World War they will make peace but not a lasting peace. They will immediately begin again preparing to strike one another.*
> *The people of the Peninsula of Europe will suffer by unnecessary wars* (World Wars I and II and many revolutions) *until the Holy Man comes. The people of Pannonia* (Pannonia was once the country comprising the region of Serbia, Austria, Hungary, & Slovenia. Archduke Franz Ferdinand, heir to the Austro-Hungarian throne, was killed in Serbia on 28 June, 1914. His assassination was the spark that ignited WWI.) *will be the cause of a great war, overcome a neighbor, and*

become an independent nation. Then will a Scourge of God come and chastise them, a lion, which will reign a long time over the nation. The Lion will come from a high mountain in the Enlightened Nation between the Rhine and the North Sea (As with most prophecies, this one moves rather quickly in the scope of time. Here the prophet is speaking of Adolph Hitler, the German Empire, and WWII. Germany is the 'enlightened nation' between the Rhine and the North Sea.), *with a great army meet them by the mouth of the Rhine River and in a fierce battle almost entirely annihilate them.*

From the Northeast, where the People live in crude Houses (This seems to describe Russia, which lies in the Northeast, where the houses would seem crude, and whose people moved into Europe during WWII and swarmed over many kingdoms while imposing Communist rule.) *they will move out in a swarm and cut their way to the midday Sea* (Arguably the Mediterranean could be described as the 'midday Sea') *and swarm over many kingdoms. There where upwards the Rivers wander* (This likely describes Africa, where the Nile River is one of only several rivers in the world that flows northwards.) *there with six Armies in the Black Sea will surrender; as soon as they have defeated the Stream from Rome, themselves will turn in the midday Sea...*

Not far from the Outflow of one Plain, the great Eagle with a Leader will again come from the Rock Island. A final battle will be delivered. The wild horde will be defeated and made to pay, when they come, but will not win the Waste nor return to their Homeland... (This seems to describe the American forces, i.e. the great Eagle from the Rock Island, when they defeat the German army, which can easily be described as a wild horde.)

One day, before the Comet shines, a lot of People from Need and Misery will be wanting a Home. The great Empire in the Sea, who are a different Folk stock and origin, will be devastated by Earthquake, Storm and Flood. This Empire will suffer much Misfortune from the sea. It will be divided into two islands and part of it will sink. The distant possession in the East will be lost through a Tiger and a Lion. (Some prophets speak of a comet coming so close to earth that we will be inundated with fireballs. Before the comet's arrival, however, sea levels will rise to flood England, or possibly the United States, which both could be considered great empires in the sea of different origin.)

Before Christian Churches are renovated and united, God will send an Eagle, who will travel to Rome and bring much happiness and good. The Holy Man will bring peace between the clergy and the Eagle and his reign will last four years. Then after his death God will send three men who are rich in wisdom and virtue. These men will administer the laws of the Holy Man and spread Christianity everywhere. Then there will be one Flock, one Faith, one Law, and one Baptism throughout the World.[68]

4th Century: St. Methodius *(Prophecy Detail - The great king, The great monarch, The Antichrist, The peace)*

Very little is known about the life of St. Methodius, but what is known comes from the writings of St. Jerome. Saint Jerome wrote that Methodius was the Bishop of Olympos in Lycia and later, the Bishop of Tyre. At the end of the persecution under the reign of Maximinus Daia in 311, Methodius suffered martyrdom, though Jerome raises questions as to whether Methodius died under Decius and Valerian at Chalcis. Over the course of time, even these scant details of the life of Methodius have proven to be unverifiable and some speculate that he may have been transported to Tyre during the persecution and suffered martyrdom there.

Of this there is certainty: Methodius was a prophet, an important theologian and a prolific writer whose theological views were diametrically opposed to those of fellow theologian Origen of Alexandria. The one area in which both men did agree, however, is that God would send a "great king" near the end of time just prior to the emergence of the Antichrist. Of the great monarch, Methodius wrote:

A day will come when the enemies of Christ will boast of having conquered the whole world. They will say "Christians cannot escape now!" But a great King will arise to fight the enemies of God. He will defeat them, and peace will be given to the world, and the Church freed from her anxieties.[69]

Methodius referred to the Great Monarch as the Roman King, no doubt a reference to the monarch as a defender of the Roman Catholic faith rather than one who presides over a Roman Empire. The Great Monarch will eventually go to the Holy Land where he will die after his reign has ended. That is when the Antichrist will appear. Methodius writes this prophetic account:

When the Son of Perdition has arisen, (the Antichrist), the King of the Romans will ascend Golgotha upon which the wood of the Holy Cross is fixed, in the place where the Lord underwent death for us. The king will take the crown from his head and place it upon the cross and stretching out his hands to heaven will hand over the kingdom of the Christians to God the Father. The cross and crown of the king will be taken up together to heaven. This is because the Cross on which our Lord Jesus Christ hung for the common salvation of all will begin to appear before him at his coming to convict the lack of faith of the unbelievers. The prophecy of David which says, "In the last days Ethiopia will stretch out their hands to God" are from the seed of Chuseth, the daughter of Phol, king of Ethiopia. When the Cross has been lifted up on high to heaven, the King of the Romans will directly give up his spirit. Then every principality and power will be destroyed that the Son of Perdition may manifest.[70]

Methodius then explained why the Antichrist will come at a time when the people of the earth were enjoying a long period of peace:

In the last period Christians will not appreciate the great grace of God who provided a monarch, a long duration of peace, a splendid fertility of the earth. They will be very ungrateful, lead a sinful life, in pride, vanity, unchastity, frivolity, hatred, avarice, gluttony, and many other vices, [so] that the sins of men will stink more than a pestilence before God. Many will doubt whether the Catholic faith is the true and only saving one and whether the Jews are correct when they still expect the Messiah. Many will be the false teachings and resultant bewilderment. The just God will in consequence give Lucifer and all devils power to come on earth and tempt his godless creatures.[71]

As with the prophesies of St. Hilarion the Great, St. Methodius seems to be describing the conditions of twenty-first century society, particularly in his description of the ingratitude, pride, vanity, unchastity, hatred, avarice, gluttony; otherwise, characteristics that seem so prevalent in modern American society.

5th or Early 6th Century: The Monk of Prémol *(Prophecy Detail – The great monarch, The angelic pontiff, Chastisements, Destruction of the Church, Restoration)*

No one knows for sure who wrote these prophecies or exactly when they were written, but they are thought to be attributable to a fifth century monk. They were unearthed sometime in the seventeenth century in Prémol, Grenoble, France. While the prophecies covered a wide range of topics, those listed here are the ones dealing with the end times.

The spirit conducted me into the heavens and said to me: "It is written that the Archangel Michael will do battle with the Dragon before the Triangle of God."

Then the spirit added, "Open the doors to your understanding; the Archangel and the Dragon are the two spirits that will contend for the kingdom of Jerusalem; and the triangle is the glory of the Almighty..."

...Is such a sacrifice not enough to appease your wrath, O Lord? But no, what then is this noise of arms? These cries of war and fear? What do the four winds bring? Ah! The dragon has appeared in all countries and has brought terrible confusion everywhere. There is war everywhere.

Individuals and nations rise against each other. Wars! Wars! Civil wars, foreign wars! What terrifying clashes! Everything is dead or in mourning; and famine stalks the earth.

The general revolution has followed. In these future happenings, will Paris be destroyed? Jerusalem! Jerusalem! Save yourself from the fire of Sodom and Gomorrah, and from the sack of Babylon. Why, Lord, do you not stop all this with Your Arm? Is the fury of men not enough without flaming ruin? (This seems to predict that Israel will be attacked by Babylon, which could mean Iraq or more likely Iran, as both countries lie in the region formerly known as Babylon...)

Must the elements also serve as an instrument of thine wrath? Stop, O Lord, stop! Thy cities are already crumbling by themselves. The elements are set loose. Cities are destroyed by fire.

Mercy, pardon for Zion! But thou are deaf to our cries, and the mountain of Zion comes crumbling down with a deafening roar!

The Cross of Christ now surmounts only a heap of ruins. And it is here that I see the king of Zion abandon his staff and his triple crown and, shaking the dust of these ruins from his feet, make haste to flee toward other shores. And that is not all, O Lord; your Church is rent asunder by her own children! (in this prophecy, Zion refers to the Catholic Church, which will apparently be physically destroyed and thus the pope, (abandoning his staff) will be forced to flee.)

The children of Zion are divided into two camps – one faithful to the fugitive pontiff, and the other inclined or disposed to the government of Zion respecting the Scepter but breaking in pieces the triple crown.

And I saw out of the Orient a significant young Man; he rode on a Lion and held a flaming sword in his hand. And France sang in front of him. And on his Path, many people fell before him, because the Spirit of God was with him. He rode into the ruins of Rome and laid his Hand in the Hand of the Pope.

And the one places the mutilated tiara upon the ardent head, determined to institute reforms that the opposing faction rejects; and confusion reigns in the sanctuary...But my Spirit wanders and my eyes become obscured at the sight of this terrible cataclysm. But the Spirit said to me that the man who hopes in God does penance, because the all-powerful and merciful God will draw the world out of confusion and a new world will commence. Then the Spirit said to me: "Here is the beginning of the end of time which begins!" And I awoke terrified. (...a new world emerging from the chastisements and upheavals.)[72]

6th Century: St. Caesarius of Arles *(Prophecy Detail – The holy pope and The great monarch)*

Born approximately in the year 470, Saint Caesarius entered the monastery of Lerins at a very young age but was sent by the Bishop to Arles to recuperate from a serious health issue. He won the affection and esteem of the local bishop, who had him ordained a deacon and a priest. Following the death of that bishop, Caesarius was the unanimous choice to succeed him. Over the next few years, he developed a reputation as a powerful preacher, theologian, and administrator. He served as bishop to the people of Arles from 502 to 542.

Following a period of political upheaval, *"he published a famous adaptation of the Roman Law known as the Breviarium Alarici which eventually became the civil code of Gaul."*[73] Despite his lasting influence, Caesarius is not well known today, but is remembered as a popular preacher whose sermons have been handed down through generations. He spoke in clear and simple language using real life examples from daily life to deliver his point, generally dealing with Christian principles and morality. He spoke openly of the real existence of, not only heaven, but of hell and purgatory as well. These sermons are a valuable thesaurus for historical students, whether of canon law, history of dogma, discipline, or liturgy.

Saint Caesarius was also a mystic who accurately predicted the French Revolution. The following prophecy deals with some of the events of the end times:

When the entire world, and in a special manner France, and in France more particularly the provinces of the north, of the east, and above all, that of Lorraine and Champagne, shall have been a prey to the greatest miseries and trials, then the provinces shall be succored by a prince who had been exiled in his youth, and who shall recover the crown of the lilies. This prince shall extend his dominion over the entire universe. At the same time there will be a great Pope, who be most eminent in sanctity and most perfect in every quality. This Pope shall have with him the Great Monarch, a most virtuous man, who shall be a scion of the holy race of the French kings. This Great Monarch will assist the Pope in the reformation of the whole earth. Many princes and nations that are living in error and impiety shall be converted, and an admirable peace shall reign among men during many years, because the wrath of God shall be appeased through their repentance, penance, and good works. There will be one common law, only one faith, one baptism, one religion. All nations shall recognize the Holy See of Rome and shall pay homage to the Pope. But after some considerable time, fervor shall cool, iniquity shall abound, and moral corruption shall become worse than ever, which shall bring upon mankind the last and worst persecution of the Antichrist, and the end of the world. There shall be a great change and as great an effusion of blood as in the time of the Gentiles: the Universal Church and the whole world shall deplore the ruin and capture of that most celebrated city, the capital and mistress of France; the altars and temples shall be destroyed; the holy virgins after experiencing many outrages, shall fly from their monasteries: the pastors of the Church shall abandon their pulpits and the Church itself be despoiled of all temporalities.[74]

St. Caesarius's prophecies seem to be among the earliest detailed writings that describe the great monarch and the holy pope. He also speaks to the fall of man following the Catholic unification of the world, an event that is believed will immediately precede the Second Coming of Christ.

6th Century: St. Columba (aka St. Columbkille) *(Prophecy Detail - Great carnage, Apostacy, Three days of darkness)*

St. Columba (aka. St. Columbkille) of Iona was born in the year 521. An Irish abbot and missionary evangelist, he was one of Ireland's most renowned saints. Before his death in 597 AD, he not only spread Christianity throughout what is today called Scotland, but revitalized monasticism. St. Columba was a miracle worker who could heal people of diseases, expel spirits, subdue wild beasts, calm storms, and raise people from the dead. In addition to performing many miracles, Columba had visions of angels, during which witnesses reported brilliant light that appeared before him. About a century after Columba's death, the author Adomnan, (also known as Eunan) wrote three volumes about his life. Two of these volumes address Columba's apparitions and his miraculous powers. The first volume of the trilogy contains a record of Columba's many prophetic revelations, some of which address the end of times. Excerpt from those passages follow:

> *Hearken, thou, until I relate things that shall come to pass in the latter ages of the world. Great carnage shall be made, justice shall be outraged, multitudinous evils, great suffering shall prevail, and many unjust laws will be administered. The time will come when they shall not perform charitable acts, and truth shall not remain in them. They will plunder the property of the church, they will be continually sneering at each other, they will employ themselves at reading and writing. They will scoff at acts of humanity, and at irreproachable humility; there shall come times of dark affliction, of scarcity, of sorrow, and of wailing; in the latter ages of the world's existence, and monarchs will be addicted to falsehood. Neither justice nor covenant will be observed by any one people of the race of Adam; they will become hard-hearted and penurious and will be devoid of piety. The clergy will become fosterers, in consequence of the tidings of wretchedness,* (that will reach them); *churches shall be held in bondage* (i.e., become private property), *by the all-powerful men* (Freemasons) *of the day. Judges will administer injustice, under the sanction of powerful, outrageous kings; the common people will adopt false principles, oh, how lamentable shall be their position! Doctors-of-science shall have cause to murmur, they will become niggardly in spirit; the aged will mourn in deep sorrow, on account of the woeful times that shall prevail. Cemeteries shall become all red* (dug up), *in consequence of the wrath that will follow sinners; wars and contentions shall rage in the bosom of every family. Excellent men shall be steeped in poverty, the people will become inhospitable to their guests, the voice of the parasite will be more agreeable to them than the melody of the harp touched by the sage's finger. In consequence of the general prevalence of sinful practices, humility shall produce no fruit. The professors of science shall not be rewarded, amiability shall not characterize the people; prosperity and hospitality shall not exist, but niggardliness and destitution will assume their place. The changes of seasons shall produce only half their verdure, the regular festivals of the Church will not be observed; all classes of men shall be filled with hatred and enmity towards each other. The people will not associate affectionately with each other during the great festivals of the seasons; they will live devoid of justice and rectitude, up from the youth of tender*

age to the aged. The clergy shall be led into error by misinterpretation of their reading; the relics of the saints will be considered powerless. Every race of mankind will become wicked! Young women will become unblushing, and aged people will be of irascible temper; the king will seldom be productive, as of old; lords will become murderers. Young people will decline in vigor, they will despise those who shall have hoary hair; there shall be no standard by which morals may be regulated, and marriages will be solemnized without witnesses. Troublous shall be the latter ages of the world, the dispositions of the generality of men I will point out, from the time they shall abandon hospitable habits - with the view of winning honor for themselves, they will hold each other as objects for ridicule. The professors of abundance shall fall through the multiplicity of their falsehoods; covetousness shall take possession of every glutton, and when satiated their arrogance will know no bounds. Between mother and daughter anger and bitter sarcasms shall continually exist; neighbors will become treacherous, cold, and false-hearted towards each other. The gentry will become grudgeful, with respect to their trifling donations; and blood relations will become cool towards each other; Church livings shall become lay property. Such is the description of the people who shall come in the ages to come; more unjust and iniquitous shall be every succeeding race of men. The trees shall not bear the usual quantity of fruit, fisheries shall become unproductive and the earth shall not yield its usual abundance. Inclement weather and famine shall come, and fishes shall forsake rivers. The people oppressed for want of food, shall pine to death. Dreadful storms and hurricanes shall afflict them. Numberless diseases shall then prevail. Fortifications shall be built narrow during those times of dreadful danger...Then a great event shall happen (three days of darkness). *I fail not to notice it: rectitude shall be its spacious motive, and if ye be not truly holy, a more sorrowful event could not possibly happen.*[75]

7th Century – Before 685 A.D.: St. Cataldus *(Prophecy Detail – The great prince)*

St. Cataldus was born in Ireland, but there is some disagreement as to the exact place. One account indicates his birthplace as Ballinameela, Canty, County Waterford, Ireland, while another says he was born in Upper Ormonde, North Tipperary in Ballycahill. There, his father was a minor prince. Cataldus, if not the only son, was at least the eldest.

According to legends, Cataldus was granted miracles from his earliest years. His mother is said to have died during childbirth but was restored to life when the infant hand of Cataldus touched her. Another legend has it that the child Cataldus fell headfirst onto a hard rock, but rather than being hurt or killed by the impact, the rock immediately softened like wax and left the impression of the child's head embedded in it. Water later drawn from the impression was said to have miraculous powers.

As a young adult, Cataldus was sent to the monastic school of Lismore and excelled as a student. He eventually became the school's headmaster and still later, an abbot of Shanrahan, a monastery not far from the school. During those years he converted many pagans with his preaching and miracles.

Upon returning from a pilgrimage to the Holy Land in circa 667 AD, Cataldus was shipwrecked at Taranto, Italy during a storm. He remained there ministering to the natives, who had fallen back into paganism after being converted by St. Mark the Evangelist. He later became the Archbishop of the region, dying in Italy around 685 AD.

In addition to working miracles, Cataldus was also a prophet, albeit a secret one. During the reign of King Ferdinand I of Naples, Cataldus appeared to a priest one night, instructing him to retrieve a small book in which Cataldus had written several prophecies. He told the priest to give the book to the king. The priest ignored Cataldus, who continued to appear to the priest until he finally complied.

The newly ordained priest found the book in 1492, exactly where Cataldus told him it would be. The book, enclosed in plates of lead and clasped with iron hooks, was given to King Ferdinand, who after reading it, immediately threw it into the fire. It is believed that this book contained the following prophecy:

> *The Great Monarch will be in war till he is 40 years of age: a King of the House of Lilies,* (i.e. France, the Fleur-du-lys) *he will assemble great armies and expel tyrants from his empire. He will conquer England and other island empires. Greece he will invade and be made king thereof. Colchis, Cyprus, the Turks and Barbarians he will subdue and have all men worship the Crucified One. He will at length lay down his crown in Jerusalem...* [76]

10th Century - Between 910 and 992: Monk Adso *(Prophecy Detail – The great monarch, The Antichrist)*

Benedictine monk Adso was an author whose work on the Antichrist became the standard for three centuries. Born of nobility, Adso was an oblate at the monastery in Luxeuil, but later entered the monastery at Montier-en-Der, eventually becoming its abbot. He was well acquainted with classical literature, a prolific writer of poetry, hymns, and letters.

His most significant work, however, was the *Letter to Queen Gerberga on the Place and Time of Antichrist (Epistola ad Gerbergam reginam de ortu et tempore Antichristi)*, which he wrote at the request of Gerberga, the wife of Louis IV of France. Adso also prophesied about the Great Monarch. He wrote:

On the Great Monarch:

Some of our Teachers say that a king of the Franks will possess the entire Roman Empire. He will be the greatest and the last of all Monarchs. After having wisely governed his kingdom, he will go in the end to Jerusalem and will lay down his scepter and his crown upon the Mount of Olives. Immediately afterwards, Antichrist will come.[77]

Yves Dupont, author of *Catholic Prophesy: The Coming Chastisement*, believes this passage implies that the Great Monarch will go to Jerusalem twice, first to start his reign and lastly to surrender it. The relinquishing of his crown indicates that he is killed by Antichristians, thereby ending the period of peace and bringing about the period of disaster brought about by the chastisement.

On the Antichrist:

Against the faithful will he (the Antichrist) rise up in three ways – that is, by terror, by gifts, and by wonders; to the believers in him will he give gold and silver in abundance; but those whom he shall fail to corrupt by presents he will overcome by fear, and those he shall fail to vanquish by fear he will seek to seduce by signs and wonders...

The ruined Temple also, which Solomon raised to God, he shall build and restore to its former state...and he shall circumcise himself, and lie that he is the Son of God almighty...Thereafter he shall send his messengers and preachers to the whole world.

Then shall all the Jews flock unto him, and thinking they shall receive Christ they shall receive the devil...Coming to Jerusalem he shall be circumcised, saying to the Jews, "I am the Christ promised unto you, who have come for your weal that I may gather and defend you that are scattered..."

Then shall be sent into the world the two great prophets Elias and Enoch, who shall forearm the faithful with godly weapons against the task of the Antichrist, and they shall encourage and get them ready for the war...But after they have accomplished their preaching, the Antichrist shall rise up and slay them, and after three days they shall be raised up by the Lord...

> *The doctors also teach, as saith Pope Gregory, that Michael the Archangel shall destroy him* (the Antichrist) *on Mount Olivet in his pavilion and seat, in that place where the Lord ascended into heaven...*[78]

It should be noted that while Adso indicates that the Antichrist will use terror and bribery to win over his followers, other prophecies indicate that he will accomplish this through his charisma and false miracles alone.

11th Century - Between 1002 and 1066: St. Edward the Confessor *(Prophecy Detail – England's departure from Catholicism)*

St. Edward was born of nobility between 1002 and 1005 in Islip, Oxfordshire. He grew up in innocence and spent his best years in exile. He took great pleasure in assisting at Mass and often involved himself in the church office at the expense of pleasures that are typically reserved for royalty.

He became King at age forty and reigned over a period of almost unbroken peace, shattered only by the Welsh uprising. His great success as King is due, in large part, to the fact that he had no personal ambition. Rather, his greatest concern was for the well-being of his people. To that end, he often gave alms to the poor and imposed unusually low taxes. He died on January 5, 1066 and his body is incorrupt. During his life, St. Edward prophesied England's departure from the Catholic faith, something that would not happen until the 1500s. He left us these words:

> *The extreme corruption and wickedness of the English nation has provoked the just anger of God. When malice has reached the fullness of its measure, God will, in His wrath, send to the English people evil spirits who will punish and afflict them with severity by separating the green tree* (England) *from its parent stem* (Roman Catholicism) *the length of three furlongs. But at last this same tree* (England) *through the compassionate mercy of God and without any national assistance, shall return to its original root* (Roman Catholicism), *reflourish, and bear abundant fruit.*[79]

If his reference to three furlongs was three centuries, then St. Edward's timeframe is wrong. We know from several other prophecies, however, that prior to the end of days, the entire world will have converted to Catholicism with the possible exception of Palestine.

12th Century: Bishop Christianos Ageda *(Prophecy Detail – Chastisements, Wars, The Great Monarch, Three days of darkness)*

Very little is known of Bishop Christianos Ageda, but the twelfth century mystic seems to have foretold of the terrible wars and conflicts that have plagued the twentieth century with astounding accuracy. Further, there does not appear to be any challenge to the authenticity of his prophecy. Bishop Christianos wrote:

> *In the 20th century France's union with England will prove to be her utter destruction: for there will be great shedding of blood by the people of the kingdom. There will be wars and fury that will last a long time; whole provinces shall be emptied of their inhabitants, and kingdoms shall be thrown into confusion; many strongholds and noble houses shall be destroyed and their cities and towns shall be forsaken of their inhabitants; in divers places the ground shall be left untilled, and there shall be great slaughters of the upper class; their sun shall be darkened and never shine again, for France shall be desolate and her leader destroyed. There shall be great mutations and changes of kings and rulers for the right hand of the world shall fear the left, and the north shall prevail over the south....*
>
> *He shall inherit the Crown of the Fleur-de-Lys... By his means the nation's religion and laws shall have an admirable change...*[80]

12ᵗʰ Century - 1094 – November 2, 1148: St. Malachy *(Prophecy Detail – The last pope, Chastisement)*

The first Irish saint declared by the Catholic Church is St. Malachy, who was born in the year 1094. He was born of Irish nobility in Armagh. Following the death of both his parents, he was ordained a priest at the age of twenty-five and, later, was named Bishop of Connor, Ireland and Archbishop of Armagh.

Malachy had the gift of prophesy and is said to have predicted, with uncanny accuracy, the papal line of succession. Some claim that this particular prophecy was a forgery, however, as the written prophecies were not discovered until 1590. Tradition has it that Malachy had a vision of the line of popes while visiting Rome. The enumerated succession indicates that following Pope Benedict XVI, Petrus Romanus (Peter the Roman) will become the final pope. The election of Pope Francis, born Jorge Mario Bergoglio in Argentina, might dispel the accuracy of that prophecy though. Some have argued that he had "Peter" somewhere in his name, because his parents were Italian immigrants who moved to Argentina, though no such association has been made.

Be that as it may, the prophecy continues:

In the final persecution of the Holy Roman Church, there will sit Peter the Roman, who will pasture his sheep in many tribulations, and when these things are finished, the city of seven hills will be destroyed, and the dreadful judge will judge his people. The End.[81]

The possible lack of authenticity of this papal prophecy, however, does not negate the other prophetic pronouncements of St. Malachy, many of which have already been proven and at least one of which speaks to the chastisement.

Ireland will suffer English oppression for a week of centuries but will preserve her fidelity to God and His Church. At the end of that time she will be delivered, and the English in turn must suffer severe chastisement. Ireland, however, will be instrumental in bringing back the English to the unity of Faith.[82]

12th Century - September 16, 1098 – September 17, 1179: St. Hildegard of Bingen *(Prophecy Details - Papal authority, The sufferings, Death of men, The comet, Peace, The Antichrist, Chastisement)*

When Hildegard joined the Benedictine Order at the Monastery of Saint Disibodenberg at eighteen years of age, she was already experiencing supernatural visions. The visions started, in fact, in 1101 when Hildegard was just three. Once a Benedictine nun, her confessor ordered her to reduce the visions to writings, which were later published in a book entitled, *Scivias (Know the Ways)*. In addition to being a mystic, St. Hildegard was a prolific writer as well as an artist, composer, pharmacist, poet, preacher, and theologian. Though her visions were not limited in scope, several focused on the end times. The more relevant of those are recounted here.

On Papal Authority:
The time is coming when princes and people will renounce the authority of the Pope. Individual countries will prefer their own Church rulers to the Pope. The German Empire will be divided. Church property will be secularized. Priests will be persecuted. After the birth of the Antichrist heretics will preach their false doctrines undisturbed, resulting in Christians having doubts about their holy Catholic faith.

(Already this prophecy can be easily applied to events that began in [the] last century. Unlike in the past, most people see the pope as a mere figurehead and not Christ's representative on earth. In addition, after World War II, Germany was divided into East Germany and West Germany and was reunited only recently after the fall of the Berlin Wall. It is quite possible that the Antichrist has already been born, because the doubters in this world seem to outnumber believers, or his birth could come in the future.)[83]

On Sufferings:

Toward the end of the world, mankind will be purified through sufferings. This will be true especially of the clergy, who will be robbed of all property. When the clergy has adopted a simple manner of living, conditions will improve.[84]

On the Death of Men:

A Powerful wind will rise in the North carrying heavy fog and the densest dust by divine command and it will fill their throats and eyes so they will cease their savagery and be stricken with great fear. After that there will be so few men left that seven women will fight for one man, that they will say to the man: "Marry me to take the disgrace from me." For in those days it will be a disgrace for a woman to be without child, as it was by the Jews in the Old Testament.[85]

On the Comet:

Before the comet comes, many nations, the good excepted, will be scoured with want and famine. The great nation in the ocean that is inhabited by people of different tribes and descent by an earthquake, storm and tidal waves will be devastated. It will be divided, and in great part submerged. That nation will also have many misfortunes at sea and lose its colonies in the east through a Tiger and a Lion. The comet by its tremendous pressure will force much out of the ocean and flood many countries, causing much want and many plagues. All coastal cities will be fearful and many of them will be destroyed by tidal waves, and most living creatures will be killed and even those who escape will die from a horrible disease. For in none of these cities does a person live according to the laws of God. (The "great nation in the ocean that is inhabited by people of different tribes" would almost certainly be the United States, even though this prophecy was recorded many centuries before the discovery of America. Or, it could refer to England. As for the comet's pressure which causes floods, this is highly feasible. The moon's gravitational pull causes tides to rise and fall; just imagine the gravitational pull of a nearby comet. Or, perhaps, if the comet were to crash into the ocean, floods and tidal waves would certainly ensue. It seems we may have witnessed a precursor to this time of tidal waves in the earthquake and tsunami disaster in Southeast Asia.)[86]

On Peace:

Peace will return to Europe when the white flower again takes possession of the throne of France. During this time of peace, the people will be forbidden to carry weapons and iron will be used solely for making agricultural implements and tools. Also, during this period, the soil will be very productive and many Jews, heathens and heretics will join the Church. (The "white flower" refers to the Holy Emperor who will come and restore peace in the world and bring it into the Catholic Faith.)[87]

On the Antichrist:

The son of perdition (the Antichrist), *who will reign very few of times, will come at the end day of the duration of the world, at the times corresponding to the moment just before the sun disappears from the horizon...*

After having passed a licentious youth among very perverted men, and in a desert, she being conducted by a demon disguised as an angel of light, the mother of the son of perdition will conceive and give birth without knowing the father. In another land, she will make men believe that her birth was some miraculous thing, seeing that she had not appointed a spouse, and she will ignore that, she will say, how the infant she had brought into the world had been formed in her womb, and the people will regard it as a saint and qualified to the title.

The son of perdition is this very wicked beast who will put to death those who refuse to believe in him; who will associate with kings, priests, the great and the rich; who will mistake the humility and will esteem pride; who will finally subjugate the entire universe by his diabolic means.

He will gain over many people and tell them: "You are allowed to do all that you please; renounce the fasts; it suffices that you love me; I who am your God."

He will show them treasures and riches, and he will permit them to riot in all sorts of festivities, as they please. He will oblige them to practice circumcision and other Judaic observances, and he will tell them: "those who believe in me will receive pardon of their sins and will live with me eternally."

He will reject baptism and evangelism, and he will reject in derision all the precepts the Spirit has given to men of my part. (That the Antichrist will reject what the "Spirit has given to men of my part" seems to mean that he will reject the spiritual authority of Catholic priests.)

Then he will say to his partisans, "Strike me with a sword, and place my corpse in a proper shroud until the day of my resurrection." They will believe him to have really given over to death, and from his mortal wound he will make a striking semblance of resuscitation.

*After which, he will compose himself a certain cipher, which he will say is to be a pledge of salute; he will give it to all his servitors like the sign of our faith in heaven, and he will command them to adore it. Concerning those who, for the love of my (*Jesus's*) name, will refuse to render this sacrilegious adoration to the son of perdition, he will put them to death amidst the cruelest torments.*

But I will defend my Witnesses, Enoch and Elias, whom I have reserved for those times. Their mission will be to combat the man of evil and reprimand him in the sight of the faithful whom he has seduced. They will have the virtue of operating the most brilliant miracles, in all the places where the son of perdition has spread his evil doctrines. In the meanwhile, I will permit this evildoer to put them to death; but I will give them in heaven the recompense of their travails.

Later, however, after the coming of Enoch and Elias, the Antichrist will be destroyed, and the Church will sing forth with unprecedented glory, and the victims of the great error will throng to return to the fold. (St. Hildegard seems to speak of Protestantism when she quotes Jesus as saying, "victims of the great error will throng to return to the fold," in other words, they will return to Catholicism in large numbers. This is interesting because St. Hildegard's prophecy was made several centuries before the Protestant church was created.)

The Man of Sin will be born of an ungodly woman who, from her infancy, will have been initiated into occult sciences and the wiles of the demon. She will live in the desert with perverse men and abandon herself to crime with so much the greater ardor, as she will think she is authorized thereby by the revelations of an angel. And thus, in the fire of burning concupiscence she will conceive the Son of Perdition, without knowing by what father. Then she will teach that fornication is permitted, declaring herself holy and honored as a saint.

But Lucifer, the old and cunning serpent, will find the fruit of her womb with his infernal spirit and entirely possess the fruit of sin.

Now when he shall have attained the age of manhood, he will set himself up as a new master and teach perverse doctrine. Soon he will revolt against the saints; and he will acquire such great power that in the madness of his pride he would raise himself above the clouds; and as in the beginning Satan said: "I will be like unto the most high," and fell; so in those days, he will fall when he will say in the person of his son, "I am the Savior of the World!"

He will ally himself with the kings, the princes and the powerful ones of the earth; he will condemn humility and will extol all the doctrines of pride. His magic art will feign the most astonishing prodigies; he will disturb the atmosphere, command thunder and tempest, produce hail and horrible lightning. He will move mountains, dry up streams, reanimate the withered verdure of forests. His arts will be practiced upon the elements, but chiefly upon man will he exhaust his infernal power. He will seem to take away health and restore it. How so? By sending some possessed soul into a dead body, to move it for a time. But these resurrections will be of short duration. (St. Hildegard tells us that the Antichrist will in fact mimic Christ by performing wild miracles, but his miracles will not be of God and in fact will be intended to deceive the world into thinking that he is the Messiah.)

At the site of these things, many will be terrified and will believe in him; and some, preserving their primitive faith, will nevertheless court the favor of the Man of Sin or fear his displeasure. And so many will be led astray among those who, shutting the interior eye of their soul, will live habitually in exterior things...

After the Antichrist has ascended a high mountain and been destroyed by Christ, many erring souls will return to truth, and men will make rapid progress in the ways of holiness.

Nothing good will enter into him nor be able to be in him. For he will be nourished in diverse and secret places, lest he should be known by men, and he will be imbued with all diabolical arts, and he will be hidden until he is of full age, nor will he show the perversities which will be in him, until he knows himself to be full and superabundant in all iniquities.

He will appear to agitate the air, to make fire descend from heaven, to produce rainbows, lightning, thunder and hail, to tumble mountains, dry up streams, to strip the verdure of the trees, of forests, and to restore them again. He will also appear to be able to make men sick or well at will, to chase out demons, and at times event to resuscitate the dead, making a cadaver move like it was alive. But this kind of resurrection will never endure beyond a little time, for the glory of God will not suffer it.

Ostensibly he will be murdered, spill blood and die. With bewilderment and consternation, mankind will learn that he is not dead, but has awakened from his death sleep.

From the beginning of his course many battles and many things contrary to the lawful dispensation will arise, and charity will be extinguished in men. In them also will arise bitterness and harshness and there will be so many heresies that heretics will preach their errors openly and certainly; and there shall be so much doubt and incertitude in the Catholic faith of Christians that men shall be in doubt of what God they invoke, and many signs shall appear in the sun and moon, and in the stars and in the waters, and in other elements and creatures, so that, as it were in a picture, future events shall be foretold in the portents.

Then so much sadness shall occupy men at that time, that they shall be led to die as if for nothing. But those who are perfect in the Catholic faith will await in great contrition what God wills to ordain. And these great tribulations shall proceed in this way, while the Son of Perdition shall open his mouth in the words of falsehood and his deceptions, heaven and earth shall tremble together. But after the fall of the Antichrist, the glory of the Son of God shall be increased.

As soon as he is born, he will have teeth and pronounce blasphemies; in short, he will be a born devil. He will emit fearful cries, work miracles, and wallow in luxury and vice. He will have brothers who are also demons incarnate, and at the age of twelve, they will distinguish themselves in brilliant achievements. They will command an armed force, which will be supported by the infernal legions.

After the Son of Perdition has accomplished all of his evil designs, he will call together all of his believers and tell them that he wishes to ascend into heaven.

At the moment of his ascension, a thunderbolt will strike him to the ground, and he will die.

The mountains where he was established for the operation of his ascension, in an instant will be covered with a thick cloud which emits an unbearable odor of truly infernal corruption...At the sight of his body, the eyes of great numbers of persons will open and they will be made to see their miserable error.

After the sorrowful defeat of the Son of Perdition, the spouse of my Son, who is the Church, will shine with a glory without equal, and the victims of the error will be impressed to reenter the sheepfold.

As to the day, after the fall of Antichrist, when the world will end, man must not seek to know, for he can never learn it. That secret the Father has reserved for Himself. (The Antichrist will ascend a mountain and be killed. This demise to the Son of Perdition is echoed in other prophecies. Only after his death will people realize the error in their beliefs.)[88]

13th Century – Between 1202 - 1226: St. Francis of Assisi
(Prophecy Detail – Destruction of the Church, Destruction of morality, The reign of the devil on earth)

He was born in Italy around the year 1181, in Assisi, duchy of Spoleto, Italy and as a young man, was known for drinking and carousing. He left school by age fourteen and became a rebellious teenager. His father was a wealthy cloth merchant who owned farmland around Assisi, but Francis wanted little to do with all that. Charming and vain, Francis learned the skills of archery, horsemanship, and wrestling and was extremely bored with what he considered the family's mundane lifestyle. Consequently, he began dreaming of a life as a knight and desired to become one. His opportunity came in 1202 when war broke out between Assisi and Perugia. Francis joined the cavalry and soon found himself captured, imprisoned and ransomed. His fate was better than that of most of his companions, who were butchered and mutilated on the battlefield, while most of the survivors were immediately sentenced to death.

While waiting for his father to make his ransom payment, Francis began receiving visions from God, and it was after about a year of imprisonment, when his release was secured, that he heard the voice of Christ. During this time, while praying before an old Byzantine crucifix at the decrepit church of San Damiano, Francis heard the voice of Christ telling him to rebuild the Church and to live a life of extreme poverty. Mistakenly thinking that Jesus was asking him to rebuild the physical building, Francis obeyed. He soon realized, however, that the call was to rebuild the spirituality of the Church. From that point, Francis devoted himself to Christianity. He began preaching around Assisi and was soon joined by twelve loyal followers.

After his epiphany at the church of San Damiano, Francis realized another critical moment in his life that completed his transformation. To raise funds needed to rebuild the church, Francis stole a horse and cloth from his father and sold them. Upon learning of the incident, his father was outraged and took Francis before the local bishop for adjudication. After hearing the facts of the case, the bishop ordered Francis to return his father's money. Francis responded by stripping off his clothes and returning both, declaring that God was now the only father he recognized.

Now free from the clutches of his father, Francis set out on a mission to restore the original values of Jesus to the decadent church. He was able to draw thousands of followers, if not by his message, then by his charisma. Those followers became known as the Order of Franciscan Friars.

Francis and his followers were preaching in as many as five villages each day, speaking of a Christianity that the common man could understand. He even preached to the animals, earning him the nickname of "God's fool."

In 1224 Francis received another vision. This one left him with the stigmata, making him the first known person to receive the holy wounds. The wounds on his hands and in his side remained with him for the balance of his life.

Francis died on October 3, 1226 in Assisi, Italy. He was only forty-four years old at the time of his death, though his order, and his good works, live on to this very day. He was canonized a saint by Pope Gregory IX on July 16, 1228. Because of his deep love of nature and animals, Francis is the patron saint of animals and the environment.

During his life, Blessed Conrad heard from those who knew Francis several prophetic statements that he uttered. These were written only twelve to twenty-two years after Conrad's death and within a hundred years of the death of Francis. As author Elizabeth Bucchianeri notes when speaking about transcription history, this is a relatively short time. The following prophecies concerning the end times are attributed to Saint Francis:

> *Act bravely, my Brethren; take courage, and trust in the Lord. The time is fast approaching in which there will be great trials and afflictions; perplexities and dissensions, both spiritual and temporal, will abound; the charity of many will grow cold, and the malice of the wicked will increase. The devils will have unusual power, the immaculate purity of our Order, and of others, will be so much obscured that there will be very few Christians who will obey the true Sovereign Pontiff and the Roman Church with loyal hearts and perfect charity. At the time of this tribulation a man not canonically elected will be raised to the Pontificate, who, by his cunning, will endeavor to draw many into error and death. Then scandals will be multiplied, our Order will be divided, and many others will be entirely destroyed, because they will consent to error instead of opposing it. There will be such diversity of opinions and schisms among the people, the religious and the clergy, that, except those days were shortened, according to the words of the Gospel, even the elect would be led into error, were they not specially guided, amid such great confusion, by the immense mercy of God. Then our Rule and manner of life will be violently opposed by some, and terrible trials will come upon us. Those who are found faithful will receive the crown of life; but woe to those who, trusting solely in their Order, shall fall into tepidity, for they will not be able to support the temptations*

permitted for the proving of the elect. Those who preserve their fervor and adhere to virtue with love and zeal for the truth, will suffer injuries and persecutions as rebels and schismatics; for their persecutors, urged on by the evil spirits, will say they are rendering a great service to God by destroying such pestilent men from the face of the earth. But the Lord will be the refuge of the afflicted and will save all who trust in Him. And in order to be like their Head, these, the elect, will act with confidence, and by their death will purchase for themselves eternal life; choosing to obey God rather than man, they will fear nothing, and they will prefer to perish rather than consent to falsehood and perfidy. Some preachers will keep silence about the truth, and others will trample it under foot and deny it. Sanctity of life will be held in derision even by those who outwardly profess it, for in those days Our Lord Jesus Christ will send them not a true Pastor, but a destroyer.[89]

13th Century – Pre 1279: Abbot Werdin d'Otrante (aka Verdino of Otranto, Verdin, The Salentino Prophet of the 13th Century) *(Prophecy Detail – The angelic pope, The great monarch, The Antichrist, The apostacy, War, Annihilation, Restoration, The great peace)*

The life of Abbot Werdin d'Otranto remains shrouded in mystery. The date of his birth is unknown and even the date of his death is uncertain, with some records indicating 1259 while his gravestone reads 1279. What appears to be certain, however, is the place of his birth which, as one of his names suggests, was in the small town of Otranto which lies in the southern region of Apulia, province of Lecce, Italy.

The text of his prophecies was entrusted to two of his students, Giacomo d'Otranto and Mauro of Palermo. The manuscripts could have been rediscovered as late as 1594, though some sources indicate that the prophecies were found in his grave by an abbot in Cosenza, in Calabria.

Likewise, there is some evidence that Werdin's body was found in 1714 in a Cistercian church, suggesting that he may have been a Cistercian who died in a monastery in Calabria that belonged to that order of monks.

Werdin's prophecies were found in a manuscript under the title, *Vaticinium Memorabile* and relate to the last days. The notes that are interspersed throughout the prophecy reflect the thoughts of Elizabeth A. Bucchianeri, author of the website The Great Catholic Monarch and Angelic Pontiff Prophecies. According to Bucchianeri, Werdin's prophecies are somewhat problematic because they are not sequential, and their nature appears cyclical.

I, Abbot Werdin d'Otranto, warned by my guardian angel that the time of my death is approaching, I have written the events that were revealed to me, and that they will happen .... *And I copy a parchment* [and place it] *into a small box of marble, recommending, by virtue of holy obedience, to Giacomo d'Otranto and Mauro of Palermo my dear disciples, to deposit* [them] *with my body in my tomb. At the time when a beautiful star will shine on the chair of Peter, elected against the expectation of men in the midst of a great electoral struggle, the star whose splendor will illuminate the universal Church, the tomb that holds my body will be opened.* (Note: as mentioned, it was thought this "star" was Clement the XI, but as Verdino's body is still "lost" and the "Angelic Shepherd will later be described as a "star" and "extinct star" in the same prophecy, this could be a prediction that Verdino's body will be discovered when the Angelic Pontiff is elected.)

This good shepherd looked at by the angels, will leave behind a lot of things. By his zeal and solicitude altars will be built, and the destroyed churches restored. (Note: The Angelic Shepherd will restore the Church after a time of destruction.)

Then a gracious young man of the posterity of Pepin, (i.e a descendant of King Pepin of France, who was the father of Charlemagne) *finding himself in a strange* (foreign) *country,* (i.e. in exile) *will come to contemplate the glory of this shepherd, which shepherd will place in a wonderful way this young man on the throne of France until then* [left] *vacant. He will crown him and call him to help his own government.* (Note: The Angelic Pope will crown the Great Monarch – this has to be a Holy Roman Emperor because the Emperor is later described as an "eagle," symbol of Imperial rule.).

After a few years, this star (Angelic Pontiff) *will become extinguished, and the* (sorrow) *will be general in the world, because with it the septuagenarian eagle will be buried at this time,* (the Great Monarch will be in his late 70s or early 80s when he dies?), *leaving its eaglet under the dominion of the nation's primaries.* (Apparently Verdino says the Great Monarch will have an heir, but, as most of the prophecies say the Antichrist will soon appear after the Great Monarch, and, if the Great Monarch dies in old age, it seems odd he would sire a very young heir that would require a regent at such a late date, so, this is one element of the Great Monarch [prophesies] that is unique.) *From this everything will turn into ruin. The beast* (Antichrist?) *whose ferocity is unheard of, which carries a bitter-filled tail of poison, will enter its abode, and an innumerable number of snakes will multiply.*

Therefore, when the time has come, they (invaders? heretics?) *will penetrate all the houses of the clergy and drown the priestly dignities in bloodshed, and such will be in all the corners of hunger and anguish, which most men will invoke the death.* (Note: as with other prophecies, it sounds like we have the persecution of the Antichrist. The Church will once more have enemies in its midst, fall into heresy and persecution just like the times before the Great Monarch and Angelic Pontiff appear. However, at this point on, it also seems like Verdino's prophecies switch back to the wars that will come before the Great Monarch and got mixed up here as it is said the Muslims will invade again before his reign.) *Of these days, many cities will perish as victims of civil and foreign wars, mainly in Italy, both in the kingdom of Naples and in Tuscany. Such cruelty to be feared, such terrible horrors, that the imagination cannot conceive of the most terrible ones! ... Otranto, my homeland, will be once again destabilized by the Mohammedan dragon. Rome will be singularly shaken. Florence of the same will be hit then; she awaits the vengeance under her apostate head. The nest of the philosophers will be equally agitated, and Genoa will be exposed to incursions of the enemy. Thus, the Lord announces it. The Turks, with the peoples that will be in those times, will* (harness?) *Venice, and will unexpectedly give you a battle. The whole kingdom of Sicily will perish. May God be propitious to his servants! Many monasteries will be landed under the poison of the eagle of the North.* (Note: there are three 'northern countries' that are represented by the symbol of an eagle, Germany, Russia with a double-headed eagle, and the United States. We could have a prophecy of the poison of Protestantism or Nazi Germany, the rise of Communism from Russia, or, corruption from the USA.) *There was a great bloodshed because of two fights between the French and the Dutch. Oh, however it is to be desired that God should remove his wrath!*

From the East will come an eagle with wings spread out in the sun, followed by a multitude of men to come in support of the son of man. (The Great Monarch "eagle" with his armies will help the Angelic Pontiff "son of man.") *Then the fortresses will fall, and the world will be in fear. On that day there will take place in the land of the lion a war between the princes, more cruel than any other than the world's desolate, and will be a flood of blood.*

The lily will lose its crown, that the eagle will steal, and the son of man will be crowned. (Note: this seems like an odd text, but if it's out of sequence, it makes sense if looked at like this: France will lose the crown of the fleur-de-lys, representing the absolute monarchy, which happened during the French Revolution, and then again in the Third Republic of France. The "eagle" will steal it = the Great

Monarch / Emperor will have to fight for it and steal back what is rightfully his. The next paragraph shows the "son of man" represents the Angelic Pontiff, see the next prophecy below. He will be crowned pope around the time or after the Great Monarch rightfully steals back his own crown and then comes to his aid. As we saw above, Vidano predicted there would be trouble around the "star" and his election to the papacy regarding an electoral struggle. Corrupt clergy will not want reform? This also corresponds with other prophecies.)

During the space of four years, nations will collide with each other, the seven will disappear, (i.e. annihilation of nations) *and a great number of people will perish. The head of the world* (Rome) *will fall into ruin. The son of man, crossing the seas, will bear on his head the marvelous sign of promise.* (The Angelic Pontiff) *And the son of man and the eagle shall prevail, and peace shall reign in the world after the victory of the son of man and of the eagle.* (Note: here we see the rise of the Angelic Pontiff as the "son of man" – the diminutive form of the word in Italian for "son" is used in the prophecy, meaning the Pontiff is a symbolic representation of Christ the true Son of Man who is the Head of the Church. The "eagle" obviously represents the Great Monarch in the role of an Emperor, and this paragraph corresponds with other prophecies that there will be a two to four year war, nations will be annihilated, and Rome will fall into ruins before the Great Restoration / Age of Peace.)[90]

14th Century – Pre 1373: St. Bridget of Sweden *(Prophecy Detail – The angelic pope, The great monarch, The Antichrist, The apostacy, War, Annihilation, Restoration, The great peace)*

Uppland's Lagman, Birger Petersson and his wife Ingeborg, were pious people. Birger went to confession every week and participated in prolonged and grueling pilgrimages to Jerusalem to enhance his understanding of the faith. Consequently, Birgitta and her siblings were also taught to live faith-filled and devout lives. However, when Ingeborg died unexpectedly, Birger sent ten-year-old Birgitta, nine-year-old Katharine, and his newborn son Israel, to live with their maternal aunt for continued care and education.

When still very young, Birgitta had a vision in her dream of "The Man of Sorrows." In response to her inquiry as to who had done this to him, The Man of Sorrows replied, "All those who despise my love." This vision was so vivid that it stayed with Birgitta her entire life.

At the young age of thirteen, Birgitta was married to Ulf Gudmarsson and together the couple had eight children, all of whom defied the odds by surviving infancy. One evening, while the couple was returning from Birgitta's years-long work assignment as lady-in waiting to the wife of the King of Sweden, Ulf became seriously ill. Birgitta prayed by his bed the entire night and then a bishop appeared to her, promising that Ulf would recover and informing her that "God had great things for her to do." Ulf did recover and worked as a Lagman in the province of Närke until his eventual death in 1344.

At age forty-one, Birgitta heard God's call for her to be His bride and asked her to found a new religious order for primarily women. Answering His call, Birgitta convinced King Magnus Eriksson to donate a palace and a significant amount of land to the new monastery. Just as she had begun the work of organizing the affairs of the Order, Jesus appeared to her and asked her to go to Rome and wait until she could convince the Pope to return to Rome from France. Birgitta complied, leaving Sweden for the last time at the end of 1349. For the rest of her life Birgitta saw visions regarding the reorganization of the Church, messages to kings and popes and many other persons in high places, instructing them to work for the Church.

Birgitta died on July 23, 1373. Though she never wore the habit of the Order that she founded, Birgitta lived her life as instructed by God and was the only woman to have founded a religious order - Ordo Sanctissimi Salvatoris. The order spread quickly and had monasteries from Scandinavia throughout Europe to Italy. Currently, there are orders in Spain, Rome, the United States, and Mexico. For unfailing devotion to the call of God, Birgitta merited canonization which was bestowed upon her by the Catholic Church in 1391.

During her life, Birgitta wrote several religious works, one of which is about her mystical revelations. In addition, *The Christian Trumpet*, a book printed 1874, attributes a separate set of prophecies *"to St. Bridget regarding the fall of Constantinople, the wars of Napoleon and the rise of a Great Monarch was allegedly discovered in the vaults of the Benedictine Fathers in the city of Naples and then preserved in their library."*[91]

These are the words of St. Bridget as they pertain to end-of-times:

> *When the Feast of St. Mark* (the Apostle), (April 25), *shall fall on Easter Sunday, the Feast of St. Anthony of Padua, (13th of June), shall occur on the Feast of Pentecost and that of St. John the Baptist,*

(24th), *shall come on the Feast of Corpus Christi, the whole world shall cry, Woe!*

For the Lily reigning in the superior part shall move the encampments against the seed of the Lions and shall surround the children of men that will fight against the Lily. At that time the sign of impiety shall be raised.

At that time will come out of the island (of Corsica?) *a terrible son of man* (Napoleon Bonaparte?), *carrying war in his powerful arm, and with the French he will fight against the Italians, Germans, Sarmatians, Spaniards, and Turks. Everything shall be upset.*

During three consecutive years there shall be fighting among the faithful The Lily, or Bourbon kings, shall lose the crown, which shall be taken up by the Eagle, (Napoleon?) *and with which shall be crowned the son of an obscure man risen from the sea, who will carry the admirable sign in the promised land. Woe! woe! woe! when the son of man shall seat himself on the throne of the Lilies* (on the throne of the Bourbons in France), *then great tribulations shall be in the Church.*[92]

(Elizabeth Bucchianeri notes that this prophecy was partially realized when Napoleon stole the crown, made himself Emperor, harassed the Pope and stole the Papal States, but adds that this sounds oddly mixed, possibly a copy of a Great Monarch prophecy of Abbot "Werdin" of Otranto where the Eagle steals back his rightful crown? She further notes that Napoleon did not carry the "admirable sign" that the Great Monarch is destined to carry, (i.e. the Cross of Christ.)

But at last the Eagle (Great Monarch?) *will come from the North to the West and shall together with her children be surrounded by the towers of Spain, and they will raise Germany up again. The Eagle will also invade Mahometan countries and will carry the admirable sign in the land of promise. Peace and abundance shall return to the world.*[93]

But shortly after new wars shall break out. Woe to you, Venice! Woe to you, Lucca and Genoa, Italian republics! Woe, because after the year 1790 you shall all be pulled down by the hands of the French.

Then in Europe there will be very many wicked men. New wars! Wars carried on with much cruelty and fierceness, many cities shall be destroyed, an innumerable quantity of men shall be killed, the very head of the world shall be shaken. (The Pope?) *This most unhappy war shall end, when an emperor of Spanish origin will be elected who will in a wonderful manner be victorious through the sign of the Cross.*

He shall destroy the Jewish and the Mahometan sect; he will restore the church of Santa Sophia (in Constantinople*), and all the earth shall enjoy peace and prosperity; and new cities will be erected in many places.*

Sweden shall see again the true light of Faith, when it will be governed by a queen born with eleven fingers.

Antichrist shall be born from an accursed woman, who will pretend to be well informed in spiritual things, and of an accursed man, from the flesh (semen) *of whom the Devil shall form his work. The time of this Antichrist, well known to me, will come when iniquity and impiety shall above measure abound. Before, however, Antichrist arrives, the gate of Faith will be opened to some nations,* (i.e. broad world-wide conversions during the Great Monarch's reign), *and the Scripture shall be verified. People without intelligence shall glorify Me,* (Our Lord is speaking here?) *and deserts shall be inhabited. Hence, when many Christians will be lovers of heresies, and wicked men will persecute the clergy and will hate justice, this should be the sign that Antichrist shall come without delay.*[94]

14th Century – Pre 1380: Saint Catherine of Siena *(Prophecy Detail – The Church in disarray, The conversion to Catholicism)*

St. Catherine was born in Siena in 1347, the twenty-third child of Jacopo and Lapa Benincasa. She was raised as an intelligent, cheerful, and intensely religious person, devoting herself to God at early age. Though her parents urged her to marry as a young teen, as was customary at the time, Catherine privately vowed to consecrate her virginity and refused to comply with her parents' wishes, instead cutting off her hair to make herself less attractive. Rather than getting married, she joined the Sisters of the Penance of St. Dominic at eighteen years of age and made her vows. She spent the next three years in seclusion, prayer, and austerity.

At some point while Catherine was in the convent, she was marked with the Stigmata and as the details of her mystical marriage spread, so did her reputation. As a result, she became highly sought after. Because of her contemplative life, Catherine developed an active apostolate. Primarily for the encouragement and spiritual instruction of her followers, she wrote many letters. These letters, however, also spoke to public affairs and that caused some opposition, resulting in slander because she spoke candidly and with the authority of one completely committed to Christ.

An investigation into her preaching, conducted by the Dominican General Chapter of 1374, resulted in Catherine being cleared of all charges. All of this made a deep impression on the pope, who enlisted Catherine to work for the crusade against the Turks and for peace between Florence and the pope. For these efforts she worked indefatigably and her influence with Pope Gregory XI played a role in his decision to leave Avignon and return to Rome.

The year 1378 was tumultuous in the Church and the Great Schism split the allegiance of Christendom first in two and then three, each sect with their own pope, and righteous people fell on opposing sides of the issues. For two years, Catherine stayed in Rome praying for the unification of the Church and pleading for the cause of Pope Urban VI. During those years, Catherine offered herself as a victim for the Church in its agony, until finally, on April 29, 1380 Catherine died. She was canonized a saint in 1461 and ranks high among the mystics and spiritual writers of the Church. Along with St. Francis of Assisi, Catherine is co-patron of Italy. The designation of doctor of the Church was bestowed upon her in 1970 by Pope Paul VI, and in 1999, Pope John Paul II proclaimed her the patron saint of Europe.

St. Catherine's spiritual director, Blessed Raymond of Capua, noted that she also had the gift of prophecy and foretold future events to him, such as the spiritual upheavals during the end of the Avignon Papacy and the beginning of the Western Schism under Pope Urban VI, adding that he would live to see them. However, he was careful to explain she never, ever gave dates or times as to when her prophecies would happen but left it all to Divine Providence.

Seeing how much her prophecies upset Raymond, she offered him a consoling prophecy of the "Great Renewal." Unlike the other prophecies that she said Raymond would live to see, this one, she indicated, would happen after his time.

She told him that the coming Renewal would be so wonderful that the very thought of it, with the mass conversions of nations, exalted her spirit. Following is that prophecy:

> *After all these tribulations and miseries, in a way beyond all human understanding, the Lord God will purify His holy Church, and awaken the spirit of His elect. Such a wondrous reform after these things will happen in the holy Church of God, and the renewal of holy shepherds, that at the mere thought my spirit exalts in the Lord, and the bride* (i.e. the Church) *who is now almost deformed and ragged, will then be beautiful and adorned with precious jewels, and crowned with the diadem of all the virtues. All the faithful peoples will rejoice in the faith of so many*

holy shepherds, and even the unfaithful nations drawn by the good odor
(of sanctity) *of Christ Jesus will return to the Catholic fold, and will be*
converted to the new Pastor and the bishop of their souls. Give thanks,
therefore, to God, who after this hurricane will give his Church an un-
speakable calm.[95]

14th Century – 1345 – 1382: John Bassigny (Bassigny wrote under the pen name, John of Vatiguerro) *(Prophecy Detail – Church persecutions, Pope in exile)*

Bassigny was of French descent having come from the Champagne region of France. Because he was proficient in the use of Latin, it is presumed that he may have been a cleric, though it is certain that he studied the Holy Scriptures, poets, and other learned men. Although he did visit the Holy Land either as a pilgrim or as part of a diplomatic mission, his prophecies originate in France and date to the mid-fourteenth century. Of his prophecies, Bassigny tried to assign years in which they would be fulfilled, but his timing was inaccurate. However, many of his prophecies were shared by Marie-Julie Jahenny who wrote in the mid-nineteenth century and garnered the approval of her local bishop in 1875. Many of those shared prophecies are being fulfilled in modern times. Bassigny wrote:

Persecutions of the Church and Exile of the Pope:
>   *The Catholic Church and the entire world shall mourn the capture,*
> *despoliation and devastation of the most illustrious and famous city*
> (Paris), *capital and mistress of the Kingdom of all the French. All the*
> *Church in all the World shall be persecuted in a lamentable and griev-*
> *ous manner; it shall be stripped and deprived of all its temporal posses-*
> *sions and there shall be nobody in all the Church who does not feel*
> *fortunate at having escaped with his or her life.*
>   *For all the churches shall be polluted and desecrated, and all pub-*
> *lic worship shall cease because of fear and because of a most rabid and*
> *uncontrolled madness. The nuns, quitting their convents, shall flee here*
> *and there, demeaned and insulted. The pastors of the Church and the*
> *hierarchy, hunted and stripped of their dignities and their positions,*
> *shall be cruelly manhandled; the flocks and subjects shall take flight,*
> *and shall remain dispersed without pastor and without leader.*
>   *The supreme leader of the Church shall change residence* (the
> pope will be in exile) *and it shall be a cause of gladness to him, as*
> *well as to his brothers who shall be with him, if they can merely find*
> *a place of shelter where each can eat the bread of suffering with his*
> *own people in this vale of tears.*

For all the malice of men shall turn against the Catholic Church, and as a result she shall be without an advocate for twenty-five months and more, because, throughout the said space of time, there shall be neither Pope nor Emperor in Rome, nor any Regent in France.

The world shall esteem only those who shall be driven by evil and vengeance. Alas! the suffering caused by all the tyrants, emperors and unfaithful princes shall be renewed by those who shall persecute the holy Church. Indeed, the mischief and profanity of the Huns and the cruel inhumanity of the Vandals shall be nothing in comparison to the new tribulations, calamities and sufferings that in a short while shall oppress the holy Church; for the altars of the holy Church shall be destroyed, the floors of the temples desecrated, the monasteries polluted and despoiled, because the hand and anger of God shall take their vengeance on the world on account of the multiplicity and continuity of sins.

Natural Disasters:

All the elements shall be debased, because it is necessary that the whole nature of the age be changed; indeed, the earth, petrified with fear, shall suffer frightening quakes in many places, and shall swallow up the living; a number of towns, fortresses and strong castles shall collapse and be flattened by earthquakes.

Days of Darkness:

The production of the land shall diminish; now the plants shall lack moisture, now the seeds shall rot in the fields, and the shoots that come up shall not produce any fruits.

The sea shall rage and shall rise against the world, and it shall swallow many ships and their crews. The air shall be contaminated and corrupt because of the malice and the iniquity of men.

In the sky shall be seen numerous and most surprising signs: the sun shall be darkened, and it shall appear the color of blood to the eyes of many people. (The Two Days of Darkness before the Three Days of Darkness? See Marie-Julie Jahenny's prophecies here.)

Stellar Occurrences:

On one occasion, for about four hours, two moons shall be seen at the same time; next to them shall appear many astonishing things worthy of awe. (Marie-Julie Jahenny also foretold a time of four hours of darkness as a warning before the chastisements strike.)

Stars shall collide with each other, and this shall be the sign for the destruction and massacre of nearly all mankind. (See: Scientists

Predict Star Collision Visible to The Naked Eye in 2022, January 9, 2017, NPR – The Two Way.)

Plagues and Famines:

The natural movement of the air shall be almost completely altered and perverted because of pestilential illnesses. Men, as well as animals, shall be struck by various infirmities and by sudden death: there shall be an unspeakable plague; there shall be an astonishing and cruel famine which shall be so great and of such an extent throughout the World and especially in the regions of the West, that since the beginning of the world no one has ever heard of the like.

The Great Monarch:

The pomp of the nobles shall disappear, even the sciences and arts shall perish, and for a short space of time the whole order of the clergy shall remain in humiliation. Lorraine shall be stripped and plunged into mourning, and Champagne shall in vain implore help from its neighbors; it shall not be given any, but it shall be turned upside down, pillaged, and shall remain grievously in devastation. It shall be Ireland, Scotland and England that shall invade and devastate it. But...shortly before or after, these provinces shall be rescued by a young captive, who shall regain the crown of the lily and shall spread his dominion over the whole World. Once fully established, he shall destroy the sons of Brutus and their isle [Britain?], such that there shall no longer be any question of it and that they shall stay forever annihilated.

The Holy Pope:

So much for the tribulations that must take place before the restoration of Christendom. But after the whole World shall have been prey to the tribulations and to such great and numerous miseries, in order that the creatures of God may not remain entirely without hope there shall be elected by the Will of God a Pope from among those that shall have escaped the persecutions of the Church, and he shall be a very holy man, gifted with every perfection and he shall be crowned by the holy angels and placed on the holy throne by his brothers who, with him, shall have survived both exile and the persecutions of the Church. This Pope shall reform the whole World by his holiness, and shall bring back the ancient manner of living, consistent with the disciples of Christ, to all the clergy, and all shall respect him because of his virtues; he shall preach barefoot and shall not fear the power of princes. Also, he shall bring back many to the holy fold through their repenting of their mistakes and of their criminal life. He shall convert nearly all the infidels, but mainly the Jews.

One Unified Catholic Church:
This Pope shall have with him an Emperor, a very virtuous man, who shall be of the remnants of the most holy blood of the kings of the French. This prince shall be an aid to him and shall obey him in all things with a view to reforming the World, and under this Pope and this Emperor the World shall be reformed, because the anger of God shall subside. There shall not be more than one law, one faith, one baptism, one way of life. All men shall have the same sentiments and shall love one another, and peace shall last for many years.

Return of the Former Ways and the End of the World:
But after the age shall have been renewed, there shall appear many signs in the heavens again and the malice of men shall reawaken. They shall return to their old iniquities and to their detestable wickedness, and their crimes shall be worse than the first; that is why God shall bring about and shall advance the end of the world. I have spoken: it is finished.[96]

It is noteworthy that a prophecy written in the Middle Ages would refer to a condition of polluted air since it wasn't until the industrial revolution and the subsequent reliance on fossil fuels that such conditions could have ever been imagined. Likewise, the references to "earthquakes" and a "raging sea rising up against the world" sound eerily similar to a tsunami that follows some quakes such as those experienced in Japan and in Southeast Asia in the recent past.

15th Century – Circa 1400: St. Vincent Ferrer *(Prophecy Detail – The chastisement, The great monarch, The importance of Confirmation and the laxity of Christians)*

St. Vincent Ferrer preached powerfully and persuasively about the end of the world with such prophetic detail that Popes referred to him as the "Angel of the Apocalypse." Ferrer was born in Valencia, Spain in 1350. At age fourteen he began the study of theology and philosophy and four years later he joined the Dominican Order of Preachers. As he matured, he developed an intense devotion to the Passion of Christ and would fast on Wednesday and Friday of every week.

For three years he read nothing but the Sacred Scripture, committing it to memory. He was an accomplished writer and in 1379 was ordained a priest at Barcelona. After becoming a Master of Sacred Theology, he was commissioned by the Order to deliver lectures on Philosophy. He earned his doctorate in theology after studying at the University of Lleida.

During this time the Catholic Church was divided between two and eventually three claimants to the papacy. Clement VII, the antipope, lived in France while Pope Urban VI remained in Rome. Ferrer followed Clement and then his eventual successor, Pope Benedict XIII.

For twenty-one years, Ferrer travelled to many countries, including Ireland, Aragon, Castile, Scotland, England, France, Italy, and Switzerland, preaching the Good News everywhere and converting many souls along the way. He displayed many mystical powers, including the gift of tongues. He is said to have raised twenty-eight people from the dead and cured many sick and infirmed people. The extensive travel and the effects of the Church schism had taken its toll on Ferrer's health, though, and he grew too ill to return to Spain. He died in 1419 in Brittany, France.

Throughout his life he made many prophetic pronouncements, including the following:

On the Chastisement:

By Revelation it is manifestly shown that the whole duration of the world rests on a certain conditional prolongation obtained by the Virgin Mary in the hope of the conversion and correction of the World. (The time of the world is prolonged for a short while for the sake of saving souls, a grace obtained by the Blessed Virgin, so this is the possible reason why the fulfillment of the various Great Monarch prophecies may extend past the dates that some of the saints gave in the past. That is, the punishments are staved off on account of her intercession. The prophecies will occur, just not exactly when we will expect.)

On the Great Monarch:

Armies from West, East and North will fight together in Italy and the Eagle (Great Monarch?) *shall capture the counterfeit king,* (usurper?) *and all things shall be made obedient unto him, and there shall be a new reformation in the world. Woe then to the shaven orders whose crowns are shaved.* (Woe to shaven orders. This refers to orders that practice, or used to practice, the tonsure, the cutting or shaving some or all of the hair on the scalp as a sign of religious devotion or humility. Possible interpretations: woe to religious who cannot disguise themselves during the times of persecutions because of their shaved heads, they will be singled out and suffer? Or, perhaps woe to those who pretend to be holy in their robes and tonsures but were hypocrites and the Great Monarch will root them out?)

On the Laxity of Christians and the Importance of Confirmation:

> *In the days of peace that are to come after the desolation of revolutions and wars, before the end of the world, the Christians will become so lax in their religion that they will refuse to receive the Sacrament of Confirmation, saying "it is an unnecessary Sacrament"; and when the false prophet, the precursor of Antichrist comes, all who are not confirmed will apostatize, while those who are confirmed will stand firm in the faith, and only a few will renounce Christ.*[97]

After a complete study of the prophecies, Yves Dupont is certain that there will be two divergent stages of unrest. An initial war will be followed by a period of peace and prosperity, but that peace will be interrupted by another war that will give rise to the Antichrist. That war, in turn, will be followed by the victory of the Church and by an additional period of peace. Dupont's assessment is largely supported by the Bible, which also describes two distinct periods: the beginning of the end, and the end of the world, sandwiched around a period of peace.

15th Century – 1401 – 1464: Cardinal Nicholas of Cusa (Sometimes attributed to St. Nicholas of Fluh) *(Prophecy Detail – Apostacy, No pope, Rebirth of the Church)*

Though this prophecy is often attributed to Nicholas of Fluh, it was actually the writings of a German philosopher, theologian, jurist, and astronomer by the name of Cardinal Nicholas of Cusa. Born in 1401, Nicholas of Cusa was one of the first German supporters of Renaissance humanism. He was often found participating in the power struggles between Rome and the German states of the Holy Roman Empire.

In 1446 he served as papal legate to Germany and accepted Pope Nicholas V's invitation to become a Cardinal in 1448. In 1459 he was named vicar general in the Papal States. He worried about the corruption in the Church during his years and prophesied about the future destruction of the Church because of the corrupt practices. Cardinal Nicholas of Cusa wrote:

> *The Church would sink still deeper until she would at last seem to be extinguished, and the succession of Peter and the other Apostles to have expired. But after that she will be victoriously exalted in the sight of all doubters.*[98]

This prophecy alludes to other prophecies that speak to the Church being without a Pope for a while until it rises again in miraculous fashion to become a very powerful and unified Church. Yves Dupont believes that the moral decay addressed in the first sentence of the prophecy refers to the poor example set by many priests of our time who are leaving the priesthood for matrimony without first being appropriately dispensed, believing themselves to be adults who were above the requirements of dispensation.

15th Century – 1482 – 1496: St. Francis of Paola (aka Wonder Worker, Francesco di Paola, Francis the Fire Handler) *(Prophecy Detail – The great monarch)*

When they had trouble conceiving children, Giacomo and Vienna d'Alession prayed to St. Francis of Assisi, commending themselves to his intercession. Eventually they were blessed with three children, the oldest of whom was Francesco, born on March 27, 1416 in Paola, Italy. When Francesco was but fifteen years of age, he left his home to live as a hermit. Four years later, Francesco was joined by two others and together, they founded the Order of the Minims, a severely ascetic order dedicated to charitable work and eating no meat, eggs, or dairy products.

Over the course of years, as Francesco had become better known to the villagers and began to gain their respect and admiration, the town's people built a church and monastery for his order. In 1446, Francesco set a Rule for the monastery which emphasized penance, charity, and humility and monastic vows of fasting and abstinence from meat.

Some twenty-eight years later, Francesco's order was officially approved by Pope Sixtus IV and the order, as well as Francesco's reputation as a healer, miracle worker, prophet, and defender of the poor and oppressed, grew exponentially. Francesco was known to raise the dead, including his own nephew. He also brought dead animals back to life, events that were witnessed by a number of people. Among his many gifts, Francesco was a prophet and foretold the taking of Constantinople by the Turks several years before it occurred.

Francesco died on April 2, 1507 at the age of ninety-one, having spent the last three months of his life alone, preparing to meet his Lord and Savior. He was canonized a saint only twelve years later by Pope Julius II in 1519. Forty-three years after his death, Protestant Huguenots pillaged Francesco's tomb, stole the body, which was found in an incorrupt state, and burned it. Catholics recovered his charred bones and distributed them to various churches to be venerated as relics.

Among his many prophecies, Francesco, now known as St. Francis of Paola, spoke of the Great Catholic Monarch, speaking of how the Monarch and his armies will found the greatest military order of the Church. His most detailed prophecies regarding the Monarch are found in seven letters written between February 5, 1482 and August 18, 1496. Relevant excerpts from the seven letters, all written to Simeon de Limena, Count of Montalto, in Calabria, Kingdom of Naples, are reprinted here:

First Letter – February 5, 1482

The first members of this holy Order shall be natives of the city of...where iniquity, vice, and sin abound. But they shall be converted from evil to good; from rebels against God they shall become most fervent and most faithful in his divine service. That city shall be cherished by God and by the great monarch, the elect and the beloved of the Most-High Lord. For the sake of that place all holy souls who have done penance in it shall pray in the sight of God for that city and for its inhabitants.

When the time shall come of the immense and most right justice of the Holy Spirit, his Divine Majesty wills that such city become converted to God, and that many of its citizens follow the great Prince of the Holy Army. The first person that will openly wear the sign of the living God shall belong to that city, because he will through a letter be commanded by a holy hermit to have it impressed in his heart and to wear it externally on his breast.

Second Letter – March 25, 1485

You and your consort desire to have children; you shall have them. Your holy offspring shall be admired upon earth. Among your descendants there will be one who shall be like the sun amidst the stars. He shall be a first-born son; in his childhood he will be like a saint; in his youth, a great sinner; then he will be converted entirely to God and will do great penance; his sins will be forgiven him, and he shall become a great saint.

He shall be a great captain and prince of holy men, who shall be called the holy Crociferi (i.e. the Cruciferi, cross-bearers) of Jesus Christ, with whom he shall destroy the Mahometan sect and the rest of the infidels. He shall annihilate all the heresies and tyrannies of the world. He shall reform the Church of God by means of his followers, who shall be the best men upon earth in holiness, in arms, in science, and in every virtue, because such is the will of the Most High. They shall obtain the dominion of the whole world, both temporal and spiritual, and they shall support the Church of God until the end of time. I say no more.

Third Letter – April 25, 1486

O comrades of Judas Iscariot! To you I say, evil prelates, greedy for robbery to devour the sheep of Jesus Christ bought back with His Most Precious Blood: what care do you have of the holy fold of Christ? Good care, you say; but what? You have no other care than to devour and eat the goods of Holy Church without ever remembering the poor of the blessed Jesus

Christ. Your benefits are not enough for you, I call evil deeds for you, not the abbeys of the monks you have tyrannized, but hospitals, giving them their income, and the poor are starving to death in the fields and on the streets.

Woe to you because God Almighty will exalt a very poor man of the blood of the Emperor Constantine, son of St. Helena, and of the seed of Pepin, (i.e. King Pepin of France) *who shall on his breast wear the sign which you have seen at the beginning of this letter* (†) (i.e. a cross). *Through the power of the Most-High he shall confound the tyrants, the heretics, and infidels. He will gather a grand army, and the angels shall fight for them; they shall kill all God's enemies. O my Lord that man shall be one of your posterity, because you come from the blood of Pepin.*

(NOTE: Apparently, this condemnation in the letter to corrupt leaders in the world and the Church is also a prophecy that this era of lack of charity, tyranny, coldness, and sin will come before the Great King. It is for this reason the King will be sent to bring renewal.)

Fourth Letter – January 13, 1489

Four hundred years shall not pass when his Divine Majesty shall visit the world with a new religious order much needed, which shall affect more good among men than all other religious institutions combined. This religious order shall be the last and the best in the Church; it shall proceed with arms, with prayer, and with hospitality. Woe to tyrants, to heretics, and to infidels, to whom no pity shall be shown, because such is the will of the Most High! An infinite number of wicked men shall perish through the hands of the Cross-bearers, the true servants of Jesus Christ. They shall act like good husbandmen when they extirpate noxious weeds and prickly thistles from the wheat-field. These holy servants of God shall purify the earth with the deaths of innumerable wicked men. The head and captain of these holy servants of God shall be one of your posterity, and he shall be the great reformer of the Church of God.

(According to this prophecy by St. Francis, God would plan to bring the Great Monarch and his new Military Order of the Cruciferi sometime in the mid-1800s. Of interest, Our Lord also revealed this to Marie-Julie Jahenny and revealed something similar to St. Margaret Mary. To Marie-Julie Jahenny, Our Lord revealed that He had prepared to send the King then (i.e. it was the 1800s), but that France was proving unworthy then to receive him, having rejected the King of His choice. Therefore, the King was removed as the first chastisement, but he would be "returned" to his subjects and that the "Lily" would "resurrect." The time for the Great Monarch had therefore been delayed to a future date due to sin and the rejection of His chosen king...)

Fifth Letter – March 26, 1490

Let, therefore, the princes of this world be prepared for the greatest scourges to fall upon them. But from whom? First from heretics and infidels, then from the holy and most faithful Cruciferi elected by the Most-High who, not succeeding in converting heretics with science, shall have to make a vigorous use of their arms. Many cities and villages shall be in ruins, with the deaths of an innumerable quantity of bad and good men. The infidels also will fight against Christians and heretics, sacking, destroying, and killing the largest portion of Christians. Lastly, the army, styled of the Church, namely, the holy Cruciferi, shall move, not against Christians or Christianity, but against the infidels in pagan countries, and they shall conquer all those kingdoms with the death of a very great number of infidels. After this they shall turn their victorious arms against bad Christians and shall destroy all the rebels against Jesus Christ. These holy Cruciferi shall reign and dominate holily over the world until the end of time. The founder of these holy men shall, my lord, be one of your posterity. But when shall this take place? When crosses with the stigmas shall be seen, and the crucifix shall be carried as the standard. May our blessed Lord Jesus Christ reign!

Sixth Letter – March 7, 1495

The time is coming when his Divine Majesty will visit the world with a new religious order of holy Cruciferi, who will carry a crucifix, or the image of our crucified Lord, lifted up upon the principal standard in view of all. This standard will be admired by all good Catholics; but at the beginning it will be derided by bad Christians and by infidels. Their sneers shall, however, be changed into mourning when they shall witness the wonderful victories achieved through it against tyrants, heretics, and infidels. Many wicked men and obstinate rebels against God shall perish; their souls will be plunged into hell. This punishment shall fall upon all those transgressors of the Divine commandments who with new and false doctrines will attempt to corrupt mankind and turn men against the ministers of God's worship. The same chastisement is due to all obstinate sinners, but not to those who sin through weakness, because these being converted, doing penance, and amending the conduct of their life, shall find the divine mercy of the Most High full of kindness towards them.

O holy Cross-bearers of the Most High Lord, how very pleasing you will be to the great God, much more than the children of Israel! God will through your instrumentality work more wonderful prodigies than he has ever done before with any nation. You shall destroy the sect of Mahomet, and all infidels of every kind and of every sect. You shall put an end to all the heresies of the world by extinguishing all tyrants. You will remove every cause of complaint by establishing a universal peace, which shall last until the end of time. You will work the sanctification of mankind.

O holy men! People blessed of the Most Holy Trinity! Your victorious founder shall triumph over the world, the flesh, and the Devil. Laos Deo et omnibus Sanctis ejus. May God and all his saints be praised.

Seventh Letter – August 18, 1496

Let your soul rejoice! for his Divine Majesty manifests through you such wonderful signs and great miracles, according to what I, by God's will, have often and again written and foretold to you. One of your posterity shall achieve greater deeds and work greater wonders than your lordship. That man will be a great sinner in his youth, but like St. Paul he shall be drawn and converted to God. He shall be the great founder of a new religious order different from all the others. He shall divide it into three classes, namely: 1. Military knights; 2. Solitary priests; 3. Most pious hospitallers. This shall be the last religious order in the Church, and it will do more good for our holy religion than all other religious institutes. By force of arms he shall take possession of a great kingdom. He shall destroy the sect of Mahomet, extirpate all tyrants and heresies. He shall bring the world to a holy mode of life. There will be one fold and one Shepherd. He shall reign until the end of time. On the whole earth there shall be only twelve kings, one emperor, and one pope. Rich gentlemen shall be very few, but all saints.[99]

16th Century – 1511 – 1535: Abbot Jacques (Joaquim) Merlin (Prophecy Detail – Church persecutions, The holy pope, Wars, The unified Church, New government order)

Though Merlin was born circa 1480, the majority of his writings, and his prophecies, are generally attributed to a twenty-four-year period beginning in 1511. Some of his prophecies have, under intense scrutiny, been attributed to Blessed Joachim de Flore, but those quoted here most likely belong to Merlin.

Born in Saint-Victurnin of the Limousin diocese, Merlin studied theology at Navarre and received his doctorate in 1499. He was ordained curate of Montmartre and appointed chief penitentiary of the cathedral of Notre Dame. There is little evidence that he was actually an Abbot, though he is often referred to as such.

In 1527, Merlin's preaching got him arrested by King Francis I who accused Merlin of being unsympathetic to the cause of Lutheranism, though the real reasons for his incarceration are much more complex. He was kept in a dungeon of the Louvre for two years. Even upon his liberation from the dungeon, Merlin was kept for another year under house arrest at his residence in Nantes. He wasn't allowed to return to Paris until 1530 at which time he was installed as both grand vicar to the bishop of Paris, and curate and archpriest of La Madeleine. He died in 1541.

Merlin's prophecies support those of other mystics who spoke of worldly tribulations and a pope in accord with the Great Monarch. Of these topics he wrote:

> *After many prolonged sufferings endured by Christians, and after a too great effusion of innocent blood, the Lord shall give peace and happiness to the desolated nations. A remarkable pope will be seated on the pontifical throne, under the special protection of the angels. Holy and full of gentleness, he shall undo all wrong, he shall recover the states of the Church, and reunite the exiled temporal powers. He shall be revered by all people and shall recover the kingdom of Jerusalem. As the only Pastor he shall reunite the Eastern to the Western Church, and thus only one faith will be in vigor. The sanctity of this beneficent Pontiff will be so great that the highest potentates shall bow before his presence. This holy man shall crush the arrogance of religious schism and heresy. All men will return to the primitive Church, and there shall be only one pastor, one law, one master — humble, modest, and fearing God. The true God of the Jews, our Lord Jesus Christ, will make everything prosper beyond all human hope, because God alone can and will pour down on the wounds of humanity the oily balm of sweetness.*

> *The heavens proclaim the glory of God, and the faithful are in joy and happiness, because the Lord has vouchsafed to be merciful to them. He shall invite his elect to the banquet of the Lamb, where melodious canticles and harmonious concerts will be heard.*

> *The power of this Pontiff's holiness will be so great as to be able to check the fury and impetuosity of threatening waves. Mountains shall be lowered before him, the sea shall be dried up, the dead shall be raised, the churches shall be reopened, and altars erected.*

> *It should be known that there will be two heads, one in the East, and the other in the West. This Pope shall break the weapons and scatter the fighting hordes. He will be the joy of God's elect. This angelic pope will preach the gospel in every country. Through his zeal and solicitude, the Greek Church shall be forever reunited to the Catholic Church.*

> *Before, however, being firmly and solidly established in the Holy See, there will be innumerable wars and violent conflicts during which the sacred throne shall be shaken. But through the favor of*

divine clemency, moved by the prayers of the faithful, everything will succeed so well that they shall be able to sing hymns of thanksgiving to the glory of the Lord. (This prophecy shares the belief that the great pope, an associate of the Holy Emperor, will come to power after the global tribulations and will help to restore peace in the world.)

This holy Pope shall be both pastor and reformer. Through him the East and West shall be in everlasting concord. The city of Babylon shall then be the head and guide of the world. Rome, weakened in temporal power, shall forever preserve her spiritual dominion, and shall enjoy great peace. During these happy days the Angelic Pope shall be able to address to Heaven prayers full of sweetness. The dispersed nation shall also enjoy tranquility. Six and a half years after this time the Pope will render his soul to God. The end of his days shall arrive in an arid province, situated between a river and a lake near the mountains...

At the beginning, in order these happy results, having need of a powerful temporal assistance, this holy Pontiff will ask the cooperation of the generous monarch of France. At that time a handsome monarch, a scion of King Pepin, will come as a pilgrim to witness the splendor of this glorious pontiff, whose name shall begin with "R."... A temporal throne being vacant, the Pope shall place on it this king whose assistance he shall ask.

When a monster shall appear in the sky, thou shalt find a ready escape towards the east, and after nine years thou shalt render thy soul to God.

A man of remarkable sanctity will be his successor in the Pontifical chair. Through him God will work so many prodigies that all men shall revere him, and no person will dare to oppose his holy precepts. He shall not allow the clergy to have many benefices. He will induce them to live by tithes and offerings of the faithful. He shall interdict pomp in dress, and all immorality in dance and songs. He will preach the gospel in person and exhort all honest ladies to appear in public without any ornament of gold or precious stones. After having occupied the Holy See for a long time he shall happily return to the Lord.

His three immediate successors shall be men of exemplary holiness. One after the other will be models of virtue, and shall work miracles, confirming the teaching of their predecessors. Under their government the Church shall spread, and these Popes shall be called the Angelic Pastors.[100]

Yves Dupont notes that the notions of kings and kingdoms referenced by Merlin may seem a bit dated, but he acknowledges that government structures change and sometimes what is modern in one century is repressed and altered in another.

The United States of America currently faces a political movement that advocates an alteration of its current Democratic Republic form of government handed down by the founding fathers, to a hybrid of socialism called Democratic Socialism that lends itself toward a rudimentary type of Communism.

More importantly, Dupont points out that the coming disaster of which Merlin speaks will be no small event. Its magnitude will devastate the earth and, if not for the presence of the Church, would destroy the entire civilization. Survivors will immediately recognize the errors of the modern age and reject all the government principals that led to them. This may be the justification of new and currently unpopular forms of government of which Merlin speaks.

17ᵗʰ Century - February 2, 1594 -December 8, 1634: Mother Mariana de Jesus Torres - Our Lady of Good Success *(Prophecy Detail – God's wrath, The corruption of Church customs, the Antichrist, Apostacy of the faith, Moral degradation)*

Thess of the Purification and Candlemas* and She made many prophetic statements. On January 16, 1611, Our Lady specifically forewarned of a crisis that would envelop the Catholic Church beginning in the middle of the nineteenth century and extending throughout the entire twentieth century.

Our Lady said that God was ready to punish the world because of the egregious sins of blasphemy, impurity, and heresy. She spoke of the *"total corruption of customs"*[101] that would take place *"due to the reign of Satan in society through Freemasonry."*[102] She vividly described how the *"sacraments would lose their importance and would not be held in high esteem among the faithful due to those who held a 'position of authority.'"*[103] There will be enormous sacrileges, including the profanation of the Holy Eucharist. The sacraments of Baptism and Confirmation will wane, and many will fail to recognize the true presence of Jesus in the Eucharist. Many will die without benefit of the Sacrament of Extreme Unction, (now known as the Anointing of the Sick) either because of the

* The significance of Candlemas will be made clear in later chapters.

negligence of their families or misconceived affection for their sick ones. Regarding the Sacrament of Matrimony, Mary warned that iniquitous laws would be passed abolishing the *"Sacrament making it easy for everyone to live in sin and encouraging the procreation of illegitimate children born without the blessing of the Church.* "[104] She cautioned that people would be used as tools of the devil to destroy the Church, adding that many souls would be lost, society would suffer greatly, and there would be a massive loss of religious vocations.

These are the prophecies as reported by Mother Mariana:

First Apparition - February 2, 1594:

> *Thus, I make it known to you that from the end of the 19th century and from shortly after the middle of the 20th century, in what is today the Colony and will then be the Republic of Ecuador, the passions will erupt and there will be a total corruption of customs, for Satan will reign almost completely by means of the Masonic Sects. They will focus principally on the children in order to sustain this general corruption. Woe to the children of these times!*

> *It will be difficult to receive the Sacrament of Baptism and also the Sacrament of Confirmation. They will receive the Sacrament of Confession only if they remain in Catholic schools, for the Devil will make a great effort to destroy it through persons in position of authority. The same thing will happen with the Sacrament of Holy Communion.*

> *Alas! How deeply I grieve to manifest to you the many enormous sacrileges – both public as well as secret – that will occur from profanation of the Holy Eucharist. Often, during this epoch the enemies of Jesus Christ, instigated by the Devil, will steal consecrated Hosts from the churches so that they might profane the Eucharistic Species. My Most Holy Son will see Himself cast upon the ground and trampled upon by filthy feet...*

> *But in those times, you will already be known, as well as the favors that I am bestowing on you. How I love the fortunate inhabitants of this sacred place! And that knowledge will stimulate love and devotion to my Sacred Statue. For this reason, today, I authoritatively order you to have this Statue made: let it be sculptured just as you see Me and placed upon the Abbess's chair, so that from there I may govern and direct my daughters and defend my Convent; for Satan, making use of both the good and the evil, will engage in a fierce battle to destroy it...*

> *Since this poor Country will lack the Catholic spirit, the Sacrament of Extreme Unction will be little valued. Many people will die without receiving it – either because of the negligence of their families or misconceived affection for their sick ones. Others, incited by the cursed Devil, will rebel against the spirit of the Catholic Church*

*and will deprive countless souls of innumerable graces, consola-
tions, and the strength they need to make the great leap from time to
eternity. But some persons will die without receiving it due to just
and secret chastisements of God.*

*As for the Sacrament of Matrimony, which symbolizes the union of
Christ with His Church, it will be attacked and deeply profaned. Freemasonry, which will then be in power, will enact iniquitous laws with
the aim of doing away with this Sacrament, making it easy for everyone
to live in sin and encouraging the procreation of illegitimate children
born without the blessing of the Church. The Catholic spirit will rapidly
decay; the precious light of Faith will gradually be extinguished until
there will be an almost total and general corruption of customs. Added
to this will be the effects of secular education, which will be one reason
for the death of priestly and religious vocations.*

*The Sacrament of Holy Orders will be ridiculed, oppressed, and
despised, for in this Sacrament, the Church of God and even God Himself is scorned and despised since He is represented in His priests. The
Devil will try to persecute the ministers of the Lord in every possible
way; he will labor with cruel and subtle astuteness to deviate them from
the spirit of their vocation and will corrupt many of them. These depraved priests, who will scandalize the Christian people, will make the
hatred of bad Catholics and the enemies of the Roman Catholic and
Apostolic Church fall upon all priests.*

*This apparent triumph of Satan will bring enormous suffering to the
good Pastors of the Church, the many good priests, and the Supreme
Pastor and Vicar of Christ on earth, who, a prisoner in the Vatican, will
shed secret and bitter tears in the presence of his God and Lord, be-
seeching light, sanctity and perfection for all the clergy of the world, of
whom he is King and Father. Further, in these unhappy times, there will
be unbridled luxury which will ensnare the rest into sin and conquer
innumerable frivolous souls who will be lost. Innocence will almost no
longer be found in children, nor modesty in women.*

*In this supreme moment of need of the Church, the one who
should speak will fall silent!*

*You will see this from Heaven, my beloved daughter, where you can
no longer suffer, but your daughters and successors will suffer, those
beloved souls already known to you who will placate the Divine Ire.
They will have recourse to Me under the invocation of Our Lady of
Good Success, whose Statue I ask and command that you have made for
the consolation and preservation of my Convent and of the faithful souls
of that time, an epoch when there will be a great devotion to Me, for I
am Queen of Heaven under many invocations.*

This devotion will be the shield between Divine Justice and the prevaricating world to prevent the release of God's formidable punishment that this guilty earth deserves.[105]

Second Apparition – February 1594:

...Tell the Bishop that it is my will and the will of my Most Holy Son that your name be hidden at all costs, both within as well as outside the cloister, for it is not fitting for anyone at the present time to know the details or origin of how this Statue came to be made. For this knowledge will only become known to the general public in the 20th century.

During that epoch the Church will find herself attacked by terrible hordes of the Masonic sect, and this poor Ecuadorian land will be agonizing because of the corruption of customs, unbridled luxury, the impious press, and secular education. The vices of impurity, blasphemy and sacrilege will dominate in this time of depraved desolation, and that one who should speak out will be silent.

A simple, humble faith in the truth of my apparitions to you, my favored child, will be reserved for the humble and fervent who are docile to the inspirations of grace, for our Heavenly Father communicates His secrets to the simple of heart, and not to those whose hearts are inflated with pride, pretending to know what they do not or infatuated with empty science.[106]

Sixth Apparition - February 1634:

In order to free men from bondage to these heresies, those whom the merciful love of My Most Holy Son will destine for that restoration will need great strength of will, constancy, valor and confidence in God. To test this faith and confidence of the just, there will be occasions in which everything will seem to be lost and paralyzed. This will be, then, the happy beginning of the complete restoration.

During this unfortunate epoch, injustice will even enter here, my closed garden. Disguised under the name of false charity, it will wreak havoc in souls. The spiteful demon will try to sow discord, making use of putrid members, who, masked by the appearance of virtue, will be like decaying sepulchers emanating the pestilence of putrefaction, causing moral deaths in some and lukewarmness in others.

The spirit of impurity that will saturate the atmosphere in those times, like a filthy ocean, it will inundate the streets, squares and public places with an astonishing liberty. There will be almost no virgin souls in the world.

> *How the Church will suffer on that occasion the dark night of the lack of a Prelate and Father to watch over them with paternal love, gentleness, strength, and prudence. Many priests will lose their spirit, placing their souls in great danger. Pray insistently without tiring and weep with bitter tears in the secrecy of your heart, imploring our Celestial Father that, for love of the Eucharistic Heart of my Most Holy Son and His Precious Blood shed with such generosity and by the profound bitterness and sufferings of His cruel Passion and Death, He might take pity on His Ministers and quickly bring to an end those ominous times, sending to this Church the Prelate that will restore the spirit of its Priests.*[107]

It doesn't take a vivid imagination to see that many of prophecies of Our Lady of Good Success, as spoken through the mouth of Mother Mariana de Jesus Torres over four hundred years ago, accurately apply to the societal conditions of the nineteenth, twentieth, and twenty-first centuries. Indeed, the twentieth century belonged to Satan as promised him by God and described in the 1884 vision of Pope Leo XIII!

17th Century – 1602 – 1665: Venerable Mary of Jesus of Agreda *(Prophecy Detail – Victory over heresy, The Blessed Virgin's role during the last days, Chastisement and Unification of the Church)*

Mary of Jesus was born of noble parents in the municipality of Agreda just after the turn of the century in 1602 and displayed signs of grace at a very early age. By the age of six, Mary had shown a significant devotion to the Virgin Mary and the sufferings of Jesus for which she attained a high degree of prayer.

At seventeen, Mary became a novice at the convent of the Poor Clares of the Immaculate Conception at Agreda, where she excelled. In the year 1620, Mary made her profession and chose perfect and cheerful surrender to God. By age twenty-five, Mary was elected abbess and confirmed in that role by the Pope. She held the position until her death in 1665. Despite her position of authority, Mary was the first to accept every menial task offered.

She slept only two to three hours per night while reclining on a board. The remainder of the night, she spent in devotional exercises. Each night she made the way of the cross while herself carrying a heavy cross. Though in charge of the convent, Mary remained humble and obedient even when her confessor treated her harshly and denied her every request.

Born with a gift of extraordinary wisdom, Mary became a prolific writer. A mystic with mysterious powers of bilocation, she was given special revelations regarding the life of the Mother of God and recorded them in a multi-volume book called *The Mystical City of God*. Over five hundred times, she found herself teaching the Indians of Texas and New Mexico, though she had never left Spain. When asked to explain this mystical power, she could not, saying only that during prayer for the welfare of the Indians, she found herself inexplicably among them.

Her mystical powers did not end there, however. A bishop testified that as Mary of Jesus prayed, she went into an ecstatic state in which her entire body would rise a bit above the ground, appearing as if weightless, and moving to even the slightest of breezes. During this ecstasy, which sometimes lasted hours, her face was beautiful, though a bit more pallid than usual.

Mary's life came to an end at 9:00 a.m. on May 24, 1667, the morning of Pentecost Sunday, and at the exact time that the Holy Spirit descended upon the Apostles. Those that surrounded her heard a voice from heaven say, "Come! Come! Come!" Many miracles occurred at her gravesite and her body remains in a state of incorruption.

Among her prophecies, Mary said the following about the end-times:

> *It was revealed to me that through the intercession of the Mother of God, all heresies will disappear. This victory over heresies has been reserved by Christ for His Blessed Mother. In the last times the Lord will especially spread the renown of His Mother: Mary began salvation and by her intercession it will be concluded. Before the Second Coming of Christ, Mary must, more than ever, shine in mercy, might and grace in order to bring unbelievers into the Catholic Faith. The powers of Mary in the last times over the demons will be very conspicuous. Mary will extend the reign of Christ over the heathens and Mohammedans and it will be a time of great joy when Mary as Mistress and Queen of Hearts is enthroned as mistress of the Queen of Hearts.*
>
> *An unusual chastisement of the human race will take place towards the end of the world.*[108]

The prophecy of Mary of Jesus of Agreda is not the only prophecy that speaks to the Blessed Virgin's role at the end of times. Mary herself spoke of these at apparitions at Fatima, Knock, Garabandal, LaSalette, Rue du Bac, and in many other places.

17th Century – Early 1600s: Balthassar Mas *(Prophecy Detail – England destroyed by water)*

I saw a land swallowed by the sea and covered with water, but afterwards I saw that little by little, the sea retreated and left the land visible, and the upper parts of the towers and the turrets of the cities rose and appeared more beautiful than before being swallowed by the sea, and it was told [to] me that was England.[109]

17th Century – Mid 1600s: Venerable Bartholomew Holzhauser (Prophecy Detail – Wars, Church persecution, The great monarch, The holy pope.)

Bartholomew Holzhauser was born in Laugna, Germany on August 24, 1613. His parents, who had eleven children, were poor, but also honest and pious people. This probably fueled young Bartholomew's desire to enter the sacred ministry. He was admitted to a free school for poor boys where he was required to earn his keep. He did so by going door to door singing and begging. After recovering from a sickness during an epidemic raging at the time, Bartholomew returned home and helped his father, who was a shoemaker.

Before long, however, Bartholomew, with the aid of friends and the Jesuits, resumed his studies. His talents, piety, and modesty offered great hope to his teachers that the young man would be very useful to the Church. Bartholomew studied hard and on July 9, 1636, he earned his doctorate in Philosophy. On May 11, 1639, he added to his credentials a baccalaureate in theology. He was admitted to the priesthood and celebrated his first Mass in the Church of Our Lady of Victory on June 12, 1639, the Feast of Pentecost.

Before long, Fr. Holzhauser earned a reputation as a confessor and was much sought after. By 1640, he was declared licentiate of theology and entered the Archdiocese of Salzburg where he was made dean and pastor of Tittmoning. Bartholomew was named pastor of St. John's at Leoggenthal and in the spring of 1655, went to Mainz where he was appointed pastor at Bingen on the Rhine. There he also served as dean of the district of Algesheim.

Fr. Holzhauser founded the Barholomites, a new religious society that he felt would address several issues of the faithful. Bartholomew believed that their faith had grown lukewarm and that their morals and discipline had relaxed in both the laity and the clergy. This union became known as the Apostolic Union of Secular Priests and its members would lead an apostolic life in the community while becoming models of priestly perfection, as well as zealous leader of the people.

Holzhauser was also a visionary who made his visions public when he presented them to Emperor Ferdinand III and to Duke Maximilian I. One such vision prophesied the execution of Charles I of England and the complete ruin of the Church that followed. He also told of a 120-year period in which the Holy Sacrifice would cease. This prophecy seems to have been fulfilled when, in 1658, England made the celebration of Mass illegal under the penalty of death. Those restrictions were partially recalled in 1778, one hundred and twenty years later. Ludwig Clarus published a book of Holzhauser's visions in 1849.

Fr. Holzhauser also published his own book on the Revelations of St. John. This prophetic book interprets the Apocalypse by likening the seven stars and seven candlesticks seen by St. John as seven distinct periods of the history of the Catholic Church from its foundation to the final judgment. The book is still held in high regard by Catholics worldwide. According to Holzhauser, seven Church ages must unfold before the final coming of Jesus Christ. The Catholic Church entered the Fifth Age around the year 1520. The Fifth Age will end with the arrival of the Holy Pope and the Great Monarch, which Holzhauser predicted will be in about the year 2038.

The following are the prophecies of Bartholomew Holzhauser as they pertain to the Fifth and Sixth Periods of the Church:

The Fifth Period:

The fifth period is one of affliction, desolation, humiliation, and poverty for the Church. Jesus Christ will purify His people through cruel wars, famines, plagues, epidemics, and other horrible calamities. He will also afflict and weaken the Latin Church with many heresies. It is a period of defections, calamities and exterminations. Those Christians who survive the sword, plague and famines, will be few on earth. Nations will fight against nations and will be desolated by internecine dissensions...

During this period the Wisdom of God guides the Church in several ways:

1) by chastising the Church so that riches may not corrupt her completely;

2) by interposing the Council of Trent like a light in the darkness, so that the Christians who see the light may know what to believe,

3) by setting St. Ignatius and his Society in opposition to Luther and other heretics;

4) by carrying to remote lands the Faith which has been banned in most of Europe...

Are we not to fear during this period that the Mohamedans [Muslims] will come again working out their sinister schemes against the Latin Church.

During this period, many men will abuse of the freedom of conscience conceded to them. It is of such men that Jude the Apostle spoke when he said, "These men blaspheme whatever they do not understand; and they corrupt whatever they know naturally as irrational animals do... They feast together without restraint, feeding themselves, grumbling murmurers, walking according to their lusts; their mouth speaketh proud things, they admire people for the sake of gain; they bring about division, sensual men, having not the spirit."

During this unhappy period, there will be laxity in divine and human precepts. Discipline will suffer. The Holy Canons will be completely disregarded, and the Clergy will not respect the laws of the Church. Everyone will be carried away and led to believe and to do what he fancies, according to the manner of the flesh...

They will ridicule Christian simplicity; they will call it folly and nonsense, but they will have the highest regard for advanced knowledge, and for the skill by which the axioms of the law, the precepts of morality, the Holy Canons and religious dogmas are clouded by senseless questions and elaborate arguments. As a result, no principle at all, however holy, authentic, ancient, and certain it may be, will remain free of censure, criticism, false interpretation, modification, and delimitation by man...

These are evil times, a century full of dangers and calamities... Heresy is everywhere, and the followers of heresy are in power almost everywhere. Bishops, prelates, and priests say that they are doing their duty, that they are vigilant, and that they live as befits their state in life. In like manner, therefore, they all seek excuses. But God will permit a great evil against His Church: Heretics and tyrants will come suddenly and unexpectedly; they will break into the Church while bishops, prelates and priests are asleep. They will enter Italy and lay Rome waste; they will burn down the churches and destroy everything....

The fifth period of the Church, which began circa 1520, will end with the arrival of the holy Pope [Peter the Roman] and of the powerful Monarch who is called "Help From God" because he will restore everything [in Christ]...

The Sixth Period:
    The Sixth Period of the church, the (status consolationis)—time of "Consolation," begins with the Holy Pope and the powerful emperor and terminates with the rise of Antichrist. (Revelations, 3: 7, 10.)

*   This will be an age of solace, wherein God will console His church after the many mortifications and afflictions she had endured in the fifth period. For all nations will be brought to the unity of the true Catholic faith.*

*   A type of this period was the sixth age of the old world, from the deliverance of the Israelites out of the Babylonian captivity, and the rebuilding of the city and of the temple of Jerusalem, down to the coming of Christ. As God gladdened His people by the rebuilding of the temple and of the holy city; as all kingdoms and nations were subjected to the Roman empire; and Caesar Augustus, the most powerful and excellent monarch, after vanquishing all his enemies, gave for fifty-six years, peace to the world; so will God pour out upon His church, that witnessed in the fifth period naught but affliction, the most abundant consolations. But this happy age will be ushered in under the following circumstances. When all is desolated with war; when the church and the priests must pay taxes; when Catholics are oppressed by heretics, and their faithless fellow-religionists; when monarchs are murdered; subjects oppressed; when riches are extirpated; when everything concurs to bring about the establishment of Republics; then will the hand of the Almighty produce a marvelous change, according to human notions seemingly impossible. For that strong monarch, (whose name is to be "the help of God,") will as the envoy of the Almighty, root up these Republics. He will subject all things to himself and will zealously assist the true Church of Christ. All heresies will be banished into hell; the Turkish Empire [Islam] will be overthrown to its foundations, and his dominion will extend from east to west. All nations will come and will worship the Lord in the one true Catholic Faith. Many righteous men will flourish, and many learned men will arise. Men will love justice and righteousness, and peace will dwell on the whole earth. For the Omnipotent will bind Satan for many years, until the advent of him who is to come, the son of perdition.*

*   In respect to perfection, this period corresponds to the sixth day of creation, on which God created man after His own image, and subjected to him, as lord of creation, all creatures of the earth. So will man be now a true image of God, (in righteousness and holiness), and the strong monarch will rule over all nations.*

The sixth gift of the spirit, the fear of the Lord will in this period be poured out upon the church; for men will fear the Lord their God, keep His commandments, and serve him with their whole heart. The scriptures will be understood after one uniform fashion, without contradiction and error, so that all will marvel they had so long misunderstood the clear sense of holy writ. The sciences will be multiplied and completed, and men will receive extraordinary illumination in natural, as well as divine knowledge.[110]

Yves Dupont notes that many of Holzhauser's prophecies confirm those of the Ecstatic of Tours. He correctly saw, over three hundred years ago, so many events that have seemingly come to pass. It is apparent that God has already set the stage for the spectacular rejuvenation which He will design.

17th Century – 1670s: Saint Margaret Mary Alacoque *(Prophecy Detail – The last effort of God's love)*

Margaret Alacoque was the only daughter born of Claude and Philiberte Lamyn Alacoque. Her birth took place in 1647 in L'Hautecour, Burgundy, a part of France now under the commune of Verosvres. Claude died when Margaret was very young, and the family's assets were held by a relative who refused to give them any part of it. As a result, the family became impoverished. During this time, Margaret took solace in visiting her local church and praying before the Blessed Sacrament, for which she acquired a special and intense love.

She made her First Communion at age nine and secretly practiced severe corporal mortification until rheumatic fever left her bedridden for four years. It was at the end of her illness that she made a vow to the Blessed Virgin to consecrate herself to a religious life. Her health was instantly restored and, in gratitude to Our Lady, Margaret added the name "Mary" as her middle name. As a youngster, Margaret also had visions of Jesus Christ, but thought they were a normal part of the human experience. Regardless, these visions prolonged her practice of austerity.

Her family regained their fortune when Margaret was seventeen and her mother urged her to socialize with her brothers in the hopes of finding a suitable man to marry. Out of obedience, she attended Carnivals and other social gatherings with them, forgetting for the moment her promise to dedicate herself to a religious life.

One night, while walking home from a ball, Margaret had a vision of Christ, scourged and bloody. He reproached her for her broken promise, but assured Margaret that *"His Heart was filled with love for her, because of the childhood promise she had made to His Blessed Mother.*"[111] This experience convinced Margaret that she needed to join a convent. On May 25, 1671, when she was almost twenty-four years old, Margaret entered the Visitation Convent at Paray-le-Monial intending to join the order. Subjected to many trials during the next several months, Margaret was admitted to wearing the religious habit, but her profession was delayed until November 6, 1672 rather than on the one-year anniversary of wearing the habit as was the custom for the time. She was assigned to the infirmary, where her lack of skill was evident. One of the novices who served with her described Margaret Mary as kind, patient, humble, simple, and frank.

It was in this monastery that Margaret Mary began to receive private revelations from Jesus. The apparitions began on December 27, 1673 and ended eighteen months later in May 1674. Of these apparitions, Margaret Mary would later say,

> *I understand that devotion to the Sacred Heart is a last effort of His love towards Christians of these latter times, by offering to them an object and means so calculated to persuade them to love Him.*[112]

The extent of God's mercy, and His many efforts to extend His mercy to mankind, was also a prevalent theme in the apparitions of Jesus to Sister Faustina.

Alacoque was pronounced Venerable by Pope Leo XII in March 1824 and was declared Blessed by Pope Pius IX on September 18, 1864. When her tomb was opened in July 1830, two instantaneous cures were reported. Her body was found to be incorrupt. It now rests above the side altar in the Chapel of Apparitions in the Visitation Monastery in France. Margaret Mary was canonized a saint by Pope Benedict XV in 1920.

17th & 18th Centuries – 1673 – 1716: St. Louis-Marie Grignion De Montfort: *(Prophecy Detail – Conversion of Mohammedans, Role of Mary)*

Born in Montfort-sur-Meu in 1673, Louis was the first of eighteen children born to Jean-Baptiste and Jeanne Robert Grignion, though many of the other children did not live past infancy. When Louis was only twelve, he entered the Jesuit College of St. Thomas Becket, where his uncle was a parish priest. He studied philosophy and theology, but it was the inspiration of a missionary that created his interest in preaching to the poor. During that time, Louis developed a keen devotion to the Blessed Mother.

Montfort also studied in Paris, living among the very poor as he did. Less than two years later, a serious illness caused his hospitalization.

Once released, he entered the Little Saint-Sulpice and was appointed librarian, providing an opportunity for him to study most of the available works on the role of the Virgin Mary in Christianity. He later published a book called *Secret of the Rosary*. This was followed by *True Devotion to Mary* and he quickly earned respect as one of the early writers about the Blessed Virgin Mary.

In the latter part of 1700, Montfort joined the Third Order of the Dominicans. There he preached the Rosary and formed Rosary confraternities. This work, and his gathering of priests to preach missions and retreats, eventually led to the formation of the Company of Mary.

Pope Clement XI recognized Montfort's true vocation as a missionary preacher, however, and gave him the title of Apostolic Missionary with an order to preach to Christians in need of guidance in Montfort's homeland of France. He quickly earned a stellar reputation as a preacher and also continued his writings with the publication of a number of classic Catholic books.

In 1715, Montfort, with the assistance of several others, opened a school which quickly grew in size to accommodate its four hundred students. The arduous nature of the work left him exhausted and he grew gravely ill, until, on April 28, 1716, at the age of forty-three, Montfort died. Thousands attended his funeral and a number of miracles were reported at the tomb. He was canonized by Pope Pius XII on July 20, 1947 and his cause for becoming a Church Doctor is underway. Montfort wrote:

> *The power of Mary over all evils will be particularly outstanding in the last period of time. She will extend the Kingdom of Christ over the idolaters and Muslims, and there will come a glorious era when Mary is the Ruler and Queen of Hearts...*[113]

This prophecy is in accord with Ven. Mary of Jesus of Agreda. Further, in his book, True Devotion to Mary, Montfort wrote:

> *I have said that this would come to pass, particularly at the end of the world and indeed presently, because the Most High and His most Holy Mother has to form for Himself great saints who shall surpass most of the other saints in sanctity as much as the cedars of Lebanon outgrow the little shrubs. These great souls, full of grace and zeal shall be chosen to match themselves against the enemies of God, who shall rage on all sides; and they shall be singularly devoted to Our Blessed Lady, illuminated by her light, strengthened by her nourishment, led by her spirit, supported by her arm and sheltered under her protection, so that they shall fight with one hand and*

build with another. With the one hand they shall fight and overthrow and crush the heretics with their heresies, the schismatics with their schisms, the idolaters with their idolatries and the sinners with their impieties...by their words and examples they shall draw the whole world to true devotion to Mary. This shall bring upon them many enemies but also bring many victories and much Glory for God alone.[114]

In these writings, Montfort confirms the prophecies of others regarding the conversion of Islam which will take place, as author Yves Dupont notes, under the reign of the Great Monarch following the invasion of Western Europe and the Christian King's defeat of the Arabs.

18th Century – 1731 – 1798: Sister Jeanne le Royer (aka Sister Jeanne Royer of the Nativity) *(Prophesy Detail – The apostacy, Persecution of the Church and Catholics, Bloody wars both civil and foreign, Church scandals, Earthquakes and other natural disasters, Faithless people, The rise of the Antichrist, A long peace)*

Her family was quite impoverished when Jeanne de le Royer entered the world in 1731. Little changed in that regard as she grew to adolescence, which may have helped shape her desire to enter the religious life early on. Her total destitution following the death of both parents when she was only fifteen or sixteen, in fact, left her with no choice but to seek admission into a convent. When she was unable to pay the required dowry, even that plan seemed to be foiled, though eventually, in 1755, she was admitted to the convent of the Urbanists at Fougères as a charitable entrant. Upon taking her vows she took the name Sister Nativite, translated, Sister of the Nativity.

Sister Nativite took on a life of penance and mortification. She fasted and self-flagellated routinely. She would occasionally line her bed with thistles and nettles to increase the discomfort of sleeping and would sip gall mixed with other equally disgusting things. Though she was plagued with numerous health problems throughout her life, she did find some comfort when a tumor on her knee was miraculously healed after her companion sisters completed a novena on her behalf.

She had a number of spiritual gifts that included the reading of hearts and visions of the future, including glimpses of the Last Judgment. Because Sister Nativite was illiterate, these visions were written down by Abbé Genet, her spiritual director, but only with the promise that he would not release them until after her death, which occurred on the Feast of the Assumption in 1798.

Abbé Genet followed her wishes and published the first edition of her visions in 1817. The second book followed two years later. A third volume of her prophecies and visions was subsequently released. All three volumes were reviewed and examined by more than one hundred theologians, seven or eight bishops and archbishops, twenty or thirty vicars-general of various diocese, doctors and professors of theology, abbots, authors and academics, more than eighty parish priests, vicars, and several other educated people of the world. No objectionable content was found in them.

The following prophecies pertain to the period of time between the French Revolution and the appearance of the Antichrist and, like so many other related prophecies, seem to have a bearing on the twenty-first century:

> *I see that the century which begins in 1800 shall not yet be the last. The reign of Antichrist is approaching. The thick vapors which I have seen rising from the earth and obscuring the light of the sun are the false maxims of irreligion and licence [sic] which are confounding all sound principles and spreading everywhere such darkness as to obscure both faith and reason.*
>
> *One day I heard a voice which said: "The new Constitution will appear to many other than what it really is." They will bless it as a gift from heaven; whereas, it is in fact sent from hell and permitted by God in His just wrath. It will only be by its effects that people will be led to recognize the Dragon who wanted to destroy all and devour all.*
>
> *One night I saw a number of ecclesiastics. Their haughtiness and air of severity seemed to demand the respect of all. They forced the faithful to follow them. But God commanded me to oppose them: "They no longer have the right to speak in my name," Jesus told me. "It is against My wish that they carry out a mandate for which they are no longer worthy."*
>
> *I saw a great power rise up against the Church. It plundered, devastated, and threw into confusion and disorder the vine of the Lord, having it trampled underfoot by the people and holding it up to ridicule by all nations. Having vilified celibacy and oppressed the priesthood, it had the effrontery to confiscate the Church's property and to arrogate to itself the powers of the Holy Father, whose person and whose laws it held in contempt.*
>
> *I had a vision: Before the Father and the Son – both seated – a virgin of incomparable beauty, representing the Church, was kneeling. The Holy Ghost spread His shining wings over the virgin and the two other persons. The wounds of Our Lord seemed alive. Leaning on the*

Cross with one hand, He offered to His Father with the other hand the chalice which the Master held in the middle. The Father placed one hand on the cup and raised the other to bless the virgin.

I noticed that the chalice was only half-filled with blood, and I heard these words spoken by the Savior at the moment of presentation: "I shall not be fully satisfied until I am able to fill it right up to the brim." I understood then that the contents of the chalice represented the blood of the early martyrs, and that this vision had reference to the last persecutions of the Christians, whose blood would fill the chalice, thereby completing the number of martyrs and predestined. For at the end of time, there will be as many martyrs as in the early Church, and even more, for the persecutions will be far more violent. Then the Last Judgment will no longer be delayed.

I see in God that a long time before the rise of Antichrist the world will be afflicted with many bloody wars. Peoples will rise against peoples, and nations will rise against nations, sometimes allied, sometimes enemies, in their fight against the same party. Armies will come into frightful collisions and will fill the earth with murder and carnage.

These internal and foreign wars will cause enormous sacrifices, profanations, scandals, and infinite evils, because of the incursions that will be made into the Church.

As well as that, I see that the earth will be shaken in different places by frightful earthquakes. I see whole mountains cracking and splitting with a terrible din. Only too happy will one be if one can escape with no more than a fright; but no, I see come out of these gaping mountains whirlwinds of smoke, fire, Sulphur, and tar, which reduce to cinders entire towns. All this and a thousand other disasters must come before the rise of the Man of Sin.

I saw in the light of the Lord that the faith and our holy Religion would become weaker in almost every Christian kingdom. God has permitted that they should be chastised by the wicked in order to awaken them from their apathy. And after the justice of God has been satisfied, He will pour out an abundance of graces on His Church, and He will spread the Faith and restore the discipline of the Church in those countries where it had become tepid and lax.

I saw in God that our Mother, Holy Church, will spread in many countries and will produce her fruits in abundance to compensate for the outrages she will have suffered from the impiety and the persecutions of her enemies.

I saw the poor people, weary of the arduous labors and trials that God sent to them, shall then be thrilled with a joy that God will infuse in their good hearts. The Church will become by her faith and by her love, more fervent and more flourishing than ever. Our good Mother the Church will witness many amazing things, even on the part of her former persecutors, for they will come forward and throw themselves at her feet, acknowledge her, and implore pardon from God and from her for all the crimes and outrages that they had perpetrated against her. She will no longer regard them as her enemies, but she will instead welcome them as her own children.

Now all the true penitents will flow from all sides to the Church, which will receive them into her bosom. The entire community of the faithful will pour out their hearts in hymns of penance and thanksgiving to the glory of the Lord.

I see in God a great power, led by the Holy Ghost, which will restore order through a second upheaval. I see in God a large assembly of pastors who will uphold the rights of the Church and of her Head. They will restore the former disciplines. I see, in particular, two servants of the Lord who will distinguish themselves in this glorious struggle and who, by the grace of the Holy Ghost, will fill with ardent zeal the hearts of this illustrious assembly.

All the false cults will be abolished; all the abuses of the Revolution will be destroyed, and the altars of the true God restored. The former practices will be put into force again, and our religion – at least in some respects – will flourish more than ever.

I see in God that the Church will enjoy a profound peace over a period which seems to me to be of a fairly long duration. This respite will be the longest of all that will occur between the revolutions from now till the General Judgment. The closer we draw to the General Judgment the shorter will be the revolutions against the Church. The kind of peace that will follow each revolution will be shorter also. This is so because we are approaching the End of Time, and little time will be left for either the elect to do good or for the wicked to do evil.

One day the Lord said to me: "A few years before the coming of my enemy, Satan will raise up false prophets who will announce Antichrist as the true Messiah, and they will try to destroy all our Christian beliefs. And I shall make the children and the old people prophesy. The closer we get to the reign of Antichrist, the more will the darkness of Satan spread over the earth, and the more will his satellites increase their efforts to trap the faithful in their net."

When the reign of Antichrist draws near, a false religion will appear which will deny the unity of God and will oppose the Church. Errors will cause ravages as never before.

One day I found myself in a vast plain alone with God. Jesus appeared to me and from the top of a small hill, showed to me a beautiful sun on the horizon. He said dolefully: "The world is passing away and the time of My second coming draws near. When the sun is about to set, one knows that the day is nearly over and that the night will soon fall. Centuries are like days for me. Look at this sun, see how much it still has to travel, and estimate the time that is left to the world."

I looked intently and it seemed to me that the sun would set in two hours. Jesus said: "Do not forget that these are not millenaries, but only centuries, and they are few in number."

But I understood that Jesus reserved to Himself the knowledge of the exact number, and I did not wish to ask Him more. It sufficed me to know that the peace of the Church and the restoration of discipline were to last a reasonably long time.

God has manifested to me the malice of Lucifer and the perverse and diabolical intentions of his henchmen against the Holy Church of Jesus Christ. At the command of their master these wicked men have crossed the world like furies to prepare the way and the place for Antichrist, whose reign is approaching. Through the corrupted breath of their proud spirit they have poisoned the minds of men. Like persons infected with pestilence, they have communicated the evil to each other, and the contagion has become general. The storm began in France, and France shall be the first theater of its ravages after having been its cradle. The Church in Council shall one day strike with anathemas, pull down and destroy the evil principles of that criminal constitution. What a consolation! What a joy for the truly faithful![115]

18th Century – circa 1760: Fr. Charles Auguste Lazare Nectou (aka Nectoux, Necktou) *(Prophecy Detail – The great monarch, Revolution, Triumph of the Church, Three days of darkness)*

Charles Nectou was born in France on November 30, 1698. As a young man he became a provincial of the Jesuits of Aquitaine and authored many ascetic writings. Many years later Nectou was named rector of the College of Poitiers where he served from 1752 to 1760. Many who knew him considered him a saint and a prophet. There are claims that he raised a dead child to life and his prophecies appear without condemnation. He rightly predicted, when Madeleine Sophie Barat was only about three years old, that she would found an order which became known as the Society of the Sacred Heart. He correctly told a young priest that he would become the archbishop of a great city and that the Jesuits would open their first college. He also prophesied the *"horrors of the French Revolution, the counter-revolutionary movement and the triumph of the Bourbons."*[116]

Fr. Nectou died on April 29, 1773, but his prophecies were preserved in the writings of the Apostolic Bikar Eillis of Edinburgh published in 1833. With regard to the chastisement, Fr. Nectou prophesied the following around the year 1760:

There will be new troubles in France. A hateful name to France will be placed on the throne. One of Orleans will be king. Only after this usurpation will the counter-revolution be made. It will not be done by strangers. Two parties will be formed in France that will wage a war to the death. One party of order and the other of disorder. One will be much more numerous than the other, but it will be the weakest who will triumph.

Then there will be a moment so terrible that we believe it the end of the world. The blood will run in several big cities: the elements will be raised. It will be like a little judgment. A great multitude will perish in this catastrophe, but the wicked will not prevail. They intend to destroy the Church entirely; time will not be given to them because this horrible period will be short-lived. When we believe everything lost, everything will be saved. During this terrible upheaval that will be general and not only for France, Paris will be completely destroyed. The destruction will be so complete that, for twenty years after, the fathers will walk with their children on its ruins, and to answer their questions, they will say to them: "My son, there was a great city here, God destroyed it because of its crimes." We will be near this catastrophe when England begins to move. It will be known at this sign, as we know the approach of summer when the fig tree begins to bud.

England, in her turn, will experience a revolution more terrible than the French Revolution, and it will last long enough for France to have time to sit down again. It will be France that will help England restore peace. When we are ready for these events which must bring about a triumph of the Church...the disorder will be so complete that we will know nothing about [the triumph being near].

When the moment of the last crisis comes, there will be nothing to do but to remain where God has placed us, shut ourselves inside and pray, while waiting for the passage of divine anger and justice. As a result of these frightful events, everything will return to order, justice will be done to everyone, the counter-revolution will be consumed.

Then the triumph of the Church will be such that there will never have been such a thing. The happy Christians who have survived...will thank God for having reserved them to contemplate such a complete triumph of the Church.

Misfortunes must happen. Blood will flow in torrents in the North and the South. The West will be spared because of its faith. But blood will flow so far north and south, that I see it flow like rain on a stormy day, and I see the horses with blood to their straps. It is mainly in the cities that blood will flow.

Religion will be persecuted. Ministers will be forced to hide at least momentarily. The churches will be closed again for a short time....Paris will be destroyed in the midst of all these calamities, so destroyed that the plow will pass there.

In these events the good will have nothing to do, because it is the Republicans who devour each other. There will come a moment when one will believe everything lost. It is then that everything will be saved, because between the cry, "All is lost" and "All is saved," there will be no interval, so to speak, the time to transfer a cake.

Foreign powers will arm themselves, march against France. Russia will come to water her horses in the Rhine, but will not pass it....Russia will convert and help France to restore peace and tranquility to the world....

After the crisis, there will be a general council, despite some oppositions made by the clergy themselves. Then there will be only one flock and one shepherd, because all the infidels and heretics will return to the Latin Church, whose triumph will continue until the destruction of the Antichrist. The triumph of the Church will be such that it will never have had such a thing [i.e. the Triumph will be so great it will have never known such a triumph before.][117]

18th Century – Sister Marianne Gaultier: *(Prophecy Detail, Three days of darkness – New social and political order, Church triumphs and becomes one with the state, Workers' guilds will replace trade unions)*

Sister Marianne was an Ursuline Nun in the Convent of Blois, France. Throughout her life she earned a reputation for sanctity and made several prophecies, including the fall of Napoleon I and his brief return from Elba. Some of the prophecies, such as those presented here, describe the latter days.

As long as public prayers are said, nothing shall happen. But a time will come when public prayers shall cease. People will say: "Things will remain as they are."

All men will be taken away gradually in small groups. Only old men will remain. Before the great battle the wicked shall be masters.

They will do as much harm as they can, but not as much as they would like, because they shall not have enough time. The good Catholics shall be on the point of being annihilated but, O Power of God, a stroke from Heaven will save them. All the wicked shall perish, but also many good Catholics.

Such extraordinary events shall take place that the most incredulous will be forced to say: "Truly, the finger of God is here." There shall be a terrible night during which no one will be able to sleep. But these trials shall not last long because no one could endure them. When all shall appear lost, all will be saved.

It is then that the Prince shall reign, whom people did not esteem before, but whom they shall then seek. The triumph of religion will be so great that no one has ever seen the equal. All injustices will be made good; civil laws will be made in harmony with the laws of God and of the Church. Education in the schools will be most Christian, and workers' guilds will flourish again.[118]

Chapter 9

The Later Prophecies: Nineteenth Through the Twenty-First Century

19th Century – 1801: Helen Wallraff *(Prophecy Detail – Pope flees Rome)*

Helen Wallraff was a stigmatist born in the year 1755. She was from a German farming family who lived near Köln and died on September 14, 1801, leaving behind this prophecy:

> *Someday a pope will flee from Rome in the company of only four cardinals...and they will come to Koeln [Cologne].[119]*

While many other prophets forewarned of a pope fleeing from Rome, Wallraff is the first to mention that he would be accompanied by four cardinals, lending credence to the interpretation of Yves Dupont, author of *Catholic Prophesy: The Coming Chastisement*, who long believed that only four cardinals would be with the pope as he fled Rome. Surely there would be a greater number of cardinals who remained faithful, but they would be isolated in various countries, according to Dupont, and unable to communicate because of the chaotic conditions of the time. Even when the pope dies in exile, the cardinals will be unable to elect a new pontiff, leading the way to the reign of an antipope.

19th Century – Early 1800s: Bishop George Michael Wittman, Mystic *(Prophecy Detail – Exile and death of the pope, Secret societies)*

Wittman was born in 1760 Germany, where he first studied with the Jesuits and then the Benedictines. In 1782 he was ordained a priest and became a professor at a diocesan seminary in 1788. From 1804 he also served as pastor of the cathedral. By 1829 he was appointed auxiliary Bishop of Ratisbon and a year later was made vicar-general, serving under Johann Michael Sailer, the ordinary of Ratisbon. Following the death of Sailer, Witmann became Bishop of Ratisbon on July 1, 1832 but died in 1833 before his preconization.

Witmann's zeal, charity, and exemplary life gained him the esteem and affection of all who knew him. Many believed him to be a living saint. During his many years as a priest, Witmann influenced some fifteen hundred candidates for the seminary, preparing them for the priesthood. He was also a significant force in helping with the discernment of Karolina Gerhardinger, aka Blessed Theresa of Jesus, who founded the School Sisters of Notre Dame.

The cause for Witmann's canonization was opened in 1956. Witmann was also a mystic who spoke many prophecies about the end times. He said in part:

Woe is me! Sad days are at hand for the Holy Church of Jesus Christ. The Passion of Jesus will be renewed in the most dolorous manner in the Church and in her Supreme Head. In all parts of the world there will be wars and revolutions, and much blood will be spilled. Distress, disasters, and poverty will everywhere be great, since pestilential maladies, scarcity, and other misfortunes will follow one another.

Violent hands will be laid on the Supreme Head of the Catholic Church; bishops and priests will be persecuted, and schisms will be provoked, and confusion reign amid all classes. Times will come, so preeminently bad, that it will seem as if the enemies of Christ, and of his Holy Church, which He founded with His blood, were about to triumph over her.... A general separation will be made. The wheat shall be winnowed, and the floor swept.

Secret societies will work great ruin, and exercise a marvellous monetary power, and through that many will be blinded, and infected with most horrible errors; however, all this shall avail naught. Christ says, "He who is not with Me is against Me, and he who gathereth not with Me scattereth." Scandals will be but too rife, and woe to those by whom they come! Although the tempests will be terrible, and will turn away many in their passage, nevertheless they cannot shake the rock whereon Christ has founded his Church. "Porte inferi non prevalebunt."

The faithful sheep will gather together, and in Unions of Prayer will offer potent resistance to the enemies of the Catholic Church. Yes, yes, the flock will become small. Many of you will see those sad times and days which will bring such evil in their train.... Great confusion will reign amid princes and nations. The incredulity of the present day is preparing those horrid evils.[120]

19ᵗʰ Century – Early 1800s: Blessed Anna Maria Taigi *(Prophecy Detail – Civil war in France, The angelic pontiff, The chastisements that will strike the earth, Three days of darkness)*

Louis Giannetti and Mary Masi baptized Anna Maria the day after her birth on May 29, 1769. By age six, her family was experiencing financial difficulties, prompting them to move from Siena to Rome. She received her early education at the hands of the Filippini Sisters. After just two years of school, however, Anna Maria abandoned her education so she could take various jobs in order to help her parents financially. At one point she even accepted work as a maid.

At a relatively young age she married Dominic Taigi, a pious, but coarse man. It was his virtue though that captured Anna Maria's attention. Despite his many faults, Anna Maria was a diligent wife who focused on his virtues and was given many opportunities to develop her own virtues of patience and charity over the course of their forty-nine-year marriage. In every way she was docile to her husband, being careful to avoid anything that might irritate him. In so doing, Anna Maria transformed her home into a sanctuary in which God was in first place.

She worked hard to ensure that her family lacked nothing. Though relatively impoverished, Anna Maria always found a way to provide for the poor. Dominic and Anna Maria had seven children but three times experienced the heartache of losing a child very early in life. She provided for the four children who reached maturity an accurate and complete religious and secular education.

She was extremely devoted to the Holy Eucharist, the Most Holy Trinity, and to the Infant Jesus. As her family grew, Anna Maria worked diligently to accomplish her primary objectives in life. First, to love and serve God in all her work, and second, to avoid even the slightest voluntary imperfection. Her success in this regard was in living a commonplace life as both wife and mother in a spirit of Christian pursuit and compliance with God's will. Though this was difficult at times, Anna Maria relied on the help and support of a good friend, Blessed Elizabeth Canori-Mora, also a wife and mother experiencing the same difficulties in her marriage. Together they were able to remain intensely spiritual despite their personal circumstances.

On December 26, 1808, Anna Maria entered the Third Order of the Most Holy Trinity and she was enriched by God with many supernatural gifts. *"The most unusual of these was the apparition of a luminous globe like a miniature sun, which shone before her eyes at all times and in which, for forty-seven years, she could see present and future events anywhere in the world as well as the state of grace of individuals, living or dead. In it she could foresee the revolutions, the wars, the designs of governments, the aims of secret societies, superstitions, and crimes, the reward of the saints, and the punishments, both temporal and eternal, prepared by God for all human transgressions.* [121]

Taigi died on June 9, 1837 and was declared "Blessed" by Pope Benedict XV in 1920. Like the bodies of so many saints and others destined for sainthood, hers is incorrupt and remains in the Chapel of the Madonna in the Basilica of San Crisogono in Rome, Italy.

Anna Maria was frequently in ecstasy and worked miracles in her life, including healing the sick. She read hearts, foretold deaths, and had mystical visions of future events that at times were so terrifying that she had to turn away from the globe that produced them. Though she never reduced her visions to writing, her accounts of those foresights were collected by visitors and passed down. Among her revelations were these:

> *God will send two punishments: one will be in the form of wars, revolutions and other evils; it shall originate on earth. The other will be sent from Heaven. There shall come over the whole earth an intense darkness lasting three days and three nights. Nothing can be seen, and the air will be laden with pestilence which will claim mainly, but not only, the enemies of religion. It will be impossible to use any man-made lighting during this darkness, except blessed candles. He, who out of curiosity, opens his window to look out, or leaves his home, will fall dead on the spot. During these three days, people should remain in their homes, pray the Rosary and beg God for mercy.*
>
> *On this terrible occasion so many of these wicked men, enemies of His Church, and of their God, shall be killed by this divine scourge, that their corpses around Rome will be as numerous as the fishes, which a recent inundation of the Tiber had carried into the city. All the enemies of the Church, secret as well as known, will perish over the whole earth during that universal darkness, with the exception of some few, whom God will soon after convert. The air shall be infested by demons, who will appear under all sorts of hideous forms.*
>
> *After the three days of darkness, Saints Peter and Paul, having come down from heaven, will preach throughout the world and designate a new Pope. A great light will flash from their bodies and settle upon the cardinal, the future pontiff. Then Christianity will spread throughout the world. Whole nations will join the Church shortly before the reign of the Antichrist. These conversions will be*

amazing. Those who survive shall have to conduct themselves well. There shall be innumerable conversions of heretics, who will return to the bosom of the Church; all will note the edifying conduct of their lives, as well as that of other Catholics.

Russia, England, and China will come into the Church. France will fall into frightful anarchy. The French people shall have a desperate civil war, in which old men themselves will take up arms. The political parties, having exhausted their blood and their rage, without being able to arrive at any satisfactory understanding, shall at the last extremity agree by common consent to have recourse to the Holy See. Then the Pope shall send France a special legate, in order that he may examine the state of affairs and the dispositions of the people. In consequence of the information received, His Holiness himself shall nominate a most Christian king for the government of France...

Religion shall be persecuted, and priests massacred. Churches shall be closed, but only for a short time. The Holy Father shall be obliged to leave Rome.[122]

19th Century - December 24, 1813 – Early 1821: Blessed Elizabeth Canori-Mora *(Prophecy Detail – Church apostacy, God's wrath, Release of demons)*

Born on November 21, 1774 to a family of nobility and wealth with deep Christian convictions, Elizabeth Canori grew to be diligent about her education. At age twenty-one, she married a young attorney named Cristoforo Mora. The couple had four daughters in their first five years of marriage, but only two survived infancy. At the same time, Cristoforo had an affair and deserted his young family, squandering the entirety of his fortune and leaving his wife and two daughters extremely impoverished.

Despite the physical and emotional abuse, Elizabeth remained faithful, believing that God brought her and Cristoforo together so that she could help save his soul. In 1801 she suffered a mysterious illness that left her near death. Inexplicably, she not only recovered, but had the first of many mystical experiences, some of which spoke to the great chastisement. A few of the more poignant prophecies are noted here.

On December 24, 1813, Elizabeth was transported to a place bathed in light. Numerous saints surrounded a humble manger, and drawing closer, she saw the Holy Child summon her.

I saw my beloved newborn Jesus bathed in his own blood. At that moment, I understood why the blood of the newborn Divine Infant had been spilled - the bad conduct of many priests and religious who did not behave according to their state, the poor education given children by their fathers and mothers.[123]

Another vision was given to Elizabeth concerning the devastating chaos and decadence into which Catholics would fall. On February 24, 1814, she wrote,

I saw many ministers of the Lord who renounced one another, furiously ripping from their person the sacred vestments. I saw the holy altars torn down by the very ministers of God.[124]

On March 22, 1814, the angels then transported Elizabeth to secret lairs where clerics conspired to topple thrones and destroy what remained of Christianity.

I saw the Sanhedrin of wolves that surrounded the Pope and two angels weeping. A holy boldness inspired me to ask the reason for their sad lamentations. Contemplating the city of Rome with compassionate eyes, they replied, "Miserable city, ungrateful people, the justice of God will chastise you."[125]

Elizabeth's visions continued and on January 16, 1815, the angels showed Elizabeth the destruction that God has in store for a world that refuses to heed his words.

Thunderbolts of divine justice flamed about me. Buildings fell into ruin. Cities, provinces and countries - the entire world was in chaos. One heard nothing save voices weakly begging for mercy. The number of dead was incalculable. His omnipotent hands were filled with bolts of lightning. His face was resplendent with indignation. His gaze alone was enough to incinerate the world. Neither angels nor saints accompanied Him - only His indignation.[126]

Elizabeth was so frightened by this vision that she later wrote, *"Had it lasted more than a moment I surely would have died."*[127]

On Christmas Day in 1816, Elizabeth saw Our Lady. She appeared very sad and Elizabeth asked Her why She lamented. *"Behold, my daughter, such great ungodliness."*[128] Upon hearing these words Elizabeth was shown,

"brazen apostates boldly seeking to wrench her Holy Son from her most pure bosom. In face of this outrage, the Mother of God did not implore God for mercy, but instead called for justice. Robed in

inexorable justice, the Eternal Father turned his indignant gaze toward the world. At that moment, nature convulsed, and the world lost its bearings as it sank beneath a misery beyond imagination."[129]

Elizabeth had a second revelation concerning God's chastisement on July 6, 1815. God's wrath was,

> *brought down on mankind by "rapacious wolves in sheep's clothing, bitter persecutors of Jesus Crucified and his bride, the Church." The whole world was in convulsion, especially the city of Rome. At the Sacred College, some had been dispersed, others humiliated and still others ruthlessly assassinated. The clergy and nobility suffered similar fates.[130]*

June 29, 1820, was the feast of Saints Peter and Paul and Elizabeth was granted another prophetic vision. This time Elizabeth,

> *beheld the Prince of the Apostles descending from Heaven in pontifical vestments and escorted by a legion of angels. With his crosier, St. Peter drew an immense cross upon the Earth; on each of its ends verdant trees appeared enveloped in brilliant light. Here the godly - religious and lay alike - found refuge from the torment. Yet woe to those religious who scorned the holy rules, because all will perish under the terrible scourge. This applies to all who embrace licentiousness and the condemnable philosophies of our day. With a wave of his right hand, He will punish them. The firmament was covered with a tenebrous blue, a terrifying sight. The wind's impetuous breath was felt everywhere as its violent roar - like that of a ferocious lion - echoed across the globe.*
>
> *Terror will reduce men and beasts to utter fear, and they will kill one another without pity. The avenging hand of the omnipotent God weigh down on these miserable souls, and He will chastise their shameless pride and impudent temerity. With a wave of his hand, He will punish them, setting loose from Hell legions of demons to scourge the world, executing the demands of Divine Justice. Because they surrendered their souls to Satan and allied themselves with him to strike against the Holy Catholic Church, God will permit these iniquitous men to be chastised by ferocious demons who will devastate every place where man has affronted and profaned Him.[131]*

Fortunately, Elizabeth's prophecy offers cause for hope among the faithful. Once the purification was complete, St. Peter descended, *from Heaven on a majestic pontifical throne. He was followed by Saint Paul, who traversed the world to imprison those malignant infernal spirits and bring them before the holy Apostle Saint Peter who, with authority, confined them to the dark netherworld from which they had been released. Then a beautiful radiance shone above the Earth, announcing the reconciliation of God and man and the remnant of faithful Catholics were led from their place of refuge to the throne of Saint Peter.[132]*

Following this, Saint Peter chose the new Pope, and the Church was converted back to the principles of the Gospel. Then, early in 1821, Jesus said to Elizabeth:

I will reform my people and my Church. I will send zealous priests to preach the Faith. I will form a new apostolate. I will send the Holy Ghost to renew the earth. I will reform the religious orders with holy men and women who possess the spirit of my beloved son Ignatius. I will give a new Pastor to my Church who, with holy zeal, will reform the flock of Christ. Finally, my Immaculate Heart will triumph.[133]

Elizabeth Canori-Mora died on February 5, 1825. Her revelations, though, were directed, not at those living with her in the nineteenth century, but rather at a people of a future century. Her words complement many other prophecies, not the least of which is the message that Our Lady of Fatima would reveal to three shepherd children almost one hundred years later in a small hamlet in Portugal.

19th Century – 1810 – 1830: Sr. Berina Bouquillon (aka Nursing Nun of Bellay) *(Prophesy Detail – Turbulent times, Religious leaders slaughtered, The great monarch, The triumph of the Church)*

Sr. Berina Bouquillon, otherwise known as the Nursing Nun of Bellay, was a stigmatist, a prophet, and a visionary. Sometime between 1810 and 1830, she made several prophecies concerning the coming of the Kingdom of God. She commended those prophetic visions to Fr. Fugence, the chaplain of the Trappist Monastery of Notre Dame des Gardes, in the diocese of Angers, France. These are her words:

Once again the madmen seem to gain the upper hand! They laugh God to scorn. Now, the churches are closed; the pastors run away; the Holy Sacrifice ceases.

Woe to thee, corrupt city! The wicked try to destroy everything; their books and their doctrines are swamping the world. But the day of justice is come. Here is your King; he comes forward amidst the confusion of those stormy days. Horrible times! The just and the wicked fall; Babylon is reduced to ashes. Woe to thee, city three times accursed!

There was also a great battle, the like of which has never been seen before. Blood was flowing like water after a heavy rain. The wicked were trying to slaughter all the servants of the Religion of Jesus Christ. After they had killed a large number, they raised a cry of victory, but suddenly the just received help from above.

A saint raises his arms to Heaven; he allays the wrath of God. He ascends the throne of Peter. At the same time, the Great Monarch ascends the throne of his ancestors. All is quiet now. Altars are set up again; religion comes to life again. What I see now is so wonderful that I am unable to express it.

All these things shall come to pass once the wicked have succeeded in circulating large numbers of bad books. [134]

19th Century - 1817 – 1828: Abbé Souffrant *(Prophecy Detail – The great monarch, Three days of darkness, The great peace)*

Abbé Souffrant was born in 1755 and ordained to the priesthood in 1780. During the years of the French Revolution, Souffrant was named vicar-general in the diocese of Nantes, Brittany. He ran into many dangers during the revolution and suffered several persecutions under the imperial regime and that of the Restoration. Souffrant had the gift of prophesy, and, according to many, including his successor, Abbé Siché, the early prophecies regarding the Revolution and its aftermath were proven true with incredible precision. The exactness of his prophecies continued into the 1830s, well beyond his death in 1828. The depth of prophetic accuracy caused Abbé Siché to leave this note in the records of the parish of Maumusson:

In the year 1821, I arrived as vicar to the venerable Monsieur Souffrant, then sixty-six, and with whom I spent six years, how sweet and agreeable his society was! At that time, he often spoke of prophecies, and people came from far away to hear him, and I saw many great people in his house who spent days and nights with him taking notes... He spoke of his ministry, he always did it with calm and moderation. It was prophecies, he was much more animated and seemed deeply convinced of what he was saying, how sorry I was for not listening and

*copying, but, I confess, I could not believe, only (until) the events oc-
curred that triumphed over my unbelief.[135]*

One might reason that accuracy in prophecies past may reflect on the
chances of exactitude of prophecies not yet fulfilled. If that is the case,
Souffrant's future prophecies may have significant implications for the
world. He wrote:

On the Great Monarch:
 *What will be his power? I cannot say it too much, but he will
have enough power to coin money. He will be near his fall when we
travel with the swiftness of a swallow.*
 *He will make a heavy fall. Then a bad republic that persecutes
religion and ends up with a catastrophe.*
 *A great number of honest people, royalists, priests, nobles, will
be eager, more eager than others, to recognize the Republic, to find
it good, to desire its maintenance.*
 *There will be several assemblies of deputies: the royalists will
put their hopes in these assemblies, but they will not bring them any
realization of these hopes.*
 *Peace is impossible: we will be afflicted with the greatest evils.
Terrible events will happen. These misfortunes that God will send us
to do penance will not be so great if we convert.*
 *These evils, and all that the Republic gives birth to, are neces-
sary to purify the area and to bring in the good grain before the
arrival of the Great Monarch.*
 *The conversion of the bourgeois would serve marvelously to di-
minish or arrest many evils.*
 *The moment of great events will be near when one travels with
the greatest speed. I do not know how these trips will be, but I see
the vehicles* (cars / wagons) *go with the speed of the bird.*
 *The coming of the Great Monarch will be very near when the
number of Legitimists who have remained truly faithful will be so
small that, to tell the truth, they will be counted.*
 In these events, the good ones (monarchists) *will have nothing
to do, because it will be the republicans, the bad guys who will loan
each other.*
 *The upheavals will be appalling. Religion will be persecuted,
and its ministers will be forced to hide in many places, at least momentarily, the churches will be closed for a while.*
 *Before the arrival of the Great Monarch, there will be great
evils, frightful disorders, misfortunes must happen.*

The blood will flow in torrents to the north and to the south, and I will see it run like rain on a stormy day, and I see the horses having blood to the straps. It is mainly in the cities that the blood will flow.

In these times and after a new republic will then be proclaimed, but that will last little and you will see three parties in France, two bad and one good. The first two will do much harm in Paris which will be destroyed, and in the rest of the North and the South of France.

These evils and ruins will, above all, ruin the great cities.

Paris will be treated with unparalleled rigor, as the center of crime and corruption. Paris will be destroyed in the midst of all these calamities, so destroyed that the plow will pass there.

The upheaval will be general in Europe and everywhere republics will be established.

The West, which was so roughly treated under the first revolution, will be spared in the events. It is because of this that the West has found favor with God, because of its faith, and the misfortunes that may happen in the West will be very little compared to other countries. It will suffer only the counterblow of the great concussions. (The west of France is meant here, Brittany and the Vendee – they suffered much during the French Revolution but will be spared many of the upheavals in the coming events. This was also foretold to Marie-Julie Jahenny). *The country sides will be spared.*

A Bonaparte will cause great sorrows to the Sovereign Pontiff and will eventually force him to flee. He may go to Russia. (May be one of the contenders who will rise up again before the Great Monarch comes. The usurpers will cause trouble.)

Cries will be uttered; those who dominate will be those of "Vive la republique!," "Vive Napoleon!," and finally "Long live the Great Monarch through whom God guards us!"[136]

On the Great Chastisement:

Invisible things will happen; thunder, lightning, earthquakes will have to convert more people than other evils, wars and massacres. There will come a moment when one will believe everything is lost. (The chastisements that will shake the earth.)

The misfortunes predicted above will be the result of our crimes. If, as God desires, we enter into his views and those of the Church, our ills will be alleviated. (Conversions and repentance for sins will lessen the chastisements.)

It is when one believes everything lost that everything will be saved; because between the cry "All is lost!" and the cry "All is saved!," there will be no interval – the time to turn (or flip) *a cake.*

The foreign powers will arm themselves and march against France.[137]

On the Great Monarch and Holy Pontiff:

Then, in this sixth age, God will comfort the Catholic priests and the other faithful by sending the Great Monarch and the Holy Pontiff.

At that time, a monk who has peace in his name and in his heart, shall pray; he will have the same mission as Joan of Arc...

Driven on all sides, he will come to take refuge in his seminary in the West of France, and the Great King whom God reserves for us, descendant of the king martyr.

They will have many difficulties with some prelates. (Some church officials may oppose the Great Monarch and his followers.) *The Great Monarch who will be* (of the) *Lys, will arrive by the South of France; he will be brought by the Holy Pontiff and the Emperor of Russia, a prince of the North who will be converted. It is especially by the care of the Sovereign Pontiff that this emperor will be determined to be recognized* (by) *him.*

The French generals, who will march for the fight, will not fire a single shot; they will lay down their arms as soon as the Great Monarch is presented to them, so surprising will his arrival be, and accompanied by dazzling proofs of his right and his virtue.

The Great Monarch is from the elder branch of the Bourbons and comes from the branch of a cut branch.

The Great Monarch will appear against all odds, when the friends of the Church and the legitimate rulers are in consternation, and so anguished, that they will be obliged to take the weapons to which God will give the most marvelous and the most brilliant success.

Brilliant and manifest signs will make the prince be recognized by everyone and overcome all obstacles. (Miracles will point out the Great Monarch chosen by God.)

The good republicans, more impressed than others, will be much more eager to submit to him than the royalists.

For the rest, few will resist; the striking signs and calamities will have sufficiently prepared the minds to receive it.

The Great Monarch will do such extraordinary things that the most incredulous will be forced to recognize the finger of God.[138]

On the Era of Peace:

Moreover, it will be the beginning of a new era of peace and triumph for the Church, an era of innumerable conversions.

The success that will be the triumph of the Church and the friends of legitimacy will take its main source in devotion to the Sacred Heart. This devotion, without stopping events, can greatly diminish the extent and intensity of the evils announced. (Not only will the Reign of the Sacred Heart begin under the Great Monarch, but devotion to the Sacred Heart will diminish the chastisements beforehand.)

A noble of the Loire-Inferior – a Breten general – will be called to take part in the events and he will play an important role for the restoration of the Holy Pontiff and the Great Monarch. He will bring him back.

France, pacified first, will restore calm and prosperity to other nations.

The Great Monarch will reform everything, make a new code, a new nobility, and all his acts will be so perfect that all the other sovereigns will be submissive to him. (Abbé Souffrant confirms there will still be other monarchs if "other sovereigns" will exist, only they will be under the rule of the Great Monarch and his ally, the Russian Emperor.)

With the Emperor of Russia, he will put an end to confusion, usurpation and injustice all over Europe.

But above all, both will re-establish the reign of religion and the authority of the Church. They will both have such supremacy over other powers that they will be like the only two monarchs.

Of course, the Emperor of Russia will convert to the Catholic faith so brilliantly that he will be regarded as another Constantine.

In concert with him, the Great Monarch will exterminate the race of heretics and the ungodly, restore order, and restore to each his good: "reddet cuique suum bonum."

There will be, so to speak, only two empires in Europe: the Eastern Empire and the Western Empire.

Russia will convert and help France restore peace and tranquility to the world. But above all, they will restore the reign of religion and the authority of the Church.

Under the reign of this Great Monarch, all justice will be done. The Catholic religion will flourish throughout the universe, except in Palestine, a country of curse.

Full of the spirit of God, he will weigh the merit of each person like gold in the scales and will do him the most scrupulous justice.

Those who possess stolen goods will be the first to return them. National assets will be taken away from their buyers.

Then he will only take the crown and place it on the head of his direct heir. (Souffrant is the only prophet to speak of an heir to the Great Monarch. All other prophecies indicate that the Great Monarch will always rule.)[139]

On the Antichrist:

> *God, at the same time, will raise up the holy Pontiff, who, supported by the Great Monarch (called "Auxilium Dei"), "The Help of God" will exterminate all the heretical sects, all the superstitions of the Gentiles, will spread and shine more than ever the reign of the Catholic Church in all the Universe, except in the infernal region of Palestine, a country of curse where the Antichrist must be born.*

> *Under the reign of the Great Monarch, religion will be honored, and God glorified as it has not been for centuries; the greatest virtue will be observed around the world and the earth will produce fruit in abundance.*

> *After the crisis, despite certain oppositions made by the clergy themselves, everything will end with a general and decisive Council to which the entire universe will submit until the last persecution, that of the Beast, or the Antichrist.* (There will be one last great council held in which all will be restored until the coming of the Antichrist.)

> *Then there will be one flock and one shepherd, because all the infidels and all the heretics, but not the Jews, whose mass will be converted after the death of the Beast, will enter the Latin Church, whose triumph will continue until the destruction of the Antichrist.*[140]

19th Century – 1820: Blessed Anna-Katarina Emmerick (aka Anne Emerich) *(Prophesy Detail – The great apostacy, Pope leaving Rome, Church in exile, Church invaded, Heretical Church established, Oppression of Clergy and Catholics, The great monarch, Intercession from the Blessed Virgin, Church victorious)*

There was nothing special about her when Anna-Katarina Emmerick was born to poor farming parents on September 8, 1774, but that would change before her death some forty-nine years later. Her education was short and from an early age Anna was drawn to prayer, and also experienced visions in which she spoke to Jesus, saw the souls in Purgatory, and saw the Holy Trinity displayed as three concentric, interpenetrating circles. Her visions would continue into adulthood.

She began working a large farm at the age of twelve and later became skilled as a seamstress. She longed to enter a convent but was unable to afford the dowry. After experiencing the disappointment of several rejections, the Poor Clares in Munster finally agreed to accept her on the condition that she learn to play the organ. She began to study under organist Söntgen, but wound up working for them in an effort to allay their poverty by relinquishing her small savings to them.

She managed to join the Augustinian nuns in Dulmen in 1802 and took her vows just one year later. She strictly observed the order's rule but was often severely sick and in great pain. For many years she ingested nothing but Holy Communion. In 1813, Anna began to exhibit marks of the stigmata. She was examined by several doctors and priests who found the wounds to be authentic. The mysterious bleeding stopped, however, at the end of 1818 and the wounds closed. Afterward, she was privileged to have visions of Jesus and the Blessed Virgin in which she was given glimpses of their earthly lives. These visions were later recorded in a series of books by a stranger named Brentano, someone she immediately recognized from her visions, who told her he was sent by God to help her express in writing the many revelations given to her. He conducted extensive interviews and wrote two volumes, one that was published ten years after his own death. Although the "Vatican does not endorse the authenticity of the books written by Brentano, [it] views their general message as 'an outstanding proclamation of the gospel in service to salvation.'"[141]

In 1820, Emmerick made several prophecies about the apostacy, the Great Monarch, the invasion and exile of the Church, Oppression of the clergy and faithful, and the final triumph of the Church. These prophecies were included in her biography *The Life of Anne Catherine Emmerich* by Rev. Carl Schmoeger, C.SS.R., first published in English in 1870.

The Great Apostasy in The Present Church - The Aging Pope:

Among the strangest things that I saw, were long processions of bishops. Their thoughts and utterances were made known to me through images issuing from their mouths. Their faults towards religion were shown by external deformities ... I saw what I believe to be nearly all the bishops of the world, but only a small number were perfectly sound. I also saw the Holy Father - God-fearing and prayerful. Nothing left to be desired in his appearance, but he was weakened by old age and by much suffering. His head was lolling from side to side, and it dropped onto his chest as if he was falling asleep ...Then I saw that everything pertaining to Protestantism was gradually gaining the upper hand, and the Catholic religion fell into complete decadence. Most priests were lured by the glittering but false knowledge of young schoolteachers, and they all contributed to the work of destruction. In those days, Faith will fall very low, and it will be preserved in some places only, in a few cottages and in a few families which God has protected from disasters and wars.

Pope Leaving Rome, The Church in Exile:

As we came nearer, however, the fire abated and we saw the blackened building. We went through a number of magnificent rooms, and we finally reached the Pope. He was sitting in the dark and slept in a large armchair. He was very ill and weak; he could no longer walk. The ecclesiastics in the inner circle looked insincere and lacking in zeal; I did not like them. I told the Pope of the bishops who are to be appointed soon. I told him also that he must not leave Rome. If he did so, it would be chaos. He thought that the evil was inevitable, and he should leave in order to save many things beside himself. He was very much inclined to leave Rome, and he was insistently urged to do so.

The Enemies of The Church Invading Italy And Rome:

I also saw the various regions of the earth. My Guide (Jesus) named Europe and pointing to a small and sandy region, He uttered these words: "Here is Prussia (East Germany), the enemy." Then He showed me another place, to the north, and He said: "This is Moskva, the land of Moscow, bringing many evils."

The False Ecumenical, Heretical Church Established in Rome:

I saw also the relationship between two popes ... I saw how baleful would be the consequences of this false church. I saw it increase in size; heretics of every kind came into the city of Rome. The local clergy grew lukewarm, and I saw a great darkness....

I had another vision of the great tribulation. It seems to me that a concession was demanded from the clergy which could not be granted. I saw many older priests, especially one, who wept bitterly. A few younger ones were also weeping. But others, and the lukewarm among them, readily did what was demanded. It was as if people were splitting into two camps.

I saw that many pastors allowed themselves to be taken up with ideas that were dangerous to the Church. They were building a great, strange, and extravagant Church. Everyone was to be admitted in it in order to be united and have equal rights: Evangelicals, Catholics, sects of every description. Such was to be the new Church ... But God had other designs.

I saw again the strange big church that was being built there in Rome. There was nothing holy in it. I saw this just as I saw a movement led by Ecclesiastics to which contributed angels, saints, and other Christians. But there in the strange big church all the work was being done mechanically according to set rules and formulae. Everything was being done according to human reason ...I saw all sorts of people, things, doctrines, and opinions. There was something proud, presumptuous, and violent about it, and they seemed very successful. I do not see

*a single Angel nor a single saint helping in the work. But far away in
the background, I saw the seat of the cruel people armed with spears,
and I saw a laughing figure which said: "Do build it as solid as you
can; we will pull it to the ground."*

*I saw again the new and odd-looking church which they were trying
to build. There was nothing holy about it ... People were kneading bread
in the crypt below ... but it would not rise, nor did they receive the body
of our Lord, but only bread. Those who were in error, through no fault
of their own, and who piously and ardently longed for the Body of Jesus
were spiritually consoled, but not by their communion. Then my Guide
(Jesus) said: "This is Babel."*

*I saw deplorable things: they were gambling, drinking, and talk-
ing in church; they were also courting women. All sorts of abominations were perpetrated there. Priests allowed everything and said
Mass with much irreverence. I saw that few of them were still godly...
All these things caused me much distress.*

Devout Catholics and Clergy Being Oppressed:

*Then I saw an apparition of the Mother of God, and she said that
the tribulation would be very great. She added that people must pray
fervently with outstretched arms, be it only long enough to say three
Our Fathers. This was the way her Son prayed for them on the Cross.
They must rise at twelve at night and pray in this manner; and they
must keep coming to the Church. They must pray above all for the
Church of Darkness to leave Rome... These were all good and devout
people, and they did not know where help and guidance should be
sought. There were no traitors and enemies among them, yet they
were afraid of one another...*

*I saw more martyrs, not now but in the future ... I saw the secret
sect relentlessly undermining the great Church. Near them I saw a
horrible beast coming up from the sea. All over the world, good and
devout people, especially the clergy, were harassed, oppressed, and
put into prison....*

*Whole Catholic communities were being oppressed, harassed,
confined, and deprived of their freedom. I saw many churches closed
down, great miseries everywhere, wars and bloodshed. A wild and
ignorant mob took violent action. But it did not last long...*

The Intercession from Blessed Virgin and King Henry, The Victors:

*I had a vision of the holy Emperor Henry. I saw him at night kneel-
ing alone at the foot of the main altar in a great and beautiful church ...
and I saw the Blessed Virgin coming down all alone. She laid on the*

altar a red cloth covered with white linen. She placed a book inlaid with precious stones. She lit the candles and the perpetual lamp. Then came the Savior Himself clad in priestly vestments. He was carrying the chalice and the veil. Two angels were serving Him and two more were following ... Although there was no altar bell, the cruets were there. The wine was as red as blood, and there was also some water. The Mass was short. The Gospel of St. John was not read at the end. (NOTE: Before Vatican II, the Holy Mass was always concluded with the reading from the Gospel of St. John. Thus, this fact was prophesied 200 years ago by Sr. Emmerick.) *When the Mass had ended, Mary came up to Henry, and she extended her right hand towards him, saying that it was in recognition of his purity. Then she urged him not to falter. Thereupon I saw an angel, and he touched the sinew of his hip, like Jacob. Henry was in great pain; and from that day on he walked with a limp....*

Very bad times will come when non-Catholics will lead many people astray. A great confusion will result. I saw the battle also. The enemies were far more numerous, but the small army of the faithful cut down whole rows of enemy soldiers. During the battle, the Blessed Virgin stood on a hill, wearing a suit of armor. It was a terrible war. At the end, only a few fighters for the just cause survived, but the victory was theirs.

The Church Shall Be Victorious, Rebuilt, And More Glorious Than Ever:

I was in such distress that I cried out to Jesus with all my might, imploring His mercy... He said, among other things, that this translation of the church from one place to another meant that she would seem to be in complete decline. But she would rise again; even if there remained but one Catholic, the church would conquer again because she does not rest on human counsels and intelligence.

When the Church had been for the most part destroyed by the secret sect, and when only the sanctuary and altar were still standing, I saw the wreckers enter the Church with the beast. There, they met a Woman of noble carriage who seemed to be with child because she walked slowly. At this sight, the enemies were terrorized, and the Beast could not take but another step forward. It projected its neck towards the Woman as if to devour her, but the woman turned about and bowed down toward the Altar, her head touching the ground. Thereupon, I saw the beast taking to flight towards the sea again, and the enemies were fleeing in the greatest of confusion. Then, I saw in the great distance great legion approaching. In the foreground I saw a man on a white horse. Prisoners were set free and joined them. All enemies were pursued. Then, I saw that the Church was being promptly rebuilt, and she was more magnificent than ever before.[142]

19th Century – Pre 1837: St. Gaspar del Bufalo *(Prophecy Detail – Three days of darkness)*

Perhaps his birth on the Feast of the Epiphany, January 6, 1786, and his baptism on the same day, was prophetic of the saintly life Gaspar would lead. He was, in fact, named for the three wise men of the Magi – Gaspar Mechior Balthazar del Bufalo. His parents, Annunziata and Antonio, insisted on it. His father was a chef to a noble family. Consequently, the del Bufalos lived in the servants' quarters of the Altieri palace located just across from the Church of the Gesu in Rome. In consideration of his early bad health, his mother had him confirmed at the age of one and a half. The family also prayed for a cure to St. Francis Xavier, whose relic was displayed on an altar of the Gesu. Despite a severe illness that threatened the boy's eyesight, Gaspar was miraculously cured of his illness, having suffered no ill effects.

As a young man, Gaspar ministered to the sick and the poor and founded a religious organization dedicated to doing works of charity. In 1808 he was ordained a priest. In that vocation he provided catechetical instruction to orphans and children of the poor, established a homeless shelter, and formed an evening society for laborers and for long-distance workers who visited Rome for the purpose of selling their produce.

For his refusal to take the oath of allegiance to Napoleon Bonaparte in 1809, Gaspar and many other priests were exiled and imprisoned for four years in northern Italy. Upon his release, Gaspar returned to Rome and, at the request of Pope Pius VII, began preaching missions with the hope of reestablishing order in an otherwise chaotic time. Despite significant hardship, he founded the Missionaries of the Precious Blood at an abandoned monastery in Giano, Umbria.

By 1821, many towns were under the control of civil authorities and great lawlessness prevailed in the Papal States, with bandits controlling many towns that comprised the coastal provinces. It was into these towns that Gaspar and his missionaries went to preach and establish mission houses. Six such houses were built in the first two years. Living among the bandits, Gaspar and his fellow priests preached repentance and a return to faithfulness. They could be found on the street corners at night, armed only with a crucifix, instructing the children and negotiating peace with the banditi. Though very popular with the people, Gaspar's success in convincing hordes of "briganti" to lay their guns at his feet after he preached to them, upset officials who profited from the bandits through

bribery. Gaspar even faced opposition from the Church after being accused of disregarding canon law because of the untraditional cross and
chain that he and his order wore. Pope Pius VII himself, who just five
years earlier had strongly supported the order, now opposed it as "ad-
verse" to the community, prompting Gaspar to offer to resign. Pope Leo
XII, however, met with Gaspar and resolved the differences between
them, making his resignation unnecessary.

Gaspar's strength began to fail in 1836, though he continued to work
indefatigably to re-evangelize central Italy until his death on December
28, 1837 at the age of sixty-one. At the time of his death, Gaspar was
ministering to the cholera-stricken people of Rome. Gaspar was beatified
by St. Pope Pius X in 1904 and canonized by Pope Pius XII on June 12,
1954. Before his death, St. Gaspar offered these prophetic words:

> *The death of the impenitent persecutors of the Church will take
> place during the three days of darkness. He who outlives the dark-
> ness and the fear of these three days will think that he is alone on
> earth because the whole world will be covered with carcasses.*[143]

This prophecy is in accord with many other prophecies about the
three days of darkness. Author Yves Dupont explained that the word
"carcasses" used by Gaspar to describe the bodies of the dead, has a very
specific meaning. Dupont believes that after the raging fires of the three
days of darkness, the carcasses of animals will be indistinguishable from
the human bodies that were burnt and blackened by the inferno.

19th Century – Early to mid-1800s: Sister Rosa Asdenti Di Taggia *(Prophecy Detail – The world at war, Precursor to the Antichrist, The great monarch)*

Rose Colomba Asdente was born in 1770, the daughter of the Count of
Luceramo, but relinquished her title of Countess to cloister in the Taggia
convent of a Dominican Sister now known as St. Catherine of Siena.
Though she had mystical powers, she remained humble and inviolable. She
was a most virtuous woman, yet there was a childish simplicity about her as
she performed her religious duties, prayers, and mortifications with exactitude.

It wasn't long, however, before so many of her prophetic predictions
had come true with uncanny accuracy. That is when she began to garner the
attention of her fellow religious and her reputation as a mystic grew well
beyond the walls of the monastery. Among her many prophecies, Sister

Rosa even predicted the circumstances of her own death, which occurred on Friday June 6, 1847, within the octave of the Most Holy Sacrament.

Following her death, the Bishop of Ventimiglia ordered that her prophetical predictions be assembled and kept in the episcopal archives. Many of her prophecies have long since been realized. The following are some of the prophecies subsequently printed in *The Christian Trumpet* in 1878 that pertain to the end-of-times.

> *Not only religious communities, but also good lay Catholics, shall have their property confiscated. Many of the nobility shall be cast into prison. A lawless democratic spirit of disorder shall reign supreme throughout all Europe. There will be a general overthrow. There shall be great confusion of people against people, and nations against nations, with clashing of arms and beating of drums. The Russians and Prussians [Germany] shall come to make war in Italy. They shall profane many churches and turn them into stables for their horses. Some bishops shall fall from the faith, but many more will remain steadfast, and shall suffer much for the Church. England shall return to the Catholic faith.[144]*

> *A great enemy of the Church, a precursor of Antichrist, will take the title of Savior. Heretics will join this precursor of Antichrist and persecute the true Church of Christ. Their cunning will be great, so great in fact that they will be able to draw many righteous men to their side. The Bishops in general will remain faithful, but all will, on account of their courage and faithfulness to the Church, suffer much, yet many Protestants will console the children of God by their conversion to the Catholic Church. Immediately preceding Antichrist there will be starvation and earthquakes.[145]*

(Bucchianeri notes that this could point to the persecution before the coming of the Great Monarch, other mystics have predicted a precursor Antichrist that will come before his arrival. The times will resemble the time of the real Antichrist, who will come after the Age of Peace).

> *The Supreme Pontiff will be stripped of temporal dominion and called only Bishop of Rome. This will take place in Italy, where there will be many marches during a very bloody war on religion...The Russians will be admonished by the Pontiff and will become more human towards the Catholics; and in the end the Turks will come to faith.*

Not only the religious, but also the good secular people will have their goods confiscated; many nobles will be imprisoned, and will dominate a spirit of democratic turn; there will be great up-heaval in Europe, and peace will not return until the white flower is returned, that is, the lily of the descendants of St. Louis on the throne of France, which will happen. The Church purged in persecutions, will rise again more beautiful. The faithful will be reduced in number, but they will be more fervent than before. A great revolution will spread over all of Europe and peace will not be restored until the white flower, the lily has taken posses-sion of the throne of France. (Great Catholic Monarch of France) *Not only religious communities, but also good lay Catholics, shall have their property confiscated. Many of the nobility shall be cast into prison. A lawless democratic spirit of disorder shall reign supreme throughout all Europe. There will be a general overthrow.*

Many terrible calamities impend over Italy. Priests and religious shall be butchered and the earth, especially in Italy, shall be wa-tered with their blood.

The persecution in Italy is to begin by the suppression of the Jes-uits; they shall be called back again; then a third time they will be suppressed and never more be revived.

During a frightful storm against the Church, all religious orders will be abolished except two, namely, the Capuchins and the Do-minicans, together with the Hospitallers, who shall receive the pious pilgrims, who, in great numbers, shall go to visit and ven-erate the many martyrs in Italy, killed during the impending per-secution.[146]

19th Century – Pre-1846: Brother Louis Rocco *(Prophecy De-tail – Corruption of morals, God's wrath, Wars, The great mon-arch, Catholic Empire)*

Not a great deal is known about Brother Louis Rocco. While much of his life remains a mystery, many of his prophecies endure. At least some of them are noted in books dealing with end-times prophecies and those appear below.

Terrible wars will rage all over Europe. God has long been pa-tient with the corruption of morals; half of mankind He will destroy. Russia will witness many outrages. Great cities and small towns alike will be destroyed in a bloody revolution that will cause the death of half the population. In Istanbul the Cross will replace the half-moon of Islam, and Jerusalem will be the seat of a King. The southern Slavs will form a great Catholic Empire and drive out of Europe the Turks, who will withdraw to North Africa and subsequently embrace the Catholic faith.[147]

On another occasion, Rocco said:

A great monarch will arise after a period of terrible wars and persecutions in Europe. He will be a Catholic: He will not be a German.[148]

This prophecy has been substantiated by any number of prophecies on the subject of the end of days. Brother Rocco died in 1840.

19th Century - September 19, 1846: Our Lady of La Salette - Melanie Calvat & Maximin Giraud *(Prophecy Detail – God's wrath, Drought, Famine, Church apostasy, Church persecution, The Antichrist, Time frame)*

On September 19, 1846, Melanie Calvat was a timid girl of fourteen who was able to neither read nor write. Since the age of nine, she had worked as a cowherd on the mountain of La Salette tending the cows of some of the wealthy peasants. That previous summer, she met Maximin Giraud, an eleven-year-old boy who also began work as a cowherd on the same plateau in the summer of 1845. Theirs was a chance meeting as it was Maximin's first cow-herding job away from home.

It was a particularly hot day and the noon heat made both children drowsy. Each fell asleep on the mountain slope of La Sallet, about six thousand feet in altitude. When they awakened, they saw a beautiful Lady. She sat on a rock in the bed of a dried stream and wept bitterly. As they stared in disbelief, the Lady began to speak to the children:

Come near, my children, be not afraid; I am here to tell you great news. If my people will not submit, I shall be forced to let fall the arm of my Son. It is so strong, so heavy, that I can no longer withhold it. For how long a time do I suffer for you! If I would not have my Son abandon you, I am compelled to pray to him without ceasing; and as to you, you take not heed of it. However much you pray, however much you do, you will never recompense the pains I have taken for you.

Six days I have given you to labor, the seventh I had kept for myself; and they will not give it to me. It is this which makes the arm of my Son so heavy. Those who drive the carts cannot swear without introducing the name of my Son. These are the two things which makes the arm of my Son so heavy.

If the harvest is spoilt, it is all on your account. I gave you warning last year with the potatoes (pommes de terre) but you did not heed it. On the contrary, when you found the potatoes spoilt, you swore, you took the name of my Son in vain. They will continue to decay, so that by Christmas there will be none left.

If you have wheat, it is no good to sow it; all you sow the insects will eat, and what comes up will fall into dust when you thresh it. There will come a great famine. Before the famine comes, the children under seven years of age will be seized with trembling and will die in the hands of those who hold them; the others will do penance by the famine. The walnuts will become bad, and the grapes will rot.[149]

This part of the conversation was universal as Our Lady spoke to the children together. Both of them heard her speak and both understood the same message. From this point on, however, Our Lady imparted to each child a secret, first to Maximin and then to Melanie. While speaking to one child the other, though standing together, could not hear Her speaking. Once the secrets had been told, Our Lady continued:

"If they are converted, the stones and rocks will change into mounds of wheat, and the potatoes will be self-sown in the land. Do you say your prayers well, my children?"[150]

Both answered, *"Not very well, Madam."*

"Ah, my children, you must be sure to say them well morning and evening. When you cannot do better, say at least an Our Father and a Hail Mary. When you have time, say more. There are none who go to Mass except a few aged women. The rest work on Sunday all summer; then in the winter, when they know not what to do, they go to Mass only to mock at religion. During Lent, they go to the meat-market like dogs. Have you never seen wheat that is spoilt, my children?"[151]

"No, Madam," they replied. Our Lady continued:

"But you, my child, you must surely have seen some once when you were at the farm of Coin with your father. The owner of the field told your father to go and see his ruined wheat. You went together. You took two or three ears of wheat into your hands and rubbed them, and they fell to dust. Then you continued home. When you were still half an hour's distance from Corps, your father gave you a piece of bread and said to you: 'Here, my child, eat some bread this year at least; I don't know who will eat any next year, if the wheat goes on like that.'"[152]

When reminded of these details, Maximin quickly replied, *"Oh yes, Madam, I remember now; just at this moment I did not remember."* Then the Lady said to them:

"Well, my children, you will make this known to all my people."[153]

As instructed by the Lady, the children said nothing of the secrets they were told. In 1851, however, they were persuaded to write down the secrets lest they be forever lost to history. The children did so and provided the secrets to Pope Pius IX for his eyes only. The Pontiff read the secrets but would not speak of them except to say, *"These are the secrets of La Salette: Unless the world repent it shall perish."*[154]

The secret messages given by Our Lady to the children remained secret for well over one hundred years. However, in 1999, the notes written to Pope Pius IX by Maximin and Melanie were retrieved from the Papal Archives in the Vatican. This is the text of the secret written by Maximin and given to Pope Pius IX:

On September 19, 1846, we saw a beautiful Lady. We never said that this lady was the Blessed Virgin, but we always said that it was a beautiful Lady. I do not know if it is the Blessed Virgin or another person. As for me, I believe today that it is the Blessed Virgin.

Here is what this Lady said to me: "If my people continue, what I will say to you will arrive earlier, if it changes a little, it will be a little later.

France has corrupted the universe, one day it will be punished. The faith will die out in France: three quarters of France will not practice religion anymore, or almost no more, the other part will practice it without really practicing it. Then, after [that], nations will convert, the faith will be rekindled everywhere.

A great country in the north of Europe, now Protestant, will be converted; by the support of this country all the other nations of the world will be converted.

Before all that arrives, great disorders will arrive, in the Church, and everywhere. Then, after [that], our Holy Father the Pope will be persecuted. His successor will be a pontiff that nobody expects.

Then, after [that], a great peace will come, but it will not last a long time. A monster will come to disturb it.

All that I tell you here will arrive in the other century, at the latest in the year two thousand."

Maximin Giraud

(She told me to say it sometime before.)

My Most Holy Father, your holy blessing to one of your sheep.

Grenoble, July 3, 1851.[155]

The following is the text of the letter written by Melanie to Pope Pius IX. While, simplistic in text like the letter of Maximin, Melanie's letter contains a bit more detail. The text of Melanie's secret follows:

Mélanie, I will say something to you which you will not say to anybody:

The time of God's wrath has arrived!

If, when you say to the people what I have said to you so far, and what I will still ask you to say, if, after that, they do not convert, (i.e. if they do not do penance, and they do not cease working on Sunday, and if they continue to blaspheme the Holy Name of God), *in a word, if the face of the earth does not change, God will be avenged against the people ungrateful and slave of the demon.*

My Son will make his power manifest! Paris, this city soiled by all kinds of crimes, will perish infallibly. Marseilles will be destroyed in a little time. When these things arrive, the disorder will be complete on the earth, the world will be given up to its impious passions.

The pope will be persecuted from all sides, they will shoot at him, they will want to put him to death, but no one will be able to do it, the Vicar of God will triumph again this time.

The priests and the Sisters, and the true servants of my Son will be persecuted, and several will die for the faith of Jesus Christ.

A famine will reign at the same time.

After all these will have arrived, many will recognize the hand of God on them, they will convert, and do penance for their sins.

A great king will go up on the throne and will reign a few years. Religion will re-flourish and spread all over the world, and there will be a great abundance, the world, glad not to be lacking nothing, will fall again in its disorders, will give up God, and will be prone to its criminal passions.

[Among] *God's ministers, and the Spouses of Jesus-Christ, there will be some who will go astray, and that will be the most terrible.*

Lastly, hell will reign on earth. It will be then that the Antichrist will be born of a Sister, but woe to her! Many will believe in him, because he will claim to have come from heaven, woe to those who will believe in him!

That time is not far away, twice 50 years will not go by.

My child, you will not say what I have just said to you. (i.e. You will not say it to anybody, you will not say if you must say it one day, you will not say what that it concerns), *finally you will say nothing anymore until I tell you to say it!*

I pray to Our Holy Father the Pope to give me his holy blessing.

Mélanie Mathieu, Shepherdess of La Salette, Grenoble, July 6, 1851.[156]

The message of Our Lady of La Salette easily comports to prophecies that both came before it and after it. It speaks to God's anger, the coming persecution of the Church, the conversion of many to Catholicism, a great king taking the throne, the reign of hell on earth, and the coming of the Antichrist.

19th Century – Pre- 1862: Ven. Mother Marie Josepha of Bourg (aka – Ven. Mother Marie De Jesus du Bourg, Mother Josepha of Bourg) *(Prophesy Detail – The great monarch, The chastisement, Plagues)*

The daughter of a martyr of the French Revolution, Anne Rose Du Bourg was born on June 25, 1788 just outside of Toulouse, France. She entered religious life at the age of twenty-one, joining the Hospitaller Sisters of Saint-Alexis de Limoges, and taking on the name Mary of Jesus.

In 1834, Mother Marie founded the Congregation of the Savior and the Blessed Virgin, receiving the congregation's final approval on February 25 of that year. She also founded the Little Sisters of the Countryside. This was an order comprised of non-cloistered nuns who gather only in groups of two and settle in small rural villages where they work as nurses, catechists, and educators. At the request of the Vatican, this group disbanded in 1891. The Congregation of the Savior and the Blessed Virgin, on the other hand, grew rapidly and realized much success until it closed the majority of its convents in 1902.

Mother Marie enjoyed the contemplative life and it is said that, in addition to receiving the stigmata, she experienced diabolical attacks, could levitate, experienced supernatural ecstasies, and offered many prophecies. In 1857 her prophecies were collected in a pamphlet called, "Inner Views." This pamphlet contains four primary revelations that conform to the revelations of Marie-Julie Jahenny, the Ecstatic of Tours, and Sister Marie Letaste.

On November 21, 1920 a cause for canonization was opened for her.

The First Prophecy – for the year 1830:

A year before the July Revolution, I was in the chapel; I was going out to visit the poor and the sick, when Jesus Christ tells me interiorly, but in a very distinct way: "Stay with Me, my daughter, I am the first poor you must visit and console!" So I had an interior view of Jesus Christ that the wicked crucify anew.

I understood that there was a conspiracy against Religion and the state; it broke out about a year later. When it took place, I begged with tears the Lord to take a glace of compassion on us, and I understood then that the royal child who was brought into exile would return later to rule France. (i.e. Henry V, the Count of Chambord, the "Miracle Child" who was exiled in 1830).

The holy Archangel Saint Michael, in particular, let me feel his presence, told me several things in advance and that he was the special protector of France, and that one day he would bring Prince Dieudonné back.

During the reign of Louis Philippe, I heard the Lord say with a threatening voice to this king: "You have despised Me; you had My people apostatized by having them work on Sundays. Youth has been delivered to the ungodly."

And I understood then that this king would be punished, and I was told that time was drawing near; and soon the revolution of 1848 broke out. The ramparts and fortresses built in defiance of the law of God (Sunday)*, could not defend the one who had elevated them for his safety according to the beautiful words of Saint Felix: "With the protection of Jesus Christ the strongest walls are only cobwebs." I understood above all that it was the profanation of Sunday which drew on France the most terrible scourges.*[157]

The Second Prophecy – for the years 1848-1850:

This revolutionary turmoil caused much blood to be shed, to commit many crimes; but, however, the wicked were still arrested, thanks to the intercession of Mary, the angels and the holy protectors of France, and by the prayer and the good works of the just. Jesus Christ was on His throne; his arm was raised to strike the earth. Mary, placed on another throne on His right hand, tried to stop His arm; she wanted to throw herself at His feet to beg for mercy; Jesus Christ stopped her and said: "My Mother, command, your prayers cannot be denied." He added, "the crimes of men went so far, that if He did not punish them, the plagues would later only be more terrible; Mary, however, always pleaded for mercy. It was [on behalf of] *France. The exterminating angels, sword in hand, were waiting for the signal to strike the Earth. Mary turned to the saints of France and encouraged them to intercede for their country; there was then a treaty between justice and mercy. Justice will punish, but mercy will come, and we will be saved! There will be a terrible crisis; but it was said to me that after this time of trial, the Lord would bring back Prince Dieudonné."*[158]

The Third Prophecy:

The Lord complained to me in a terrible way; He complains of this fury to seek pleasure; he complains of the scandalous dances, the indecency, and the luxury of adornments, and if He warns against in the Holy Gospel even a single bad look, even a single bad desire, is it any wonder that He punishes, by terrible punishments, the corruption of morals, which is the necessary consequence of all these abuses, the source of so many crimes, and which leads, with the ruin of good morals, that of health and the loss of souls. The peoples, as always, have imitated the bad examples of the great: there is no longer a dike at the torrent of furious passions (i.e. a dike to stop the evil torrent); *divine authority is entirely unknown; men and children despise the laws of God, those of the family* (i.e. the divine rules God set for family life are disregarded); *also the order is only factitious,* (i.e. the divine norms regarding society are disregarded) *the force and the constraint alone maintain it still.*[159]

The Fourth Prophecy:

The Lord's chastisements will fall upon us in various ways. Plagues, troubles, bloodshed. There will be in France a terrible reversal! However, these days will be shortened in favor of the righteous. God will elevate a model king, a Christian king, to the throne. The son of Saint Louis will love religion, goodness, justice. The Lord will give him light, wisdom and power. He Himself has prepared him for a long time and made him pass into the crucible of trial and suffering, but He will recall him from exile. He, the Lord, will take him by the hand, and on the appointed day He will place him back on the throne. His destiny is to repair and regenerate; then consoled religion will flourish, and all peoples will bless the reign of Prince Dieudonne; but then evil will take over and last more or less until the end of time. The light from above was not given to me for the last events of the world of which the Apocalypse speaks.[160]

19th Century – mid 1800s: Brother Anthony of Aachen (aka Brother Anthony of Aix-la-Chapelle) - *(Prophesy Detail – The great war, Civil wars, The great monarch)*

Brother Anthony was a monk who, in the mid-nineteenth century, lived in Alsace-Lorraine, the name given to the 5,067 square miles of territory that was ceded by France to Germany in 1871 after the Franco-German War. He was known far and wide as a great prophet who most often proved to be right in his prophetic pronouncements. He spoke frequently of a future event in Europe that would pit good people against bad people. He was very clear that he was speaking not of good nations and bad nations, but of good and bad people from a variety of nations. With regard to the great war, Anthony said:

> *Someday war will break out in Alsace. I saw French in Alsace with Strasburg at their rear and I saw Italians fighting with them* [as allies of the French]. *Suddenly, great transports of troops arrived from the French side. A two-day battle ended with the defeat of the Prussian* [German] *Army. The French pursued the Prussians over the Rhine in many directions. In a second battle, at Frankfurt the Prussians lost again and retreated to Siegeburg, where they joined with the Russian army. The Russians made common cause with the Prussians. It seemed to me as if the Austrians were also helping the French.*
>
> *The battle of Siegeburg was more horrible than any before, and its like will never occur again. After some days the Russians and the Prussians retreated past the Rhine below Bonn, to the left bank of the Rhine. Steadily pressed by their opponents they retired in Cologne which had been so bombed that only one-fourth of the city remained intact. Constantly in retreat, what was left of the Prussians moved to Westphalia where the last battle went against them. People rejoiced because they were freed from the Prussians.*
>
> *After the battle of Westphalia, the French returned to their country. All exiles returned to their homes. There was now peace between the French and Germans. Then a new emperor was elected, and he*

met the Pope. Meanwhile deadly epidemics broke out in the regions that war had broken out and many more people died. When I begged God to take the terrible vision away, I heard God's voice say "Prussia must be so humiliated that it will never again bring sorrow to the Church." In the following year the Russians will war with the Turks driving the latter out of Europe and taking Constantinople. The new German Emperor will mobilize for war, but the Germans will not go beyond their frontiers. Soon after the Russian Turkish war, England too shall be visited by war.[161]

That civil wars will be fought between the good and bad people of a nation is a concept supported by many other Catholic prophets, including dozens of canonized saints, or those named blessed and venerable. The prophecy of Antonius is one example.

19th Century – 1854: Blessed Pope Pius IX – *(Prophecy Detail – The age of peace, Revolution, Church persecution, The great monarch)*

Giovanni Maria Mastai Ferretti was born on May 13, 1792, the ninth child of a noble family, and was baptized immediately after his birth. His education was at the Piarist College in Volterra and in Rome. He had occasion to meet Pope Pius VII while still a theology student and entered the Papal Noble Guard. That venture didn't last long, however, as an epileptic seizure brought it to an abrupt end. But, after pleading with the Pope, he was elevated and even garnered the Pope's support in his theological studies. He was ordained a priest on April 10, 1819.

His first assignment was as rector of the Tata Giovanni Institute in Rome, but he was later appointed Archbishop of Spoleto when he was just thirty-five years of age. After demonstrating his liberalism, organization skills, and charity, he was moved to the prestigious diocese of Imola and was elevated to cardinal in pectore. In 1840 he was announced as Cardinal-Priest of Santi Marcellino e Pietro. There he earned a reputation for visiting prisoners in jail and developing programs for street children.

Ferretti was elected pope in 1846 and many faithful Catholics hoped that he would be a champion of reform and modernization. Some even wanted him to advocate for Italian independence. Instead, he shifted toward conservatism, to the dismay of his supporters and to the delight of the establishment. He served in the papacy until 1878, making him the longest reigning pope in Church history. During his reign he convoked the Vatican Council in 1868, emphasized Mary's role in salvation, promulgated the dogma of the Immaculate Conception, and canonized the Twenty-Six Martyrs of Japan.

Pope Pius IX died in 1878 and his cause for canonization was opened on February 11, 1907. He was declared venerable by Pope John Paul II on July 6, 1985, and beatified by him on September 3, 2000.

During his reign as Pope, Pius IX made several prophetic statements, some of which addressed the end times. The relevant prophecies follow:

> *We expect that the Immaculate Virgin and Mother of God, Mary, through her most powerful intercession will bring it about that our holy mother, the Catholic church after removal of all obstacles and overcoming of all errors will gain in influence from day to day among all nations and in all places, prosper and rule from ocean to ocean, from the great stream to the ends of the earth; that she will enjoy peace and liberty...that all erring souls will return to the path of truth and justice after the darkness of their minds has been dispelled, and that there will be then one fold and one shepherd...[162]*

> *There will be a great prodigy which will fill the world with awe. But this prodigy will be preceded by the triumph of a revolution during which the Church will go through ordeals that are beyond description.[163]*

19th Century – Post 1820: Antonius *(Prophesy Detail - The great war, Civil wars)*

Antonius was a German immigrant who was born in 1820 in Cologne, France. There is very little information about his life, but the following prophecy, one that is almost identical in detail to the prophecy of Brother Anthony of Achen, has been attributed to him.

> *I saw a new war in Alsace. Suddenly from the French side out of Metz and Nancy, large troop transports, where after the battle began, which lasted two days, and which ended by winning over the Prussian commander. The French follow the Prussians over the Rhine in many directions. In a significant battle by Frankfurt, the Prussians were beaten heavily. They pulled back to Siegeburg, where they ran into the Russians. The Russians treated the Prussians badly. It appears to me that the Prussians helped the French. The battle by Siegeburg has never been equaled for horror. After several days the Russians and Prussians disengage and begin to pull back below Bonn on the west side of the Rhine River. The city of Cologne was shot at; only a quarter of the town*

was unaffected. They left shortly afterwards, and the people were glad and clapped and their faces beamed.[164]

19th Century - Pre-1862: Abbess Maria Steiner *(Prophesy Detail – Chastisement, Three days of darkness, Pope in exile, Need for prayer)*

Stigmatist and prophet Maria Steiner died in 1862, leaving behind several prophetic writings. Sometime in the nineteenth century, Steiner wrote these words regarding the end-of-times:

> *I see the Lord as He will be scourging the world and chastising it in a fearful manner so that few men and women will remain. The monks will have to leave their monasteries, and the nuns will be driven from the convents, especially in Italy. The Holy Church will be persecuted, and Rome will be without a shepherd. But the Lord showed me how beautiful the world will be after this awful punishment.*[165]
>
> *Unless people obtain pardon through their prayers, the time will come when they will see the sword and death, and Rome without a Shepherd.*[166]

19th Century - Maria Martel of Tilly (aka: Maria de Tilly) Apparitions of the Virgin Mary *(Prophecy Detail – Schism in the Church, Destruction of Paris, Suffering of England, Natural disasters, Two and three days of darkness)*

About fourteen miles south of the English Channel, between the towns of Bayeux and Caen in France, lies the small town of Tilly. It was a town of very little significance until March 18, 1886. On that day, three nuns of the Order of the Sacred Heart, and sixty of their students, witnessed the Blessed Virgin Mary descend from the sky and hover over a big elm tree across an open field. The sixty-three witnesses to this apparition all reported seeing the,

> *...beautiful Lady within an oval-like aura of brilliant greens, reds, pinks, blues, and yellows which emitted "rays." Her dress appeared to have been "opulent and Turkish" in style, but it scintillated and changed colors.*[167]

The apparition was not limited to only those in the schoolhouse. Many others in the area had also seen the Blessed Mother descend. As word spread, a great concourse of curious and devout alike filled the field, looking for signs and awaiting another appearance of the Virgin Mary. Most knelt and prayed while awaiting another miracle from the heavens. Among those who heard about the apparitions was Marie Martel. A pure and pious woman, she wanted to see for herself what all the talk was about. When she finished working, she rushed to the field. Upon arriving, she saw the Virgin near an elm tree dressed in white with a blue belt, golden roses placed on Her bare feet. She wore a white banner with the words, "I am the Immaculate" emblazoned across it. It was to this woman that the Virgin spoke for the first time on the feast of Our Lady of Mount Carmel in July 1896.

Marie Martel was born in 1872 and, in 1902, at the age of thirty, became a tertiary of St. Francis after having made a retreat a few years earlier. While making her First Communion at the age of twenty-four, she was graced with an apparition of the Blessed Virgin.

Marie had several discussions with the Virgin Mary over the course of the next three years. Several of those discussions revealed prophecies that have been borne out, such as the death and canonization of Pope Leo XII, and the two eruptions of Mt. Pelée, a volcano in France. She participated in many other discussions with the Mother of God that included the following prophecies about the end-of-times.

Marie Martel died in France on October 24, 1913 leaving us much to ponder about the coming chastisements.

July 1896:

In the month of July 1896, feast of Our Lady of Mount Carmel, for the first time I heard the voice of the Blessed Virgin, who said to me: "Penance! My child, Penitence! My child, do you want to be happy in this life or the other?" Right away, I said, "O my good Mother, I want to go with you right now, if you want to." The Blessed Virgin tells me: "My child, you will have much to suffer here, if you are faithful to the mission that you have to fulfil, I promise you will be happy in the other life." And the last word of the Blessed Virgin was this: "My dear children, I beg you to pray well and to do penance. It is through prayer and penance that you will appease the vengeance of heaven."[168]

The following month, the Blessed Virgin Mary was photographed as a reflection in the eyes of the visionary during her ecstasies. This phenomenon was repeated in many future apparitions as well.

January 1897:

"My children, pray, because great evils will strike you. The war will soon be declared on all sides against the Church. A schism is

being made." The Blessed Virgin begs, her eyes turned to the sky, and then, turning to me, she says to me: "Oh ! Paris, Paris did not respect the laws of my Divine Son ... It will be punished and destroyed by fire ... There will be few people who will remain ... Those who remain will not recognize themselves ... Paris will be destroyed by fire, if it refuses to convert ... this is the punishment that is reserved for it!" England will be punished. I saw ships sinking, on which England was written.

January 27, 1897:

I heard the Blessed Virgin who said to me: "My child, you must pray well, especially for Martinique, because it will be chastised, and it will be by a rain of fire from the sky, that will not be able to be extinguished. Many will perish; those who stay, if they refuse to convert, a second strike will be carried, and the plague will prevail." The Blessed Virgin showed me the catastrophe, I saw the fire on the sea, which reached the ships. The fire consumes these ships ... it was a shower of fire.

(NOTE: this came to pass when Mount Pelée [erupted] on May 8, 1902 and utterly destroyed the town of St. Pierre in Martinique. 28,000 people died within a few minutes. A second eruption then happened on May 20, 1902 which killed 2,000 rescue workers and survivors. It was a mega-volcanic catastrophe that shocked France and the world and is considered the worst volcanic disaster of the twentieth century.)

May 1897:

"My child, for you the world will be cruel. There are some who will try to crush you, to trample you; they will spit in your face. Above all, be calm and say nothing. You will be well humiliated. What I have told you is the truth. If God has not yet struck, (i.e. has not yet chastised the earth) *it is because, in His goodness as Father, He has waited for the return of sinners; and today what has He received from this expectation? What blasphemies ... And yet my Divine Son, in his goodness, has made known to them all the misfortunes that threaten them, by warnings He sends them. Now God will strike if you refuse to pray, to do penance and to convert. Oh! Pray, my dear children, for I will soon not be able to stop this divine anger, which will be sent from the Divine Master. The first blow will be on Paris: theatres will blow up; victims will burn; the blood will flow."* (Marie Martel saw Montmartre spared, Versailles destroyed, and Fontainebleau preserved). *"You must pray well. You are in dangerous days, and there will be some preserved. A*

disaster will pass in a festival that will be given; and the other is nothing next to it." (i.e. This is a possible reference to the Charity Bazaar disaster of Paris that happened that year which shocked everyone, which will be nothing compared to what's coming). *"Many will see me rise above danger, and the angels will be with me. The catastrophe is going to be so terrible that the world will pray better ... I see them coming by God in a more distant time ... Oh! How many weeping mothers! They will shriek to the sky when they see their children writhing in the flames! Oh! It is there that these mothers will forget the feasts of Baal and all their pleasures; and during these days of mourning, the world will pray better. Many will come to prostrate themselves before the divine tabernacles and ask God's forgiveness ... Ah! What repentance! But unfortunately! It will be too late!... Since the world does not want to pray, that's how God will strike!"* And then the word "Penance!" was repeated. *"A great miracle is going to take place, and many more will follow. Do not be discouraged. You must pray, pray well."*

The Blessed Virgin also says that in a festival that would be given for little children, there would be many victims, who would shout, who would resound in the air. (NOTE: It seems a great fire or calamity will break out at a festival given for children. Apparently, the chastisements of Paris will begin with the tragic destruction of this festival.) *"And most of these children, it is the mothers who lead them where my Divine Son does not want, and it is there that these mothers will beat their chests, when they will see their children writhing in the flames."*

Marie then said to Our Lady, *"Have mercy on Paris! Hold the arm of your divine Son! ... After it has passed, they will not think about it! ... Forgive us! ... Forgive us all!"*

Marie, who feels no fatigue, takes her rosary. Then Our Lady recommends blessed candles in anticipation of the time of darkness.[169]

(NOTE: Is this a reference to the Two and Three Days of Darkness in which only blessed candles will light? According to the approved mystic Marie-Julie Jahenny, they must be one hundred percent wax, or they will not light. Beeswax is the material approved by the Church. The candles must also be blessed on Candlemas, which is celebrated each year on February 2)

June 1901:

The Sacred Heart of Jesus said to me: "My child, from this day, I take you to be, near my people, my intermediary, to ask each of my children to come, every Friday of the year, spend an hour with the Divine tabernacles: that is to say, an hour of worship, (adoration) to repair all the outrages, of which My Heart is showered every day, from My own children.

On Sundays, most of them profane My Holy Day, which I have reserved for Myself, and others blaspheme Me, and even come to sit at My holy table, to receive My Sacred Flesh and My Precious Blood, (i.e. in the state of mortal sin)*: They come to make Me undergo a new agony. It is necessary to pray for these unfortunate ones, so that they become converted. My Holy Mother must be implored for them." The good Jesus also told me that I had to start with the poor, to ask to do the hour of adoration. Our Lord [said] "And above all, my child, do not fail to fulfil the mission that I have just given you, and sometimes you will find many troubles and trials: even you will laugh at yourself, you will find yourself in trouble. My child, place slander underfoot; because for all that comes from heaven there are more difficulties than for things that come from the earth. Child be brave! Take courage! Answer My call!*

"Say to those who apologize for not being able to come every week, that they come on the first Friday of each month, and especially that it is necessary to be well prepared, to come to receive Me, to repair all the outrages of which I am showered, as well as My Father, who is ready to strike the whole of France. She (France) is the most guilty! It is she who has received the most graces and blessings, and I have received only ingratitude! The world will be chastised if it refuses to pray and do penance. France will be chastised ... The trials will come ... At the moment when the law on the Congregations will pass that religious who will (be forced) *leave! The schism against the Church is being made ..."*[170]

Elizabeth A. Bucchianeri notes that Marie-Julie Jahenny received the same revelation about an evil secular law passed in France that will force religious and clergy out of the country. It is a diabolical law that leads to a great apostate schism. That is when the chastisements will start in earnest.

July 7, 1901:

All the balls started from the sun, as if they had come out from behind it. When they started from the bottom of the sun, they were a little elongated like lemons, then they grew bigger; but they diminished as they came towards us, until they became very small. They swayed then, one meter of earth (...) Everyone was covered: they (i.e. the strange balls) *were in countless quantities. There were some green ones, some rose, some dark blue, some black some yellow, color of flame, fire ... some came in large numbers to us, others went to all sides.*

I saw a lot of the sun, and falling on the Church especially, it hurt me a lot. My heart was tight...I also saw several times below the sun [something] *like a mourning curtain, there was no cloud at all and the sky was all pink. This black was only below the sun; it disappeared quickly and reappeared again_... that's when I heard a voice telling me that the black I saw, that's how the darkness will be! And the balls that look like flames, it's the fire for Paris and for different places! This is how the fire of heaven will fall.*

We will do penance. We refuse now, but we will do penance ... We must pray ... but a lot, to stop the arm of Divine Justice. The voice was that of the Sacred Heart. With all the other balls that I saw fall, the Voice also said to me: "Here are all the punishments of all kinds, and then also great misfortunes threaten you. The good ones will also pay for the bad ones."

The voice was very severe. I would have preferred not to hear it. How sad it was![171]

August 15, 1901:

The Blessed Virgin says: "My children, all the balls [of fire] *you see are nothing compared to the misfortunes and punishments of all kinds, which have been announced, and of which they mock so much ...It will be necessary to repair the outrages committed on all sides. Most of them, on Sundays, do not go to Mass: that is what insults my Divine Son! The others blaspheme: that is what insults my Divine Son! Many others already outrage the Holy Tabernacle.*

"Pray, pray, my children ... You [are] *all about to be tested: the good ones will pay for the culprits, I will protect many, especially those who have always trusted me. All the animals that you saw, that's how it will come in many places! They will devour whatever they find in their path. Many people will be devoured."*

I saw a lot of ships gobbled up. This is how everyone will do penance! The fire on Paris was announced again, and that's when I saw a big banner, on which was written "War, plague, famine, plagues of all kinds." I saw a cross surrounded by little angels. Oh! How beautiful they were!

Afterwards, I saw Saint Radegonde (i.e. St. Radegund). *It was the first time I saw her. She rested her feet on a banner, held by two little angels, and on which was written "Saint Radegonde." How beautiful she was! She was all dressed in white: a beautiful white coat, with a gold border. She was crowned.*

Afterwards, I saw the Sacred Heart. Oh! How much I was seized, seeing the Heart of Jesus bleeding! The Sacred Heart said to me, "You must ask for adorers for every Friday, and you must begin with the poor." (i.e. The request for the hour of adoration and reparation before a tabernacle.) *At that moment, the blood flowed, I could not behold it anymore, it hurt to see!*

And always the Voice complained "Here, and in many other places, you do not hasten to make Me adored. At all costs, it is necessary before the punishments, to appease the arm of the Divine Justice, I will bless all those who will make adoration to Me. Come tomorrow morning recite the rosary!"

I went the next morning [August 16], *as the Sacred Heart had told me. During the recitation of the rosary, I heard the word "Penance!" several times. When I asked the Sacred Heart for Tilly's triumph, the Sacred Heart replied, "It will be at the moment of the great shock, which will pass. There must not* [be] *despair; you must pray a lot."*[172]

October 2, 1901:

The Sacred Heart has also announced great misfortunes, of which we are much threatened. "In many different places, little children will be slaughtered, even in the arms of their mothers. Many people will be destroyed by water, others by fire from the sky... All these punishments are terrible ... What priests, who have fled, will be massacred! ... The blood will flow freely ... you must also pray a lot for the Holy Father, the Pope, and for all the clergy ... He is not valiant! When all these punishments will pass, they will all be in great terror! That's why we must pray! I see a lot of everything giving up. They (the clergy) *will forget all the commitments they made. They will suffer, and even they will forget their Father of Heaven. All those who will remain peaceful, and who patiently wait for all these misfortunes, will be the blessed of My Father. This is the last time that I warn you of all that will happen: War, plague, famine, plagues of all kinds. Everyone will have to suffer, plus one less. Your souls must wake up. It's time! It's the test!"*

And then the voice of the good Jesus also told me that it was the last time He asked for the hour of adoration. I heard these words again: "France is guilty; she will be punished and punished. It takes blood to repair the outrages with which My Heart is showered. France is making a huge wound to My heart. She does not content herself, she enlarges it every day. Pray, my children! Come near My tabernacle. Come to adore this Heart, which suffers horribly because of your ingratitude! Oh! Come comfort My Heart! It is the channel, through which all the graces, which loves to spread in souls, overflow. It is also the road, which leads in the way to Heaven."

I asked a lot to quell the divine wrath. I prayed the good Jesus to soften all these punishments; I was very scared ... Good Jesus looked to the right and to the left, and blessed us, as if to say to us: Goodbye! His face became radiant and beautiful. And then, a great light has enveloped everything: the vision is lifted. I did not see anything anymore.

When I found myself in the middle of all this world, it seemed very sad to me, and yet, on the other hand, I was happy, because everyone was praying well; I thought that was why the good Jesus had looked right and left: it was probably to hear the prayer of all His children ... [173]

December 2, 1901:

I went to the Field, as the voice had asked me...I got on my knees, and I began the rosary. It was during the Sorrowful Mysteries that I saw before me a very bright light, and at that moment I perceived all the Angels that surrounded our good Mother, when she showed herself in this blessed place. I also saw many lilies, and stars falling on the angels, and also falling on us.

At that moment, I heard the voice of our good Mother, who told me that we had to pray a lot for the Holy Father, and then for the clergy. The voice of our good Mother was very sad! It seemed to me that her heart was very big, for the voice was sobbing: "You must pray for everything that happens in a large part of the clergy. O my children! These things are appalling! When I see the enemies of my Son who lead my children to death; when I see these enemies present their deceitful promises to many who carry the priesthood of my Divine Son, (i.e. these enemies will lead priests astray) *I see them, these souls,* (the wayward priests) *descend into the hollow of abysses, and I also see the Divine wrath that will strike! All the words that I brought to the earth, most rejected them, and even trampled on them. My words have been blasphemed! They refuse to believe them! ... A moment will come when all that I have brought to earth will be preached by the beloved of my Divine Son, and all those who have blasphemed them will be struck... The Heart of my Divine Son is so outraged that sometimes He Forgets His Blessed Mother! He is ready to split heaven, to sift them all, in the sieve of His holiness. All the misfortunes, which I have come to announce on the mount of La Salette, will arrive. The clergy trod on my words at their feet; they laughed; they did not want to do anything; they did not want to hear me! And today their hearts are going to be tortured, for lack of faith in my words. Here, they turned a deaf ear to my call! But Divine Justice will wake them up ... Their hearts are harder than stone! Only the punishments that will strike them will make them see their cowardice against me!"*[174]

January 31, 1903:

Our Lady said "Oh, my children, pray, pray, indulge in penance. I can no longer retain divine justice. Pray for the King who is coming. In these days you live under a regime of crime ... but France will go to the Sacred Heart. You must come to this place and pray for the King to come. This is the monarchy which will ensure the recovery of France in a new era because the royalty of France is traditionally a Christian regime."[175]

May 3, 1903:

Our Lady said, "The triumph will come, it will not be long (in coming) *... I pray, I beg my Divine Son, with the heart of the tenderest of the mothers, so that He removes the plagues ... O my children, pray, pray a lot! ... It will be necessary to pray a lot during the months of August and September ... It is necessary to pray for the future King ... and for the Sovereign Pontiff ... The Republic will fall. It is the reign of Satan! ... Another world and another reign will come ..."*

(Note: France did not then, and does not now, have a king. The reference to a future king refers to the Great Monarch and Angelic Pontiff. This is a confirmation of the prophecy of Marie-Julie Jahenny with regard to the Masonic Republic of France being from hell.)

July 20, 1903

The Blessed Virgin tells me: "Take courage, my children, I assure you: I will do here (at Tilly) what I have never done in the whole world ...The King of France in the Great Glorious Kingdom of Christ King Master of the Nations." A monastery was there once. It is dead. He will resurrect another, of a new kind...The French Royalty, incarnated by Saint Louis and Joan of Arc, was decapitated in Louis XVI and buried with Charles X ... it will be resurrected by Tilly.[176]

In addition to these prophecies, Yves Dupont also records these words which he attributes to Marie Martel:

I see a great darkness and lightning. Paris will be almost entirely destroyed by fire. Marseilles also will be destroyed, and other cities as well.[177]

19th Century – St. John Bosco (aka Giovanni Melchiorre Bosco and Don Bosco) Between May 24 and June 24, 1873: *(Prophecy Detail – Darkness, Pope in exile, Wars)*

Giovanni Melchiorre Bosco was born in Becchi, Italy, on August 16, 1815 at a time of massive upheaval. The Napoleonic Wars had just ended, leaving his hometown ravaged. In addition, the area was in the midst of a drought as well as a famine. When John was only two years old, his father died, leaving his mother, Margherita Occhiena, to alone raise her three boys. Together they attended church and led devout lives. Despite their intense poverty the family always found a way to help the less fortunate.

At the age of nine, John had the first of several vivid dreams that would have a profound impact on his life. In his dream he came upon several boys who were playing and swearing. Among the boys were a majestic man and a woman of equal majesty. The man told John that he would *"conquer the boys"* only through meekness and charity. The Lady added, *"Be strong, humble and robust. When the time comes, you will understand everything."*[178]

A short time later, after viewing the performers and magicians in a traveling circus, John taught himself magic as a means of attracting others and holding their attention. He later staged his own magic show after which he recited a homily that he heard earlier that day. At the conclusion of his "show" he invited the boys to pray with him. After this experience he discerned the call to enter the priesthood.

He found a priest to provide the required education of which poverty had deprived him. The education, however, was not without consequence as it caused one of John's brothers to whip him for his disloyalty to his farming roots. Undeterred, John left home at the age of twelve, taking work in a vineyard to earn his way. Two years later John befriended Fr. Joseph Cafasso, who offered his assistance in getting John a place in the seminary, and in 1841, John was ordained a priest and assigned to the impoverished area of Turin. Known as Fr. "Don" Bosco, John immediately went to work with the poor children.

One of the things that struck John was the extraordinary number of children between the ages of twelve and eighteen who were in prison under deplorable conditions. He vowed to work with children to prevent them from ending up there. He took to the streets where the children played and worked, grabbing their attention with his magic.

Fr. Bosco preached, but also tried to find work for some of the boys and lodging for some others. He enlisted his mother's help and together, "Mamma Margherita" and Fr. Bosco found lodging for eight hundred boys. Many of these boys he encouraged to become priests, and helped those truly interested in doing so with their studies.

In 1859, Fr. Bosco established the Society of St. Francis de Sales, organizing fifteen seminarians and one teenage boy into the group. The purpose of the group was to keep them out of trouble by carrying on his charitable work and developing their faith.

Fr. Bosco died on January 31, 1888, though his organization still functions today. Pope Pius XI declared him blessed in 1929 and he was canonized to sainthood on Easter Sunday in 1934 with the title "Father and Teacher of Youth."

John Bosco is one of the greatest saints of the nineteenth century. He was also a visionary who was able to detail future events with remarkable accuracy. One of his prophecies concerning the end-of-times is quoted here:

> *It was a dark night, and men could no longer find their way back to their own countries. Suddenly a most brilliant light* (faith in God and in His power) *shone in the sky, illuminating their way as at high noon. At that moment from the Vatican came forth, as in procession, a multitude of men and women, young children, monks, nuns, and priests, and at their head was the Pope.* (It seems to allude to the suppression of monasteries and schools run by religious and to the Pope's exile.)

> *But a furious storm broke out, somewhat dimming that light, as if light and darkness were locked in battle.* (Perhaps this means a battle between truth and error, or else a bloody war.) *Meanwhile the long procession reached a small square littered with dead and wounded, many of whom cried for help.*

> *The ranks of the procession thinned considerably. After a two hundred-day march, all realized that they were no longer in Rome. In dismay they swarmed about the Pontiff to protect him and minister to him in his needs.*

> *At that moment two angels appeared, bearing a banner which they presented to the Supreme Pontiff, saying: "Take the banner of Her who battles and routs the most powerful armies on earth. Your enemies have vanished: with tears and sighs your children plead for your return."*

> *One side of the banner bore the inscription: <u>Regina sine labe concepta</u>* [Queen conceived without sin]*, and the other side read: <u>Auxilium Christianorum</u>* [Help of Christians]*.*

> *The Pontiff accepted the banner gladly, but he became distressed to see how few were his followers.*

But the two angels went on: "Go now, comfort your children. Write to your brothers scattered throughout the world that men must reform their lives. This cannot be achieved unless the bread of the Divine Word is broken among the peoples. Teach children their catechism and preach detachment from earthly things. The time has come," the two angels concluded, "when the poor will evangelize the world." Priests shall be sought among those who wield the hoe, the spade, and the hammer, as David prophesied: 'God lifted the poor man from the fields to place him on the throne of His people.'"

On hearing this, the Pontiff moved on, and the ranks began to swell. Upon reaching the Holy City, the Pontiff wept at the sight of its desolate citizens, for many of them were no longer. He then entered St. Peter's and intoned the Te Deum, *to which a chorus of angels responded, singing:* Gloria in excelsis Deo et in terra pax hominibus bonae voluntatis [Glory to God in the highest, and peace on earth to men of good will.] *When the song was over, all darkness vanished, and a blazing sun shone. The population had declined greatly in the cities and in the countryside; the land was mangled as if by a hurricane and hailstorm, and people sought each other, deeply moved, and saying:* Est Deus in Israel [There is a God in Israel].

From the start of the exile until the intoning of the Te Deum, *the sun rose 200 times. All the events described covered a period of 400 days.*[179]

19th Century – 1872-1873: The Ecstatic of Tours *(Prophecy Detail – War and revolution in Italy, France, and across Europe, the Pope in exile, the Church without a leader, Priests and bishops martyred, Return to God, Great leader frees the Church, Three days of darkness.)*

The Ecstatic of Tours is a nom de plume used by a French nun who lived in nineteenth century France. Her revelations were published by her spiritual director in the book, *La Veille de la Victoire du Christ*, translated, *On the Eve of the Victory of Christ*. Her prophecies were made in 1872 and 1873. This and her prophecies are all that is known of her. While her prophecies seem to be confined to Europe, it has been understood by scholars, through analysis of similar prophetic statements, that the turmoil from the catastrophic events described in Europe will be more universal in nature, setting up a new political order across the globe. In 1872 and 1873, the Ecstatic of Tours said:

Before the war breaks out again, food will be scarce and expensive. There will be little work for the workers, and fathers will hear their children crying for food. There will be earthquakes and signs in the sun. Toward the end, darkness will cover the earth.

When everyone believes that peace is ensured, when everyone least expects it, the great happening will begin. Revolution will break out in Italy almost at the same time as in France. For some time, the Church will be without a Pope. England too will have much to suffer.

The revolution will spread to every French town. Wholesale slaughter will take place. This revolution will last only a few months, but it will be frightful; blood will flow everywhere because the malice of the wicked will reach its highest pitch. Victims will be innumerable. Paris will look like a slaughterhouse. Persecutions against the church will be ever greater but will not last long. All churches will be closed but only a few for a very short time in those towns where disturbances are the least. Priests will have to go into hiding. The wicked will try to obliterate anything religious, but they will not have enough time.

Many bishops and priests will be put to death. The archbishop of Paris will be murdered. Many other priests in Paris will have their throats cut because they will not have time to find a hiding place.

The wicked will be the masters for one year and a few months. In those days France will receive no human assistance. She will be alone and helpless. At this juncture, the French people will turn back to God and implore the sacred heart of Jesus and Mary Immaculate. They will at last confess that He alone can restore peace and happiness.

The French people will ask for the good king. He who was chosen by God. He will come; this savior whom God has spared for France. This king who is not wanted now because he is dear to God's Heart. He will ascend to the throne. He will free the church and reassert the Pope's rights.

The council will meet again after the victory. But this time men will be obliged to obey. There will be only one flock and one shepherd. All men will acknowledge the pope as the universal father, king of all peoples. Thus, mankind will be regenerated.[180]

19th Century – 1873 – 1877: St. Mariam Baouardy (aka Sister Mary of Jesus Crucified, The Little Arab, the Lily of Palestine) *(Prophecy Detail – Wars, Three days of darkness)*

The first twelve children born to Giries Baouardy and Mariam Shahine died in infancy. Consequently, when the poor Greek Melchite Catholic couple gave birth to little Mariam on January 5, 1846, it seemed to them an answered prayer to the Virgin Mary. Unfortunately, Mariam's parents died just two years later, leaving the child to be raised by her father's brother.

When Mariam was just eight, her uncle moved to Alexandria, Egypt, where he arranged Mariam's marriage five years later. The thirteen-year-old child had other plans, however, wanting instead to enter a convent. Her refusal to go along with the arranged marriage earned her the scorn of her uncle, who hired Mariam out as a domestic servant where she was required to do the most menial jobs.

It was on this job that Mariam was befriended by a Muslim servant who, after hearing of her sufferings, wanted to marry her and tried to convert her to Islam. Holding steadfast to the precepts of her Catholic faith again cost Mariam greatly, as the Muslim boy cut her throat, and dumped her limp body in an alley where she lay dying. Against all odds, and through the intervention of *"a beautiful lady...wrapped in a blue dress,"*[181] who appeared to Mariam and stitched her wound, she lived. She recalled the words the Virgin spoke to her as She treated her slashed throat. *"Be happy even if you suffer and suffer for God, He sends you only what you need, accept always good."*[182] The Virgin then warned Mariam about the temptations of the devil and encouraged her to engage in love of neighbor. The Blessed Virgin prophesied that Mariam would live in a convent in France and would die in the habit of Carmel in Bethlehem. Miriam never returned to her uncle's house and from that moment, dedicated herself to becoming a nun.

To support herself she worked as a domestic and was employed by a Christian family. During this phase, she also devoted a great deal of time to prayer. In 1860, she moved in with the Sisters of Saint Joseph. It was in this convent that Mariam started to experience supernatural events, which caused the Sisters to refuse to let her join their order. In 1867 she became a lay sister at Carmel at Pau, France and later entered the cloister, taking the name Mary of Jesus Crucified. She made her final profession on November 21, 1871.

She continued to experience supernatural events and at one point, as the Blessed Mother had prophesied, Mariam had to battle demonic possession, which lasted for forty days. Additionally, she received the stigmata, was observed levitating, and received the gifts of prophecy and knowledge of conscience. Her guardian angel would frequently speak through her, but over the years, Mariam became known, not for her supernatural abilities, but rather for her devotion to the Holy Spirit.

Mariam assisted with the founding of the missionary Carmel of Mangalore in India and built a Carmelite monastery in Bethlehem in 1875. She died of gangrene on August 26, 1878 following an injury received at the construction site of the Bethlehem monastery. Pope John Paul II beatified her in 1983 and Pope Francis canonized her on May 17, 2015.

Between the years 1873 and 1877 Mariam had several visions resulting in her contribution of several prophecies regarding the end times.

Of a vision on May 26, 1873 she wrote:

> *I saw France as a field watered by the rain, lit and warmed by the sun. But the earth was covered with weeds, among which, however, there were some good ones. I said to Jesus, "Lord, why are You leaving these weeds?"*
>
> *"I leave them," replied the Divine Master, "because the good are still too weak. They have their roots tied to the bad ones. If I tear out the bad ones, the good ones will be damaged, and they will wither. When the good will be stronger, I will pull out all that is bad. (...) Now its* (France's) *peace is built on the sand. Later, I will establish peace built on the firm rock and nothing will shake it. France is the center of My heart."*

Elizabeth A. Bucchianeri, author of the blog The Great Catholic Monarch and Angelic Pontiff Prophecies, notes that the reference to "the firm rock" may "indicate that once France turns away from the sand of the world and returns to 'the rock', that is Christ, His Church, and her ancient holy mission to defend the Church, the Age of Peace will be established and France will never lose this peace."[183]

During subsequent visions of 1873, St. Mariam saw a terrible futuristic war. The fighting seemed endless, prompting Mariam to ask when the horrible war might end. Following a long silence, the answer came.

> *Ah, it will be long, because everyone has to go, big and small: we are all corrupt!*[184]

In this same ecstasy, Mariam saw two massive armies engaged in fighting. She also saw two cisterns, one filled with blood and one empty. The empty cistern was so vast that even the blood of three quarters of the men could not fill it. At that moment she heard the Voice say,

You see, it is necessary that this cistern be filled to calm the justice of God...[185]

In a vision on February 16, 1874, Mariam was warned that France will be the Queen of all Kingdoms, but only after the bloody war and the three days of darkness.

Yesterday, I nelt before God, and I prayed for our Mother the Holy Church and for France.

Then the voice of Our Lord said,

Yes, I will delight in the bosom of France, she will still be the queen of all kingdoms. But before then, France must be made absolutely nothing so that I am at the head of armies, so that all nations say between them, from generation to generation: Really, it is the Most-High who is at the head of France. All nations will cry out with one mouth, one voice, the same tone, even the ungodly.[186]

Bucchianeri again explains that *"Our Lord is saying France must be reduced to a state of abjection so that when the Lord steps in, the whole world will recognize that it is indeed the Lord that has miraculously intervened."*[187]

To the words of Jesus, St. Mariam adds the following prophetic words:

Little lambs, do not be afraid of God. He will strike the earth, there will be earthquakes; fear nothing; resort to God alone, remain in him, trust in Him and fear nothing; His mercy is immense. He will want to spread it (His Mercy) over men, but justice stops mercy...

On August 14, 1874, Saint Mariam had another vision pertaining to the war.

It will be a terrible massacre. We will walk in blood up to the knees. I think that in this great war that will come, they will take all the priests to fight ...I do not know whether it is in this way that the priests will perish, for it must remain very soon after the Event, and it seems to me that they will be placed before them, at the height of danger.

Bucchianeri points out that other mystics have foretold of the clergy being persecuted in France, but this is different as St. Mariam seems to suggest that the clergy will be forced to take up arms in service to the military, though she is uncertain if this is how they perish.

In 1878 St. Mariam told Father Prosper Chirou that an evil government would rise in France, persecuting the Church prior to a second German invasion.

> *There will be a bad government in France. The religious will be hunted. It will take leagues to confess. The Germans will return to France, but they will be crushed* (reference to WW III?). *We will be forced to say, "God's finger is there." Yes, yes, soon France will triumph, soon she will be the queen of kingdoms. She did too much good in the missions for God to abandon her.*[188]

In a vision on July 6, 1875, Mariam reported hearing the following words:

> *Comfort yourself, will come a time to come, it is far from here, where France will become queen. But before, it must undergo many humiliations, even more than it has ever had. After the Lord will triumph and be the head of the kingdom. There will come a time, which seems far, very far in the eyes of man, but in the eyes of God it is not far, where France will be Queen too. She will rule Syria...*

On August 31, 1876, Mariam had another vision of wars, revolutions, three days of darkness, and the death of the clergy. She reported it this way:

> *I saw clouds, storms, rains of all things, falling on the earth, and nothing happened to this house. All nations will be shaken by war and revolution. In the darkness, for three days, the evil followers will be annihilated, so that only a quarter of humanity will survive. At that time, the clergy will be well diminished, because most of the priests will be dead for the defense of the faith or for their homeland. The cause of the terrible disasters that will melt on France, here it is: one will commit sins and outrages towards the Blessed Sacrament, and the Incarnation will be considered like a fable...The power of the enemy will not last forever. The church will live again and blossom forever...Happy man who perseveres despite everything! And woe to him who weakens at the first obstacle...Little flock, do not be afraid, be small. Do not fear thunder, nor rain, nor mountains, nothing will touch the elect of the Lord! Walk underground. If you want to be great, be small. Do not look for the greatness of the creature; whoever raises you today will lower you tomorrow.*[189]

On December 2, 1877, Mariam said:

> *The Lord showed me everything! I saw the Dove of fire! Address the Dove of fire, the Holy Spirit who inspires everything. I was told, "Follow me." I saw all the trees and mountains leap. Peace is my share. Peace and the cross are my share, but the cross and discouragement are the portion of the enemy and those who listen to the enemy.[190]*

Here Mariam seems to say that *"one escapes the cross, but those who follow the Holy Spirit will experience peace; those who are the enemies of God or who listen to the enemy will know only discouragement as well as bearing the cross."*[191]

19th Century – 1884: Pope Leo XIII *(Prophecy Detail – The Lord provides the devil with up to 100 years to attempt to destroy the Church.)*

Vincenzo Gioacchino Raffaele Luigi Pecci was born in Rome on March 2, 1810. He was the sixth of seven children born to Count Ludovico Pecci and Anna Prosperi Bruzzi. To his family, religion was the highest grace on the planet, through which eternal salvation was earned. As a young man Vincenzo studied in the Jesuit College in Viterbo, and by age eleven his love for Latin was already well known. His mother died in 1824 and Vincenzo returned to Rome where he attended Jesuit Collegium Romanum. He entered the Jesuit order in 1828 at age eighteen. He gained the attention of the Vatican in 1834 when he gave an award-winning student presentation on papal judgments which was attended by several cardinals. He received his doctorate in theology and civil and Canon Law in 1836.

On February 14, 1837, Vincenzo was appointed personal prelate by Pope Gregory XVI though he was only twenty-seven years old and was not yet ordained a priest. His ordination took place on December 31 of that same year and he was appointed legate (provincial administrator) shortly thereafter. At the age of thirty-three, Vincenzo was appointed Archbishop. In that position, Pecci developed excellent relations with the royal family, a relationship he exploited for the benefit of the Church.

Pecci rose quickly up the Church hierarchy, serving as Archbishop of Perugia from 1846 to 1878, using that position to call a provincial council to reform religious life in his dioceses. He developed several activities in support of Catholic charities; founded homeless shelters for boys, girls, and elderly women; opened soup kitchens operated by the Capuchins; opened branches of a bank, Monte di Pieta, which focused on low-income people, providing them with low-interest loans; and forged many other achievements, including a strong defense of the papacy against the secular government moving to take over church and school buildings.

On December 8, 1869, he organized an ecumenical council known as the First Vatican Council. He defined the Church as the mother of material civilization because it upheld human dignity for working people, opposed the excesses of industrialization, and developed large-scale charities for the needy.

Following the death of Pope Pius IX, the conclave assembled in Rome and elected Pecci on the third ballot. He chose the name Leo XIII and was crowned on March 3, 1878. He was sixty-eight years old and served for twenty-five years before his own death at the age of ninety-three, making him the oldest pope in history.

After celebrating Mass in the Vatican's private chapel on October 13, 1884, a Mass attended by a few cardinals and members of the Vatican staff, Pope Leo XIII began to leave the altar when he had a remarkable vision. He stopped quickly at the base of the altar and stood there for several minutes as if in a trance. According to eyewitnesses the Pontiff's face was ashen white. He fell to the ground, leaving the impression that he had died. "He had no pulse...and the Holy Father was feared dead. Suddenly, Pope Leo awoke and said, *'What a horrible picture I was permitted to see!'*"[192] Now in a state of full awareness, Pope Leo rushed to his office where he immediately composed the Prayer to St. Michael the Archangel. When asked for an explanation by those who witnessed the pope's trance, Leo said that he,

> *...suddenly heard voices – two voices, one kind and gentle, the other guttural and harsh. They seemed to come from near the tabernacle. As he listened, he heard the following conversation:*
>
> *Satan – I can destroy your Church.*
> *Jesus – You can? Then go ahead and do so."*
> *Satan – To do so I need more time and more power.*
> *Jesus – How much time? How much power?*
> *Satan – 75 to 100 years, and a greater power over those who will give themselves over to my service* (meaning the Masons and Communists).
> *Jesus – "You have the time, you will have the power. Do with them as you will.*[193]

The Pope found this conversation so troubling that in 1886, he decreed that the prayer he composed along with the Salve Regina (Hail Holy Queen) be recited at the conclusion of every low Mass throughout the entire world. This practice was adopted, but was discontinued by Pope Paul VI in 1968. In his book, *The Last Warnings: The Year 2017 and Thereafter*, Jerald James notes, *"This is where Satan started the ball rolling with the infiltration of both Mason and Communist into the Catholic Church. Infiltration of the Church becomes serious in the early 1900s."*[194]

The conversation between God and the devil, or good and evil, gives insight into what purports to be a troubling negotiation between God and Satan. Indeed, the twentieth century seemed to have belonged to Satan. The planet was engulfed in two world wars, we saw the rise of communism who's philosophy shook Christianity, the Armenian Genocide and the Holocaust, the atomic bomb, the spreading of national and international secularism, a decline in Church attendance and religious vocations, a sexual revolution, the legalization of abortion up to the moment of birth in some cases, the rise of gay marriage, the legalization of marijuana and other drugs, assisted suicide, cloning, the overt attack on Christianity in America, and many other insensitivities and abominations. Some insist that Pope John XXIII started the decline of the Church with his Second Vatican Council. Others say that Pope Paul VI *"let the devil develop a church that is called Catholic but is not. The devil has twisted and distorted church teachings so much that there truly is a brand new Church, a new order (Novus Ordo) and the true Church has been reduced in population to a mere shell of what it once was...*[even so] *it will survive."*[195] What is clear is that, as Pope Leo XIII prophesied, the twentieth century was owned by the devil.

19th & 20th Centuries – 1874-1925: Marie-Julie Jahenny, (aka Marie de la Fraudais) *(Prophecy Detail – Satan's free reign, Plagues, Diseases, Two days of darkness, Three days of darkness, Earthquakes and other natural disasters)*

Marie-Julie Jahenny was the first of five children born to Charles and Marie Boya Jahenny, but she was the only one of the five that exhibited extraordinary powers. Little did these pious, hard-working peasants know that little Marie-Julie had been chosen by God for a very special mission;

> *to spread the love of the cross, to make sacrifices and suffer for the salvation of sinners, to prepare the world for the prophesied*

chastisements, and to announce the coming of the Great Monarch and the Angelic Pontiff who would restore the glory of Christendom in an unprecedented and miraculous manner.[196]

Marie-Julie first heard the voice of Jesus when she was just a young girl in church. Jesus asked her to stay with Him just a little longer. She complied, and in that moment, developed a deep love and devotion to the Blessed Sacrament and the tabernacle where she would keep long hours in prayer. As she grew, she entered the Third Order of St. Francis. She remained modest and approached the altar with angelic devotion when receiving Holy Communion.

On February 22, 1873, Marie-Julie suffered a serious illness during which the Blessed Virgin appeared to her to inform her that she would have much to suffer. The Blessed Mother appeared to Marie-Julie again on March 15, asking her if *"she would be willing to suffer the same agonies her Son had endured to save mankind."*[197] Marie-Julie said yes, at which time Mary informed her that she would receive the Five Wounds of Jesus. Six days later, she began to receive the stigmata.

The first wound was the crown of thorns, appearing on October 5, 1873. On November 25, she received the shoulder wound from the carrying of the cross. On December 6, the scourge wounds bloodied Marie-Julie's back, and on January 12, 1874, Jahenny received the wrist wounds where the Roman soldiers bound Jesus's hands. On that same day appeared a wound over Marie-Julie's heart. On January 14, she received additional scourge marks on her ankles, legs, and forearms, and a few days following, she received two additional scourge marks on her side.

On February 20, the Blessed Mother told Jahenny that *"she was to become the spiritual bride of Christ. A wound appeared around the ring finger of her right hand: a special mark showing that she had been chosen as the Spiritual Spouse of Christ."*[198]

Then, Marie-Julie told of a stigmatic miracle that others could witness as it happened. After being told by Mary that she would receive a special mark on her chest, she announced that it would appear on December 7. On that day, family, friends, and other witnesses were *"stunned to see a cross and flower appear on her chest with the words: O Crux Ave, (Hail to the Cross) accompanied by the most extraordinary perfumes emanating from her body."*[199] The sign remained for witnesses to examine even after the ecstasy was over.

The stigmatic wounds bled every Friday at first, but then only on Good Friday after a period of time. Marie-Julie was told of several other miracles that others would be able to witness, and all occurred just as she foretold.

Monseigneur Fournier, Bishop of Nantes, opened an investigation to authenticate these miracles. Doctor Imbert-Gourbeyre, a professor at the Faculty of Medicine at Clermont-Ferrand, was asked to examine the stigmatic wounds. His conclusion indicated the authenticity of the wounds and eliminated fraud as a possibility. On quick order, the Bishop authenticated the stigmata.

The graces bestowed on Marie-Julie by God did not stop with the stigmata, however, as her heart was pierced with a golden nail to signify the special union between her and God her Father. She was also granted a "mystical sun" in which she could see visions. She could distinguish blessed objects from those that were not blessed, and consecrated from unconsecrated Hosts. She could discern souls and could fast for months at a time, eating and drinking nothing but the Blessed Sacrament. She frequently suffered the Passion of Christ and was often physically attacked by Satan. She possessed a supernatural spiritual knowledge and was given the gift of prophecy. She was persecuted by friends and neighbors who didn't believe in her gifts and was, at one point, even denied the Sacraments until a Vatican commission under Pope Leo XIII lifted the wrongfully imposed ban. Through all this, her stigmata and other gifts are still recognized as approved by the Catholic Church.

Over the course of fifty-one years spanning two centuries, from 1874 to 1925, Marie-Julie Jahenny issued a great many prophecies. On August 30, 1880, Marie-Julie was given a vision of the Ascension of Jesus. Satan appeared before Him and demanded more power. Jesus promised a period of freedom where Satan would be free to tempt mankind without limit. She saw that the devil's evil conquests would be so great in number that he would have an army of followers greater than that of God. Satan's pinnacle of power would come just as a disastrous anti-cleric civil war broke out in Paris and spread throughout France then all of Europe. Marie-Julie was then told that we have already entered Satan's age.

The following are Marie-Julie Jahenny's prophecies on the two and three days of darkness, the warning signs leading up to them, and how to prepare for them. These prophecies are not presented in the order in which they were received, but rather have been grouped by topic.

There will be bright precursory signs before God's Justice strikes the earth. (October 27, 1877)[200]

God will give his warning signs in nature during the first months of the year when the days are short but beginning to grow. (June 15, 1882)

Brittany will see the first warning – "still in the hard season when the wheat has not yet reached the third node of growth" (winter wheat - i.e. still in winter circa February and March), *there will be a four hour darkness lasting from 12:00 Noon to 4:00 PM - the sun will be veiled as if in mourning - darkness will be so great, no eye will see anything. It is only a warning - no destruction will happen - but it is a warning that God's justice is about to be released.* (Oct. 5, 1882)

The earth will shake from this place until sunrise, the space of six days. A day of rest and (on) the eighth day, the trembling will begin again. France and England will respond with their cries of despair. The land will shake so hard that the people will be thrown up to 300 steps. The thunder will sound more brightly than in the months that will lead up to the end of the world, with a strange noise. (March 8, 1881)

There will be "strange thunder" that does not seem normal - then lightning without thunder which will last for half a day.[201] (However, it will still come from a natural origin, not supernatural) (March 19, 1878)

This is one of the first warnings that will come at the beginning of the year during the cold months.[202]
Part of Brittany will be tested then it will not reach all of France. Only the lands around the shrine of St. Anne in Brittany will not experience this warning of this day of semi-darkness and lightning - everywhere else will be in a fright as for a whole day the fire of lightning will do much harm, even in the private homes of sinners, and the thunder will scold.
This day of semi-darkness and lightning is not related to the three days of darkness which will happen later.
"Thunderings" will come before the justice of God strikes. (July 30, 1925)

The prophecy of these dark days was also revealed to St. Catherine Laboure, and also St. Mary of St. Peter of Tours - St. Mary of Tours wrote them down and they were hidden - when these hidden scrolls are brought to light again, then the time of the warning of lightning will be close.[203] (June 15, 1882)

There will be one major earthquake, but this time it will last 43 days – it will shake many buildings of Paris to the ground – mega tsunamis will occur.[204] (Sept. 29, 1879 and March 15, 1882) (This is probably the last of the Major warnings that will happen right between the two and three days of darkness, which will occur thirty-seven days apart from each other.)

In the end, Paris will be destroyed by a hail of fire.[205] (April 27, 1877)

Stay away from this city of Sodom which will be destroyed by God's justice.[206] (April 6, 1877)

If Paris does not convert, it will be burned. The heat will be so intense the stones will be crumbled and cannot be reused.[207] (Nov. 28, 1881)

The fire of heaven will fall upon this Sodom and mix with the fire of hell. Even water will take on the burning nature of Fire. The National Assembly will be destroyed, and the city will resemble a huge sand or quarry pit. This sign of destruction will last until the end of time.[208] (unknown date)

Only 88 people will be saved during the destruction of Paris.[209] (Aug. 9, 1881)

The church of Our Lady of Victories will survive the destruction of Paris.[210] (Jan. 27, 1882)

The good will suffer with the guilty as Heaven needs sacrificial suffering for God to pour out His grace to cleanse and restore the kingdom.[211] (July 25, 1882)

The chastisements will be so great that France will be practically depopulated, especially Paris, the larger cities, and in the south of France. Only a few who hide underground will be safe. Pray a "Miserere" for Paris, for Lyon and Toulouse. No coffins for the people - the massacres will be great. A person will have to travel leagues before they see another soul.[212] (Sept. 20, 1881)

Do not expect improvement, on the contrary, you will see evil growing continuously, unjust disorders multiplying...until the time that I rise up in My turn.[213] (Aug. 4, 1904)

The Two Days of Darkness:

In the following prophecies, the Holy Spirit said to Marie-Julie Jahenny: There will be two days of horrible darkness, distinct from those advertised (i.e. different from the 3 days). The sky will be purple and red, so low that the clump of tall trees will be as lost. These two days will warn you, as an authentic proof of His goodness, as proof of descent from the wrath of God on earth. You will not be free from the darkness. So far, no soul has mentioned it, because those are not many who were made aware. To resist all these signs, holy water is a strength and consolation, and the candle, but with wax. All those that are not of this paste will not help. (i.e. must be 100% pure wax, which means blessed 100% beeswax candles)

The sky will turn red and purple - the sap of the fruit trees will be burnt and not produce fruit the following year. Black rain will fall as a burning hailstone but will not destroy the homes of the faithful or destroy the land that will produce food for the faithful.

In Brittany, in these two days of darkness, under the lowering sky, it will seem light, but no one will be able to see, because they cannot put out their face by day when opening a door; there will be an envoy of God, in the form of a hot flash, which will obscure the human eye. - "The Lord is urging me to pass on His words and His wishes. The day of these darknesses will still be bearable, despite the darkness ... But if the day is calm, the night will be violent, and during the two nights, cries will come out where they know not, they will hear nothing, nor walk on earth, covered with Justice. At night, the blessed candle, the candle should not be put out. During the day, they will be able to go without it, a grace that comes from beyond the Heart of God."[214] (Sept. 20, 1880)

After these Two Days, there will be a thirty-seven to forty-day period, after which the three days of darkness will occur.

Our Lord said to Jahenny:
I shall come over the sinful world in a frightful rumbling of thunder during a very cold winter night. A very hot southerly wind shall precede the thunderstorm, and heavy hailstones shall dig deep into the soil. From a mass of fiery clouds devastating lightning will come forth in zigzags, setting fires and turning everything into ash. The air

will be filled with poisonous gases and deadly vapors which, in great whirlwinds, will uproot the works of the audacity, the folly, and the will of the city of "Darkness."[215] (Nov. 28, 1881)

The Three Days of Darkness:

There will come three days of complete darkness. Only blessed candles made of 100% beeswax will give some light during this horrible darkness. One candle will last for three days, but they will not give light in the houses of the Godless. Lightning will penetrate your houses, but it will not put out the blessed candles. Neither wind, nor storm, nor earthquake will put out the blessed candles. Red clouds, like blood, will cross the sky, and the crash of thunder will shake the earth to its very core. The ocean will cast its foaming waves over the land, and the earth will be turned into a huge graveyard. The bodies of the wicked and of the righteous will cover the face of the earth. The famine that follows will be severe. All plant-life will be destroyed as well as three-fourths of the human race. This crisis will be sudden, and the punishment will be worldwide.[216] (Oct. 27, 1876 and May 23, 1876)

The candle's light will be the only thing that will protect us from the fire falling from the sky and the lightning that will enter the houses.[217] (March 24, 1881)

[Note: A prophecy of the Breton Stigmatist indicates that the three days of darkness will be on a Thursday, Friday, and a Saturday. Days of the Most Holy Sacrament, of the Cross and Our Lady.]

The lightnings of heaven will succeed with a rapid violence. Fire from heaven will travel the earth to an appalling width: the vengeful lightning will burn any point that produces the fruit. Cultivated lands will be devastated by the power of this fire; grasslands will be burned and reduced to a land completely stripped. The fruit will not appear, all the branches of trees will be dry to the trunk. For three days the sky will be on fire with the Divine wrath. The earth will not produce food for many years after it, the fruit trees will not produce for three years.[218] (Nov. 30, 1880)

During these three days and two nights, the demons will appear under the most hideous forms. You will hear in the air the most horrible blasphemies. The lightning will enter your homes, but will not extinguish the candles; neither wind, nor the storm can put them out. Red clouds like blood will ride across the sky. The crash of thunder will shake the earth. Sinister lightning will cut across the dense clouds, in a season when they never occur. (In winter, or the end of March?) *The earth will be shaken down to the foundations. The sea will raise thundering waves that will spread across the continent. Blood will flow in such abundance that the earth will become a vast cemetery. The corpses of the wicked and the righteous ones will litter the ground. The famine will be great. Everything will be in turmoil and three-quarters of men will perish. The crisis will break out suddenly. The chastisements will be common in the world to swell up and will succeed one another ceaselessly.*[219] (Jan. 4, 1884)

The Virgin Mary said to Jahenny:

My children, mind my words ... In these days of mourning, there will be another earthquake as strong as many others, less strong than in many other places. It will be easy to notice; everything will shake except the piece of furniture on which will burn the wax candle. You will all group around, with the crucifix and my blessed image. This is what shall take fear away from you, as these days will cause many deaths. Here is a proof of my goodness, those who make me well served and invoke me, and that will keep in their homes my blessed image, I will keep safely all that belongs to them. During these three days, I will protect their cattle from starvation. I will keep them because there must not be a single door ajar. The hungry animals shall be satisfied by me, without any food.[220] (Sept. 20, year unknown)

The Earth will be covered in darkness, and Hell will be loosed on Earth. The thunder and lightning will cause those who have no faith or trust in my Power, to die of fear. During these three days of terrifying darkness, no windows must be opened, because no one will be able to see the earth and the terrible color it will have in those days of punishment without dying at once...The sky will be on fire, the earth will split... During these three days of darkness let the blessed candle be lighted everywhere, no other light will shine...[221] (Sept. 20, 1882)

Our Lord said to Jahenny:

When, on a cold winter night, thunder is heard loud enough to shake even the mountains, then quickly shut all doors and windows. ...Your eyes must not profane the terrible event by curious glances. Gather together in front of the Crucifix. Place yourselves under the protection of My Most Holy Mother. Do not let any doubts enter your hearts concerning your salvation. The more confident you are, the more inviolable the rampart with which I wish to surround you. Light blessed candles; say the Rosary. Persevere for three days and two nights. The following night the terror will abate. After the horror of this long darkness, the sun will shine with all its light and warmth. It will be a great devastation. I, your God, will have purified everything. The survivors must give thanks to the Blessed Trinity for their protection. Magnificent shall My Kingdom of peace be, and My name shall be invoked and praised from sunrise to sunset. (Source: "World Trends" Newsletter, Issue 47 B, by Yves Dupont. His sources, the books of Marie-Julie Jahenny's prophecies by Fr. P. Roberdel)

No one outside a shelter... will survive. The earth will shake as at the judgment and fear will be great. Yes, We will listen to the prayers of your friends, (i.e. the friends of Marie-Julie Jahenny, those devoted to her and her Mission of the Cross) *not one will perish. We will need them to publish the glory of the cross.*[222] (December 8, 1882)

France itself will lose half its population. Four towns of France will disappear - there will be villages without a soul.[223] (Sept. 16, 1904)

Those destined to see and live through the chastisements and God's wrath will see things no other century has seen - the living will envy the dead - the punishments will be so great.[224] (Sept. 29, 1878)

God's Justice will spare nothing. He is cultivating the earth to plant a "new seed"[225] (May 25, 1877)

The earth will be depopulated by two thirds to three quarters - but God will repopulate the earth again during the Age of Peace.[226] (Sept. 29, 1879 and March 15, 1882)

The Lord then shall "bring forth the sun to console after it had been obscured."[227] (Sept. 29, 1880)

After the great blow, the chastisements of God that will leave many dying for fear, the Triumph will come.[228] (May 19, 1898)

Following are some of Jahenny's additional prophecies that relate to the end times. These prophecies are listed chronologically:

The chastisements will begin when respect is no longer paid to the Sacred Heart and charity grows cold.

Marie-Julie Jahenny was told she would live to see the beginning of the chastisements[229] (she lived to see WWI and WWII) (Oct. 27, 1876)

Cries of despair will break out in the months of the Sacred Heart and Precious Blood (June & July) *– It will be the sign of civil war - it will start in Paris. The bloodshed will begin - and the government will flee and take off like a bird to another country when it sees the carnage begin, to leave France free in its revolution with nothing to stop it.*

Churches will then be closed and pillaged, holy statues toppled, crosses torn down, tabernacles violated.[230] (April 27, 1877)

Before the sinister warnings appear on earth, everyone will feel in their heart that "the time must not be far off" for the chastisements to occur and will feel God's Justice in their hearts. (i.e. a palpable interior warning that grave things are about to happen.)

A blood rain will fall from an extraordinary cloud and coagulate on the earth for seven weeks. A terrible "burning" will happen from the earth and will send off a terrible heat and poisonous stench – No one must open their doors or windows for the seven weeks.[231] (March 9, 1878)

The Church will be defiled, the clergy grow corrupt – much suffering, torture and bloodshed will be needed to cleanse it before it is granted the Triumph. A pope will suffer torments beyond his powers, he will be discarded and cast aside.

A great apostasy will occur - the infamies of the corruption will spread across the world and cause the greatest scandal. Woe to priests who ascend the altar with a veiled conscience.[232] (i.e. corrupt intent) (March 19, 1878)

A great persecution will break out - many faithful religious will be made martyrs - traps will be set in monasteries and cloisters. A pope will suffer torments beyond his powers, he will be discarded and cast aside. (March 19, 1878)

The corrupt clergy will be infected with the spiritual "Plague of Degradation" - the lack of true charity and love and respect for each other. If the clergy do not correct themselves God will punish them by making them subjects of scandal - God will send all a serious warning[233] (August 5, 1878)

The evil ones will plot conspiracies against the Church to overthrow it.[234] (August 19, 1878), (Oct. 14, 1878) and (July 23, 1925)

The events of the chastisements will resemble the events leading up to the day of judgment.[235]
Many demonic false miracles and visionaries will suddenly appear around the world - when this sudden proliferation of false mystics and wonder workers appear – It is a sign God is getting ready to strike the earth.[236] (August 26, 1878)

Everyone will feel an "inquietude" in their hearts before the chastisements strike.[237] (August 27, 1878)

Much courage and blood will be needed to save the Church in peril.[238] (Sept. 19, 1878)

A time of martyrdom is coming.[239] (Oct. 14, 1878)

A time of genocide is coming when evil leaders will plot in secret using the pretext of stopping "rebellion" to round up Christians, (Catholics), *and march them into churches where they will be martyred, in the places where the Blessed Sacrament resides.*
The Prophecy of the "Bloodthirsty century" - Catholics will be rounded up, the pretext of stopping a rebellion will be used - defending secular "freedom" will be the pretext - Catholics will be martyred in Churches.[240] (Oct. 23, 1878)

The Church will be abandoned - deprived of the Pope, prayer, all offices, "exiled from God and the saints" – "They" intend (meaning some evil force or group) *to take away the crucifixes and the statues of saints from their shrines to break them and profane them.*[241] (Mar. 29, 1879)

Scandals from the clergy will pass before our eyes – pray to the Divine Mercy! We must expect to see it all – crime is carried to the altar, the Church will fail in its mission and not try to convert sinners, the Lord is offended by those who should serve Him.[242] (Sept. 29, 1879)

Those who "assemble in and fill the lodges" are waiting for the moment to rise up and sling the mud of scandal upon the Church.[243] (Sept. 29, 1879 and Mar. 15, 1882)

Religious will be forced out of religious schooling institutions so secular schools may be put in their place. The religious will not be able to earn their living this way and will have to rely on Divine Providence.[244] *(*Sept. 29, 1879 and Mar. 15, 1882)

The evil ones will aim to pass a law in France (and beyond) (i.e. an anticlerical law against the Church). *The ministers of God will be robbed in everything except what is absolutely necessary - they will be forced out of their habits and into common clothes to escape persecution - the enemies of the Church will attempt to turn churches into the theatre or places of infernal dances - priests will lack courage to defend the faith - priests will be bribed to leave the Church.*

There will be a terrible heaven-sent famine. Fire will fall from the sky and consume the food of a Protestant country with a Muslim population (aka Germany?) *In France: for three years, the potatoes will rot at the time of the seed, the corn will not grow or stop halfway. Fruits will blacken: a worm will eat the inside, before they reach the size of a finger.*[245] (Sept. 29, 1879)

The civil unrest will come during the economic hardship - France will be flooded with people who are jobless, unable to find "asylum" or "refuge" - agitators will go through the country and rile the workers up to revolt.[246] (Sept. 29, 1879 and Mar. 15, 1882)

Shortly before the revolutionary plans of the evil men are put into effect – Our Lady will appear in the surrounding mountains of La Salette to give a warning.[247] (Sept. 29, 1879 and Mar. 15, 1882)

Our Lady will appear in Amiens with the Holy Infant to warn the people - a sign will appear in Heaven, and the sorrow-filled voice of a little child will announce the horrors that are about befall the country. The child will speak for 27 minutes. The warning is not just for France but is "universal" - a warning for all nations.[248] (Sept. 29, 1879, Mar. 15, 1882, and Nov. 16, 1882)

A terrible prodigy will happen when the "murder attempts happen" and the "crimes are being committed" – a black and blue rainbow will appear - when the crimes are being committed it will rain a red rain that will coagulate on all the houses and stick like paint. It will fall on the ground but will not be drinkable. A sign of terror will then appear - a cross in the sky will form in this red rain and bear the marks of Christ - all will be struck with a mark of terror that will not be effaced - after three days, the rain will go through the whole universe.[249] (Apr. 8, 1880)

The suppression of the works of God and the triumph of evil men will occur when devotion to the Sacred Heart is suppressed and attacked - men will not want to admit that it is through the Sacred Heart which will come the promised peace. (Apr. 12, 1880)

The evil ones will be furious against devotion to the Sacred Heart.[250] (mixed dates)

A new diabolical worship service or universal ecumenical style service will be introduced by Satan - the ministers shall wear red cloaks, or simply red, they will have a little bread and water for the service, but no valid consecration. They will be permitted to say it everywhere, under the open sky, and in "all houses" (i.e. possibly a cryptic reference to all places and churches of worship of all denominations)

In the years when the "universal service" is introduced or about to be introduced, Satan will make "many revelations," (i.e. send out many false mystics and visionaries.) *He will be so cunning with his plans this time that it will be difficult to expose his false messages, he will sound very much like authentic mystics. He will attempt to get people to be lost through these false revelations, or lose time trying to expose them all - also, cause nothing but strife and contention through the false mystics as the faithful attempt to expose them for the fakes they are.*[251] (June 28, 1880)

Satanic possessions and obsessions will be many before the crisis hits - also many satanic apparitions that will bring "happy messages" - (no doubt to fool people to follow the fake "happy" religion).[252] (mixed dates)

The Pope will be attacked, held prisoner, all ecclesial authorities will feel the persecution - they will be permitted to practice their ministry at first, then, they will be dragged out of their seats- the order will then come for them to flee. Evil ones will take their place - a new set of ceremonies will be put in place but will be against the Faith and the holy laws. An evil law will be passed where parents will be forced to let these evil authorities corrupt their children, but it will only last 44 days - the martyrdom will occur during this time - after which will come the chastisements of God.[253] (August 10, 1880)

The suppression of church bells and the suppression of funeral services will be demanded - They will erase all memory of the first religion and they will instruct in an impious religion ...[254] (Sept. 6, 1880)

Warning signs will be given in nature at the beginning of each year.

This chastisement will leave its victims as those without life, they will still breathe with the ability to speak, the flesh raw like after a deep burn. This malady will be very contagious, and nothing will stop it. It is a punishment from God to bring many (souls) back. This malady will attack the heart first, then the mind, and at the same time, the tongue. It will be horrible. The heat that will accompany it will be a consuming fire, so strong that the affected parts of the body will be of an unbearable redness. After seven days, this malady, like the seed sown in a field, will rise rapidly and make immense progress. There is only one remedy that will cure it, and, it must be taken in time or it will not work: white haw-thorn leaf tea[255] * (Sept. 20, 1880)

"I will attack the Church, I will throw down the Cross, I will divide (or cause division among) the people, I will deposit in hearts a major weakening of the faith and there will be a great betrayal."

* On September 20, 1880, Jahenny was given a prophecy about a "burning plague." On August 5, 1880, she was given the remedy. This is the prophecy of August 5, 1880. "My children, this is the only remedy that can save you: You know the leaves of thorns that grow in almost any hedges (white hawthorn). The leaves of this thorn will stop the progress of the disease. You must pick the leaves, not the wood. Even dry, they will retain their effectiveness. Put them in boiling water and leave them there for 14 minutes, covering the container so that the steam remains. When the malady first attacks, you must use this remedy three times a day. My children, this disease will be very serious in Brittany. The thought of God there will be less great... (i.e. they will not think of God as much as before and therefore will be struck hardest with this malady.) The malady will produce a continual uprising of the heart, (blood pressure? Increased heart rate?) vomiting. If the remedy is taken too late, the affected parts will become black, and in this black, there will be yellowish pale streaks."

The Blessed Virgin Mary provided Jahenny with the following prayer that must be prayed over the leaves of the white hawthorn bush prior to preparing the remedy.

The Most Holy Virgin: "Oh! my beloved little children using these little flowers and small plants say to me:

'Holy Queen of Heaven, Health of the sick, prodigy of power, spread your blessings on this infusion, Mother most powerful, show us that you are our Mother by relieving our miseries.'

My little children, taking this little flower, invoke me:

'O Immaculate Mary, O Our Mother, O Our Mother look upon us and make your blessing manifest in this suffering.'"

A short prayer offering up their work for those who care for the sick that they can say, Our Lady says: "My dear child, it is not necessary to say so long (a prayer). Simply:

'O! my good Mother, look at my little work for the sick or afflicted, bless it.'"

Satan to the Lord - "I will become for some time, the Supreme Master of all things, I will have everything under my empire, even Your temple and (all of) Yours entirely." (Sept. 29, 1880)

Demons will congregate – many in the form of man – they will bring about false miracles – many of these demons even wear the habits of the true servants of God – they will have a strange, ferocious hunger for human flesh and blood – they crave the death

and bloodshed of the true faithful[256] (i.e. they plot the genocidal persecution.) (Sept. 29, 1880)

Monasteries will be looted, the Mass parodied, funeral services forbidden. (mixed sources)

Lourdes will be profaned, the cloister of Paray-le-Monial will burn. However, it seems Our Lady will protect places where her miraculous statues are venerated.[257] (mixed dates)

This plague [the burning plague] *will strike so fast that people will not have time to prepare their souls to meet their Creator.*[258] (Nov. 30, 1880)

An evil man or leader will rise three times against the church and religious (i.e. the three crisis periods - see the prophecies for France) - *religious will be forced to hide in private homes of Christian families, but even they will not be safe as evil men will break in and search. This black persecution will last until the Great Monarch is sent by God.*[259] (Nov. 30, 1880)

In their aberration, they [priests] *will break their oaths. The Book of Life contains a list of names that rends the heart. Because of the little respect it has for the apostles of God, the flock grows careless and ceases to observe the laws. The priest himself is responsible for the lack of respect because he does not respect enough his holy ministry, and the place which he occupies in his sacred functions. The flock follows in the footsteps of its pastors; this is a great tragedy. The clergy will be severely punished on account of their inconceivable fickleness and great cowardice which is incompatible with their functions. A terrible chastisement has been provided for those who ascend every morning the steps of the Holy Sacrifice. I have not come on your altars to be tortured. I suffer a hundredfold more from such hearts than any of the others.*

I absolve you from your great sins, My children, but I cannot grant any pardon to these priests. (June 1881)

A false apostate religion resembling Islam will be established by force by authorities - Catholics who have lost grace will happily enter into it. It will be a "happy happy" religion of a "merry heart" that will be completely divested of the Sacraments of the Church. To escape the threat of death and the sufferings caused by persecutions, many will enter into this false religion to save themselves. Many bishops will enter and lead souls to Hell. The youth will be spoiled at this time - the purification of souls will be terrible.[260] (June 9, 1881)

The Church will suffer a persecution the likes of which Hell has never unleashed before. The bishops will have fled, churches closed, holy souls will weep over the ruins and abandonment. There will be a hellish attack against the devotion to the Sacred Heart.[261] (July 21, 1881)

A "Book of the Second Celebration" will be established by the "infamous spirits" who wish to crucify Christ anew and who await "a new Messiah" - (i.e. this diabolical new rite of worship will be an endeavor of Antichrist precursors). *Many holy priests will refuse this book "sealed with the words of the abyss," but there are those who will accept and use it.*[262] (July 21, 1881)

The evil government from Paris will pass anticlerical laws against the faith and the Church - the government intended to turn the holy places of worship into a theatre, and of hellish abomination - weak clergy will join with the government. Many bishops will join the hellish regime, particularly in Paris, the south and east of France.[263] (Aug. 9, 1881)

There will be few true priests - many have grown corrupt and will join the revolutionaries - they cannot wait to throw off their habits and spread horror and abomination among the people - in the days of terror there will be priests inside and outside of France who will think of nothing of breaking the seal of the confessional, to spoil the Faith and defile the Church.[264] (Sept. 19, 1881)

It is time to look up to Heaven because in all the corners of the Earth you will find the Antichrist, as in the time of the last judgment, that will travel the whole world to pervert, to weaken by their threats the faith of Christians.

The guilty men who start it all will suddenly be gone, it will be as if they were never there - when they are gone then the resounding cry will come from Paris. It will be the cries of the ungodly cheering the entrance of this bloody hour. These cries will continue for several days then spread through the country – Do not build a house or remain in France, it will be thrown over. Only Brittany will be spared.[265] (Sept. 20, 1881)

Epidemics will also be terrible in the south of France, Valence, Lyon, Bordeaux, and the lands leading up to Paris. Very few will escape it - the corpses will spread a stench that kills.[266] (Oct. 5, 1881)

The cries from Paris that will initiate the carnage will first start with a horrific blasphemy - then there will be shouts, hateful songs, confused cries - the poor innocent people caught in the city will not have time to escape. Streets will be closed, and passages blocked - it will be the time of massacre. The terrible Thunderstorm and lightning will come and last two days, but nothing will stop the two-day massacre. Christians will die by bullets; some will die by the guillotine.[267] (Dec. 23, 1881)

The sanctuary of Sacre Coeur will be used for their diabolical counsels of these evil men - from there they will plan their treachery, form organizations to close churches, close religious orders, and shut down the famous sites of apparitions.[268] (Sept. 29, 1881 and Mar. 15, 1882)

The devil will appear in apparitions - woe to those who will make pacts with the "personages" in these diabolical visions - in the months leading up to the great crisis, many souls will be possessed, the world will become insane with fear and the devil will travel around and attempt to make people give up their Faith and deny the cross.[269] (Dec. 14, 1881)

Sacre Coeur will serve as a theatre for the impious and all those involved with human laws.[270] (Jan. 27, 1882)

Do not follow the crowd! Many will abjure their faith and trample on the cross to save themselves during the persecutions - do not follow their example. Do not trample on the cross! Your courage will soften the executioners.[271] (Feb. 2, 1882)

There will not remain in France a religious house or monastery in which one can escape the tyrants that will come during this epoch.

Bad Christians will not be content with the loss of their own souls during the apostasy - they will hunt for souls, try and make others sin against their Christian faith and duty.

Do not be a cowardly Christian - those who are cowardly and will not stand for the Faith will be as guilty as those who want to destroy everything and who will attempt to overthrow Christ's reign.

Our Lord will give His warning signs in the first months of the year when it is not yet spring.

The massacres will happen during the cold months. (Winter?) *During these massacres - the earth will become deluged with blood as during Noah's time when the earth was deluged with water.*

Plagues [the burning plague] *and diseases never seen before will fall upon France - the great plague will start from the Centre* (Paris).[272] (June 15, 1882)

The evil leaders will pass a law requiring the bishops to send out a summons or an order for the priests who have hidden themselves underground in the private homes of the faithful to give themselves up. The laws will be so implacable they will never be able to undo them. The bishops will be forced to answer. Then, the evil lawmakers and administrators will not stop there - they will next order all religious orders to leave France. The Jesuits will suffer in particular from these evil men. They will also try to go for the head of the Pope. However, there will be some good people who will resist all these evil laws. However, there will be many weak bishops who will fail and succumb to the evil government - their weak faith will give a bad example and will cause the damnation of many souls.[273] (July 25, 1882)

Before the chastisements of France strike - many souls will lose the faith. France will be covered with masses of guilty men who "from the bottom of the lodges" will work to glorify Satan and raise him places of worship.[274] (Warning of Freemasonry and masonic lodges?) (August 22, 1882)

In several cities the pastors (bishops) *will hold meetings on what to do about these godless laws - however only three bishops will remain faithful and support what they know is God's will*

It is a red revolution - many priests will fall and send out letters attempting to sway the faithful there is nothing wrong with the government's laws. The Pope will attempt to appeal to the faithful not to follow their example and hold fast to the Faith, but few will listen. Many souls will be lost.[275] (Oct. 12, 1882)

It is the time of great schism - a certain bishop will head up the schism and the heart of his diocese will revolt against the Church and refuse to submit to Rome. A few men will enter a false religion - then many bishops will follow and all their flocks with them - it is a sacrilegious religion. The French bishops will start it and then others will follow. These apostate bishops will be against the Great Monarch chosen by God.[276] (Oct. 26, 1882)

Civil unrest will be manufactured by those who rule (i.e. government conspiracy) - *they will deprive the workers of their work and employment. When that happens - unrest will be caused by agitators - they will cause fire blood and murder and use the "violent powder" to destroy the "strongest walls ever built."*[277] (Nov. 23, 1882)

The Blessed Sacrament will be desecrated and trampled upon and thrown in the mud. The faithful and the priests will try to save them, pick them up from the roads and carry the Sacrament away hidden in their breasts.[278] (Oct. 17, 1883)

When the crisis breaks out, it will explode suddenly and the punishments will be shared by all and will come one after the other without interruption. The earth will become like a vast cemetery - the bodies of the good and the wicked will litter the ground. The famine will be great, and confusion will be everywhere.[279] (i.e. because not only will there be the revolts, but also God's great chastisements.) (Jan. 4, 1884)

Priests in great numbers will separate themselves from the voice of authority - there will be a scandalous freedom of disunion, levity, and will spread in all the dioceses of France.[280] (April 24, 1884)

At the time of the fatal events in France - there will be a great number of apostasies, and the clergy will be the first to have started most of them.[281] (Nov. 14, 1884)

Our Lady weeps her warnings of La Salette were not heeded - she now warns as a result bishops will become apostates, false apostles, and break from Rome and the Pope - they will heed the evil government and also will promote the lies of the schism, and will encourage the faithful to save their lives during the persecutions by joining the schism. Priests will be swayed. Many souls will head to the abyss because of this.[282] (Sept. 19, 1901)

Jesus said to Jahenny:

I give you a warning even today. The disciples who are not of My Holy Gospel are now in a great work of the mind to form as the second facsimiles when they will make to their idea and under the influence of the enemy of souls, a Mass that contains words odious in My sight. -- When the fatal hour arrives when they will put to the test the Faith of My eternal priesthood, it is these sheets that they will give to celebrate in this last period. The first period, it is that of My priesthood which exists since (or after) *Me. The second, is the period of persecution when the enemies of the Faith and of Holy Religion have formulated - and they are strongly enforced - these sheets as the book of the second celebration, these infamous spirits or, infamous mind) are those who crucified Me and who are waiting for the reign of the new Messiah to make them happy. - Many of My holy priests will refuse this book sealed with the words of the abyss. Unfortunately,* [they] *will be the exception, it will be used.*[283] (Nov. 27, 1901 or 1902)

Parents will corrupt their children before they reach the age of reason - they will be raised irreligious - (basically set on the path of damnation before they reach the age of reason). *It would have been better if these children had never been born.*[284] (Sept. 24, 1903)

Children are raised so they lose their innocence early before the age of reason, they are raised as adults.[285] (Oct. 2, 1903)

Our Lady said to Jehenny:

The French people will become very miserable. All the doors have been wide open to all languages, to the foreigners, to all those who wish to enter this cursed Sodom (Paris) *where the Justice of my Divine Son, is suspended over it.*[286] (Jan. 5, 1904)

Satan is joyful, he travels all over the world...in the enclosure of his houses where the disciples who follow his doctrine live, where he reveals his satanic secrets to them to lose their souls. He gives his advice and the (leaders of his hell-hounds) *drink long draughts of his doctrines that are made up of sacrileges and spells.*[287] (Jan. 5, 1904)

My beloved children, all is engaged in an irreparable loss, I mean the salvation of souls of children. The nourishment of these poor little souls should be for them the bread of love of their Immaculate Queen, the Queen of Heaven. ... After the delivery of young adolescent souls to Satan, the enemy of souls, I mean to say that most of these children have entered the path of corruption and these souls have not received a drop of this perfume of my virtues of purity; it is in very immense pain, because if you saw the number, you would be frightened and even struck as if by a mortal blow. Evil parents have corrupted their children.[288] (Feb 8, 1904)

When the evil persecutions against the true Faith breaks out and the genocidal revolution, it will be the corrupted youth that will cry out for the death of the Christians and "death to Christ." They will be the worst enemies against Christ and be the most active at the time of the bloodshed, in the desecrations of churches, graveyards, and the Blessed Sacrament, and will tear down the crosses and submit them to profanation.[289] (July 19, 1906)

The Antichrist has commenced his appearance on earth, but he will multiply. Soon, he will run through the earth; He will possess souls and above all many priests, monks and nuns. He will enter these souls; He will make them do unheard wonders.[290] (Oct. 19, 1911)

They will go to the point of effacing the arts and to remake them under a hideous form, terrible and all that they prepare and approach.[291] (Nov. 16, 1920)

The forerunner of the great chastisements is when the great attacks against the Church occur, and will be accompanied by their indoctrination of the children to take away the Name and all knowledge of God from the children.[292] (Nov. 11, 1924)

Plots are hatched by the evil ones -- they will wait for the moment when this leader will give the order so their plots may be put into effect.[293] (Nov. 11, 1924)

Our Lord said to Jahenny:

If you knew the infamous correspondences that are under the influence of Satan. They sell My Holy Church, they sell in secret the head of the priest, they sell in secret the poor earth that they subject to a horrible punishment. It has not seen it did not understand and today it makes a hellish trade that the world has never seen before take place. All is delivered up, everything is sold, and plots being hatched, every day, the hunger for human flesh to devour, the thirst for human blood makes all their bodies seethe with unrest and a desire to reach the goal as soon as possible. All this is happening in the room of hell (Chamber of Deputies-National Assembly in France), *under the chairmanship of souls sold to the spirit of evil.*[294] (Nov. 13, 1924)

The evil one will make more laws more infamous than the ones before. They will send out letters or a summons and will ask for reinforcements to aid in the bloodshed. This evil one in power will be the first to feel God's Divine Justice and suffer the punishment of God first in the chastisements - there will be a terrible earthquake that will shake the earth to the heavens and swallow these culprits up, entombing them and sending their souls to the Abyss. (This is probably related to the "week-long earthquake" then the 43-day earthquake that is foretold. See the prophecies above). *The "Burning Face Plague" will be wiping out the other evil people in or around the same time, but the people of God will know about the white hawthorn remedy, and, will also have the Divine Heart, the Immaculate Heart and the Cross as a safe refuge, plus, the Crosses of Pardon, medals, and our sacramentals. God will also strike the bodies of the wicked and reduce them to dust, their corpses would be too pestilent and corrupt to leave - God will literally reduce them to dust so the earth is not defiled by them and the land is left for the pre-destined who will repopulate the earth.*[295] (July 23, 1925)

Evil on earth is growing - Divine Justice will be forced to send more punishments – the sacrifices and prayers of the faithful lessen the punishments - Heaven calls for sacrifices to appease the Divine Justice![296] (Aug 14, 1928)

20th Century – September 8, 1914: Marcelle Planchon (aka Sister Marie France/Our Lady Queen of France)

September 8, 1914:

Young Marcelle Planchon was praying in the Notre Dame des Armees chapel at Versailles, France when her prayer was interrupted by a miraculous image. The Blessed Virgin chose this twenty-three-year-old woman to convey a special request of urgent significance just as the enemy approached Paris during World War I. The Virgin said:

> *If, in union with my Divine Son, I love all the nations which he has redeemed with His Blood, see how I particularly cherish your dear fatherland. My Son wants you to make images and statues representing me thus, and to be invoked under the name of "Our Lady Queen of France." If you respond to this new desire of His Divine Heart, France will become particularly mine again. I will take it forever under my maternal protection and my Son will be pleased to spread abundant blessings over it.*[297]

Our Lady appeared a second time to Marcelle later that same day. She was initially surrounded by clouds which dispersed, displaying a blue coat, dotted with lilies and edged in white ermine. On Her head was a crown with three lilies signifying Her royalty. Just as Marcelle took in this miraculous image it changed. The Blessed Mother opened Her arms and was now dressed in a white dress with a blue belt falling in a tricolor scarf. She was standing on a globe inscribed with the word "France." One foot crushed the head of a serpent, signifying that France would not be conquered by Satan as long as Mary was Queen. She looked toward heaven and asked Marcelle to pray for France. Following this She led Marcelle in prayer, saying, *"My Son, forgive her* (France), *she still loves you since she never stopped loving me."*[298] She asked Marcelle to include this prayer with Her image as She appeared with Her arms spread down to Francepart, and to add the words, *"See how I cherish my people."*[299] Mary then offered a second prayer to be recited before the requested statue of Our Lady of France.

> *O Mary conceived without sin, our good Mother who wanted us to invoke You under the term so consoling to our hearts, Queen of France, see prostrate at your feet your unhappy Subjects. Have mercy on us, be our Advocate with Your divine Son, our beloved King. We know that we have greatly offended Him, outraged even, that we have despised His commandments, trampled on the holy laws of His Church; but we also*

know, O lovable Sovereign, that You are all powerful on the Heart of this King of love who Himself only asks to forgive; therefore grant us this national and individual Peace so much desired by all for the greater glory of Your dear Son. So be it! Amen![300] *

December 31, 1914:
Marcelle's next vision took place at the Chapel of Armies. This time, it was not the Blessed Virgin, but Her Son, Jesus, who appeared to her. Standing on the high altar dressed in a white tunic and a tricolor "stole,"

*Elizabeth Bucchianeri incorporates into her blog, the following fascinating [quote] from Alain Denizot's book, *The Sacred Heart and the Great War*. (Editions: New Latin editions):

On the same day of September 8, 1914 when the vision of Our Lady Queen of France occurred in Versailles, the Blessed Virgin appeared on the Marne in the afternoon facing the German army which was heading to Paris and stopped its advance. More than 100,000 men saw it and some, including a German priest, testified to it. It is said this was the secret of Marshal Foch, but at the time, it was then forbidden to speak of this vision, under penalty of death.
Here are several accounts of some of the supernatural occurrences that happened on the Marne:
1) A specific testimony from Madame Tripet-Nizery, widow of Captain Tripet who died in action on September 4, 1916: she declared that being a nurse in the ambulance of the École Polytechnique, from the end of 1914 to June 1916, she received a wounded man who had participated in the Battle of the Marne on the French side. He confided to her: "When we were ordered to leave, a woman in white, in front of the trench, was dragging us."
2) Le Courrier, newspaper of Saint-Lô, published on January 8, 1917 a letter dated January 3, 1915. A German priest, wounded and taken prisoner at the Battle of the Marne, died in a French ambulance where there were religious. He said to them: "As a soldier, I should remain silent; as a priest, I think I have to say what I saw. During the battle, we were surprised to be driven back because we were legion compared to the French, and we expected to arrive in Paris. But we saw the Blessed Virgin all dressed in white, with a blue belt, tilted towards Paris... She turned her back on us and, with her right hand, seemed to repel us."
3) Two German officers, prisoners and wounded, testified as the dead priest had done on January 3, 1915. One of them says: "If I were on the front, I would be shot, because it was forbidden to tell, under pain of death, what I am going to tell you: you were surprised by our sudden retreat when we arrived at the gates of Paris. We could not go further, a Virgin stood before us, arms outstretched, pushing us whenever we were ordered to move forward. For several days we did not know if it was one of your national saints, Geneviève or Jeanne d'Arc. [Joan of Arc] Afterwards, we understood that it was the Blessed Virgin who nailed us on the spot. On September 8, She pushed us away with such force, that all of us, as one man, fled. What I tell you, you will no doubt hear it later, because we are perhaps 100,000 men who have seen it."[301]

Jesus displayed the wounds of His Passion and His Resplendent Heart of light in the middle of His chest. He was flanked by Saint Michael and Saint Joan of Arc, both protectors of France. Speaking to her of France, Jesus said, *"See how I cherish her, when will she fulfill my dearest desire? I want to see the image of my Heart painted on its flag."*[302]

June 20, 1914:

Once again, Marcelle prayed in the Chapel of Armies, her eyes fixed on the tabernacle. As before, Christ appeared to her in supernatural clarity, wearing the same tricolor stole that he wore some six months earlier. This time, He wore a golden crown decorated with lily flowers. Over His shoulders was a purple cloak just like a Bourbon king would wear. His feet rested on a globe inscribed with the word "France" written in gold letters.

With his left hand, He revealed His Sacred Heart "crowned with thorns and bloody," on the white part of the stole. Written on the red portion of the stole were the words, "He wants to reign over France."

Elizabeth A. Bucchianeri, points out, "when Christ revealed the devotion to His Sacred Heart to St. Margaret Mary, He also requested His Sacred Heart to be placed on the royal standard of France, which would have ensured its protection, but Louis XIV did not comply, neither did his successor until Louis XVI consecrated the country to the Sacred Heart in his prison cell, but it was almost too late to the detriment of the country. It is rather surprising that Our Lady and Our Lord would appear here with a stole in the colors of the French Republic as it is revealed in the visions of Marie-Julie Jahenny that Heaven considers the tricolor 'impure colors' of the diabolical Masonic Republic that supplanted the White Flag of the Catholic Monarchy, the flag Heaven promises to restore to France. It is possible at this point [that] Heaven was giving the democratic government another chance to do the right thing. The Republic had already built the basilica of Sacre Coeur as a 'propitiation' church after the horrors of the Franco-Prussian war in the mid-1800s, the national Church the Sacred Heart had requested from the kings along with having His Heart placed on the flag. Marie-Julie Jahenny revealed the future of France was now saved thanks to the building of the national church dedicated to the Sacred Heart; one of the conditions fulfilled, even if it was fulfilled by the Republic and not the Monarchy as Heaven would have liked. So, a grace was given. Now, the Republic must have been given a chance to place that Heart on the flags as requested, even if it is the tricolor. God always gives nations a chance to do what is right. So far, the Republic of France has refused. It may continue to refuse as the other Great Monarch prophecies predict the Republic will be swept away to make room for the restoration of the Monarchy."[303]

Marcelle became Sister Marie France and was one of the first members of the Pious Union of Adorers of the Heart of Jesus, a lay sister organization. The society's objective was to pray and sacrifice for the reign of the Sacred Heart and the salvation of France. The order did not have official status from the Church until 1939 when it was officially authorized. Sr. Marie France vowed to offer herself as a victim on June 11, 1915 and all the sisters of the society vowed the same, placing themselves at the disposal of Jesus for His work of Salvation.

The visions of Sister Marie France continued as did her mystic experiences, but she told no one about it except her fellow sisters, as in humility she did not wish to be noticed but rather only hidden. *"A handful of her prophecies have been transmitted thanks to the Mother Superior of the Pious Union of Adorers, Sr. Marguerite Marie, who wrote a few in her diary"[304]*

These are the prophecies of a Great Monarch:

France will no longer be called France but "New France." It will be thanks to Brittany that it will not be cursed by God. (It is interesting to note here that Marie-Julie Jahenny said that Brittany will be spared much of the chastisements because of the strong devotion to Our Lady there.) *They will wonder for a long time why there remained a green leaf on the dead branch of France. Versailles, which will carry as its motto "between heaven and earth," will see the Virgin Mary enthroned Queen of France, by the King of the Sacred Heart.*

This one will come on foot to the gates of the castle and will give his crown to King Louis XVI and the diadem to Marie Antoinette, before the people of France who will be in such bad health that he will have tears in his eyes. This king will be more like a priest than a monarch. He will have his cathedrals rebuilt with the help of all nations.[305]

In 1933 Sr. Marie France contracted tuberculosis and after a period of excruciating pain, she died. She was only forty-one years of age. Her doctor testified *"that her pains were abnormally acute and that she displayed all her reason, as well as a calm and moderate temperament."[306]*

Following her service, Sister Marie France was buried in the same tomb as Sister Marguerite Marie, the mother superior of the congregation. In 1934, frescoes representing the apparitions were painted in the chapel of Notre Dame des Armées in Versailles. The Pious Union died out and went extinct for lack of nuns who wished to join this congregation.

While many of the faithful supported Marcelle in her revelations, the ecclesiastical authorities never declared an investigation as World War I consumed them. Nonetheless, Sister Marie France was not condemned by the Church, and the local bishop of Versailles, Mgr. Roland-Gosselin, (bishop from 1931-1952) authorized the printing of the Image of Mary, Queen of France, as well as the revealed prayer, to which he gave indulgences. Because the message is not specifically condemned by the Church, *"the story of this apparition may be spread by the faithful."*[307]

20th Century – 1906: St. Joseph Freinademetz *(Prophecy Detail – Missionaries expelled from China, The Apostasy, China invaded by coalition of forces led by Russia, Almost all of China converts to Christianity)*

Joseph Freinademetz was born on April 15, 1852, one of thirteen children of Giovanmattia and Anna Maria Freinademetz. They were very poor farmers living in Oies, a section of the town of Badia in the mountains of the Alps. After finishing the fourth grade, Joseph was apprenticed to a Mr. Thaler, an enterprising tailor who lived about forty miles away from his parents' home. It was Thaler who set young Joseph on a path to the priesthood. There, Joseph earned a place to sleep by doing household chores. He decided to continue his education but was forced to beg for food in order to survive. Despite the hardships, Joseph graduated elementary school with honors and received academic and singing scholarships for eight years of education, including his theological courses. On July 25, 1875, Joseph was ordained a priest and assigned to the community of San Martin de Tor, near his own home, though he always felt a calling to be a missionary. To that end, in August 1878, Joseph obtained the permission of his bishop and his parents to move to Steyl for missionary training.

In March of 1879, Joseph and his confrere, Johann Baptist von Anzer, boarded a ship to Hong Kong, a journey of five weeks. After setting up a chapel, the two accepted a new assignment and in 1881 moved to the southern province of Shantung. Though a large province of twelve million, there were only 158 baptized Catholics. Freinademetz went to work immediately, educating Chinese laymen and priests, writing a catechism in their native language. By 1898, Freinademetz had contracted tuberculosis. At the urging of his bishop and other priests, he went to Japan to recuperate, but returned to his mission before fully recovering. In 1907, with the departure of Bishop Anzer, Freinademetz was placed in charge of the administration of the diocese.

Throughout his years as a missionary, he was arrested and severely beaten many times, but it was caring for those suffering during the outbreak of typhus that eventually caused his death on January 28, 1908, when Joseph was himself infected with the dreaded disease. He was only fifty-five years old. Joseph was canonized a saint by Pope John Paul II on October 5, 2003.

Two years prior to his death, Freinademetz prophesied the following:

> *All foreign missionaries shall soon be expelled from China. You will have to walk hundreds of miles before you can find a priest. Even then, your journey will often be fruitless. Some priests and some Catholics shall apostatize. A war shall break out once all foreign missionaries have been expelled. Then, some foreign powers shall occupy the whole of China and shall divide it into zones. One of the occupying powers will be pitiless, and very hard on the people. But during this period, nearly the whole of China shall turn to Christianity.*[308]

Yves Dupont, author of *Catholic Prophecy: The Coming Chastisement*, believes that Russia will prove to be the pitiless occupying power, but after invading China, there is a period of civil unrest, chaos and anarchy in Western Europe, limiting Russia's ability to sustain occupation in China. As communism collapses, Russia seeks the aid of the United States and other powers to keep its foothold in China. Those nations comply and together, they defeat China and occupy the land.

20th Century – 1909 - 1914: Pope Pius X *(Prophecy Detail – Persecution of the Church)*

Giuseppe Melchiorre Sarto was born in Riese, Kingdom of Lombardy-Venetia (now Italy) in 1835. He was one of ten children born to the impoverished Giovanni Battista Sarto and Margarita Sanson. He studied Latin with a village priest and at the age of fifteen was given a diocesan scholarship to attend the Seminary at Padua. Giuseppe was ordained a priest eight years later. He was elevated to the position of Bishop of Mantua by Pope Leo XIII in 1884, the position of cardinal in 1893, and assumed the position of Patriarch in 1894. With the death of Pope Leo XIII in July, 1903, Cardinal-Patriarch Giuseppe Melchiorre Sarto was elected Pope on August 4, 1903 after five votes of the Conclave taking the name Pius X.

In 1909, while attending an audience with some members of the Franciscan order, he fell into what has been described as a trance. Moments later, his eyes opened, he jumped to his feet saying,

> *What I have seen is terrifying! Will I be the one, or will it be a successor? What is certain is that the Pope will leave Rome and, in leaving the Vatican, he will have to pass over the dead bodies of his priests!*[309]

In 1914, Pope Pius X had another vision:

> *I have seen one of my successors, of the same name, who was fleeing over the bodies of his brethren. He will take refuge in some hiding place; but after a brief respite, he will die a cruel death. Respect for God has disappeared from human hearts. They wish to efface even God's memory. This perversity is nothing less than the beginning of the last days of the world.*[310]

20th Century – May 13 – October 13, 1917: Our Lady of Fatima, (aka Our Lady of the Rosary) *(Prophesy Detail: Spread of Communism, Wars, Church apostasy, Chastisements)*

In the year 1917, Our Lady appeared to three young shepherd children in the small village of Fatima, Portugal. She appeared to them once each month beginning in May and ending in October, at which time She performed an astonishing miracle for all to see.

In May, Our Lady identified Herself by saying simply, *"Do not be afraid, I will do you no harm. I am from Heaven."*[311] She told the children that She would return on the thirteenth day for six months and asked them to come as well. She promised that all three children would go to heaven and asked if the children would be willing to suffer much for Jesus, to which they replied, "yes." Mary then told them to pray the Rosary every day for peace in the world and for an end to World War I, which raged on.

As promised, Our Lady appeared to the children again on June 13, reminding them to pray the Rosary every day. She answered some of their questions, noting that She would take Francesco and Jacinta to heaven very soon, though Lucia would be here for quite some time before being taken. Then Our Lady said,

> *Jesus wishes to make use of you to make me known and loved. He wants to establish in the world a devotion to my Immaculate Heart. I promise salvation to those who embrace it, and those souls will be loved by God like flowers placed by me to adorn His throne.*[312]

On July 13, Our Lady again reminded the children to pray the Rosary every day. Lucia told the Lady that no one believed them when they spoke of their vision and asked for a sign by which the others might also believe. Mary promised the children to identify Herself on October 13 and to perform a miracle for all to see and believe. Mary then said,

Sacrifice yourselves for sinners and say many times, especially whenever you make some sacrifice: "Oh Jesus, it is for love of you, for the conversion of sinners, and in reparation for the sins committed against the Immaculate Heart of Mary."[313]

As She spoke these words, She stretched out Her hands, emulating rays of light that seemed to penetrate directly into the earth, exposing to the children a sea of fire.

Plunged in this fire were demons and souls in human form, like transparent burning embers, all blackened or burnished bronze, floating about in the conflagration, now raised into the air by the flames that issued from within themselves together with great clouds of smoke now falling back on every side like sparks in huge fires, without weight or equilibrium, amid shrieks and groans of pain and despair.[314]

The children were horrified and cried out. Mary said,

You have seen Hell where the souls of poor sinners go. To save them, God wishes to establish in the world devotion to My Immaculate Heart. If what I say to you is done, many souls will be saved and there will be peace. The war is going to end, but if people do not cease offending God, a worse one will break out during the pontificate of Pius XI. When you see the night illumined by an unknown light, know that this is the great sign given you by God that he is about to punish the world for its crimes, by means of war, famine, and persecutions of the Church and of the Holy Father. To prevent this, I shall come to ask for the consecration of Russia to my Immaculate Heart, and the Communion of Reparation on the First Saturdays. If my requests are heeded, Russia will be converted and there will be peace. If not, she will spread her errors throughout the world, causing wars and persecution of the Church. The good will be martyred, the Holy Father will have much to suffer, various nations will be annihilated. In the end, My Immaculate Heart will triumph. The Holy Father will consecrate Russia to me, and she will be converted, and a period of peace will be granted to the world. Do not tell this to anybody.... When you pray the Rosary, say after each mystery, "Oh my Jesus, forgive us, save us from the fire of hell. Lead all souls to Heaven, especially those who are in most need."[315]

To prevent the children from going to the site of the apparitions on the thirteenth of August, the government had the children arrested. The secular Administrator threatened to boil the children alive if they did not reveal the secrets that the mysterious lady had imparted to them. Though terrified, the children would not betray Our Lady. They remained silent even as each was taken away, one at a time, to their promised death. But the children were not killed. Rather, they were released, and Mary appeared to them a few days later on August 19. Our Lady told the children,

> *Pray, pray very much, and make sacrifices for sinners; for many souls go to hell, because there are none to sacrifice themselves and to pray for them.*[316]

On September 13, Mary once again appeared as scheduled. This time she reminded the children to:

> *Continue to pray the Rosary in order to obtain the end of the war. In October Our Lord will come, as well as Our Lady of Sorrows and Our Lady of Mount Carmel. Saint Joseph will appear with the Child Jesus to bless the world...In October, I will perform a miracle so that all may believe.*[317]

Our Lady did appear on October 13 and told the children that She wanted a chapel built on that site in Her honor. She continued:

> *"I am the Lady of the Rosary. Continue always to pray the Rosary every day. The war is going to end, and the soldiers will soon return to their homes...*[To get to Heaven, people] *must amend their lives and ask forgiveness for their sins...Do not offend the Lord our God anymore because He is already so much offended." When She was finished speaking, She opened Her hands launching a ray of light in the direction of the sun.*[318]

Then, she performed the great miracle that she had promised. Though it had been pouring rain for several hours, seventy thousand drenched and mud-soaked people were on hand to witness it. Included in that number were many government officials and members of the secular press who were there only to gloat to the crowd that the whole affair had been a hoax perpetrated by three delusional or perhaps evil children. But not even the atheistic media could deny what happened next. First, the rain stopped, and the clouds parted, exposing the magnificent sun. Though brilliant in appearance, people were able to look directly at it without hurting their eyes.

Then, *"without warning, it began to turn in the sky as if projecting in each direction bands of light of each color that lit and colored the remaining clouds, the sky, the trees, and the crowd. It stayed for some moments then it went back to its normal position where it remained still for another short while. As the seventy thousand gazed upon the sky and, in particular, the sun, the children remained focused on the Lady of the Rosary,"*[319] whose vision, though ascended, was now instantly replaced with a vision of St. Joseph holding the Child Jesus. Jesus, Joseph, and Mary all blessed the crowd three times. Then the children saw Our Lady of Sorrows and then Our Lady of Mount Carmel, who held the baby Jesus upon Her knee.

While the children were witnessing these sights, the crowd of seventy thousand realized that their clothes were now completely dry, and they began to pray. Within seconds, however,

> *...the sun looked as if it stood out from the sky, appearing to fall on the now terrified crowd below. Most of the assembled fell to their knees and begged mercy. Though still intensely bright, people could look directly at the sun without hurting their eyes. As the crowd gazed at the burning orb, it seemed to "dance," then whirled like a giant wheel of fire. It did this for some time before stopping; then it quickly rotated again. Then brilliant colors began to reach down to the earth making all that could be seen tinted by the spectrum of colors. No one knew what to make of this and many continued to stare in utter amazement when, in an instant, the "fiery orb seemed to tremble, to shudder, and then to plunge precipitately, in a mighty zigzag, toward the crowd." Many observers thought this was the end of the world. Terrified cries were heard from the crowd as some knelt in prayer and others ran for cover. Many critics of the children's "fantasies" were now believers who fell prostrate to the ground...After about ten minutes the sun began to return to its rightful position in the sky following the same circuitous zigzag route with which it descended.*[320]

The message of Fatima may well be one of the most important in history. The Mother of God provided a roadmap to victory over eternal damnation. Pray the Rosary daily and sacrifice for the conversion of sinners. Make the Five First Saturday's devotion as reparation for sins against the Immaculate Heart of Mary and stop offending the Lord our God. Yves Dupont notes that the message was given shortly before Communism took over in Russia. The message has been supported by many others both before and after Her apparitions at Fatima including by Our Lady Herself in several additional post-1917 apparitions "in Beauraing, Banneux, Osnabruck, Girkalnis, Bonate, Caderosa, Heede, Pfaffenhofen, Montichiari, Espis, Gimigliano, Sisov, Sicily, Nededah, Garabandal, San Damiano, Mexico, Quebec, New Norcia, and many others. Some have been approved by the Church, some are still being investigated, others have been the object of a negative judgment, and still others have been condemned."[321]

20th Century – 1911-1922: Venerable Anne de Guigné (aka: Anna de la Foi) *(Prophecy Detail – Discord in the Church, Questionable fashions)*

Anne de Guigné was born on April 25, 1911, the first of four children born to Count Jacques de Guigné and Antoinette de Charette. Though wealthy and powerful, Jacques was called to service as a second lieutenant in the Thirteenth Battalion when the first World War broke out in 1914. Antoinette was the daughter of Francois de Charette, a rather famous general who led France in the battle of Patay. She was a direct descendant of Robert, Count of Clermont, the sixth son of French King Louis IX, and she recalled the stories that were passed down about the hardships of war. So, when the mayor of Annecy-le-Vieux unexpectedly arrived in July 1915, Antoinette knew it couldn't be good news. The mayor informed Antoinette of her husband's heroic death, struck down on July 29, 1915 as he was leading an attack against the German army.

Up to that point, four-year-old Anne had been a difficult child. She was disobedient, arrogant, and jealous, but her behavior dramatically changed at that point. Telling her mother that her father was now with the angels, Anne led a bitter fight to become a better daughter and person. She was no longer a rude and jealous child, but rather worked hard to help and please her mother who was stricken with grief. She prayed intensely and imposed on herself endless sacrifice.

> *One would see her becoming red in the face and clenching her little fists in order to control her temper when difficulties arose. Little by little, these crises became less frequent and her family began to have the impression that she was content with everything. Her love for her mother, whom she wished to comfort, was thus to become her path towards God.[322]*

The intensity of her spiritual life was marked by her own reflections and by a significant number of testimonies from her friends and family members.

Anne longed for the day when she could make her First Communion. It was her heart's desire that prepared her soul with joy. Because she was too young, she needed to first pass a test administered by the bishop. She passed with ease, prompting the examiner to say, *"I wish we could all have the same level of religious instruction as this child."[323]*

Young Anne was no stranger to suffering. She developed rheumatism at an early age and would frequently be heard offering her pain to Jesus while telling others that she had no pain. In December of 1921 she contracted meningitis, which left her bedridden. Still, her prayer was for God's will. When her family and friends prayed for her recovery, she would be quick to add, *"and may all other sick people recover!"*[324]

In December 1921, while attended by a nun, little Anne said, "Sister, may I join the angels?" Upon receiving the desired permission, she thanked the nun. Her suffering, however, continued for several more days. Her condition worsened, her pain grew more intense, and Anne slipped into a coma. Finally, on Saturday, January 14, 1922, Anne de Guigné passed peacefully at home, ending her torment. On March 3, 1990, Saint Pope John Paul II declared the little girl Venerable.

There is one end-times prophecy attributed to Anne de Guigné as follows:

> *There will be discord within the Catholic Church. In those days, men will wear women's clothes, and women will put on men's clothes.*[325]

20th Century – Countess Francesca de Billiante *(Prophecy Detail – Wars, Destruction)*

Countess Francesca de Billiante prophesied the following sometime in the twentieth century, regarding a great war with Russia and China overpowering Europe:

> *I see yellow warriors* (China?) *and red warriors* (Russia?) *marching against Europe. Europe will be completely covered with a yellow fog that will kill the cattle in the fields. Those nations which have rebelled against the law of Christ will perish by fire. Europe will then be too large for them who survive. May the Lord grant to my grandchildren the grace of persevering in the true Faith.*[326]

20th Century – 1930s: Saint Maria Faustina Kowalska *(Prophecy Detail – God's divine mercy and the Final Judgment, Days of darkness)*

Helena Kowalska was born in Glogowiec, Poland on August 25, 1905. She was the third of ten children and was baptized in the parish church of Swinice, Warckie. She loved prayer and work and was obedient to her parents. Even at an early age she showed a special compassion for the poor. She received the Holy Eucharist for the first time at age nine, but had already felt a calling to a religious vocation two years earlier. She wanted, in fact, to enter the convent after completing just three years of school, but her parents refused to give her their permission.

When Helena turned sixteen, she left home and found work as a housekeeper, thereby supporting herself and helping her family. After receiving a vision of the Suffering Christ, however, she fulfilled her dream of a religious vocation by entering the Congregation of the Sisters of Our Lady of Mercy. On August 1, 1925, Helena took the name Sister Maria Faustina of the Most Blessed Sacrament. She lived with the Congregation in various religious houses for thirteen years and worked as a cook, porter, and gardener.

To observers, Sister Faustina had an apparently insignificant and dull life, but within herself, she hid an extraordinary union with God. It was the process of contemplating God's mercy that helped her develop a childlike attitude of trust in God and show mercy toward her neighbors.

As a result, she was chosen by Jesus as the Apostle and Secretary of His Mercy. She was entrusted by God to deliver to the world His message of mercy, and she recorded these in a diary entitled *Divine Mercy in My Soul*. Her work sheds light on the mystery of Jesus's Divine Mercy and serves as a source of scholarly theological research.

Sister Faustina contracted tuberculosis, from which she suffered immeasurably. She died at the age of thirty-three on October 5, 1938 and is known as one of the great mystics. In 1968 the Catholic Church initiated her beatification process and she was canonized on April 30, 2000 by Pope John Paul II. Her remains rest in the Sanctuary of the Divine Mercy in Krakow-Lagiewniki.

Over the course of the hundreds of visions and locutions she received throughout the years, several messages related to the final judgment and the end of days. Those diary entries follow:

> *Secretary of My mercy, write, tell souls about this great mercy of Mine, because the awful day, the day of My justice is near....* **(Diary, 965)**

> *Then I saw the Mother of God, who said to me ... "I gave the Savior to the world; as for you, you have to speak to the world about His great mercy and prepare the world for the Second Coming of Him who will come, not as a merciful Savior, but as a just Judge. Oh, how terrible is that day! Determined is the day of justice, the day of divine wrath. The angels tremble before it. Speak to souls about this great mercy while it is still time for* [granting] *mercy. If you keep silent now, you will be answering for a great number of souls on that*

terrible day. Fear nothing. Be faithful to the end. I sympathize with you." (Diary, 635)

"Write down these words, my daughter. Speak to the world about My mercy; let all mankind recognize My unfathomable mercy. It is a sign for the end times; after it will come the day of justice. While there is still time let them have recourse to the fount of My mercy. Let them profit from the Blood and Water which gushed forth for them ..." (Diary, 848)

"Write: before I come as just Judge, I first open wide the door of My mercy. He who refuses to pass through the door of My mercy must pass through the door of My justice..." (Diary, 1146)

"Today I am sending you with My mercy to the people of the whole world. I do not want to punish aching mankind, but I desire to heal it, pressing it to My Merciful Heart. I use punishment when they themselves force Me to do so; My hand is reluctant to take hold of the sword of justice. Before the Day of Justice, I am sending the Day of Mercy." (Diary, 1588)

"Write this: before I come as the Just Judge, I am coming first as the King of Mercy. Before the day of justice arrives, there will be given to people a sign in the heavens of this sort: All light in the heavens will be extinguished, and there will be great darkness over the whole earth. Then the sign of the cross will be seen in the sky, and from the openings where the hands and the feet of the Savior were nailed will come forth great lights which will light up the earth for a period of time. This will take place shortly before the last day." (Diary, 83)

"...Tell sinners that no one shall escape My Hand; if they run away from My Merciful Heart, they will fall into My Just Hands. Tell sinners that I am always waiting for them, that I listen intently to the beating of their heart...when will it beat for Me? Write, that I am speaking to them through their remorse of conscience, through their failures and sufferings, through thunderstorms, through the voice of the Church. And if they bring all My graces to naught, I begin to be angry with them, leaving them alone and giving them what they want." (Diary, 1728)

"...I bear a special love for Poland, and if she will be obedient to My will, I will exalt her in might and holiness. From her will come

forth the spark that will prepare the world for My final coming."
(Diary, 1732)

*"...I am prolonging the time of mercy for the sake of sinners. But woe to them if they do not recognize this time of My visitation. My daughter, secretary of My mercy, your duty is not only to write about and proclaim My mercy, but also to beg for this grace for them, so that they too may glorify My mercy." **(Diary, 1160)***

*"You will prepare the world for My final coming." **(Diary, 429)**[327]*

20th Century - 1936: Therese Neumann, The Mystic of Konnersreuth *(Prophecy Detail – God's wrath, Time frame)*

German born mystic and stigmatist Teresa Neumann was a member of the Third Order of St. Francis. Born in Bavaria in 1898 in the late hours of Holy Thursday and early Good Friday, she was baptized as Therese in honor of St. Teresa of Avila. Though suffering from many illnesses and ailments including blindness (of which she was cured), temporary deafness, paralysis, and a condition that made even an act as simple as eating very painful, she remained cheerful.

In 1923, she was unable to either eat or drink for twelve days. Later, this condition extended "to the incredible phenomenon of inedia, whereby a mystic subsists only on the Eucharist. Neumann's abstinence from all food and drink except Communion – well-documented by certain observers – lasted from 1926 to [the time of her death] in 1962."[328] She often went without sleep, and instead would lapse into a state of "exalted repose," an unconscious state during which she would have visions of Jesus during His Passion. During these visions Neumann was observed levitating at least a half meter above the ground and bleeding from wounds of dramatic stigmata. She bled profusely from wounds on her right hand, both feet, and from her eyes, all of which was captured on camera.

Considered one of the greatest mystics of the twentieth century, Neumann could also speak in ancient languages without training, and displayed the gifts of prophecy, healing, and bilocation. During a state of exalted repose in 1936, Neumann said, *"The furies of hell are now set loose. Divine punishment is inevitable."*[329]

Shortly after the end of World War II, an American soldier asked Neumann if the United States would ever be invaded or destroyed by war. In one account of her response, Neumann said, *"No,"* and added, *"at the end of this century America will be destroyed economically by natural disasters."*[330]

20th Century - September 7, 1910 – 1943: Berthe Petit *(Prophecy Detail - God's wrath)*

Franciscan tertiary and mystic Berthe Petit was born on January 23, 1870 in Enghien, Belgium. Throughout much of her adult life, she had the respect of many of the cardinals, bishops, and theologians of the time. Berthe had a substantial number of visions and locutions of Jesus and Mary which started at an early age. Just after receiving her first communion, she told her teacher, a nun, *"I must suffer a great deal, I must be like Jesus."* When the nun asked who told her that, young Berthe replied, *"The little Host which is Jesus."*[331]

In a vision on February 7, 1910, Bertha saw the image of *"Two Hearts fused together, surmounted by the symbolical dove of the Holy Spirit, and on the following day were seen surmounted by luminous rays of light."* Jesus spoke to the seer saying:

> *My desire that this picture, guided by My hand, be spread far and wide, simultaneously with the invocation. Wherever it will be venerated, My Mercy and My Love will be made manifest and the sight of Our Hearts, wounded by the same wound, will encourage tepid and weak souls to come back to their duty.*[332]

Jesus appeared and spoke to Berthe many more times over the ensuing months and years about this and several other matters. Initially, the mystic's revelations were solely in the religious realm, but on July 12, 1912, Berthe began to receive revelations of a political nature. It was on that day Jesus warned her of the impending assassination of the heir to the Catholic empire of Austria-Hungary. He said:

> *A double murder will strike down the successor of the aged sovereign, so loyal to the faith. It will be the first of those events full of sorrows, but from whence I shall still bring forth good and which will precede the chastisement.*[333]

There is no doubt now, nor was there any doubt at the time, that the aged sovereign was eighty-two-year-old Archduke Franz Josef I and the subjects of the double assassination were Archduke Franz Ferdinand and his wife Sophia, the Duchess of Hohenburg. The day following the assassinations, on June 29, 1914, Jesus again spoke to Berthe:

Now begins the ascending curve of preliminary events, which will lead to the great manifestation of My justice.[334]

In fact, this preliminary event was the spark that ignited World War I which began just five weeks later, on August 4, 1914, when the Germans stormed Brussels in violation of Belgium's neutrality. Before the day was over, Germany and Great Britain were at war. In a subsequent revelation, Jesus said to Berthe:

The proud race and its ambitious ruler (Kaiser William II) *will be chastised on the very soil* (Belgium) *of their unjust conquest...The worst calamities which I predicted are unleashed. The time has now arrived when I wish mankind to turn to the Sorrowful and Immaculate Heart of My Mother. Let this prayer be uttered by every soul:* **"Sorrowful and Immaculate Heart of Mary, pray for us"** *so that it may spread as a refreshing and purifying balm of reparation that will appease My anger. This devotion to the Sorrowful and Immaculate Heart of My Mother will restore faith and hope to broken hearts and to ruined families. It will help to repair the destruction. It will sweeten sorrow. It will be a new strength for My Church, bringing souls, not only to confidence in My Heart, but also to abandonment to the Sorrowful Heart of My Mother.*[335]

Shortly thereafter, Pope Pius X died and was replaced by Pope Benedict XV, who promptly mourned the bloodshed of the war without pointing the finger of blame, and denounced the violence as a crime against religion, humanity, and civilization. His First Encyclical, Ad Beatissimi Apostolorum, issued on November 1, 1914, criticized the war between nations of Christian people. The Encyclical was followed by the Pontiff's letter of May 3, 1915, in which he recommended that all Catholics and the world,

pray with confidence to the Sorrowful and Immaculate Heart of Mary, the most gentle Mother of Jesus and ours, that by her powerful intercession she will obtain from her divine Son the speedy end of the war and the return of peace and tranquility.[336]

But it wasn't until Cardinal Disire Mercier, the Primate of Belgium, and Cardinal Alphonsus Bourne, the Primate of England and Archbishop of Canterbury, took action that things began to change. On March 7, 1916, as the war raged, Cardinal Mercer announced that he would dedicate his diocese and the country of Belgium to the Sorrowful and

Immaculate Heart of Mary during Good Friday ceremonies. Cardinal Bourne did the same on September 15. On that very day, Britain achieved its greatest success of the war and subsequently,

> *each time public devotions were performed in England, the British armies swept forward to unexpected victories, so much so that Marshal Ferdinand Foch, the Commander in Chief of the Allied forces in France, observed in his "Memories" that, strangely enough, the English seemed scarcely aware of how those successes could have come about. "I will never repeat it too often," he wrote, "that the English fought in a most extraordinary way. They won victory upon victory. At the beginning of October, they had broken the formidable Hindenburg line at its strongest point. But still more wonderful, these victories were won almost unknown to themselves."[337]*

However, when the war began to turn against the Allies in the spring of 1918, Jesus again spoke to Berthe, explaining the reversal of fortunes this way:

> *It is a necessary trial for after My protection has helped them to conquer, they attributed the glory to their own prowess. Reverses are now showing these soldiers how human means alone are powerless to repel the surge of invasion.[338]*

At this point, Jesus sent a message to Cardinal Francis Alphonsus Bourne through Berthe in which He asked the Cardinal

> *...to exert an ever-increasing activity in favor of the Sorrowful and Immaculate Heart of My Mother. Let him hasten what he calls his "first step" so that a still more solemn consecration may be timed for the feast of the Sorrows of My Mother – that great feast of Her Heart as Co-redemptrix.[339]*

Jesus promised Berthe that He would turn the tide of the war when his servant obeyed. Cardinal Bourne clearly heeded the warning and consecrated England to the Sorrowful Heart of Mary for the second time on August 15, 1917. The following spring, the war did indeed turn once again in favor of the Allies and with the number of German desertions skyrocketing, chaos prevailed throughout Central Europe. Once more, Jesus revealed to Berthe:

Were it not for my intervention, obtained by My apostle Francis through recourse to the Sorrowful and Immaculate Heart of My Mother, the victory would have belonged to those who strained every nerve during so many years to prepare and organize a great war for the attainment of their own ambitions...Material force would have overborne justice and right and this more especially so for your own country (Belgium). *For why should I come to the help of a people in France intent on persecuting My Church? That is why trials will continue until the day when, humbly acknowledging her errors, this nation will render Me My rights and give full liberty to My Church.*[340]

Later in the month Jesus warned:

The world is hanging on the edge of utter cataclysm. My justice cannot preside over the machination of those who work in their own interests to forward a peace totally unworthy of the name, and which can never be genuine except through My intervention.[341]

Three weeks later, on November 11, 1918, the war ended, giving the victory to the British. Ten million had died and many more were maimed.

On May 24 of the following year, the Archbishop of Westminster again consecrated Britain to the Sorrowful and Immaculate Heart of Mary, but Jesus had not yet had the final word. That came in July 1919 when the Lord spoke these prophetic and ominous words to Berthe:

Internal strife is more rampant than ever in our country. It is being fanned by the evil seed sown by the invader. It is fed by egoism, pride and jealousy – malevolent germs which can only generate moral ruin...Time will prove that a peace established without Me and without him who speaks in My name (the Pope) *has no stability. The nation* (Germany) *which is considered to be vanquished but whose forces are only momentarily diminished, will remain a menace for your country and likewise for France. Confusion and terror will steadily spread through every nation. Because this peace is not Mine, wars will be rekindled on every side – civil war and racial war. What would have been so noble, so true, so beautiful, so lasting in its fulfillment is consequently delayed. Humanity is advancing towards a frightful scourge which will divide the nations more and more. It will reduce human schemes to nothingness. It will break the pride of the powers that be. It will show that nothing subsists without Me and that I remain the sole Master of the destinies of nations.*[342]

In fact, Jesus's words, though Berthe could not possibly have known it at the time, were rightfully critical of the armistice that was signed between the warring factions. Pope Benedict had placed equal blame on both sides in denouncing the war in 1914 and Germany refused to acknowledge any sole guilt and responsibility for the war. Protests organized by the German people called for Germany to refuse to sign the Treaty of Versailles. Germany ignored the protesters' cries and the peace agreement was in fact signed, further dividing Germany and causing some to denounce the Armistice. Winston Churchill was among the detractors, writing that *"the economic clauses of the Treaty were malignant and silly to an extent that made them obviously futile."*[343]

Petit spent the balance of the World War I years in Switzerland where she continued to receive revelations that foretold of calamities that would befall the Allies.

The previous revelation proved to be most prophetic, as the "war to end all wars" was followed on short order by the outbreak of an even greater war, World War II. On April 25, 1942, Berthe received another revelation from the Lord:

> *A frightful torment is in preparation. It will be seen that the forces launched in such fury will soon be let loose. It is now or never, the moment for all of you to give yourselves to the Sorrowful Heart of My Mother. By Her acceptance of Calvary, My Mother has participated in all My sufferings. Devotion to Her Heart united to Mine will bring peace, that true peace so often implored and yet so little merited.*[344]

Later, Jesus said:

> *It is hearts that must be changed. This will be accomplished only by the Devotion proclaimed, explained, preached and recommended everywhere. Recourse to My Mother under the title I wish for Her universally, is the last help I shall give before the end of time.*[345]

Jesus concluded in a later vision:

> *It is as a Son that I have conceived this devotion for My Mother. It is as God that I impose it.*[346]

Berthe's life and her sufferings were coming to an end, but the Lord was not yet finished with her. During a pilgrimage to the shrine of St. Anne in Alsace, Jesus revealed to Berthe her greatest mission, *"to obtain the Consecration of the world to the Sorrowful and Immaculate Heart of Mary.* "[347] With her health quickly waning, Berthe knew that she would not live to fulfill this mission, but she carried on until the end.

The great mystic, in excruciating pain, was given the last rites of the Church and finally succumbed to the sufferings to the effects of her great pain, passing into eternity on Friday, March 26, 1943 even as the sufferings of World War II were at their peak.

Even today, almost eighty years after her death, many people around the globe wonder if the punishment of which Jesus foretold to Berthe Petit will in fact be a Third World War, one that takes place in this nuclear age. Such an event would certainly have the potential to destroy many nations, fulfilling the prophecies of the great chastisement to come.

20th Century – 1931 - 1940: Pope Pius XII *(Prophecy Detail – Church persecution, End of times)*

Born in Rome on March 2, 1876 to a Catholic family of penetrating piety, Eugenio Maria Giuseppe Giovanni Pacelli already had ties to the papacy. His grandfather, Marcantonio Pacelli, served Pope Pius IX in several high-ranking positions, while his cousin, Ernesto Pacelli, was a key financial advisor to Pope Leo XIII.

Pacelli was ordained to the priesthood on Easter Sunday in 1899, not in a public ceremony with the other candidates, but rather alone in the privileged chapel of the Vicegerent of Rome. In 1930, after many high-level assignments, Pacelli was made a cardinal-priest and within a few months was appointed Cardinal Secretary of State by Pope Pius XI. In 1935 he was named Camerlengo of the Holy Roman Church. Following the death of Pius XI, Pacelli was elected Pope, taking the name of Pius XII.

It was not as Pope Pius XII, but rather as Cardinal Pacelli, that he had several visions. The first of these was in 1931, just fourteen years after the apparitions of Our Lady of Fatima to the three shepherd children. At that time, he said:

> *I am worried by the Blessed Virgin's messages to Lucy of Fatima. This persistence of Mary about the dangers which menace the Church is a Divine warning against the suicide of altering the Faith, in Her liturgy, Her theology and Her soul...I hear all around me innovators who wish to dismantle the Sacred Chapel, destroy the universal flame of the true Faith of the Church, reject Her ornaments and make Her feel remorse for Her historical past.*

A day will come when the civilized world will deny its God, when the Church will doubt as Peter doubted. She will be tempted to believe that man has become God. In our churches, Christians will search in vain for the red lamp (the red lamp burning in Catholic Churches signifies that God is really present before them in the Most Blessed Sacrament) *where God awaits them. Like Mary Magdelene, weeping before the empty tomb, they will ask, "Where have they taken Him?"* (The implication is that the Most Blessed Sacrament will no longer be able to be found in the "Catholic" Churches)[348]

In 1940, Pope Pius XII issued another prophetic warning when he said:

We believe that the present hour is a dread phase of the events foretold by Christ. It seems that darkness is about to fall on the world. Humanity is in the grip of a supreme crisis.[349]

20th Century – 1937 – 1945: Apparitions of Heede *(Prophecy Detail – The great chastisement)*

Tucked into the district of Pinneberg in Schleswig-Holstein, Germany, is the little town of Heede. Until 1937 nothing too special had occurred here. That changed, however, on November 1 when eleven-year-old Anna Schulte, Greta Gauseforth, Greta's thirteen-year-old sister Margaret, and Susanna Bruns attended the feast of All Saints in the yard of their local parish. It was only Greta and her sister Margaret, though, that noticed the "floating light," moving in a churchyard cemetery about one hundred feet away and about three and a quarter feet above the ground. As they moved in for a closer look, the light began to take the shape of a woman. That's when they recognized that it was the Virgin Mary holding the Christ Child. The heads of both Mary and the Christ Child were adorned with beautiful crowns.

It was Margaret who was able to speak first. *"It's there,"* she exclaimed, *"between the two cypresses!"* Neither Mary nor Jesus spoke. Adele wasn't able to see the figures and, in frustration, insisted on returning home. Margaret and Grete, however, told their mother of the vision and she alerted the parish priest, Fr. Staelberg.

Most villagers were unfazed by the news, thinking that the girls were making up the story. But when the girls' lifestyles changed dramatically toward the pious, some began to wonder. Rather than amusing themselves with pleasure, the young girls opted for long fervent prayer, hoping that Mary and Jesus would appear to them once again. The Blessed Mother and/or the Savior of the World did appear again, as many as one hundred times. The girls reported receiving many messages.

Nov 2, 1937:
Our Lady appeared on November 2, this time without the Baby Jesus. She didn't speak but She clasped her hands in prayer.

Nov. 5, 1936:
Our Lady appeared on a white cloud. She held the Baby Jesus and stood atop a white cloud. A luminous halo measuring about eleven to fifteen inches surrounded Her. The girls estimated Her age to be about eighteen or nineteen and this time, Our Lady asked the girls questions. According to the children,

> *She wore a golden crown, richly worked...a long white dress fitted at the waist by a cord...a non-transparent white veil falls on each side, doing some folds, and hides her hair...On her left hand, covered by the veil, sits the Christ Child. She raises her arm.*

Nov. 7, 1937:
The villagers were no longer skeptics and approximately five thousand people turned out for this apparition. In fact, several priests who attended were able to see Mary just as the children did.

Nov. 8, 1937:
The next day more than seven thousand crowded the field but civil authorities would not allow Fr. Staelberg to accompany the girls. Instead, a priest from Herkenhoff attended and reported the following:

> *Suddenly, the* (four) *girls fell to their knees, all together, without one or another making a signal to her companions ... They posed several questions to the apparition. After a quarter of an hour – during which they continued to be constantly stiff, eyes fixed on a precise point – their questions seemed unanswered, even when they spoke. When Greta was alongside me later, she told me that she had wondered how the Mother of God feels. The response she received was a sad countenance. Greta said, "The Mother of God was very sad and very bright."*

April 5, 1939:
Margaret was alone for this apparition and noted, *"I saw the Mother of God directly in front of me, standing two feet away, and asked her how*

she would like to be invoked." She replied, "*'as Queen of the Universe and Queen of the Poor Souls in Purgatory.'*" When asked what prayer She would like to honor Her, she indicated the *"Litany of Laurentanas"* (The Litany of Loreto).

May 12, 1939:

During this apparition Greta asked, *"Will we have diseases?"* Our Lady answered, *"Not yet."* Then Greta asked, *"Can we come here every day?"* Our Lady responded, *"Yes."* But then the number of occurrences decreased. By this time, Adolf Hitler ruled Germany and forbade participation in this type of "superstitious nonsense." This invoked fear in many people, causing them to stay away from Heede. In short order, the Gestapo forcefully took the children to an insane asylum and strictly forbade any pilgrimages to Heede. The children were released from the asylum after a month and promptly resumed their visits to the field in violation of the orders of the Gestapo. Mary continued to appear to them in "secret locations." Later that year, Greta Ganseforth received the stigmata.

October 19, 1940:

During this apparition, Our Lady gave the four girls a "secret," warning them, *"Do not say anything to anyone other than the Holy Pope of Rome."* The message was later placed in a sealed envelope and given to Bishop Berning who hand-carried it to Pope Pius XII.

The Virgin also showed them visions of future catastrophes and warned them that a horrifying event described as a "Minor Judgment" was in store for the future.

> *The world will have to drink the dregs of the chalice of Divine wrath for their innumerable sins through which they have wounded the Sacred Heart of Jesus* (Then she admonished them). *Pray...pray much, especially for the conversion of sinners.*

Our Lady, who generally appeared very solemn and even crying, encouraged the girls to say the Rosary often.

November 3, 1940:

This was the last apparition of the Blessed Mother that the girls would receive. It happened at eight thirty in the evening. Each girl received a "secret" from the Blessed Virgin who then said:

> *Be good and faithful to the will of God. Pray often – especially the Rosary. Now farewell, my children, until we meet in Heaven.*

On July 23, 1942, Bishop Berning delivered a homily after which he said the following:

> *From Heede came a rich blessing. I could see that Marian devotion dramatically increased; that sacramental life, in particular, has flourished dramatically in this parish.*

While the Marian apparitions stopped, Greta Ganseforth began receiving visits from Our Lord beginning in 1945. These apparitions included the Angel of Justice. Her spiritual director ordered her to record any mystical events in her diary. Though she never saw Our Lady again, she did hear her voice, speaking to her from a brilliant light on numerous occasions. These are some of the warnings that she recorded in her diary.

When a school dance was being planned for October 21, 1945, which apparently was going to exceed Catholic norms for decency, Greta, at the request of Jesus, sought to have the dance cancelled or at least modified so that it would not create a near occasion for sin. Greta warned the parents as Our Lord declared:

> *If they proceed with that dance, all involved will have to answer to Me at their Judgment.*

The dance was promptly cancelled. Following the cancellation and a number of miraculous healings, other parish priests and clergymen finally came to believe that the girls had indeed been visited by Jesus and His Blessed Mother.

In a subsequent apparition, Jesus had this dire warning:

> *Men did not listen to My Most Holy Mother when she appeared to them at Fatima and admonished them to do penance. Now I, Myself, am coming at the last hour to warn and admonish mankind!*
>
> *The times are very serious! Men should at last do penance, turn away from their sins and pray, pray much in order that the wrath of God may be mitigated. Particularly the Holy Rosary should be prayed very often. The Rosary is very powerful with God. Worldly pleasures and amusements should be restricted.*
>
> *Men do not listen to My voice. They harden their hearts; they resist My grace. They do not wish to have anything to do with My Mercy, My Love, My merits. Mankind is worse than before the deluge. Mankind is suffocating in sin. Hatred and greed rule their hearts. This is the work of the devil. They live in great darkness. Through the wounds that bled, Mercy will again gain victory over*

justice. My faithful souls should not be asleep now like the disciples on Mt. Olive. They should pray without ceasing and gain all they can for themselves and for others.

This generation deserves to be annihilated but I desire to show myself as merciful. Tremendous things are in preparation; it will be terrible as never before since the foundation of the world. All those, who in these grave times have suffered so much, are martyrs and form the seed for the renovation of the Church. They were privileged to participate in My captivity, in My scourging, in My crown of thorns, and My Way of the Cross.

That which will shortly happen, will greatly surpass everything that has ever happened until now.

The Blessed Virgin Mary and all the choirs of angels will be active during these events. Hell believes that it is sure of the harvest, but I will snatch it away from them. I will come with My peace. Many curse me now, but these sufferings will come over mankind that they may be saved through it ... Many expiate all they can for those who curse Me now ...

With a few faithful I will build up My kingdom. As a flash of lightning this Kingdom will come ... much faster than mankind will realize. I will give them a special light. For some this light will be a blessing; for others, darkness. The light will come like the Star that showed the way to the wise men. Mankind will experience My love and My power. My beloved, the hour comes closer. Pray without ceasing!

Those who are not in the State of Grace (when the Minor Judgment happens) – *it will be frightful for them.*

On March 7, 1946, the bishop authorized the sculpting of a statue of Mary, Queen of the Universe. The statue was then placed in the church cemetery as directed by the seers. Then, on June 3, 1959, following years of investigation, the Bishop of Osnabruck said:

The apparitions are undeniable proof of the seriousness and authenticity of these manifestations ... In the apparitions and messages of Heede we find nothing contrary to the Faith. Indeed, their similarity to the approved apparitions of Fatima, Lourdes, and La Salette give good indications of their authenticity.

With those words, the local bishop approved the authenticity of the apparitions for faith expression. Formal approval is still pending, but there is no question that the bishop recognized these events as supernatural.

20th Century – 1945-1959: Ida Peerderman/Our Lady of All Nations *(Prophecy Detail – Death of a pope, Massive flood affecting Europe, Devastating world war)*

Born in Alkmaar, Netherlands on August 13, 1905, Ida Peerdeman was the youngest of five children. As a young adult she worked as a secretary and her life was rather ordinary and unspectacular. That all changed, however, when on March 25, 1945, Peerdeman reported seeing a woman surrounded in light who identified herself as "The Lady" and "Mother." The apparitions continued over a period of fourteen years, finally ending on May 31, 1959.

While initially not accepted as authentic, Peerdeman was undeterred and a movement advocating the supernatural origination of her visions was initiated. In December 1979 the movement received the support of a member of the wealthy and influential Brenninkmeijer family. The Lady of All Nations Foundation purchased property in Diepenbrockstraat, Amsterdam, which became the center of the apparition believers. It is also the place where Peerdeman decided to live. She spent the rest of her life promoting the messages she received from Our Lady.

Peerderman died on June 17, 1996. Devotion to Our Lady of All Nations was officially approved by the Bishop Henry Bomers of Haarlem in 1996. It was then reaffirmed by his successor Bishop Jozef Punt in 2002. It is Bishop Punt under whom such jurisdiction resides. These decisions overturn an earlier decree that the visions were "not supernatural" and therefore the subject of some controversy because the new decree was not formally approved by the Congregation. It should be noted, however, that the congregation also did not object to the ruling. Regardless of the controversy, the visions have now met the first stage in being officially recognized by the Vatican.

Throughout the fourteen years of the apparitions, Our Lady of All Nations gave to Peerdeman several prophecies related to the end times. The prophecy that follows was taken from a commentary written by Emmett O'Regan for *Prophecy in Catholic Tradition*. O'Regan is also the author of *Unveiling the Apocalypse*.

December 7, 1947 – the Thirteenth Apparition – The Cross
I see the Lady, and I hear, "Rome threatened!"
After that a big "4" appears before me and around it a circle. Then that image vanishes, and a Cross appears before me with four equal beams. A circle appears around that, too, and in the center of the Cross I read "I H S." It is as if I would take this Cross up and I show it around

me. Now I suddenly see crowds of people standing around us. They are looking at it, but many with aversion.

Then I see heavy, thick clouds appearing over Europe and under them huge waves engulfing Europe. Then I see the Lady standing in a glaring, bright light. She is dressed in white. She keeps her arms extended, and from her hands emanates a thick beam of rays. I have to hold up my hand and that beam of rays seems to come into my hand. I feel it aglow and tingling. The Lady smiles at me and points at that hand, while she nods in approval. I do not know what this means. Then the Lady's face becomes drawn and she looks very sad. She points at those heavy clouds and waves, and she says, "They will first have to perish by that flood, and only then ..." and then I see those words written down. After "only then," I see many dots, as if something is to follow which must remain hidden. Then the Lady's face brightens, and I see the water evaporate as steam. For a moment the sun seems to break through. Again, the Lady points out the earth to me, and I notice that everything has cleared up. And now I see lots of bones of human beings scattered over the ground, parts of skulls, arms and legs. It is a horrible sight. I hear the Lady say, "This is the perdition. But go and work, work ..." Then she points upwards and says, "Read." Then I see letters appear and I read, "Righteousness." After that I feel a terrible pain in my hand; it feels as heavy as lead. Then I hear the Lady say, "Just read on" and I see in large letters before me, "Love of Neighbor." I see dripping icicles appearing all over it. Then I hear that voice saying, "Read on!" But when I want to read, I cannot read anything, because of the flames playing around the letters. For a moment the flames clear away, and I read "Justice."

After this the Lady points and I see a soldiers' cemetery with countless rows of white crosses. I see them fall over, one after the other—all falling backwards. Once again, the Lady points and I see new white crosses appearing. As far as my eyes can reach, they are rising out of the ground. Then I hear the Lady say, "This is the message I bring today."

After this I see her slowly disappear in the light. I feel a great emptiness around me, and it is as if everything on earth looks dreary.[350]

O'Regan notes that the threat against Rome signifies the death of a Pope while "the letters IHS that Ida sees in the midst of the Cross of course refers to the Christogram bearing the first three letters of Jesus's name in the Greek alphabet - iota, eta and sigma (the "H" shape in the

Greek alphabet is actually the capitalization of the letter eta - which is sounded as an "e").

"Then after the threat presented towards Rome, Ida sees clouds forming over Europe, which is then engulfed by massive tidal waves. It is almost certain that this is one and the same event seen by other seers as chiefly affecting America. But here the focus is on its effects on the homeland of the visionary - Europe, and more specifically the Netherlands."

Dr. Simon Ward believes the effects of the mega-tsunami will devastate England with waves of forty feet traveling five hundred miles per hour. Thirty-three-foot waves will hit Lisbon and La Coruna within three hours of the strike in Britain. The impact will be felt in all of Europe. *"Even Britain's more sheltered shores, in the North Sea and Irish Sea, will be struck by smaller but still significant swells, causing widespread flooding in major coastal cities."*[351]

O'Regan continues, *"If the Cumbre Vieja mega-tsunami could cause sea surges which would even affect London, then it would have a far worse effect on the Netherlands* (the homeland of Ida Peerdeman) - *a large portion of which lies below sea level. Indeed, many other parts of Western Europe* (such as Denmark and parts of France and Germany) *have land areas below or close to sea level, making these locations extremely susceptible to large tsunami events."*[352]

The remainder of the Peerdeman prophecies are taken from the blog The Great Catholic Monarch and Angelic Pontiff Prophecies written by Elizabeth A. Bucchianeri, who also authored several other titles on the end-of-times.

July 29, 1945 – The Third Message – England and America Will Come Back to Our Lady

A large number of men of all sorts are now standing before me: gentlemen, simple fellows, also priests and religious, dressed in black. Among them there are good people but also some not so good. The Lady invites them to come with her. She shall guide them. Now I see a long and difficult road before me, at the end of which there is a bright light. "This way," says the Lady, and with a broad gesture she indicates to the men that they have to walk along this road. It is difficult and challenging. On both sides they are falling away. The Lady is watching with motherly concern and keeps smiling at them. Then I see written before me, "Into life again, with Christ." After this the Lady looks sad and says, "England will find her way back to me." She pauses for a moment and then says slowly and softly,

"America too." Then the Lady slowly disappears, and I see a peculiar haze hanging over the world.[353]

January 3, 1946 – The Sixth Message - Visions of England and Europe at War, The Return of Joan of Arc, The Great Monarch.

I hear that voice say, "England, be on your guard!" Then I see England and in England a large church. I am given to understand Westminster Abbey. Then I see a bishop; he is not of our Church. I am given to understand that [he] is a bishop of England. After this I see the Pope sitting before me; he looks very serious. Then I see that bishop again—this has to do with England. The Lady points out England to me, and then I see the word "Fight" above the head of that bishop. A strange feeling overcomes me; it is as if everything within me were to change—I cannot explain how. I suddenly look up to my left and see the Lady again. She is dressed all in white, standing slightly above me. She is pointing something out to me. I look and I see England lying before me once more. The Lady says to me, "There will be a fight all over Europe and beyond." A heavy, paralyzing feeling and a great spiritual weariness take hold of me. The Lady says, "It is a heavy spiritual fight."

Then the Lady says to me, "Come," and she points at my hand. It is as if a Cross were placed in it. Now the Lady indicates what I should do. I move the hand with the Cross in it over the earth, and I have to let the Cross be seen. Then the Lady says to me, "Yes, look at that Cross." I do so and as I am looking, the Cross leaves my hand and I make a fist. I must look at that too. Then the Lady says, "Now look at the Cross again." And the Cross is again lying in my hand. Then the Lady moves her finger to and fro in warning and says, "That Cross they want to change into other crosses." Now I see several things whirling around before my eyes: communism and a new kind of movement that will arise, a combination of the swastika and communism.[354]

The Lady says, "The Christians will become weary, because of all the fighting." She emphasizes the word "weary," and I feel a spiritual weariness coming over me. The Lady points at something in front of me and then I see a stretch of sand, a desert. A pulpit is placed in it. Then that pulpit disappears again and for a moment I see that desert before me again. I hear a voice calling something in a foreign language of former times. This repeats itself a few times before my eyes, very quickly. Then the Lady points out something again, and I see the Vatican. It is as though it were spinning around in the midst of the world. In the Vatican I see the Pope with his head raised and two fingers uplifted. He is looking ahead seriously. Then I beat my breast three times.

Next, I suddenly see someone on horseback, in full armor. When I ask who it is, I am told, Jeanne d'Arc (St. Joan of Arc). All of a sudden, I see a big cathedral rising up behind her. I ask what church it is, and I hear within me: that is the Cathedral of Reims. Then I see a procession going in the direction of that church. It is a procession of former times with someone on horseback. He is carrying a shield and a sword and is surrounded by shield-bearers. I hear: Bourbon. I get the feeling: that is for later on.[355]

(Elizabeth Bucchianeri notes the similarities between this and other visions such as the apparitions of Tilly that state St. Joan of Arc will return to aid France. Marie-Julie Jahenny mentions the army of the Great Monarch to come, it will be like a procession – Reims is where the French kings were crowned. Marie-Julie foretold the Great Monarch will be crowned quite rapidly. "Bourbon" is the name of the direct line of the French kings, and here, the apparition of Our Lady of all Nations is in accordance with the other prophecies that state the Great Monarch will be a King of France, and be the last of his line. Marie-Julie Jahenny, Ven. Mother Josepha of Bourg and the "Ecstatic of Tours" all declared Henry V, "Prince Dieudonné," the exiled "Miracle Child," who was the last of the direct Bourbon line, was and is the Great Monarch).

After that I have to look into my hands, and I represent humanity. "They are empty," I tell the Lady. She is watching and then I must join them, while I look up at her. The Lady smiles at me. It is as though she moves down a step, and she says, "Come." Then it is as if I were going with her across the world. Suddenly a terrible tiredness comes over me, and I tell the Lady, "I am so tired, so hopelessly tired." I feel that way throughout my entire body. But the Lady takes me along further and further. Then I look ahead of me and see the word "Truth" written in very large letters. I read it aloud and then we continue again. The Lady shakes her head. She looks very serious and sad and says to me, "Do you see love of neighbor?" I look again into my hands and say, "Those hands are empty." She takes me by the hand again and we go on. As I see an unending emptiness before me, I hear the Lady ask, "Righteousness, justice, where are these?"

Then once more I see the Cross standing in the midst of the world, and the Lady points at it. I have to take it up, but I turn my head away. It is as if I were humanity and would throw the Cross away from me. "No," says the Lady, "that must be taken up and placed in the center.

There will be a certain category of people who will fight, will fight for this, and I shall lead them on to it." As she says this, a terrible pain seizes my whole body, such that I groan and say to the Lady, "Oh, this is so painful!" After that I hear a voice crying out very loudly, "Jericho!" And the Lady has gone back to her place above me. She looks down, looks down at me and says, "What I have told you must be made known. There will be no peace beforehand."

After that I see the Pope before me again with quite a number of clerics and other gentlemen around him. "They seem to be in conference," I say. They are having fierce discussions, and it sometimes seems that they are angry. The Lady says, "This is the spiritual fight which is going about the world. This is much worse than the other, and the world is being undermined."

Then I go, so to speak, across the world, and it is as if I burrow into the ground. It is as if I go further and further below the surface, passing through all kinds of tunnels. It suddenly comes to an end, and all at once I hear the words, "I am here." Then I hear a voice saying, "Ego sum," and then I softly say, "And the world is small." After this the Lady says, pointing with her finger, "Go and spread it."[356]

(Bucchianeri finds it interesting that Ida would, in later years (May 31, 1969), visit the famous Chapel of Rue du Bac in Paris at the convent of the Sisters of Charity where St. Catherine Labouré received the famous visits of Our Lady in 1830 and the command to have the Miraculous Medal struck. At the time Ida visited this chapel, the visits of Our Lady of All Nations had stopped and she was receiving the Eucharistic Visions. On this occasion after receiving Communion, she received the very strong interior inspiration: *"What began here, will be continued by 'The Lady of All Nations'"*[357])

February 7, 1946 – The Seventh Message – Warning to Europe, New Disasters for the World,

Then all at once I see Rome before me again and the Pope seated. In his hand the Pope has an open book which he lets me see. I cannot see what kind of book it is. Then the Pope shows that book in all directions. I hear the Lady say, "But much has to be changed there." She points towards where the Pope is. She looks very serious and shakes her head. Again, the Lady raises three fingers and then five fingers. Suddenly a feeling of confusion seizes me, and I hear the Lady say, "New disasters are again coming upon the world."[358]

February 25, 1946 – The Eighth Message – Truth, Faith and Love Need to Come back – A Prophecy of Natural Disasters, Famine, Political Chaos

"You must warn them; Truth has been lost." The Lady says to me, "Look," and she traces a semicircle, a curve, over the world. She seems to write in it, and I read the words aloud. "Truth"—this is in the middle. Then she writes a word on the left, and I read "Faith," then on the right, and I read "Love." The Lady points to it and says, "Go and spread it!" Then she points at the curve again, and says, "That has to come back. To all appearances it is there, but in reality, it is not." And she looks terribly sad. After this I have to say, "Disaster upon disaster, natural disasters." Then I see the words "Hunger" and "Political Chaos." The Lady says, "This goes not only for your country, but for the whole world." I feel a terrible pain and say, "That is yet a period of pressure and pain, which is still going on throughout the world." I then see the word "Hopeless." It suddenly gets light around me, and I see the Lady, so to speak, coming down. She points out to me those three words, "Truth" "Faith" and "Love." The Lady laughs and says to me, "But there is a lot to be learned."[359]

March 29, 1946 – The Ninth Message – Religion Under Attack

The Lady said, "Religion will have a hard struggle, and they want to tread it under foot. This will be done so cunningly that scarcely anyone will notice it. But I am warning," and she looks very serious and points at the chalice. I hear her say, "Christus Regnum," (Christ's Kingdom) and then I see Jerusalem lying before me—this I am given to understand. There is a fight there. All of a sudden, I see Armenian priests before me. Then I hold up two fingers. Again, I see the Lady seated on her chair with everything around her, and now I see the Church of England, a Russian Church, an Armenian Church and many other churches. They continuously whirl around through one another. The Lady looks worried and I hear her say, "Rome, be on guard!"[360]

June 9, 1946 – The Tenth Message – Demons and Cosmic Disasters Befall the Earth

Our Lady holds the Christ Child, He begins to cry: "You people who are for Him, be watchful! I cannot warn you enough."[361]

Then I look again at that place, but the Child is suddenly gone. The Lady looks dejectedly into the world and says, "These are not to be found among men: Righteousness, Truth and Love"' After that it is as if the Lady stares intently in front of herself, and she says,

"Disaster upon disaster! For a second time I tell you this: as long as these are missing, there can be no true peace. By praying and especially by working for the good and not just praying. Working and keeping watch."

Then I suddenly see that the Lady has stepped aside. Now I am shown a very repulsive sight. From the other direction something like demons are coming towards me, figures whirling around through one another, with horns on their heads, awkward paws and horrible faces. Then I hear the Lady say, "I predict a great, new disaster in the world." This the Lady says very sadly and warningly. Then she says, "If people would only listen ... Seemingly things will go well for a short time."

Next, I see the globe, and the Lady points at it. I see glaring lights and rays, and the globe seems to explode on all sides. Then the Lady points at the sky. She stands to my right, that is, in the West, and she points to the East. I see a great number of stars in the sky, and the Lady says, "That is where it comes from."

(Bucchianeri notes: "Sounds like a cosmic chastisement – Our Lady would later warn of meteors. Fire falling from the sky?! Again, very similar to what other mystics and apparitions have foretold.")

"There will be a struggle in Rome against the pope." I see lots of bishops sitting around the Pope, and then I hear, "Catastrophic."[362]

August 30, 1947 – The Twelfth Message - Politico-Christian Struggle in Italy, Secret Meetings in the Vatican.

Then all of a sudden, I see a large room in the Vatican, and the Pope is seated there. Something seems to be going on in the Vatican. The Lady says, "Secret meetings are being held there. This is happening several times. They assemble in secret." The Lady points at somebody, and I am given to understand that is an envoy from America. In front of the Pope there are all sorts of papers. The Lady says, "The Pope is kept informed of everything. He is completely informed about what is going to happen. It is said that there is peace, but in reality, it is not so. It is all camouflage before the world." Then twice I have to move my right hand over my left, and I hear, "That will happen twice." And I see a kind of point of time.

December 26, 1947 – The Fourteenth Message - Vision of the World Torn in Two – a War in Jerusalem, the Middle East – the Hellish Invention of Biological Warfare

Now I see a round dome. I am given to understand that is a dome of Jerusalem. I hear now, "In and around Jerusalem heavy battles will be waged." All at once I see Cairo clearly, and I get a strange feeling about it. Then I see various Eastern peoples: Persians, (i.e. Iranians), *Arabs and so on. The Lady says, "The world is, so to speak, going to be torn in two."*

Now I see the world lying before me and in it a great crack appearing, a break winding right over the world. Heavy clouds are hanging over it, and I feel great sorrow and misery. I hear the Lady say, "Great sorrow and misery will come." Then I see Eastern places with white-roofed houses.

Then I see lines of young men passing by me; they are soldiers. I hear that voice say, "Stand by our boys with spiritual aid." Then I see white graves arise, lots of small white crosses. Then I feel a pain in my hand, and I see America and Europe lying side by side. After this I see written: "Economic warfare, Boycotting, Currencies, Disasters."

(Bucchianeri notes that it "seems like she is predicting our own times, the wars in the Middle East seem to be escalating – we are also seeing economic warfare, boycotts, currency fluctuations and the introduction of new 'crypto-currencies' and also natural disasters."[363])

I have to look at the sky, and something seems to be launched into it. There is something flying past me so rapidly that I can hardly see it. It is shaped like a cigar or a torpedo, and its color is like that of aluminum. All of a sudden, I see something shooting off from the back. I feel about with my hand, and different terrible sensations come over me. At first a total numbness. I live and yet I do not live. Then I see horrible images of people before me. I see faces, wide faces, covered with dreadful ulcers, something like leprosy. Then I feel terrible deadly diseases: cholera, leprosy—everything those people have to suffer. Then that is gone again, and I see tiny little black things floating about me. I try to feel what it is, but that is not possible. It seems to be very fine matter. With my eyes I cannot discern what it is. It is as if I would have to look through something, and below I now see brilliant white fields. Upon those fields I see those little black things, but enlarged, and it is as if they are alive. I don't know how to describe this properly. I ask the Lady, "Are these bacilli?" (i.e. bacteria) She answers very seriously, "It is hellish." Then I feel my face and my whole body swelling. It feels like my face gets very bloated, and everything is stiff and swollen. I cannot move. I hear the Lady say, "And that is what they are inventing," and then very softly, "that Russian, but the others as well." After this the Lady says emphatically, "Peoples, be warned!" And then the Lady goes away.[364]

(Bucchianeri explains that this prophecy might refer to the "burning face" plague foretold by the Old Testament and other mystics [and may come about as a result of] biological warfare. Since Marie-Julie Jahenny has foretold [of] a "burning face" disease that incubates and spreads fast during the time of the upheavals of war in France, warfare seems to be the source of it. According to the visions of Our Lady of All Nations, it apparently will be invented by a Russian, but "others" are also working on germ warfare.)

March 28, 1948 – The Fifteenth Message - A Warning of What is Coming – Possible Hidden Reference to the Three Days of Darkness

Our Lady said to Ida, *"Justice will be the point at issue. Within a very short time grave things are going to happen. These will be preceded by chaos, disorder, doubt and despair. Above St. Peter's heavy clouds will hang, which will be dispersed with much struggle and difficulty. Otherwise, perdition. All Christians must join forces. That will be accompanied by great pain and misery. Join forces, all of you, for the struggle begins. The gates are opening. The Eastern peoples are holding their hands before their faces in Jerusalem. They will wail over their city. There is a large well in which you all can wash yourselves."*

(Once again, Bucchianeri indicated the possibility that "the 'large well' related to Jerusalem could be a reference to Zachariah Ch. 13 where it is foretold a fountain will be opened to the House of David to wash the inhabitants of Jerusalem. It will happen when the Lord shall destroy all idols, false prophets and the unclean spirit from the earth. This renewal will happen when God has allowed two thirds of the earth to perish, and the last third to be tried by fire, according to verses 8-9 of Zachariah. This sounds exactly what has been foretold of the Three Days of Darkness – before it happens, there will be wars, chaos, doubt, then when the Days of Darkness hit, two thirds of the earth will perish, the last third will be a predestined generation that has made it through the fire. Of interest, the Great Monarch destined to restore the earth will be the last king of France according to the Great Monarch prophecies, and Tradition states the French kings descend from the House of David.")

Then I see written: "Righteousness," "Love" and "Justice."
The Lady says, "As long as these words are not kept before people's
eyes and are not lived in their hearts, there will be no peace in
sight." Then I see a Cross planted in the ground. A snake is wrig-
gling around it, and everything around me is growing black and
dark. Next, I see a sword hanging over Europe and the East. From
the West a light is coming. I hear the Lady say very seriously,
"Christian peoples, the heathens will teach it to you."

Then I see the Pope and around him a reinforced bodyguard.
There are also other people around him; it seems to me they are all
clerics—bishops and cardinals. While pointing at these clerics, the
Lady says, "Snares and traps." Having said this, the Lady looks at
me intently. Heavy clouds are hanging over St. Peter's. Then the
Lady says to all those who are sitting around the Pope, "Be right-
eous and act according to your teaching. Cover your eyes with your
hands and search your hearts." Then it is as if I would again receive
a Cross in my hand, and it hurts. It is so heavy that I can scarcely
hold it. The Lady says, "Grip it tightly." It is as if large rays would
stream forth from it. Then suddenly the Lady is gone, and so is the
light.

February 11, 1951 – The Twenty Seventh Message - Feast of Our Lady of Lourdes – Our Lady Warns the World is Entering a Time of Upheaval

Our Lady says to Ida, *"'Listen carefully, child. Changes have al-*
ready been made, and others are in progress. I, however, want to bring
the Son's message. The doctrine is right, but the laws can and must be
changed. I want to tell you this on this very day, for the world is under-
going great upheaval—nobody knows in which direction. That is why
the Son wants me to bring this message.' Let everyone come back to the
Cross; only then can there be peace and tranquility. Our Lady then
*gives the prayer that must be said before the Cross: '**Lord Jesus Christ,***
Son of the Father, send now Your Spirit over the earth. Let the Holy
Spirit live in the hearts of all nations, that they may be preserved from
degeneration, disaster and war. May the Lady of All Nations, the
Blessed Virgin Mary, be our Advocate. Amen.'

'Child, this is so simple and short that everyone can say it in
one's own language, before one's own crucifix; and those who have
no crucifix say it to themselves. This is the message which I want to
give this very day, for I am now coming to say that I want to save
souls. All of you, cooperate in this great work for the world. If only
every child of man would try to live up to this for oneself.' And then

the Lady raises a finger and says, 'Especially in the first and greatest commandment, Love.' I now see this word written in large letters. 'Let them begin with that,' the Lady says. Then I see a certain group of people; the Lady looks at them very compassionately and says, 'And then the little ones of this world will say: how can we begin with that? For it is the great ones who do this to us.' The Lady says this very lovingly, as if she had great pity on the people around her. But then the Lady's face changes, and she says very emphatically, 'And then I say to the little ones: if you practice love among your-selves in all its refinement, even the great ones will not have a chance. Go to your crucifix and say what I recited to you, and the Son will answer it.

'A great natural disaster will again take place. The great ones of this world will always disagree with one another. People will seek here and there. Watch out for the false prophets. Seek and ask only for the true Holy Spirit. For it is now a war of ideas. The fight no longer concerns races and peoples; the fight concerns the spirit. Un-derstand this well.

'You can save this world. I have said more than once: Rome has its chance. Seize the present moment. No church in the world is built-up like yours. But move with the times and insist upon your modern changes concerning religious, priests, seminarians, and so on and so forth. Keep an eye on that. Carry through with it to the smallest detail! The doctrine remains, but the laws can be changed. Let the people of this world benefit more from the Remembrance of my Son.

'I showed you in the dream how the practice of frequent com-munion can be carried through. This I tell you for the Netherlands and for all countries in which it is not so. For Germany I want to say: they shall work hard, hard in this country to bring the people, who have strayed far, far away, back to this center, the Cross. Priests are too few, but lay people are many. Conduct a great cam-paign among the laity to call them forward for this goal. Work here above all with great love and charity. The great ones of Germany shall help and not turn away from the Church. Deutschland jedoch liegt mir sehr am Herzen. Die Mutter Gottes weint über die Kinder Deutschlands. (Our Lady spoke this in German: 'My heart is greatly concerned for Germany. The Mother of God weeps for the people of Germany.') *For France, Belgium, the Balkans and Aus-tria I say the following: do not let yourselves be brought to the wrong spirit. For Italy I say: great ones of Italy, do you know your task? To England I say: I will come back, England. To America I say: do not push your politics too far; and seek the True Spirit. I*

*am glad that America is better disposed to the faith at the moment.
For Africa I say: say that I would like to have a seminary there. I
will help the Dominicans. ....Further, I would like to say to all Eastern and Asian peoples, whether they know the Son or not: We are
taking care of them. '"[365]*

March 28, 1951 - Twenty-Ninth Message – The Prayer Must be Prayed, Beware of Communism and False Prophets

Our Lady then gives an urgent message [that] *this new prayer
and image must be spread "Otherwise the world will fall into degeneration. Otherwise the world will destroy itself. Otherwise there will
be war upon war and no end to destruction.*

*"Rome must know her task in this time. Does Rome realize which
enemy is lying in wait and creeping like a snake throughout the
world? And by this I do not mean communism alone; other prophets
will come—false prophets. That is why those means should be made
use of. I stand as the Lady before the Cross, as the Mother before my
Son, Who, through the Father, entered into me. And this is why I
stand before my Son, as the Advocate and bearer of this message to
this modern world. "[366]*

August 15, 1951 – The Thirty-Fifth Message – More Disasters Result from a World Falling Into Degeneration

*I have said: disasters will come, natural disasters. I have said: the
great ones will disagree with one another. I have said: the world is falling into degeneration. That is why the Father and the Son now sends
the Lady back into the world as she was. The Lady was once known as
Mary. The world is falling into degeneration, is in degeneration. The
Netherlands is on the brink of degeneration; that is why I have put my
foot on it. From the Netherlands I want to give my words to the world.
My other foot is placed on Germany. Die Mutter Gottes weint über die
Kinder Deutschlands. They have always been my children, and that is
why, from Germany too, I wish to be brought into the world as the Lady
of All Nations. I shall help you and all who see to this. I even want the
outspreading to penetrate into those countries which are cut off from
others. There also will the Lady of All Nations give her blessing. See to
this; do not hesitate. For I myself never hesitated. I went before the Son
on the way to the Cross. This image shall precede. This image shall be
brought into the world. Do you realize, Rome, how much everything is
being undermined? Years will pass by, years will elapse. But the more
the years, the less faith; the more the years, the greater the apostasy.*

The Lady of All Nations stands here and says, I want to help them, and I may help them.[367]

(Of this final end-times prophecy, Bucchianeri notes with interest that Our Lady would announce later in the Fifty-Second Message that the Fifth Marian Dogma must be declared in the year 1960 – which was not done. She also [points out that] 1960 was the year Sr. Lucia of Fatima directed that the Third Secret of Fatima warning the world was to be opened, and that did not happen either at the time. It appears Our Lady of All Nations here in the Thirty-Fifth Vision was giving a warning what would happen if the Church dragged its heels with regards to proclaiming her as Coredemptrix, Mediatrix, and Advocate. Our Lady had said until the new Marian Dogma is declared, there would be no true peace, but war upon war and the world going to destruction – and as we can see, we have seen the years elapse since she asked for this, and, there indeed is less faith and now, a growing apostasy which has been foretold by other mystics.)

20th Century – 1957: Sister Lucy's Last Public Interview (Prophecy Detail – The great chastisement, The final battle between the devil and the Virgin Mary)

Lucia Dos Santos was the oldest of the three children who saw Our Lady of the Rosary in Fatima, Portugal in 1917. As promised by Our Lady, she was the only one of the visionaries who would survive to old age. Over the years, Lucia continued to have visions of the Virgin Mary, though she was able to speak about them less and less as a result of an order of her bishop. On December 26, 1957, however, she granted a public interview to Fr. Augustin Fuentes, a Mexican priest named vice-postulator of the cause of beatification for Francisco and Jacinta, the other two visionaries and Lucia's first cousins.

In the interview, Lucia told Fr. Fuentes that Our Lady told her:

The last means that God will give to the world for its salvation are the Holy Rosary and My Immaculate Heart.[368]

The following text of that interview has the approval and imprimatur of Archbishop Sanchez of Santa Cruz, Mexico and is reprinted here in its entirety.

Father, the Blessed Virgin is very sad because no one has paid attention to her Message, neither the good nor the bad. The good, because they continue on the road of goodness, but without paying mind to this Message. The bad, because of their sins, do not see God's chastisement already falling on them presently; they also continue on their path of badness, ignoring the Message. But, Father, you must believe me that God is going to punish the world and chastise it in a tremendous way.

The chastisement from Heaven is imminent. The year 1960 is on us, and then what will happen? It will be very sad for everyone, and far from a happy thing if the world does not pray and do penance before then. I cannot give more details, because it is still a secret. By the will of the Blessed Virgin, only the Holy Father and the Bishop of Fatima can know the secret. Both have chosen, however, not to open it in order not to be influenced by it.*

This is the third part of the Message of Our Lady, which still remains secret until 1960. Tell them, Father, that the Blessed Virgin said repeatedly – to my cousins Francisco and Jacinta as well as to me – that many nations would disappear from the face of the earth, that Russia would be the instrument of chastisement from Heaven for the whole world if the conversion of that poor Nation is not obtained beforehand. ...

Father, the Devil is fighting a decisive battle against the Virgin and, as you know, what most offends God and what will gain him the greatest number of souls in the shortest time is to gain the souls consecrated to God. For this also leaves unprotected the field of the laity and the Devil can more easily seize them.

Also, Father, tell them that my cousins Francisco and Jacinta made sacrifices because they always saw the Blessed Virgin was very sad in all her apparitions. She never smiled at us. This anguish that we saw in her, caused by offenses to God and the chastisements that threaten sinners, penetrated our souls. And being children, we did not know what measures to devise except to pray and make sacrifices.

For this reason, Father, it is my mission not just to tell about the material punishments that will certainly come over the earth if the world does not pray and do penance. No, my mission is to tell

---

*In 1943, the Bishop of Fatima, José Correia da Silva, authorized Sister Lucia to write down the Third Secret during her bout with pleurisy, which threatened her life. On June 17, 1944, this document was officially placed in his hands. When Sister Lucia gave the letter to Bishop da Silva, she told him that he could read it, but he refused. Instead, he ordered the sealed document to be kept in the safe of the Episcopal Curia. Pope Pius XII also chose not to read the message and left it in the care of Bishop da Silva until 1957, when the sealed envelope was sent to Rome at his request.

everyone the imminent danger we are in of losing our souls for all eternity if we remain fixed in sin.

Father, we should not wait for a call to the world from Rome on the part of the Holy Father to do penance. Nor should we wait for a call for penance to come from the Bishops in our Dioceses, nor from our Religious Congregations. No, Our Lord has often used these means, and the world has not paid heed. So, now each one of us must begin to reform himself spiritually. Each one has to save not only his own soul, but also all the souls that God has placed on his pathway.

Father, the Blessed Virgin did not tell me that we are in the last times of the world, but I understood this for three reasons:

The first is because she told me that the Devil is engaging in a battle with the Virgin, a decisive battle. It is a final battle where one party will be victorious and the other will suffer defeat. So, from now on, we are either with God or we are with the Devil; there is no middle ground.

The second reason is because she told me, as well as my cousins, that God is giving two last remedies to the world: the Holy Rosary and devotion to the Immaculate Heart of Mary. And, being the last remedies, that is to say, they are the final ones, means that there will be no others.

And the third, because in the plans of the Divine Providence, when God is going to chastise the world, He always first exhausts all other remedies. When He sees that the world pays no attention whatsoever, then, as we say in our imperfect way of talking, with a certain fear He presents us the last means of salvation, His Blessed Mother.

If we despise and reject this last means, Heaven will no longer pardon us, because we will have committed a sin that the Gospel calls a sin against the Holy Spirit. This sin consists in openly reject-ing – with full knowledge and will – the salvation that is put in our hands.

Also, since Our Lord is a very good Son, He will not permit that we offend and despise His Blessed Mother. We have as obvious tes-timony the history of different centuries where Our Lord has shown us with terrible examples how He has always defended the honor of His Blessed Mother.

Prayer and sacrifice are the two means to save the world. As for the Holy Rosary, Father, in these last times in which we are living, the Blessed Virgin has given a new efficacy to the praying of the Holy Ro-sary. This in such a way that there is no problem that cannot be resolved by praying the Rosary, no matter how difficult it is - be it temporal or above all spiritual - in the spiritual life of each of us or the lives of our families, be they our families in the world or Religious Communities, or even in the lives of peoples and nations.

I repeat, there is no problem, as difficult as it may be, that we cannot resolve at this time by praying the Holy Rosary. With the Holy Rosary we will save ourselves, sanctify ourselves, console Our Lord and obtain the salvation of many souls.

Then, there is devotion to the Immaculate Heart of Mary, our Most Holy Mother, holding her as the seat of mercy, goodness and pardon and the sure door to enter Heaven. This is the first part of the Message referring to Our Lady of Fatima, and the second part, which is briefer but no less important, refers to the Holy Father.[369]

20ᵗʰ Century – June 18, 1961 – June 18, 1965: Our lady of Garabandal in Apparitions to Mari Loli Mazon, Jacinta Gonzalez, Mari Cruz Gonzalez, and Maria "Conchita" Concepcion Gonzalez *(Prophecy Detail – The tribulation, The warning, The illumination of conscience.)*

In 1961, the small hamlet of San Sebastian de Garbandal boasted a population of some three hundred people who lived in eighty dwellings. It was hardly a speck on the map, that is, until the evening of June 18, 1961. On that day, four girls reported having had a vision of an Angel. Eleven-year-old Mari Loli Mazón, Jacinta González, Maria "Conchita" Concepcion González, and twelve-year-old Mari Cruz González* were playing together in the southern part of the village when they heard the sound of thunder. They turned to see an Angel, with a dazzling appearance, standing before them. The Angel said nothing and vanished within a few seconds. Frightened, the children ran to the village church. Their ashen-white faces prompted a series of questions from others who quickly discovered the truth.

The Angel appeared to them eight more times over a period of twelve days, finally speaking to the children on July 1. *"Do you know why I have come,"* the Angel asked the children. *"It is to announce to you that tomorrow, Sunday, the Virgin Mary will appear to you as Our Lady of Mount Carmel."*[370] After preparing the children for an apparition from the Blessed Virgin, the Angel disappeared.

*None of the children are related though three of them share a common surname.

The news spread throughout the small village like wildfire and on Sunday, July 2, a number of visitors, including several priests, were on hand to witness the apparition. At about six o'clock in the evening, the children, with the crowd in tow, departed for the spot where they had been seeing the Angel. The Virgin, flanked by two Angels, was already waiting. A large eye that seemed to the children to be the eye of God, was suspended above the apparition. The children spoke to Our Lady and prayed the rosary. The children said that during this vision, Our Lady told them that:

> *We must make many sacrifices, perform much penance and visit the Blessed Sacrament frequently. But first we must lead good lives. If we do not, a chastisement will befall us. The cup is already filling up and if we do not change, a great chastisement will come upon all humanity.*[371]

Over the next four years Mary appeared to the children about two thousand times; occasionally She would appear several times in a single day. Each appearance was preceded by three interior calls. On the third call the children would run to the apparition site and fall into ecstasy. While in ecstasy, the children could not feel pin pricks and their pupils would dilate. Also, during this time, it was impossible to lift them. They could lift each other with ease, as they often lifted one after the other to kiss the Virgin, but even the strongest onlooker could not lift the ecstatic children off the ground. Before experiencing ecstasy, the children would fall hard to their knees on the rocky path without flinching. Those close by could hear the horrible sound of the children's knees hitting the rocks. Still, they were unhurt. At times, their stiffened bodies would fall backward without bracing themselves. Despite their heads hitting the rocks with significant force, the children were unhurt. Many of the witnesses, including several priests, witnessed the girls running backwards along the rocky path at great speeds, their feet elevated off the ground. On one occasion a priest reported that he witnessed the children cross a wide stream, two of them using the foot bridge, the other two walking on air. It was also noted that while in ecstasy, the girls could hear the private thoughts of other people.

On August 8, 1961, Fr. Luis Maria Andreu, a Jesuit, was observing the girls in ecstasy when he too was able to see the Blessed Virgin and a great Miracle that was to come. He yelled out four times, *"Miracle."* While no one else in the crowd was privy to the vision, they could clearly see the priest's tear-soaked face altered during this time. Later that evening, as he was being driven home by friends, he said, *"What a wonderful present the Virgin has given me! How lucky to have a mother like that in Heaven! We shouldn't be afraid of the supernatural... Today is the happiest day of my life!"*[372] Then Fr. Luis bowed his head, and despite not having been sick, died. It was said that he died of joy.

Among the discussions that Our Lady had with the children were several prophecies pertaining to the end times. This is a summary of those prophecies:

The Tribulation:

On June 19, 1962, at 10:30 in the evening, the Blessed Mother appeared to Jacinta Cruz, Mari Cruz and Mari Loli and showed to them a series of event that would take place before God's Warning. The onlookers, standing a distance away at the request of Our Lady, could hear the scream of the children as they witnessed these events roll before their eyes like a movie. The vision lasted for fifty minutes. Everyone was so frightened by the reaction of the girls that most made their Confessions and received Holy Communion the following morning thinking that the world might be coming to an end. The girls wouldn't speak of the vision for some five years until the silence was broken beginning in 1967 and culminating in 1978 when Mari Loli revealed the following:

"Although we continued to see the Blessed Virgin, we saw a great multitude of people who were suffering intensely and screaming in terror. The Blessed Virgin explained to us that this tribulation would come because a time would arrive when the Church would appear to be on the point of perishing. It would pass through a terrible trial. We asked the Virgin what this great trial was, and She told us it was 'Communism.' Russia will suddenly and unexpectedly overrun and overwhelm a great part of the free world. It was all related to communism and what is going to happen in the Church and to the people because all these things are to have repercussions amongst the people. When communists will create such confusion that people will not know right from wrong."

In 1979, Jacinta added, "These difficult events will take place before the Warning, because the Warning itself will occur when the situation will be at its worst." Conchita, who was not present during the apparition of June 19, said that the duration of the tribulation is unclear, but "The pope will go to Russia, to Moscow and after his return to the Vatican, hostilities will break out in different parts of Europe."[373]

The Warning (Illumination of Conscience):

On January 1, 1965, Our Lady told Conchita that God would send a great "Warning" of supernatural magnitude described as a "Mystical Experience" or an "Illumination of Consciences." Conchita said:

First, a World-Wide Warning that will happen in the sky...like a collision of two stars that do not fall down...it will frighten all humanity regardless of where one happens to be at the time...it will be a thousand times worse than earthquakes...like a fire that will not burn our flesh...it will last a very short time, although to us it will seem to be a very long time...no one can prevent it from happening...It will be recognized as coming from God...it will resemble a punishment...it is meant to be a purification...like the revelation of our sins and what we will feel in our hearts will be worse than sorrow. It will not kill us; if we die it will be caused by the emotion within us. The date was not revealed, only that it will happen before the announcement of the miracle. The Warning is a thing that comes directly from God and will be visible throughout the entire world in whatever place anyone might be.[374]

The following is a compilation of what the four children said at various times regarding their revelation of the Warning:

Maria "Conchita" Concepcion Gonzalez:

The Warning is something supernatural and will not be explained by science. It will be seen and felt. The Warning will be a correction of the conscience of the world. For those who do not know Christ, they will believe it is a Warning from God. The most important thing about that day is that everyone in the whole world will see a sign, a grace, or a punishment within themselves, in other words, a Warning.

They will find themselves all alone in the world no matter where they are at the time, alone with their conscience right before God. They will then see all their sins and what their sins have caused.

We will all feel it differently because it will depend on our conscience. The Warning will be very personal, therefore, we will all react differently to it. The most important thing will be to recognize our own sins and the bad consequences of them.

Your experience of the Warning will be different from mine because your sins are different from mine. This will be a Warning to see what you have done with your sins. It will be like a purification before the Miracle to see if with the Warning and Miracle we will be converted.

The Virgin told me that before the Miracle, God will be sending us a Warning so as to purify us or prepare us to see the Miracle and, in this way, draw enough grace to change our lives toward God. It is a phenomenon which will be seen and felt in all the world and everywhere; I have always given as an example that of two stars that collide.

This phenomenon will not cause physical damage, but it will horrify us because at that very moment we will see our souls and the harm we have done. It will be as though we were in agony, but we will not die by its effects but perhaps we will die of fright or shock to see ourselves. No one will have doubts of it being from God.

I, who know what it is, am very much afraid of that day. The Virgin told us that the Warning and Miracle will be the last warnings or public manifestations that God will give us. This is why I believe that after them we will be near the end of time.

To me it's like two stars that crash and make a lot of noise and a lot of light, but they don't fall down. It's something that's not going to hurt us but we're going to see it. In that moment, we're going to see our conscience. You're going to see everything wrong that you're doing and the good you're not doing.[375]

Marie Loli Mazon:

Everyone will experience it wherever they may be, regardless of their condition or their knowledge of God. It will be an interior personal experience. It will look as if the world has come to a standstill, however, no one will be aware of that as they will be totally absorbed in their own experience.

It is going to be something like an interior feeling of sorrow and pain for having offended God. God will help us see clearly the harm we are causing Him and all the evil things we do. He will help us sense this interior pain because often when we do something wrong, we just ask the Lord's forgiveness with our lips, but now (through the Warning) *He will help us sense physically that deep sorrow.*[376]

Jacinta Gonzalez:

The Warning is something that is first seen in the air everywhere in the world and immediately is transmitted into the interior of our souls. It will last for a very little time, but it will seem a very long time because of its effect within us. It will be for the good of our souls, in order to see in ourselves our conscience, the good and the bad that we've done.[377]

The Great Miracle:

Our Lady told the children that within twelve months after the Warning, a great miracle will take place at grove of the pine trees overlooking the Garabandal village. Conchita was told both the nature and exact time of the great miracle but cannot reveal it until eight days prior. This is the same miracle that Our Lady allowed Fr. Luis Andreu to witness just prior to his death on August 8, 1901. On August 10, 1971, Conchita was talking to a group of Americans when she offered the following information about the event:

> It will take place on or between the eighth and sixteenth of March, April or May. It will not happen in February or June.
> It will be on a Thursday at 8:30 p.m.. It will coincide with a great Ecclesiastical event in the Church. It will be on the Feast-day of a young martyred Saint of the Eucharist. It will last fifteen minutes. All those either in the village or on the surrounding mountains, which will serve as a "natural" amphitheater, will see it. The sick who come to Garabandal on that day will be cured, unbelievers will be converted. It will be the greatest miracle that Jesus has ever performed in the world. On the day after the miracle, the body of Fr. Luis Andreu will be removed from his grave and will be found to be in-corrupt. As a consequence of the miracle, Russia and other countries will be converted. There will remain a permanent sign at "The Pines" as a proof of Our Lady's tremendous love for all her children. It will be capable of being filmed, photographed and televised.
> Our Lady has promised the great miracle in Garabandal so that all may believe the Apparitions and be obedient to the messages. As the punishment which we deserve for the sins of the world is great, the miracle must also be great, for the world needs it.[378]

Our Lady granted Conchita permission to announce the date of the miracle eight days in advance. The miracle will provide the second opportunity (the Warning is the first) for people to change their lives before the chastisement.

The Permanent Sign:

On September 14, 1965, Conchita said:

> The sign that will remain forever at the Pines, will have never been seen before on earth, and is something we will be able to photograph, televise and see, but not touch. It will be evident that it is not a sign of this world but from God.[379]

The Conditional Chastisement:

On June 20, 1962, at half past ten in the evening, the four girls went to the cuadro. As was the case on the night prior, the people remained at a distance at the request of Our Lady. No one except the children went beyond the last house in the village. The Virgin then gave the children a vision of a terrible chastisement from God, telling them that the punishment was conditional and could be averted if mankind heeds Her message.

> *If it happens it will be more terrible than anything we can possibly imagine because it will be the result of the direct intervention of God. It will have nothing to do with wars, revolutions, or the hardness of men's hearts.*[380]

Conchita would later say that Our Lady assumed a look of great sadness:

> *We have never seen Her look so serious. She said, "The cup is already filling." She spoke in a very low voice. Our Lady made us see how the great chastisement for all humanity would come and how it comes directly from God. In a certain moment not a single motor or machine will function. A terrible heat wave will come, and men will suffer a burning thirst. Desperately they will look for water but with the intense heat it will evaporate. With this, there will enter into the people a desperation and they will attempt to kill each other, but in those moments their strength will fail, and they will fall to the ground. God then will make them see that it is He who directly has permitted all this. Finally, we saw a multitude of people enveloped in flames – desperately they threw themselves into the seas and lakes but upon entering the water, far from putting out the flames the water was boiling and seemed to help the flames burn more. I asked the Blessed Virgin to take all our children with Her, but She said that when this happens, they will all be adults.*[381]

Conchita later wrote:

> *I cannot reveal what kind of punishment it is except that it will be a result of the direct intervention of God, which makes it more terrible and fearful than anything we can imagine. It will be less painful for innocent babies to die a natural death than for those babies to die because of the punishment. All Catholics should go to confession before the punishment and the others should repent of*

their sins. When I saw it (punishment), *I felt a great fear even though at the same time I was seeing Our Blessed Mother. The punishment, if it comes, will come after the Miracle.*[382]

20th Century – 1973-1981: Sister Agnes Sasagawa *(Prophecy Detail – The great chastisement, Three days of darkness)*

Agnes Sasagawa was born prematurely to Buddhist parents in Joetsu City, Japan on May 28, 1931. As a young child she suffered poor health, most likely a consequence of her premature birth. To further exacerbate her health issues, a botched operation on her appendix rendered her immobile for about ten years.

While under the care of a Catholic nun at the Institute of Handmaids of the Eucharist, Agnes was given a vial that contained water from the miraculous Spring of Lourdes. Her health began to improve upon drinking the water. This miracle was enough for Agnes to convert to Catholicism. Over the course of the next few years, Agnes lost her hearing, but was undeterred in her new faith. She entered the convent near Akita, Japan on May 12, 1973.

Exactly one month after becoming a nun, on June 12, 1973, when she opened the tabernacle for adoration of the Blessed Sacrament, she saw a very strong light emanate from it, filling the entire chapel. This happened for three days. Upon a closer inspection, she noticed "spiritual beings" kneeling in worship to the Eucharist. This happened to her on more than one occasion. When she asked, the other Sisters reported that they had seen nothing out of the ordinary.

Concerned, she mentioned these apparitions to her local bishop, John Ito, who urged her to keep it in her heart. That same month Sister Agnes began to experience the stigmata. The initial pain would begin on Thursdays, but it wasn't until Friday that a cross of blood would appear on her left hand, a wound that remained through Saturday.

In the chapel was a wooden statue of the Virgin Mary. While praying before the statue, Sister Agnes noticed tears running down Our Lady's face. Sister Agnes heard the statue call her name. It was then, July 6, 1973, that Sister Agnes witnessed the first apparition of the Blessed Virgin Mary.

The phenomenon of the weeping statue was witnessed by Sister Agnes and many others on 101 occasions. Other nuns in the convent also reported seeing stigmata on the statue, which reportedly started before the tears and ended after the tears had stopped.

In all, the Blessed Mother appeared to Sasagawa three times. It was in the third appearance, however, that Sister Agnes received a terrifying and sobering message of chastisement and a call to prayer and repentance. Many believe that this message of Our Lady of Akita is the final part of the third secret of Fatima.

The first message was received by Sister Agnes Katsuko Sasagawa on June 6, 1973. It was a call for prayer and sacrifice for the glory of the Father and salvation of souls. The second message, August 3, 1973, was for prayer, penance, and courageous sacrifices to soften the Father's anger.

The third message was received on October 13, 1973 after Sister Agnes witnessed the statue become animated for an extended period. This phenomenon was also witnessed by a number of nuns at the convent. Following is the third message of Our Lady of Akita:

> *As I told you, if men do not repent and better themselves, the Father will inflict a terrible punishment on all humanity. It will be a punishment greater than the deluge, such as one will never have seen before. Fire will fall from the sky and will wipe out a great part of humanity, the good as well as the bad, sparing neither priests nor faithful. The survivors will find themselves so desolate that they will envy the dead. The only arms which will remain for you will be the Rosary and the Sign left by my Son. Each day recite the prayers of the Rosary. With the Rosary, pray for the Pope, the bishops and the priests. The work of the devil will infiltrate even into the Church in such a way that one will see cardinals opposing cardinals, and bishops against other bishops. The priests who venerate me will be scorned and opposed by their Confreres. The Church and altars will be vandalized. The Church will be full of those who accept compromises and the demon will press many priests and consecrated souls to leave the service of the Lord. The demon will rage especially against souls consecrated to God. The thought of the loss of so many souls is the cause of my sadness. If sins increase in number and gravity, there will no longer be pardon for them.*
>
> *I have prevented the coming of calamities by offering to the Father, together with all the victim souls who console Him, the sufferings endured by the Son on the Cross, by His blood and by His very loving Soul. Prayer, penance, and courageous sacrifices can appease the anger of the Father.*
>
> *Live in poverty, sanctify it and pray in reparation for the ingratitude and the outrages of so many men.*[383]

Finally, on October 6, 2019, an aging Sasagawa had an apparition from her angel. That the apparition took place on the opening day of the Amazon Synod, one that some feel may have provided some confusing messages, may be coincidence. During the apparition, the angel offered Sister Agnes one more suggestion of repentance:

Put on ashes and pray a repentant Rosary every day.[384]

While Sister Agnes believes that the message may have been directed only to her, it is not bad advice for the balance of the world. The Vatican has not yet approved this final apparition as authentic.

20th Century – 1980: Fr. Bernardo Martinez/Apparitions of Cuapa, Nicaragua *(Prophecy Detail: Continued sufferings for Nicaragua, Request to pray the Rosary with Biblical meditations, Renew first Saturday devotions. In subsequent apparitions in later years the Virgin Mary spoke of the destruction of atheistic Communism. She also requested the propagation of the devotion to the shoulder wounds of Christ.)*

Bernardo Martinez was born in Cuapa, Nicaragua on August 29, 1931. His family, which included two brothers and three sisters, was struggling financially, so Bernardo was raised by Dona Eloisa James, his maternal grandmother. Though uneducated and illiterate, Dona had grounded common sense and a good memory. She taught Bernardo how to say his prayers and instilled in him a strong faith. Bernardo's mother died when he was eighteen, so he continued to live with his Dona until she died in 1974. As a result of his pious upbringing, Bernardo felt a calling to the priesthood, but that idea was vehemently opposed by his family. For the sake of familial peace, Bernardo did as they asked. Instead, he worked as a farmer and became a member of a Neocatechumenal community. There, he was given the keys to, and entrusted with the care of, the small chapel.

Beginning in 1980, while in the chapel, forty-seven-year-old Bernardo was blessed with apparitions of the Blessed Virgin Mary. At the request of Bishop Pablo Antonia Vega, Bernardo reduced to writing all of the events that took place in the Valley of Cuapa. This is his story in his own hand.

It was in the old chapel that the signs started on a date that I don't remember, maybe at the end of March. Upon entering the sacristy, I saw that there was light. I later blamed it on Ms. Auxiliadora Martinez because I thought she had left it on. Another day, I entered the chapel and I found the light on again, it may have been in the first days of April. I wanted to reproach Mrs. Socorro Barea. I did not think that these signs came from Heaven, this is the reason why I wanted to tell these ladies, because of the cost of electricity, to pay more attention to the light because we had very little money.

The keys had been entrusted to me, and whoever is in charge of the keys to a house must take great care of them. It was my concern. But when I wanted to go and reprimand them on the way to their home ... I couldn't tell them anything. I understood that they were not responsible. I would have blamed them unfairly. So, I decided to say nothing and pay the expenses myself.

On April 15, 1980, I saw the statue, all lit. I thought it was the boys playing in the square who had broken the roof tiles, so that the light lit up the statue. I thought that they [the church] *should be reimbursed for the tiles and the repair costs, because that had already happened before. I approached to look and saw that there was no hole in the roof. I went back to the statue to see if someone had put a phosphorescent string on it. I examined the hands, the feet, the neck...it was none of that. The light came from nowhere: it emanated from her. It was a great mystery to me, the light emanated from her to such an extent that one could walk without tripping.*

I arrived late. It was dark. It was almost eight in the evening. I realized that it was a strange thing, something not ordinary, in myself I say to myself, "The Blessed Virgin comes to reprimand us." I decided to ask their forgiveness because I was so moved to have seen it all lit. I saw it very beautiful, the statue, now I don't see it anymore. I went to ring the church bell, and because I was an hour late, and with the incident of light, the prayer of the rosary was even more late. Everything I had seen was etched in my mind and I thought "I am at fault."

As these thoughts crossed my mind, I remembered something my grandmother said to me when I was a child: "Never be a light in the street, and darkness at home." I understood my sin: I wanted others to make peace, but I was a source of discord at home. I say this because I had helped solve a problem in the city of Cuapa. There was a division among the residents, many of whom opposed the arrival of the Cubans for the literacy program. Little by little, talking to the priest, we settled everything calmly.

For his own impatience, and to anyone who may have been hurt by it, Bernardo made a public apology. He recounted the story of the light on the statue and asked that the group keep it a secret. Unfortunately, the secret was not kept, and Bernardo became the brunt of ridicule. The community priest was also told the "secret" and confronted Bernardo, asking to be told everything, including how the seer prayed. Bernardo told the priest that ever since he was young, his grandmother taught him to say the rosary and to call on Mary when he was having misfortunes, saying, *"Don't let me go, my Mother."* He recounted how it was that he learned to love Her, *"the love of my soul. She has guided each of my steps since my childhood. And thanks to that, since childhood, my love for her has always remained. She* [his grandmother] *taught me this from memory because she couldn't read."*

The priest responded by asking Bernardo to pray to the Blessed Virgin, asking if she expected something from him. So, Bernardo prayed, saying:

> *Very Holy Mother, please do not expect anything from me. I have a lot of problems in church. Make yourself known to another person because I want to avoid any problems. I already have a lot. I don't want any more.*

As time elapsed, the story of the light seemed to fade in people's memories, but Bernardo continued to pray as he had before. Rather than an affirmative response, however, Bernardo was made to,

> *understand that the Virgin wanted to prepare me as a farmer prepares the soil. After this public confession that I made before my brothers to whom I asked for forgiveness, a change took place in me... She prepared me for this transformation.*
>
> *On May 8, 1980, I felt sad due to financial, employment and spiritual problems. I even told myself in the morning that I wanted to die. I no longer wanted to exist. I had worked a lot for the townspeople, and I realized that they didn't like anything. I no longer wanted to continue. In the chapel, I had swept, dusted, washed the altar cloths, and blades, and in exchange I had been flouted, called an idiot. Even my own family, my blood brothers, said that if I had not succeeded financially, it was because of my commitment to the sacristy. I was a sacristan voluntarily. I have been working in the house of God since I was old enough to use rags and brooms ... I felt humiliated. I was doing it to serve the Lord.*
>
> *At night I slept badly. I was very hot... I had little lunch and said to myself, "I will go fishing in the river so that I will be cool and calm." I left early in the morning with a bag and a machete and headed for the river. I felt happy, content in a pleasant environment. I had forgotten everything. When it was noon, I did not want to leave,*

so much did I feel at peace. I did not feel hungry. Suddenly it started to rain, and I took shelter under a tree where I began to pray the Rosary. I was all wet and my clothes were soaked. I picked up the fish from the sand, put them in a bag, and went under a mango tree to see if any fruit was ripe.

I then went to a hill to cut a branch to pick berries, then I went to a jocote tree. The hours had passed like minutes. I say to myself: "It's late." I remembered that I had to feed the animals and that I had to go to town to pray the Rosary with people at five o'clock... when suddenly I saw a lightning bolt. I thought, "It's going to rain." But I was intrigued because I couldn't see where the light was coming from. I stopped but I saw neither rain nor anything. Then I headed for a rocky place (...). It was then that I saw another flash in the middle of which She appeared.

I wondered if it was an illusion or if it was the same luminous statue as in the chapel. But I saw her eyes blink. How beautiful she was... She was standing on a cloud like foam, above a pile of stone...The cloud was very white, the rays melted with the sunlight. Barefoot...her dress was long and white. She had a gold belt around her waist. Her sleeves were long. She was covered with a pale veil, with borders embroidered with gold. Her hands were joined on her chest. It looked like the statue of the Virgin of Fatima. I remained motionless, unable to run or scream. I was not afraid, I was amazed."

The Virgin stretched out her arms and emanating from her hands were rays of light that reached Bernardo's chest.

"It was when She emitted Her light that I was encouraged to speak. I ask her, "What is your name?" She answers in a soft voice: "Mary," then I ask her where she comes from. "I come from Heaven. I am the Mother of Jesus" Hearing this, I asked her, remembering the priest's request "What do you want?" She replied, "I want you to recite the Rosary every day...I want it to be prayed permanently, as a family, including with children old enough to understand; let it be prayed at a defined time when there are no problems with work in the house."

She tells me that the Lord does not like prayers that we make hastily or mechanically. For this reason, she recommended to pray the Rosary meditated with the Gospel to put into practice the Word of God. When I heard that, I said to myself "How is that," because I did not know that the Rosary was biblical. That's why I asked her, "Where are the meditations?" She told me to look for them in the Bible and went on to say, "Love each other. Fulfill your obligations.

Make peace. Do not ask our Lord for peace because if you do not do it there will be no peace. Repeat the first five Saturdays. You received many graces when you all did this."

Before the war, we used to do this. We went to Confession and Communion every First Saturday of the month. But since the Lord had set us free from the bloody battles in Cuapa, we no longer continued this practice.

Then she said: "Nicaragua has suffered a lot since the earthquake. It is threatened with more suffering. It will continue to suffer if you don't change." (Our Lady was referring to the devastating earthquake in Managua in 1972. Ten thousand people were killed, and property damage was in the millions. The prediction of another earthquake may have been a reference to the one that struck the region in 1992. Although not as deadly, it was followed by a tsunami that caused significant destruction.)

And after a brief pause, she said, "Pray! Pray, my son, the Rosary for the whole world. Tell believers and non-believers that the world is threatened by grave dangers. I ask the Lord to appease His Justice, but if you do not change, you will hasten the arrival of the third world war."

After saying these words, I realized that I had to tell people and I said to her, "Madam, I don't want any problems, I already have a lot of them in church. Ask someone else." She replied, "No, because Our Lord chose you to give the message."

The cloud rose and threw her arms in the air, like the statue of the Assumption that I have seen so many times in the cathedral of Juigalpa. She looked up at the sky, and the cloud that supported her raised her. She was like in a niche of light, and at a certain distance, She disappeared from my sight.

I then gathered the machete, the bag, and the branches and went to cut the coyoles thinking that I would not say anything to anyone about what I had seen and heard. I went to pray the Rosary in the chapel, without saying anything.

When I got home, I felt sad. My problems were growing. I prayed the Rosary again, asking the Most Holy Mother to free me from temptation, because I thought it was a temptation. During the night, I heard a voice asking me to speak. I awoke again, and I prayed the rosary again. I couldn't find peace. I didn't tell anyone because I didn't want people to talk about it. They were already speaking because of the statue I had seen lit. I thought, "Now it will be worse. I will no longer know peace."

I did not return to the place of the apparitions. The mangoes and jocotes were lost. I went to the river, but by another road. I go there every day to bathe and give my calf a drink. During this period of secrecy, a great weight seemed to have fallen, fell on me, and I heard something like a voice telling me to speak. But I didn't mean [to do] it. To forget my growing suffering, I tried to amuse myself. But nothing managed to interest me. I was looking for my friends in order to entertain myself, young and old friends, but to the best of my joy, I heard the voice and my sadness returned. I had become pale and thin. People asked me what was wrong if I was sick.

Eight days passed thus. On May 16, I was on my way to feed the calf. I crossed the pasture without finding the calf. I was walking with a stick in my hand...I saw a flash of light. It was noon. In full light, because as I said, it was a hot sunny day, there was an even stronger light than daylight. In that flash, She appeared. I saw Her in the same way as I had seen Her on May 8. She stretched out her hands and in the extension of her hands, the rays of light appeared to me. I stayed to watch it. I remained silent thinking, "It's Her! It is the same. The same Woman appeared to me again." I thought she was going to blame me for keeping from you what she asked me to say. I felt guilty for not talking about it the way she wanted it, and at the same time, in my mind, I said to myself, "I haven't been where she usually appears but She appears to me anywhere and now She's here. I'm going to be in good shape, She'll follow me wherever I go."

So, she said to me with her soft voice, but in a reproachful tone, "Why didn't you say what I asked you to say?" I replied, "Madam, it's that I'm scared. I am afraid of being ridiculed by people, afraid that they will laugh at me, that they will not believe me. Those who will not believe this will laugh at me. They will say that I am mad."

"Do not be afraid. I will help you. And talk to the priest." Then there was another flash, and She disappeared.

Then I continued on foot and discovered the calf that I had not seen before. I took her to the river, gave her some water, and returned home.

I got ready to go to the chapel while praying the Rosary. I thought I should speak to Mrs. Lilliam Riz from Martinez and Mrs. Socorro Barea from Marin. This is what I did. I trust them more than other people in the Cuapa community. I took them aside and told them everything I had seen and heard. They berated me...I promised that in the future I would speak. I went home to rest. The next day, at dawn, I felt a strange happiness. All the problems seemed to be resolved.

On May 17, everyone who came to my house heard what I had to say to them. Some believed me, others listened out of curiosity and pretended to believe me, others did not believe me and laughed. But it didn't matter to me. When the time came, we prayed the Rosary and then I told them everything.

Once again, I noticed the same thing; some believed, others did not, some listened, surprised, surprised. Others analyzed, others remained silent, others laughed and called me crazy, each according to how he felt, but nothing mattered to me. I felt the happiness of saying everything.

On May 19, I went to Juigalpa in the morning and told the priest what the Lady expected from me. I tell him everything I have seen and heard. He listened to me and said, "Could it be someone who wants to scare you in the hills?" I answered, no because it would be impossible in the river and in the hills where I will cut the cane as well as in the middle of the pastures where I pass because nobody can hide there. They would be exposed.

He said to me, "Perhaps it is a temptation that is persecuting you?" I replied that no, that I did not know. Because with him I could not say what I had seen and heard, but as regards temptation, I did not know because I did not know. He told me to go back and pray the Rosary at the place where the apparitions had taken place, to make the sign of the cross when I saw Her and not to be afraid, because whether it be good or bad nothing would happen to me. He also asked me, in the future, not to speak to anyone about what I would see or hear. But what I had already seen, I can tell the people of Cuapa. I consider this apparition as an extension of that of May 8 and I call it, that of the reprimand.

Bernardo returned to the site of the apparition as the priest had instructed but Our Lady did not return. That night, however, She did appear to Bernardo in a dream at the site of the apparition.

She gave me the same message as the first time. Then I entrusted her with certain intentions, because now people entrusted me with certain requests. She replied, "Some will be answered, others will not." She raised her right hand, indicating the space and said, "Look at the sky." I looked in that direction...She presented something like a film in the sky, which I will describe.

I saw a large group of people dressed in white walking towards the east. They went, all bathed in light and joy, they sang. I heard them, but I did not understand the words they said. It was a heavenly celebration. It was such happiness. Such incomparable joy that I have never seen it in any procession. Their bodies radiated light. I felt transported. I couldn't explain it to myself in my wonder. She said to me, "Look, here are the first communities of the beginnings of Christianity. These are the first catechumens. Many of them were martyrs. Do you want to be a martyr? Would you like to be a martyr?" At the time, I did not know exactly what it meant to be a martyr, I now know, having asked, that it is the one who openly confesses Jesus Christ in public, who is a witness ready to give his life. She asked me and I answered yes.

Then I saw another group. People were also dressed in white with luminous rosaries in their hands. The grains were very white and threw multicolored fires. One of them had a large open book. He read and after listening, they meditated silently. They seemed to be in prayer. After a moment of silent prayer, they prayed the Our Father and ten Hail Marys. I prayed with them. When the Rosary was finished, the Blessed Virgin said to me, "These are the first to whom I have given the Rosary. This is how I want you to pray the Rosary." I answered yes to the Lady. Some people told me that they may have been Dominicans. I do not know the religious and to date have never seen anyone of this order.

Then I saw a third group, all dressed in a brown dress. I thought I recognized Franciscans. Likewise, they prayed the Rosary. As they passed, after having prayed, the Lady said to me again, "They received the Rosary from the hands of the first."

After that, a fourth group arrived. It was a huge procession, dressed like us. They were so numerous that it would have been impossible for me to count them. Previously, I had seen many men and women, but this time it was like an army in battle with Rosaries in hand. They were dressed normally, in all colors. I was very happy to see them.

On July 8, 1980, about forty of us went to the place where the apparitions had taken place. We prayed and sang, but I did not see Her. In my prayers, I begged Her to see Her again.

At night, while sleeping, I had a dream. I dreamed that I was at the place of the apparitions, praying for the world. In my dream, I remembered that the Virgin asked me to pray for Nicaragua and for the whole world because of serious threatening dangers. I then remembered what the priest had told me when I had entrusted to him the message of the Virgin,_in particular, to pray for the men and women religious, the priests, and the Pope. Remembering all this, I began to pray, I began to entrust them. And I entrusted the whole of humanity to the Rosary.

There was a boy from Cuapa unjustly imprisoned, accused of being a counterrevolutionary against the Communist government. Her sister asked me to petition for him. She was very sad because she couldn't speak to him alone when she visited him in prison. After I finished the rosary, I realized that I had forgotten to pray for this boy, and I thought: "I will pray for him, but the Rosary takes me so long."

I thought in my dream the same way as in the place of the apparitions. I say to myself "I have to go home, otherwise I will be late. I'm going to say three Hail Mary's." In the dream, I knelt down and folded my arms. I looked up again, praying for the innocent boy. When I looked down and looked at the rocks where the Blessed Virgin had appeared, I saw an Angel.

He was dressed in a long white tunic. He was tall and very young. His body seemed to be bathed in light. He had a physique and a male voice. He wore no ornament, coat or crown. He was simple but beautiful. His feet were not on a cloud. They were bare. He had a warm, friendly demeanor and seemed very serene. I felt a respect for him, but my feeling towards him was different from what I felt before the Lady...With Her, I dare ask Her questions, talk to Her and make requests. With the Angel, I speak with difficulty.

I heard the Angel say to me, "Your prayer has been heard." After a moment of silence, he added, "Go and tell the prisoner's sister to console him on Sunday, because he is very sad; to advise him not to sign a document that they will urge him to sign, a paper in which he assumes his responsibility for some sum of money; she shouldn't worry; she can talk to him for a long time; she will be treated in a friendly manner; tell him to go to the Juigalpa Police headquarters on Monday to complete all stages of his release because he will be released that day; to take 1,000 córdobas as the amount of the fine."

I tell him that I had another request written by a cousin who lives in Zelaya. She had come to see me in Cuapa to ask me to speak to the Blessed Virgin about two concerns: a problem at home, alcoholism and another work problem due to the changes brought about by the Revolution. She wanted to know how to deal with her father and brother's alcoholism, because they got violent when they drank too much. She also wanted to know how to solve the problems she encountered in her teaching job. She had explained to me that she did not want to lose her job; that gradually led her to renounce her faith. It made her suffer a lot, because she didn't want to lose her job, much less deny her faith...I did not go into details.

The Angel replied, "The people around them should be patient with them, and not complain when they are drunk." Later, he added, "Go and tell them to stop this vice; to do it little by little. In this way, this desire will leave them." He told me to warn my [male] cousin that they were going to attack him; and that they would shoot him in the foot, injuring him in the left heel. Later, they would kill him. On hearing this, I was so afraid that I said to the Angel, "Could we not avoid my cousin, this misfortune, by reciting many Rosaries?" He replied, "No, he will die, but if he listens to your advice, his life can be prolonged." He then added, about my [female] cousin, "She shouldn't be afraid, and she should trust in Our Lord, it could do a lot of good for people."

He went on to say, "Don't turn your back on problems and don't curse anyone." And the Angel at the end, disappeared. I woke up. I immediately began to pray the Rosary, without being distracted by this dream. Then, I remembered its contents. I remembered everything. Everything was printed. I did not know what to think. But I choose to speak to the inmate's sister in secret because I feared that he would ignore his duty.

People said '\"Bernardo is crazy. You have to take him to the asylum." That's why I was afraid. I tell Madame Socorro to send her that it concerned her personally. I tell her the next day. She asked me how it would be possible since she was not allowed to speak with him. I tell her to trust the Lord, to go there and do whatever the angel asked. Together we prayed the Rosary for her brother who was in prison.

We went to see him on Sunday, July 13. She was alone with him for a long time, thanks to which she was able to tell him not to sign the document. They were all kind to her. When she returned to Cuapa the same day, Sunday afternoon, she asked for a loan of 1000 córdobas from a man who does not lend anything without guarantee. He gave it without any guarantee, without bail, and added, "If you want more, I'll give you more."

They presented the document to the boy, but he refused to sign it. Madame Socorro went to the Juigalpa police station on Monday to take all the necessary steps to eventually release him. She found the people at the station quite friendly. They released the brother by fining him 1000 córdobas. She tells them that she was poor, that they could lower the fine a little. They reduced it by 200 córdobas. Everything was accomplished.

They left quickly and returned to Cuapa where, arriving at my house, they expressed their gratitude to me. I told them not to thank *me, but rather to thank the Lord and the Blessed Virgin. I suggested that they pray the Rosary.*

Madame Socorro was very happy and asked me if she could tell people about it. I say yes. Many believed thanks to this event. And for me as for others, this providential outcome was perceived as a grace. He left prison on Monday July 14, and the next day I went to Zelaya to tell them about the message received. I spoke to three of them. She believed me and told me that she would continue to work as a teacher. My uncle listened and promised me that he would try to give up his vice little by little. Then I quickly went on horseback to my cousin's ranch, but he didn't believe me. He believed nothing. He listened out of politeness.

He was indifferent and even harsh because, in an insulting tone of voice, he said to me "Cousin, are you looking for an opportunity to have a drink?" I returned home with a feeling of sadness and prayed the Rosary for him.

A few days later, I heard that he had been robbed and assaulted at his home. I went back to Zelaya to give him advice and tell him to sell his ranch and return to Cuapa so he could avoid these incidents. He paid no attention to me despite what I had told him during the previous visit. It was already partly accomplished: I told him about a theft. They stole two mules from him. I told him about a break-in. They broke a door to him one night and stole it again. I told him that his left heel would be injured. It was so.

During this second visit to Zelaya, he showed me his wound, but did not believe it. He says it was a fluke. It hadn't brought about any change in him. Sad, I went back to Cuapa again, inconsolable! I insisted on praying the Rosary for him.

Two months and a day later, on September 9, 1980, his sister-in-law who lived in Cuapa and believed nothing I said, received a telegram informing her that my cousin had been found murdered.

The same day at midnight, according to the fourth vision, his corpse arrived in Cuapa. Everything the Angel had told me turned out to be correct. I made an appointment with the Lady, but it was cancelled. We couldn't go because the river was too deep, it was in flood. The current was too strong, and the river overflowed from its bed due to the strong wind. It rained abundantly all night and the day after the seventh day as well as all night the following day. It rained non-stop all day the eighth day of August. It was impossible to cross! I was accompanied by a group of women. Arriving at the edge of the river despite our will, it was impossible for us to cross. It would have been impossible, even on horseback."

In the rain, the group stuck in front of the river began to sing and pray the Rosary and became joyous, despite their circumstances. Once it was possible to cross, they joined at the place of the apparitions. The priest followed them. Up to that time Bernardo was convinced the priest never really believed him. Arrived at the place of the apparitions, the priest was astonished - *"I dreamed of this place last night ...*

The Lady did not appear. The priest told Bernardo to *"Pray, and She will appear again."*

On September 8, 1980, I went to the place of the apparitions in the hope of accomplishing what I had not achieved in August. I accompanied many people again, there were also children. We prayed the Rosary, and as soon as we were finished, I saw a bright light. We only saw this light. It was clear and there was no sign of rain. I say to myself internally, "The lady is about to arrive!" The other sign was the great inner joy that I know when I am about to see Her.

I then saw a second bright light, during which She always appears, and I saw her on a cloud. In this way, the Virgin Mary appeared. I saw her as a child. Magnificent! But small! She was dressed in a pale cream tunic, without veil, crown, coat, ornament, or embroidery. The dress and the sleeves were long, surrounded by a pink cord. Her brown hair fell on her shoulders.

The eyes were a light brown, almost the color of honey, while She radiated light. She looked like the Lady, but She was a child. I looked at her astonished, without saying a word, then I heard her voice which seemed to be that of a child. In a very beautiful voice, she gave the message, completely identical. First of all, I thought, since it was a child, that it would be easier to see her for those who accompany me. It was my concern. I thought, "The others should also see Her!" I tell her, "Let yourself be seen, so that everyone will believe You. These people who are gathered here, want to meet You." People could hear me, but they couldn't hear Her.

I spoke to her trying to persuade her to show up, but after listening to me She said, "No, you just have to give them the message; for the one who believes, it will be enough, and for the one who does not believe, even if he saw me, he would not believe with any advantage." Her words were fulfilled. I can now see an individual's disbelief or faith. The people who came do not try to see a sign, the message is enough for them, they receive it. Some have great needs, they do not ask for a miracle, they do not ask for healing, they prefer to trust the Lord. There are others who by signs have come to believe. I knew a man, who, filled with joy, said to me, "Bernardo, I now believe that the Virgin appeared. You're very lucky! I see her too." And he indicated the place. It is in the old chapel, where the altar was before. A few meters away there was another man who, when he saw me pass nearby, said to me full of indifference, "It is true that She is there. But it is nothing more than the beings of other planets. Who are they?"

This happened on May 7, 1981, the day before the first anniversary of the first appearance. I no longer insisted that She show herself, but rather told her about the church that people wanted to build in her honor. Father Domingo told us that it was a decision he could not make and that we had to tell the Blessed Virgin. She replied, "No! The Lord does not want material churches, He wants living temples that are yourselves. Restore the sacred temple of the Lord. The Lord takes pleasure in being present in you. Love each other. Forgive each other. Make peace. Don't just ask for it, do it."

At that moment, the shadow of a doubt came to my mind. I decided to entrust Her with this doubt: I did not know whether or not I should continue the catechumenate. I wanted Her to advise me. She said to me, "Always continue firmly in the catechumenate. Little by little, you will understand everything that the catechumenate means. As a community group, meditate on the Beatitudes in silence." Later she added, "I will not be back on October 8, but on October 13." Then the clouds rose as for each apparition.

On the 13th which was Monday we were about fifty people towards the place of the apparitions. Everyone prays and sings the rosary, when suddenly a luminous circle forms on the ground. The light came from above. It was like a fire which, falling on the ground, dispersed. Seeing that this light fell on the heads of those who were there, I turned to see what was happening and saw that a circle had also formed in the sky. We say to ourselves "His kingdom is in heaven as on earth." This circle gave colored lights that did not appear on the ground. Nothing like this is known here. A young girl, holding her mother by the hand, tried to get away from her, saying that the Lady was calling her. The mom held her even harder and didn't let her go. The mother told me about it after the apparitions were over.

It was three o'clock in the afternoon. We could feel a little breeze that was sweet like a cool wind that didn't offend us. During this phenomenon, we remained silent and continued to look at this circle on the ground like a midday sun. Suddenly, a light similar to the other apparitions appeared to me. I looked up and saw the Lady. The cloud was above the flowers we had placed, and above the feet of the beautiful Madonna. She stretched out her hands and sent rays of light to all of us.

Seeing her with her arms outstretched, I say to people, "Look at her, She is here!"

And no one contested me. I then asked the Lady to let herself be seen, that the people who were here wanted to see her. She replied, "No, not everyone can see me." And I tell people again that She was on the pile of stones above the flowers. I heard a few people cry. Some mumbled alone.

A lady named Mildred said to me, "I only see a shadow over the flowers." I turned to the Lady to ask again that she let herself be seen and She said, no to me.

So, I turned back to the people. "Look at the flowers on the stones!" No one contested. So, I say to her, "Lady, let them look at you to believe because many do not believe. They tell me that it is the devil who appears to me, that the Virgin is dead, like any mortal. But Lady, let them see you ..." She says no. And raising her hands to the chest, just like the image of the Virgin of Sorrows, these images that we see in the processions, during Holy Week, Her face became pale like that of the statue, her coat became grey, and then the sad look, and She cried. I cried too. I was trembling to see her like that and said to her "Lady, forgive me for what I said, I am the one who is guilty! You are saddened because of me. Excuse me! Excuse me!"

She replied, "I am not saddened and angry because of you."

I asked her, "And why are you crying? I see you cry."

She said to me, "It saddens me to see the hardness of the hearts of these people. But you will have to pray for them to change. Pray the Rosary. Meditate on the mysteries. Hear the Word of God communicated in these mysteries. Love each other. Forgive each other. Make peace. Do not ask for peace without making it because if you do not do it there is no point in asking for it. Fulfill your obligations. Practice the Word of God. Look for ways to please God. Serve your neighbor because in this way you will please Him."

When she finished giving her message, I remembered the request from the people of Cuapa. I said to her, "Lady, I have a lot of requests, but I forgot. There are many. You, my Lady, know them all."

Then She said to me, "They ask me things that are unimportant. Ask for Faith so that everyone has the strength to carry their cross. The suffering in this world cannot be removed. Suffering is the Cross that you have to bear. It's life. If there are problems with the husband, wife, children, brothers, speak, discuss, so that they may be resolved in peace. Do not use violence. Never use violence. Pray for the faith that will give you patience." In this way, She allowed me to understand that, if with faith, we ask to be released from suffering, we will only be released if suffering is not the Cross that we have to bear. But if suffering is a person's Cross, that weight will turn into glory. This is why She tells us to ask for faith to receive strength and patience. Then she said to me, "You will no longer see me in this place."

I thought I would never see her again and I started to lament, "Don't leave us, Mother! Don't leave us, Mother! Don't leave us, Mother!" [Our Lady replied,]

"Do not be sad. I'm with you all even if you don't see me. I am the Mother of all of you sinners. Love each other. Forgive each other. Make peace, because if you don't, there will be no peace. Do not use violence. Never turn to violence. Nicaragua has suffered greatly since the earthquake, and it will continue to suffer if all of you do not change. If you do not change, you will hasten the arrival of the third world war. Pray, pray, my son, for the whole world. Serious dangers threaten the world. A Mother never forgets Her children. And I have not forgotten that you are suffering. I am the Mother of all you sinners."

Bishop Bosco M. Vivas Robelo, Auxiliary Bishop and Vicar General of the Archdiocese of Managua, sensing Bernardo's transparency and the importance of the message of Heed to the faithful, authorized the publication of the narration of the apparitions of the Blessed Virgin Mary in Cuapa, and in 1982, he issued an official letter for this approval. Without taking a formal, personal position on the apparitions, he authorized Bernardo to speak of them openly. That is when the visionary became subject to "all kinds of blackmail, persecutions and temptations." Officials of the atheistic government regime offered him bribes in exchange for his silence. Official televised news reports called him crazy and hysterical. Women were sent to tempt him.

It became necessary for other Catholics to protect Bernardo from an army of invading photographers. He was attacked by regime police in his home in an attempted kidnapping, but pilgrims camping out at his house prevented it.

A year later, in 1983, the apparitions were approved by Pablo Antonio Vega Mantilla, the Bishop of Juigalpa. And then, on August 20, 1995, after completing his course of study at the seminary, Bernardo became a priest. He was sixty-four years old when he fulfilled the calling to the priesthood that he had received so many years before.

Fr. Bernardo died in the year 2000 and was buried in the little old chapel of Cuapa where Our Lady first appeared to him.

20th & 21st Centuries – June 24, 1981 – 1985: Ivanka Ivankovic, Mirjana Dragicevic, Vicka Ivankovic, Ivan Dregicevic, Ivan

Ivankovic, Milka Pavlovic and the Apparitions at Medjugorje
(Prophecy Detail – Chastisement, Prayer and fasting)

For Ivanka Ivankovic (age 15), Mirjana Dragicevic (age 16), Vicka Ivankovic (age 16), Ivan Dregicevic (age 16), Ivan Ivankovic (age20), and Milka Pavlovic (age 12), the day began as any other Wednesday. June 24, 1981 would prove to be anything but ordinary, however, as late in the afternoon of this feast of St. John the Baptist, as the six youths walking in the stony area called Podbrdo on Mount Crniça saw the figure of a beautiful and luminous woman holding a child. The children understood the woman to be the Virgin Mary. The woman did not speak but did motion for the children to approach her. Rather than getting closer, however, the children became frightened and turned to run. Once home, they told the adults what they had seen, but the adults were also frightened, not by the thought of an apparition, but rather by the consequences of such a vision in the Socialist Federal Republic of Yugoslavia. They instructed the children to say nothing of their vision.

With so many people knowing of the apparitions, however, secrecy was not a possibility and the news spread quickly. By the following day, a rather curious group gathered on Apparition Hill, as it has become known, hoping to share a glimpse of a new vision. Four of the children, Ivanka, Mirjana, Vicka, and Ivan Dregicevic, also assembled at the site. Though Ivan Ivankovic and Milka were not at the site, and would never experience another apparition, the children were joined by two others: Maija Pavlovic, Milka's older sister who was ten, and ten-year-old Jakov Colo. The children were not disappointed as Our Lady appeared to them on a cloud, this time without the Child Jesus. She was, however, equally bright and beautiful. This group of six children would experience many visions over the next several years.

Rather than being overwrought with fright as they were the day prior, all six children ran swiftly along an unmarked trail laced with rocks, brambles, and weeds. Despite the obstacles, they were not hurt, had no scratches, and reported feeling "transported" by a mysterious force. The children now stood before the smiling lady who, according to the youngsters, was *"dressed in a shiny silver-gray dress with a white veil covering her black hair; She has loving blue eyes and is crowned by twelve stars. Her voice is sweet 'like music.' She has [a] few words with the youngsters, prays with them and promises to come back.* "[385]

By Friday, June 26, more than one thousand people joined the children, all attracted by a bright glow. When the woman appeared, Vicka, at the urging of some elders, tossed a bottle of holy water at Her saying, *"If you are the Madonna stay with us, if you are not, go away!"* The woman smiled and Vicka mustered up the courage to ask Her name. *"I am the Blessed Virgin Mary,"* She responds, and then repeats the word *"Peace"* several times. When the apparition ended, the children returned home, but the Virgin appeared again, only to Marija. She was crying and stood in front of a cross. She gave Marija this warning:

> *The world can only be saved through Peace, but the whole world will have peace only if it finds God... Reconcile yourselves, be brothers ....*[386]

In all, the Virgin Mary appeared in Medjugorje over two thousand times, many times to the group of children and many more times to individuals of the group. The apparitions that began on June 24, 1981 continued through March 18, 2020. As of this date, all visions have ceased. Throughout those years, Our Lady imparted messages addressing various issues and also gave the children ten secrets. Some of those secrets have since been disclosed and some of those secrets addressed the end times and the coming chastisement.

The following summary of the end-times prophecies contained within the portion of those secrets that have been made public is reprinted here from the website, medjugorje.com:

> *The Blessed Virgin Mary has told the visionaries of Medjugorje that She would impart to them Ten Secrets. Very little is known about these secrets, though we do know that some of them have to do with chastisements for the world. We also know that the third secret will be a visible, lasting sign that will miraculously be placed somewhere on Apparition Hill. It will be permanent, indestructible, and beautiful. Also, both Mirjana and Vicka have stated that part of the seventh secret no longer exists because of the prayers and fasting of the people responding to Our Lady's call.*
>
> *Our Lady has entrusted secrets to* [the six visionaries] *them that will, once revealed, bring about sweeping conversions throughout the world. Three of the visionaries have all ten secrets, while the other three have nine.*
>
> *Three of the visionaries, Mirjana, Ivanka, and Jakov, have all ten secrets and no longer see Our Lady on a daily basis. Mirjana received the 10th secret in 1982, Ivanka in 1985, and Jakov in 1998. The other three visionaries, Ivan, Marija and Vicka, each have nine secrets and* [were still seeing] *Our Lady on a daily basis, as of June 1, 2009.* (Update: All visions have now stopped.)
>
> *Mirjana was the first visionary to receive all ten secrets. Our Lady has given her the responsibility of revealing the secrets. Mirjana knows the day and date of each of the secrets. Our Lady told Mirjana to choose*

a priest to reveal the secrets to the world. Mirjana chose Father Petar Liubicic. Ten days before the first secret is to be revealed, Father Petar will be given a parchment containing the Ten Secrets. When Father Petar receives the parchment, he will only be able to read the first secret. During the ten days, Father Petar, along with Mirjana, is to spend the first seven days in fasting and prayer. Three days before the event takes place, he is to announce it to the world. At the proper time, he will be able to see and read the second secret, and then the third, etc., according to the schedule of Heaven. Mirjana said that Father Petar doesn't have the right to choose whether to say or not to say them. He accepted this mission and he has to fulfill that according to God's Will.

Before the visible sign is given to mankind, there will be three warnings to the world. The warnings will be in the form of events on earth. Mirjana will be a witness to them. Ten days before one of the admonitions, Mirjana will notify a priest of her choice. Fr. Petar was the priest she chose. The witness of Mirjana will be a confirmation of the apparitions and a stimulus for the conversion of the world.

After the admonitions, the visible sign will appear on the site of the apparitions in Medjugorje for all the people to see. The sign will be given as a testimony, confirming the apparitions and in order to call people back to faith.

The ninth and tenth secrets are serious. They concern chastisement for the sins of the world. Punishment is inevitable, for we cannot expect the whole world to be converted. The punishment can be diminished by prayer and penance, but it cannot be eliminated. Mirjana says that one of the evils that threatened the world, the one contained in the seventh secret, has been averted thanks to prayer and fasting. That is why the Blessed Virgin continues to encourage prayer and fasting: "You have forgotten that through prayer and fasting you can avert wars and suspend the laws of nature."

After the first admonition, the others will follow in a rather short time. Thus, people will have some time for conversion. That interval will be a period of grace and conversion. After the visible sign appears, those who are still alive will have little time for conversion. For that reason, the Blessed Virgin invites us to urgent conversion and reconciliation. The invitation to prayer and penance is meant to avert evil and war, but most of all to save souls.

According to Mirjana, the events predicted by the Blessed Virgin are near. By virtue of this experience, Mirjana proclaims to the world: "Convert as quickly as possible. Open your hearts to God."

In addition to this basic message, Mirjana related an apparition she had in 1982 which we believe sheds some light on some aspects of Church history. She spoke of an apparition in which Satan appeared to her. Satan asked Mirjana to renounce the Madonna and follow him. That way she could be happy in love and in life. He said that following the Virgin, on the contrary, would only lead to suffering. Mirjana rejected him, and immediately the Virgin gave her the following message, in substance:

> *Excuse me for this, but you must realize that Satan exists. One day he appeared before the throne of God and asked permission to submit the Church to a period of trial. God gave him permission to try the Church for one century. This century is under the power of the devil, but when the secrets confided to you come to pass, his power will be destroyed. Even now he is beginning to lose his power and has become aggressive. He is destroying marriages, creating division among priests and is responsible for obsessions and murder. You must protect yourselves against these things through fasting and prayer, especially community prayer. Carry blessed objects with you. Put them in your house and restore the use of holy water.*[387]

The apparitions of Medjugorje have not yet been officially approved by the Vatican, but neither have they been discounted by them because the messages contain nothing contrary to Church teachings. It is not uncommon for such events to be approved several years after the apparitions cease.

20th & 21st Centuries – February 2, 1995 – December 23, 2008: Fabio, Jessica, and Annamaria Gregori in Civitavecchia, Italy (Prophecy Details: Warnings of great danger for the Nation of Italy, the Apostasy, the potential for a nuclear World War III, Period of great trial for the Church)

It was just about 4:21 in the evening of February 2, 1995 when five-year-old Jessica Gregori walked into her backyard. She was there but a minute when her father, Fabio, heard her crying out. He was busy placing his eighteen-month-old son Davide into the car so that they could to go to Mass where his wife Annamaria waited for them. When he heard his daughter scream the word "blood" he ran to the backyard to see what had happened. There, standing in front of a small grotto that he had built to house a statue of the Blessed Virgin Mary, he saw Jessica. She looked unhurt, but turned to him and said, *"Papa, papa, the Madonna is crying!"*[388] Looking toward the statue he could see that Our Lady was indeed shedding tears of blood.

Though perplexed, Fabio took his daughter to the car and drove to church where the family reunited with their wife and mother. After hearing of the incident, Annamaria wasn't surprised. Just days earlier, on January 18, she had a dream that *"referred to a painful event that would take place on the day of Candlemas,"*[389] a feast celebrated every year on February 2 of the Church calendar.

The phenomenon of the weeping statue would repeat itself some thirteen times until February 6, 1995. Crowds of people witnessed the events and Fabio was forced to hire security agents to guard his yard around the clock. They too saw the statue shed tears of blood and provided sworn statements to that effect during the investigation that followed.

One witness to the events, the parish priest, contacted the diocesan bishop, Msgr. Girolamo Grillo, but he preferred to remain ignorant of the happenings and tore up the priest's report. In fact, Grillo was openly hostile to the concept of a miracle, something that prompted negative media reaction and prompting the government officials to get involved. The Judiciary investigated the family thoroughly, and conducted examinations on the liquid, on the statue, and on the homes of the Gregori family and their relatives. Fabio himself had pushed for the investigations and even offered to mortgage his house to pay for very expensive DNA testing that he felt was necessary to determine the source of the tears.

At the conclusion of the government investigations, Bishop Grillo confiscated the statue and kept it at his home. The bishop later told Archbishop Carlo Maria Vigano, the former Papal Nuncio to the United States, the following story:

> *It was 8:15 in the morning. After celebrating Holy Mass, [he] acceded to his sister's request to pray before the sacred image, which he had been keeping in a closet. With the people who were present that day, [he] began reciting the "Hail Holy Queen." When they said the line, "Turn then most gracious advocate, thine eyes of Mercy toward us," the statue began to weep blood. The shock was so great that [he] had to receive first aid from a cardiologist.*[390]

After this, Bishop Grillo's attitude toward the phenomenon changed. He ordered a stop to the DNA testing and *"established a Theological Commission and began an ecclesiastical process to study and verify the event."*[391] No longer a judge, Grillo became a witness to the miraculous events. Pope John Paul II took a personal interest in the miracles. It was then that the statue was confiscated by the Judiciary. This action prompted Pope John Paul II, on April 10, 1995, to send Cardinal Andrzej Maria Deskur, his close friend, to preside over a prayer vigil set for the local cathedral as reparation for the government seizure of the statue. The Pope also instructed the cardinal to bless a statue identical to the weeping statue and give it to the Gregori family. This was a very important sign of his support and closeness. Subsequently, this statue would display the phenomenon of exuding a very fragrant oil before numerous witnesses. It also wept tears of water from March 28 through April 2, 2005 during the Pope's final agony, and then again in 2006 on those same days. On March 31, 2006, Bishop Grillo witnessed the tears of the statue and provided public testimony of the occurrence to the press.

On June 11, 1995, the Judiciary released from their custody the original statue, prompting Pope John Paul II to secretly venerate and crown her in his Vatican apartment. He did it secretly so as to not interfere with the Diocesan Commission's investigation, but on October 8, 2000, he confirmed in writing that he had done so. On June 17, 1995 the original statue was publicly venerated by the faithful in the parish church in Civitavecchia and on May 15, 2005, the tenth anniversary of the final time that the statue wept, the diocesan bishop issued a decree for the construction of a shrine.

The Gregori family began getting locutions and hearing voices of God the Father, Jesus, and Mary beginning on February 6, 1995, but a few months later, on July 2, they received a series of apparitions from Jesus, Mary, and the Angels. These ended on May 17, 1996. The Blessed Virgin also appeared recently, on December 23, 2018, leaving a message on that day as well.

On May 17, 1995, Mary revealed to Fabio that the blood the statue wept was the Blood of Jesus *"shed for all the children who turn away from Her Immaculate Heart, to give you salvation."*[392]

Young Jessica, when asked about the messages of Our Lady of Civitavecchia, replied:

> *The main message is that they want to destroy the family. And then the apostasy in the Church and the risk of a third world war.*[393]

There is also a warning of grave danger, especially for Italy, and the offering of a means of salvation.

> *Your Nation is in grave danger. In Rome darkness is descending more and more on the Rock that my Son Jesus left you on which to build up, educate and spiritually raise his children. Bishops, your*

task is to continue the growth of God's Church, since you are God's heirs.[394]

There is also a strong call for people to return to the sacramental life. Go to Confession regularly, receive Communion, attend Eucharistic adoration, and develop a daily prayer routine. The messages encourage placing oneself in the presence of Jesus in the Eucharist for at least fifteen minutes each day and to pray the Holy Rosary, *"a powerful weapon to defeat Satan,"*[395] daily. Finally, the apparitions are a call to the *"sanctification of daily life by transforming all the gestures of family life into 'acts of love' which 'save souls from Satan.'"*[396]

The Blessed Mother said during her apparitions:

> *Listen to my Son Jesus, true God and your brother. Listen to and build up his Word, revealed to the Holy Church so that you may become true children of God, so that you may do God's will in your daily life for your sanctification. The world is becoming more and more a prisoner of Satan's darkness and evil, without sparing numerous servants of the Church. Children, the Church has entered the period of great trial, and in many of you the faith will become unstable.*[397]

She spoke of the danger of a third world war, which may be nuclear war, but can be stopped by:

> *...weapons stronger than those used, which are love, prayers, humility, the Rosary and true conversion of your hearts to God through our Heavenly Mother who is holding you all in Her arms, close to Her Immaculate Heart. Consecrate yourselves to me, to my Immaculate Heart, and I will protect your Nation under my mantle now full of graces. Listen to me, please, I beg you! I am your Heavenly Mother, I beg you: do not make me weep again seeing so many of my children die for your faults by not accepting me and allowing Satan to act. Let yourself be guided in your steps with the simplicity with which a child puts his hand in the Hand of his Father. My Immaculate Heart will transform your sufferings into joys which you accept with true love, for these are trials which the Lord Jesus allows.*
>
> *Through you I can spread the light of faith in these days of great apostasy. You are the light of the Lord, because you are children totally consecrated to Me. Let yourselves be guided by Me...If you listen to Me with true love, and fulfill my requests by walking the path that I point out to you in your mind and heart, through you I*

*can realize the great divine Design of the great triumph of my Im-
maculate Heart.*[398] (September 8, 1995)

On August 27, 1995, during an apparition in the garden of the Gregori house, Our Lady transmitted an alarming message. While referring
to what had been revealed in her appearance at Fatima in 1917, She said:

> *My children, the darkness of Satan is now obscuring the whole
> world and it is also obscuring the Church of God. Prepare to live
> what I had revealed to my little daughters of Fatima...After the pain-
> ful years of Satan's darkness, the years of triumph of my Immaculate
> Heart are now imminent.*[399]

As in virtually all of her apparitions, the Virgin Mary identified herself in Civitavecchia, saying:

> *The Lord has clothed me with His Light and the Holy Spirit with
> His Power. My task is to take all my children away from Satan and
> bring them back to the perfect glorification of the Most Holy Trin-
> ity... My wish is that you all consecrate yourselves to my Immaculate
> Heart so that I can lead you all to Jesus, cultivating you in my heav-
> enly garden... I present myself to you as Our Lady of the Immaculate
> Heart, Queen of Heaven, Mother of Families, Bearer of Peace in
> your hearts... Convert, my sweet children, because time is running
> out.*[400]

The apparitions that took place in Civitavecchia were approved by
the local bishop. According to Archbishop Vigano, there is plenty of reason to believe that they have also been accepted by the Vatican, although
no official document to that effect has been issued by the Vatican.

Throughout the ages there have been thousands of prophetic utterances by hundreds of prophets. Some prophecies were received in
dreams, some in locutions and some in visions. Many spoke of the things
that would happen at the end of the age; the apostasy within Christ's
Church, the illumination of conscience, the minor chastisements, the two
and three days of darkness, the great chastisement, the rise to power of a
great monarch and a holy pontiff, the unification of the entire world and
its conversion to Catholicism, and other events leading up to the second
coming. In many cases, Jesus sent His own Mother to deliver the messages. In others, He appeared Himself. Regardless of the messenger, regardless of the person receiving the message, and regardless of the century in which the message was sent, that message is consistent

throughout time, and it is meant for the salvation of souls. God is taking great pains to make sure souls are not condemned. Why? If being saved is simply a matter of being baptized with water and in the Spirit, and the acceptance of Christ as Lord and Savior, why would Jesus be so concerned about losing souls? Finally, from what is God trying to save souls?

Part IV

Hell is Real and it Matters!

There is no question that the place the Bible describes as hell is real. It exists outside of both time and space so it is only natural that the concept would be difficult for the human mind to absorb. Regardless, *"Studies of religious belief in America reveal that a majority of those surveyed, in one study a full seventy-one percent, believe in the existence of hell."*[401] However, of those who believe in hell, only one percent of those surveyed expect to end up there. Christians, and especially Catholics, however, should doubt neither the existence of hell nor the ease with which one might find himself a permanent resident.

The concept of hell is relevant to any discussion of the final punishments that God will inflict upon the earth and upon His creation. It matters because, with the great chastisement, we are nearing the end point of our existence and of our own ability to avoid final damnation. In short, it is time to choose.

That hell exists is a tenet that "has always been held by Christendom; and it has the support of reason...scripture and tradition."[402] Hell is mentioned, in the abstract if not by name, several times in the Old and New Testaments of the Bible as well as in public revelations. Jesus spoke freely of the existence of hell. He also told how difficult it is to enter the kingdom of heaven, and by exclusion, how easy it is to attain final damnation. Should Catholics presume to think, then, that they would not suffer such a fate? There is a reason why presumption is considered a sin by the Church. It *"can lull us to sleep. We must recall St. Augustine's warning, when he spoke of the two men who were crucified with Jesus: 'Do not despair. One of the thieves was saved. Do not presume. One of the thieves was damned.'"*[403] Award-winning journalist and author, Dr. Paul Thigpen, reminds us that our earthly choices matter and will ultimately lead us to one of two very different destinies. *"Hell,"* he says, *"is the final guarantee that what we do here and now really matters."*[404]

The concept of hell is, after all, one of the fundamental tenets of our faith. The Apostles Creed tells how, following His death on the cross, Jesus descended to the dead, but on the third day, rose again and ascended into heaven. It continues that Jesus *"will come again to judge the living and the dead."* If heaven, to the exclusion of hell, is the only option for Christians following our mortal death, then why would a judgment be needed? This phrase is not simply a collection of words to a meaningless Catholic prayer; they are a fragment of the words that define the essential convictions of our Catholic faith.

The Catholic catechism teaches that God created man to know, love, and serve Him. God could have programmed man to love him, but he chose to give us the gift of ultimate dignity, the gift of free will. With it, man is free to obey God or not, to worship God or not, and to love God or not. God gave his creation free will because, as we all know, forced love is not love at all. Love is a gift that must be given consciously and freely, and God asks it and expects it of us.

Justice requires, even for a merciful God, that unconfessed mortal sin be punished. To allow otherwise would indicate a failure of justice which defeats God's very purpose of being a merciful and just God. In such a case, *"the ongoing existence of hell and its occupants would just as readily reflect on the glory of God's holiness and his righteous opposition to evil."*[405] A final judgment that included no option of damnation may appeal to human beings, but what we prefer is utterly irrelevant to God, as our desires have no bearing on justice. *"The fact that we have an intuitive sense for what strikes us as 'fair' or 'just' plays no part whatsoever in coming to a conclusion on whether or not there is an eternal hell. The fact that we may not enjoy the thought of eternal conscious punishment doesn't make it go away! The fact that you 'feel' the existence of hell is inconsistent with your concept of God doesn't mean there isn't one."*[406]

So, while man is free to choose to obey and love God or to ignore His commandments and thereby rebuke Him, man is also subject to the rewards and consequences of those choices. God can certainly forgive the sin that might lead His creation to hell, but,

> *He cannot in justice simply ignore it. Forgiveness is a gift, and for sin to be forgiven, there must be an acceptance of the gift, or it will have no consequences. Those who admit no guilt refuse to accept forgiveness. The Church teaches that to refuse God's forgiveness, to say to Him, "I don't need or want you or your mercy," is in fact the unforgivable sin of which Jesus speaks in the Gospel.*[407]

Dr. Paul Thigpen notes that *"hell is one of the great mysteries of human existence."*[408] It would be impossible for human beings to grasp the concept of hell without Divine Intervention. Consequently, God had intervened so as to provide an explanation of hell that might make sense to His creation. The following two chapters will explore the reality of hell based not only on biblical references, but on private revelations as well.

Chapter 10

Biblical References to Hell

W e, as Catholics, must believe in the reality of hell because *"Jesus Himself did so."*[409] Jesus not only spoke of hell, but He reminded those to whom He spoke that they *"could end up there forever."*[410]

In the New Testament, the word most commonly used in reference to what we refer to as "hell" is Gehenna.* This is the Greek equivalent word for a valley lying immediately southwest of Jerusalem called, "the Valley of Hinnom." This valley is still visible today from the Mount of Olives, the site of Jesus's arrest following His betrayal by Judas. At one time in history the Valley of Hinnom was used to offer human sacrifices, primarily children and typically by fire, to the pagan god, Moloch.[411]

Hell is described in various places in the Bible, but the most graphic portrayal is contained in the Book of Revelation 14:9-11.

> *A third angel followed them and said in a loud voice, "Anyone who worships the beast or its image, or accepts its mark on forehead or hand, will also drink the wine of God's fury, poured full strength into the cup of his wrath, and will be tormented in burning sulfur before the holy angels and before the Lamb. The smoke of the fire that torments them will rise forever and ever, and there will*

*Other words used in the Bible to refer to hell include the Hebrew word "Sheol" that refers to the grave or the realm of the dead; "Hades" from the pagan Greek also refers to the realm of the dead. "Tartarus" is a Greek word referring to a realm of punishment below Hades. Other words used in reference to hell include "abyss," "destruction," "eternal destruction," "corruption," "death," and "the second death."

be no relief day or night for those who worship the beast or its image or accept the mark of its name."

Thus, St. John's describes hell as a burning fire that torments its inhabitants for eternity without relief. He continues by describing the type of person who will suffer such a fate.

But as for cowards, the unfaithful, the depraved, murderers, the unchaste, sorcerers, idol-worshipers, and deceivers of every sort, their lot is in the burning pool of fire and sulfur, which is the second death.[412]

The Gospel of Saint Matthew speaks to the final judgment of the Second Coming when God will separate the righteous from the sinners as a shepherd separates the sheep from the goats. He will say to the righteous on his right:

Come, you who are blessed by my Father. Inherit the kingdom prepared for you from the foundation of the world. For I was hungry and you gave me food, I was thirsty and you gave me drink, a stranger and you welcomed me, naked and you clothed me, ill and you cared for me, in prison and you visited me...I say to you, whatever you did for the one of the least brothers of mine, you did for me.[413]

To the others on his left he will say:

Amen, I say to you, what you did not do for one of these least ones, you did not do for me. And these will go off to eternal punishment, but the righteous to eternal life.

St. Matthew also speaks to the concept of hell in recounting the words of Jesus when his Apostles asked Him to explain the parable of the weeds in which the Kingdom of Heaven is likened to a man who sowed good seed in his field only to have the enemy come at night and sow weeds among the wheat. The owner of the field allowed the wheat and weeds to grow together until the harvest when the wheat was collected and stored, while the weeds were tied in bundles for burning.

He who sows good seed is the Son of Man, the field is the world, the good seed the children of the kingdom. The weeds are the children of the evil one, and the enemy who sows them is the devil. The harvest is the end of the age, and the harvesters are angels. Just as weeds are collected and burned with fire, so will it be at the end of the age. The Son of Man will send his angels, and they will collect out of his kingdom all who cause others to sin and all evildoers. They will throw them into the fiery furnace, where there will be wailing and grinding of teeth. Then the righteous will shine like the sun in the kingdom of their Father. Whoever has ears ought to hear.[414]

Likewise, the Gospel of Saint Mark speaks to the concept of hell, and the necessity to avoid it at all costs, in rather graphic terms recounting the words of Jesus:

Whoever causes one of these little ones who believe to sin, it would be better for him if a great millstone were put around his neck and he were thrown into the sea. If your hand causes you to sin, cut it off. It is better for you to enter into life maimed than with two hands to go into Gehenna, into unquenchable fire. And if your foot causes you to sin, cut it off. It is better for you to enter into life crippled than with two feet to be thrown into Gehenna. And if your eye causes you to sin, pluck it out. Better for you to enter into the kingdom of God with one eye than with two eyes to be thrown into Gehenna, where their worm does not die, and the fire is not quenched.[415]

St. John's Revelations once again makes reference to the fire of hell;

The beast was caught and with it the false prophet who had performed in its sight the signs by which he led astray those who had accepted the mark of the beast and those who had worshiped its image. The two were thrown alive into the fiery pool burning with sulfur.[416]

There are many more references to hell in both the Old and New Testaments of the Bible. Most repeat the detail that has been shared in the preceding references. While not taking the space to elaborate on all those references, the citations are provided as a means of verification by the reader. While not an exhaustive list, references to hell may be found in Psalms 9:17; 2 Thessalonians 1:9; Matthew 13:50; Acts 2:27; Jude 1:7; Proverbs 15:24; Proverbs 23:14; Proverbs 15:11; Matthew 16:19; 2 Peter 2:4; Rev 20:13-14; Matthew 10:28; and Ezekiel 18:20.

Both the Old and New Testaments of the Bible make it clear that there is a hell and it is a place of fire and eternal torment for those who disrespect God's commands and sin unrepentantly. These are not the only glimpses that are given of God's equitable justice. A plethora of people, including saints and those whose cause for sainthood is already underway, as well as priests, laymen, and other holy people, have been granted visions of hell throughout the centuries. They have documented and otherwise preserved their visions to share with all this warning for what awaits those who cavalierly violate God's commands. Their stories are told in the next chapter.

Chapter 11

Private Revelations of Hell

S ome people have been through hell, literally. Some have had visions of hell while others have reported having guided tours. These reports fall strictly in the realm of private revelations, and they *"must be treated accordingly. Even when the claim is made by a canonized saint, we cannot for that reason assume that the revelation is authentic or approved by the Church...And even when such a private revelation has in fact been approved by the Church as worthy of belief, we still must not place it on the same level as the scriptural accounts of hell."*[417]

That is not to say that these private revelations serve no useful purpose. In the words of Saint Paul in his letter to the Romans, God, *"will render to every man according to his works,* [either] *eternal life or wrath and fury."*[418] Perhaps, then, these visions might be considered credible for many reasons. First, they support the biblical description of hell as a place of *"damnation* [described] *in the most gruesome and terrifying terms, with everlasting darkness, fire, and worms (Mt 8:12; Mk 9:47) and much more."*[419] Second, these visions help us understand how our behavior and actions in this life will have consequences in the next. Finally, the visions remind us of just how deceiving human appearances can be. In other words, there is no way to make a final prediction of the last judgment of our neighbors and friends based on their outward appearance. None of us are able to read their hearts as God alone will. Jeramiah 17:10 tells us that *"I the Lord search the mind and test the heart, to give to every man according to his ways, according to the fruit of his doings."*[420] For God *"sees not as man sees; man looks on the outward appearance, but the Lord looks on the heart (1 Sm 16:7)"*[421]

Reading about these visions serves as warnings to mankind. Though, despite the horror and fear that these warnings may instill, we are provided hope through those visions that tell of God giving even the most wicked among us one final chance to repent of our sins. Not all will take advantage of the benevolent opportunity God has provided, as some of the visions clearly demonstrate, but they serve as a reminder of just how merciful God is despite the warnings to not presume upon that mercy.

Saint Maria Faustina Kowalska

Sister Faustina, a sister of Our Lady of Mercy, was born in Poland in 1905 and spent most of her time in the convent in the service of others. Over a number of years, she was given extraordinary visions from Jesus, and had extensive conversations with him. Jesus spoke to Faustina about His great mercy and shared with her a special prayer which we now know as the Chaplet of Divine Mercy. Faustina recorded her conversations, as instructed, in a diary that is over six hundred pages. Both the diary and the image of Divine Mercy, as revealed to her by Jesus, have been published, providing the world both a glimpse into her divine revelations as well as a powerful devotion to Jesus' Divine Mercy. On one occasion, Jesus allowed Faustina to visit hell and purgatory. This is her account of hell:

> *Today, I was led by an angel to the chasms of hell. It is a place of great torture; how awesomely large and extensive it is!*
> *The kinds of tortures I saw: the first torture that constitutes hell is the loss of God; the second is perpetual remorse of conscience; the third is that one's condition will never change; the fourth is the fire that will penetrate the soul without destroying it – a terrible suffering, since it is purely spiritual fire, lit by God's anger; the fifth torture is continual darkness and a terrible suffocating smell, and despite the darkness, the devils and the souls of the damned see each other and all the evil, both of others and their own; the sixth torture is the constant company of Satan; the seventh torture is horrible despair, hatred of God, vile words, curses, and blasphemies.*
> *These are the tortures suffered by all the damned together, but that is not the end of the sufferings. There are the special tortures destined for particular souls. These are the torments of the senses.*
> *Each soul undergoes terrible and indescribable sufferings, related to the manner in which it has sinned. There are caverns and pits of torture where one form of agony differs from another. I would have died at the very sight of these tortures if the omnipotence of God had not supported me.*
> *Let the sinner know that he will be tortured throughout all eternity, in those senses which he made use of to sin. I am writing this at*

the command of God, so that no soul may find an excuse by saying there is no hell, or that nobody has ever been there, and so no one can say what it is like.

I, Sister Faustina, by the order of God, have visited the abyss of hell so that I might tell souls about it and testify to its existence. I cannot speak about it now; but I have received a command from God to leave it in writing. The devils were full of hatred for me, but they had to obey me at the command of God.

What I have written is but a pale shadow of the things I saw. But I noticed one thing: that most of the souls there are those who disbelieved that there is a hell. When I came to, I could hardly recover from the fright.

How terribly souls suffer there! Consequently, I pray even more fervently for the conversion of sinners. I incessantly plead God's mercy upon them. O my Jesus, I would rather be in agony until the end of the world, amidst the greatest sufferings, than offend you by the least sin.[422]

The Children of Fatima

During the apparitions of Our Lady of Fatima to Lucia dos Santos, Francesco, and Jacinta Marto, in 1917, She gave the children three secrets. One of those secrets, disclosed years later by Sister Lucia, at the behest of her local bishop, was a vision of hell. On June 13, 1917, Our Lady taught the children a new prayer, one we now commonly recite at the end of each decade of the Rosary: "*O my Jesus, forgive us our sins, save us from the fires of hell, lead all souls to heaven, especially those in most need of thy mercy.*" Our Lady followed up on this theme in later apparitions to the children, telling them in August to "*pray, pray very much, and make sacrifices for sinners; for many souls go to hell, because there are none to sacrifice themselves and to pray for them.*" In other appearances, Our Lady continued to urge the children to pray and make sacrifices for those who might lose their souls to hell.

Sister Lucia, the only one of the three Fatima visionaries to live to adulthood, became a Discalced Carmelite nun. She described the events of the June 13, 1917 apparition this way:

She [Our Lady] continued: "Sacrifice yourselves for sinners, and say many times, especially whenever you make some sacrifice: 'O Jesus, it is for love of you, for the conversion of sinners, and in reparation for the sins committed against the Immaculate Heart of Mary."

As Our Lady spoke these words, she opened her hands once more, as she had done during the two previous months. The rays of light seemed to penetrate the earth, and we saw, as it were, a sea of fire.

Plunged in this fire were demons and souls in human form, like transparent burning embers, all blackened or burnished bronze, floating about in the conflagration, now raised into the air by the flames that issued from within themselves together with great clouds of smoke, now falling back on every side like sparks in huge fires, without weight or equilibrium, amid shrieks and groans of pain and despair, which horrified us and made us tremble with fear. It must have been this sight which caused me to cry out, as people say they heard me. The demons could be distinguished by their terrifying and repellent likeness to frightful and unknown animals, black and transparent like burning coals.

Terrified, and as if to plead for succor, we looked up at Our Lady, who said to us, so kindly and so sadly: "You have seen hell, where the souls of poor sinners go. To save them, God wishes to establish in the world devotion to my Immaculate Heart. If what I say to you is done, many souls will be saved, and there will be peace."[423]

Saint Teresa of Avila

St. Teresa of Ávila was born in Avila, Spain in 1515. She was a Carmelite nun, a mystic, an author of spiritual writings and poems, and in 1970 was elevated by Pope Paul VI to Doctor of the Church, becoming the first woman in Church history to achieve that status. In addition to founding numerous convents throughout Spain, Teresa was the originator of the Carmelite Reform that restored a contemplative and austere life to the order.

In her autobiography, *The Life of Teresa of Jesus*, the saint provided details for some of her mystical visions, including one in which she was plunged into hell. Saint Teresa tells it this way:

...The entrance seemed to be by a long narrow pass, like a furnace, very low, dark and close. The ground seemed to be saturated with water, mere mud, exceedingly foul, sending forth pestilential odors, and covered with loathsome vermin. At the end was a hollow place in the wall, like a closet, and in that I saw myself confined. All this was even pleasant to behold in comparison with what I felt there. There is no exaggeration in what I am saying.

...It was utterly inexplicable. I felt a fire in my soul. I cannot see how it is possible to describe it. My bodily sufferings were unbearable. I have undergone most painful sufferings in this life and, as the physicians say, the greatest that can be borne, such as the contraction of my sinews when I was paralyzed – without speaking of others

of different kinds, yes, even those of which I have also spoken, inflicted on me by Satan. Yet all these were nothing in comparison with what I felt then, especially when I saw that there would be no pause, nor any end to them.

These sufferings were nothing in comparison with the anguish of my soul, a sense of oppression, of stifling, and of pain so keen, accompanied by so hopeless and cruel an affliction, that I do not know how to speak of it. If I said that the soul is continually being torn from the body, it would be nothing – for that implies the destruction of life by the hands of another. But here, it is the soul itself that is tearing itself in pieces. I cannot describe that inward fire or that despair, surpassing all torments and all pain. I did not see who it was that tormented me, but I felt myself on fire, and torn to pieces, as it seemed to me; and, I repeat it, this inward fire and despair are the greatest torments of all.

Left in that pestilential place, and utterly without the power to hope for comfort, I could neither sit nor lie down; there was no room. I was placed as it were in a hole in the wall, and those walls, terrible to look on in themselves, hemmed me in on every side. I could not breathe. There was no light, but all was thick darkness. I do not understand how it is; though there was no light, yet everything that can give pain by being seen was visible.

Our Lord at that time would not let me see more of hell. Afterwards I had another most fearful vision, in which I saw the punishment of certain sins. They were most horrible to look at, but because I felt none of the pain, my terror was not so great.

In the former vision Our Lord made me really feel those torments, and that anguish of spirit, just as if I had been suffering them in the body there. I do not know how it was, but I understood distinctly that it was a great mercy that Our Lord would have me see with my own eyes the very place from which His compassion had saved me. I have listened to people speaking of these things, and I have at other times dwelled on the various torments of hell (though not often, because my soul made no progress by the way of fear). I have also read of the various tortures, and how the devils tear the flesh with red-hot pincers.

But all is as nothing before this that I saw. It is a wholly different matter. In short, the one is a reality, the other a picture; and all burning here in this life is as nothing in comparison with the fire that is there.

I was so terrified by that vision – and that terror is on me even now while I am writing – that although it took place nearly six years ago, the natural warmth of my body is chilled by fear even now when I think of it. And so, amid all the pain and suffering that I may have had to bear, I have always thought that all we have to suffer in this world is as nothing in comparison to the suffering of hell. It seems to me that we complain without reason.[424]

Saint Hildegard of Bingen

Born in Germany in 1098, St. Hildegard was a Benedictine abbess, a poet, a musician, a composer, a playwright, a healer, a scientist, a mystic, a visionary, and a Doctor of the Church. In her book entitled, *Scivias*, the saint provides insight into twenty-six of her visions. One of these visions was of hell and another was of the devil. Those two visions are described in her own words:

Behold! A pit appeared, immense in breadth and depth. The opening was like the mouth of a well, with flames and smoke and a noxious stench pouring out from it...And once more I heard the One who had spoken to me before, saying: "...The pit of immense breadth and depth that appeared to you is hell. It lies broad with vice and deep with damnation, as you can see. It does indeed have an opening like the mouth of a well, with flames and smoke and a noxious stench pouring out from it, because in its rapacious hunger for souls, it displays to them sweetness and gentleness, yet with wicked deceit it leads them to the miseries of damnation."

There burns a flame with black smoke rising up, and a foul odor. These dreadful tortures were prepared for the Devil and those who followed him in turning away from [God,] the Supreme Good, not desiring to know It or understand It. For this reason, they have been cast out from all good – not because they were ignorant of the good, but because in their great arrogance they despised it....

This outer darkness, filled with various torments, was created when the Devil was cast down. These evil spirits, rather than possessing the glory that had been prepared for them, were subjected to the agony of a multitude of punishments. Having lost the brightness they had possessed they now suffered the deepest darkness.

How? When the spirit [Lucifer] exalted himself on high like a serpent, he was cast into the prison of hell because it was not possible that any creature could prevail over God. How could two hearts possibly beat in one breast? In the same way, two gods could not exist in heaven. Because the Devil and those who followed him chose pride and presumption, he discovered that the pit of hell was prepared for him. In addition, the people who imitate the demons' actions receive a share of their torments, according to what they deserve....[425]

Following are the words Saint Hildegard used to describe her vision of the Devil:

Lying on its back before the crowd of people dressed in white, as if across the road, was a monster who looked like a worm, amazingly huge and long. It provoked a feeling of horror and fury beyond words...Now that worm was black and covered with bristles, full of open sores and abscesses. Its body displayed five parts from the head down through the abdomen to its feet, like stripes. One was green, one was white, one was red, one was yellow, and one was black. They were full of deadly poison.

Even so, the monster's head had been so powerfully crushed that the left side of its jawbone was dislocated. Its eyes were bloody outside and fiery inside. Its ears were round and covered with bristles. It had the nose and mouth of a viper, the hands of a man, and the feet of a viper. Its tail was stubby and horrifying.

A chain was riveted around the neck of the worm, binding its hands and feet as well, and securely fastened to a rock in the abyss. In this way the monster was restrained so that it could not move around as its wicked will wished. Tongues of fire issued from its mouth, dividing four ways; One part ascended to the clouds, another breathed forth among people of the world, another among spiritual people, and the last descended into the abyss....

The flame that issued deep into the abyss inflicted various agonies on those who had worshipped Satan instead of God, without having been washed by the font of Baptism or knowing the light of truth and faith. I saw piercing arrows come whistling loudly from its mouth. Black smoke breathed out from its breast. Scalding liquid boiled up from its loins. A hot whirlwind blew out from its navel. And the filth of frogs poured out of its bowels.

The assault of all these foul discharges terrified people. And the hideous stench that came out of the monster infected many people with its own perversion. Then behold! There came a host of souls, gleaming brightly. They stomped on the worm and tortured it severely. But they could not be harmed by its flames or its poison....

We see, then, that the power of God remains without failing, immoveable for all eternity. His power displayed in saving souls oppresses the Devil so violently that he cannot by any means, within or without, steal redemption from the faithful, or prevent them from entering the joyful place from which Satan perversely exiled himself.[426]

Blessed Anne Catherine Emmerich

Catherine Emmerich was born in Germany in 1774 and had mystical experiences from an early age. She entered religious life as an Augustinian and was able to diagnose the sick without any medical training, prescribing treatments that healed the affliction. When the government closed her convent, Emmerich was forced to live with a poor widow. By 1813 her own medical condition had become so poor that she became bedridden. Shortly thereafter, she received the stigmata, including the marks of the thorns on her head and crosses on her breast.

From 1820 to 1824, German poet Clemens Brentano, who converted because of his experiences with Emmerich, resorted to writing her visions and mystical experiences. He read each of his notes to her at the end of each day for her approval. Brentano published the compilation of those notes in a book entitled, *The Dolorous Passion of Our Lord Jesus Christ According to the Meditations of Anne Catherine Emmerich.* The book is noted for its remarkably vivid detail of the passion, death, and resurrection of Jesus. One of the visions recorded in the book describes Jesus's descent to the dead following his death on the cross and his entry into three infernal regions: limbo, purgatory, and hell. The following is Emmerich's description of hell and its comparison to heaven:

> *When Jesus, after uttering a loud cry, expired, I saw his heavenly soul under the form of a bright meteor pierce the earth at the foot of the Cross, accompanied by the angel Gabriel and many other angels. His Divine nature remained united to his soul as well as to his body, which still remained hanging upon the Cross. But I cannot explain how this was, although I saw it plainly in my own mind....*
>
> *Finally,* [after he visited limbo and purgatory,] *I beheld him approach the center of the great abyss, that is to say, hell itself. The expression on his face was most severe.*
>
> *The exterior of hell was appalling and frightful. It was an immense, heavy-looking building, and the granite from which it was formed, although black, was of metallic brightness. The dark and weighty doors were secured with such terrible bolts that no one could behold them without trembling.*
>
> *Deep groans and cries of despair could be plainly heard even while the doors were tightly closed. But, oh, who can describe the dreadful shouts and shrieks that burst upon the ear when the bolts*

were unfastened, and the doors flung open? And, who can depict the dejection of the inhabitants of this wretched place!

The form in which the heavenly Jerusalem is generally represented in my visions is that of a beautiful and well-regulated city. In it, the different degrees of glory to which the elect are raised are manifested by the magnificence of their palaces, or the wonderful fruit and flowers with which the gardens are embellished.

Hell is shown to me in the same form, as a city, but all within it is, on the contrary, close, confused, and crowded. Every object tends to fill the mind with sensations of pain and grief. The marks of the wrath and vengeance of God are visible everywhere. Despair, like a vulture, gnaws every heart, and discord and misery reign everywhere.

In the heavenly Jerusalem all is peace and eternal harmony, because the beginning, fulfillment, and end of everything is pure and perfect happiness. The city is filled with splendid buildings, decorated in such a manner as to charm every eye and enrapture every sense. The inhabitants of this delightful dwelling are overflowing with rapture and exultation, the gardens gay with lovely flowers, and the trees covered with delicious fruits which give eternal life.

In the city of hell, on the other hand, nothing is to be seen but dismal dungeons, dark caverns, frightful deserts, and fetid swamps filled with every imaginable species of poisonous and disgusting reptile. In heaven you behold the happiness and peaceful union of the saints; in hell, perpetual scenes of wretched discord, and every species of sin and corruption, either under the most horrible forms imaginable, or represented by different kinds of dreadful torments.

Everything in this dreary abode tends to fill the mind with horror. Not a word of comfort is heard, or a consoling idea allowed entrance. One dread-inspiring thought – that the justice of an all-powerful God inflicts on the damned nothing but what they have fully deserved – is the absorbing, terrifying conviction that weighs down each heart.

Vice appears on its own grim, disgusting colors, being stripped of the mask under which it is hidden in this world. The infernal viper is seen devouring those who have cherished or fostered it here below. In a word, hell is the temple of anguish and despair, while the kingdom of God is the temple of peace and happiness. This is easy to understand when seen; but it is almost impossible to describe clearly.

The dreadful explosion of oaths, curses, cries of despair, and frightful cries that, like a clap of thunder, burst forth when the gates of hell were thrown open by the angels, would be difficult even to imagine. Our Lord spoke first to the soul of Judas, and the angels then compelled the demons to acknowledge and adore Jesus. They would have infinitely preferred the most frightful torments to such a humiliation, but all were obliged to submit.

Many were chained down in a circle that was placed around other circles. In the center of hell, I saw a dark and horrible-looking abyss. Into this Lucifer was cast, after being first strongly secured with chains. Thick clouds of sulfurous black smoke rose from its fearful depths and enveloped his frightful form in its dismal folds. In this way the Devil was effectively concealed from everyone looking on.

God himself had decreed this arrangement. I was likewise told, if I remember rightly, that he will be unchained for a time fifty or sixty years before the year of Christ, 2000. The dates of many other events were pointed out to me that I do not now remember. But a certain number of demons are to be let loose much earlier than Lucifer, in order to tempt men, and to serve as instruments of the divine vengeance. I should think that some must be loosened even in the present day, and others will be set free in a short time.

It would be utterly impossible for me to describe all the things that were shown to me. Their number was so great that I could not organize them sufficiently to define and make them intelligible. In addition, my sufferings are very great; and when I speak on the subject of my visions, I behold them in my mind's eye portrayed in such vivid colors that the sight is almost enough to cause a weak mortal like myself to die.[427]

Saint Catherine of Siena

Saint Catherine was born in Siena, Italy in 1347 and was a Third-Order Dominican. She was a mystic, a spiritual writer, and was named a Doctor of the Church. A published work entitled *The Dialogue of Divine Providence*, which was dictated to others while Catherine herself was in a state of ecstasy, details her conversations with God. Included in her work is a locution describing the condemned souls upon their death, during their stay in hell, and on the day of their final judgment. In the following excerpt, God speaks to Catherine in the first person:

They have disparaged my mercy. So, with justice, I send them to damnation, with their cruel servant sensuality, and the cruel tyrant the Devil, whose servants they made of themselves through their own sensuality. In this way, together they are punished and tortured, as together they have offended me. They are tormented, I say, by my ministering devils whom my judgment has appointed to torment those who have done evil.

My daughter, the tongue is not sufficient to tell the pain of these poor souls. There are three principal vices. First is self-love. It gives rise to the second, love of reputation, which itself leads to the third: pride, with injustice and cruelty, and with other filthiness and iniquitous sins, that follow upon these.

So, I say to you that in hell, the souls have four principal torments, from which arise all the other torments. The first is that they see themselves deprived of the vision of me. This is such pain to them that, were it possible, they would rather choose the fire and the tortures and torments, and to see me along with them, than to be without the torments and not see me.

This first pain then revives in them the second, the worm of conscience, which gnaws unceasingly, knowing that the soul is deprived of me, and of the conversation of the angels. Instead, through sin the soul has been made worthy of the conversation and sight of the devils. The vision of the Devil is the third pain and intensifies in them their every agony.

The saints in heaven exult in the sight of me, refreshing themselves with joy in the fruit of their toils borne for me with such abundance of love and displeasure with themselves. In the same way, the sight of the Devil renews these wretched ones to torments. In seeing him, they know themselves more, that is to say, they know that, by their own sin, they have made themselves worthy of him. So the worm of conscience gnaws more and more, and the fire of this conscience never ceases to burn.

The sight is even more painful to them because they see him in his own form, which is so horrible that the heart of man could not imagine it. And if you remember well, you know that I showed him to you in his own form for a little space of time, hardly a moment, and you decided (after you returned to yourself) that you would rather walk on a road of fire, even until the Day of Judgment, than to see him again. With all this that you have seen, even you do not know fully how horrible he is. For by divine justice, he appears more horrible to the soul that is deprived of me, and more or less according to the gravity of that soul's sin.

The fourth torment that they suffer is the fire. This fire burns yet does not consume, for the substance of the soul cannot be consumed, because it is not a material thing that fire can consume. But I, by divine justice, have permitted the fire to burn them with torments, so that it torments them, without consuming them, with the greatest pains in various ways according to the variety of their sins: to some more, and to some less, according to the gravity of their fault.

Out of these four torments issue all others, such as cold and heat and gnashing of teeth and many others. They did not correct themselves after the reproof I gave them in this life concerning their injustice and false judgment. Nor did they change after the second reproof they received at the moment of death, but instead refused to hope in me or grieve for the offense done to me, but only for their own pain. So they have in this way miserably received eternal punishment.

Now it remains to tell of the third reproof, which is on the Last Day, Judgment Day. In the general judgment, the pain of the miserable soul is renewed and increased by the reunion of the soul with its body. It is an unbearable reproof that will cause humiliation and shame.

Know that on Judgment Day, the Word, my Son, will come with my divine majesty to reprove the world with divine power. He will not come like a poor child, as he did when he entered the womb of the Virgin, was born in a stable among the animals, then died between two thieves. At that time I concealed my power in him, letting him suffer pain and torment as a man – not that my divine nature was separated from his human nature, but I allowed him to suffer as a man to satisfy for your guilt.

No, he will not come in that way when he comes on the last day. Instead, he will come with power, to judge the world himself. He will render to everyone his due, and there will be no one in that day who will not tremble.

For the miserable ones who are damned, just to see him will cause such torment and terror that the tongue cannot describe it. To the just, it will cause reverent fear with great joy. This is not because his face changes, because he is unchangeable; but to the eye of the damned, it will appear that way, because of their terrible and darkened vision.

The sun, which is so bright, appears dark to the diseased eye, but light to the healthy eye. It is not the defect of the light, but the defect of the diseased eye, that makes it appear one way to the blind and another to the man who can see. In the same way, those who are condemned will see his Face in darkness, in humiliation, and in hatred, not through any defect in my divine majesty, with which he will come to judge the world, but rather through their own defect.

Their hatred is so great that they cannot will or desire any good. Instead, they continually blaspheme. And do you know why they cannot desire good? Because their life has ended, their free will is now bound.

For this reason, they cannot attain merit, because the season for doing so has passed. If they finish their life by dying in hatred with the guilt of mortal sin, their souls, by divine justice, remain forever bound with the bonds of hatred and forever obstinate in that evil. In this state, being gnawed by themselves, their pains always increase, especially the pains of those who have been the cause of damnation to others....

I have told you of this dignity of the righteous, so that you may know better the misery of the damned. For this is another of their pains: the vision of the bliss of the righteous, which is to them an increase of pain, just as to the righteous, the damnation of the damned is an increase of exultation in my goodness. As light is seen better in contrast to darkness, and darkness in contrast to light, so the sight of the Blessed increases their pain.

With pain they await Judgment Day, because they see that following it will come an increase of pain in themselves. And so will it be: When that terrible voice shall say to them, "Arise, you dead, and come to judgment," the soul will return to be reunited with the body, in the just to be glorified, and in the damned to be tortured eternally.

The very sight of my truth, and of all the blessed ones, will severely reproach them and make them ashamed. The worm of conscience will gnaw the core of the tree – that is, the soul – and also the outward bark, which is the body. They will be reproached by the Blood that was shed for them, and by the works of mercy, both spiritual and corporal, which I did for them through my Son, and which they should have done for their neighbor, as the Holy Gospel teaches.

They will be reproved for their cruelty towards their neighbor, for their pride and self-love, for their filthiness and avarice. And when they see the mercy that they have received from me, their reproof will seem to be intensified in harshness. For at the time of death, only the soul is reproved. But at the general judgment, the soul is reproved together with the body, because the body has been the companion and instrument of the soul – to do good or evil as the free will pleased.

Every work, good or bad, is done by means of the body. And therefore, in justice, my daughter, glory and infinite good are rendered to my chosen ones with their glorified body, rewarding them for the toils they bore for me, together with the soul. But to the perverse ones will be rendered eternal pains by means of their body, because their body was the instrument of evil.

For this reason, their body being restored, their pains will revive and increase at the sight of my Son. In contrast to their miserable sensuality with its filthiness, they will behold their human nature (that is, the humanity of Christ) united with the purity of my Deity, and this mass of their Adam nature raised above all the choirs of angels – while they themselves, by their own fault, are sunk into the depths of hell.

They will also see generosity and mercy shining in the blessed ones, who receive the fruit of the Blood of the Lamb, with the pains that they have borne remaining as ornaments on their bodies, like the dye upon the cloth. This will be not by virtue of the body, but only out of the fullness of the soul, representing in the body the fruit of its labor, because it was the companion of the soul in the working of virtue. As the face of the man is reflected in the mirror, so the body will reflect the fruit of bodily toils, in the way that I have told you.

The pain and humiliation of the darkened ones, on seeing so great a dignity – of which they are deprived – will increase. Their bodies will appear as the sign of the wickedness they have committed, with pain and torture. And when they hear that terrible command, "Go, cursed ones, to the eternal fire," the soul and the body will go to be with the Devil without any remedy or hope.

Each one will be wrapped up in various kinds of earthly filth, according to his evil works. The miser will be filthy with avarice, wrapping himself up with the worldly goods he loved so inordinately, burning in the fire. The cruel one will be filthy with cruelty; the lewd man with lewdness and miserable lust; the unjust with his injustice; the envious with envy; and the hater of his neighbor with hatred. And inordinate self-love, which gave birth to all their disorders, will be burned with intolerable pain, as the head and principle of every evil, in company with pride. In this way, body and soul together will be punished in various ways....

The Devil, dearest daughter, is the instrument of my justice to torment the souls who have miserably offended me. And I have appointed him in this life to tempt and harass my creatures, not so that my creatures will be conquered, but so that they may conquer, proving their virtue, and receive from me the glory of victory. No one should fear any battle or temptation of the Devil that may come to him, because I have made my creatures strong and have given them strength of will fortified in the Blood of my Son. Neither Devil nor any other creature can move that free will, because it is yours, given by me.

You can freely choose, then, to hold it or leave it, as you please. It is an instrument, and if you place it in the hands of the Devil, right away it becomes a knife, with which he strikes you and slays you. But if you do not give this knife of your will into the hands of the Devil – if you do not consent to his temptations and harassments – you will never be injured by the guilt of sin in any temptation.

In fact, you will even be strengthened by it, because the eye of your intellect will be opened to see my love that allowed you to be tempted, so that you could arrive at virtue by being tested. For you do not arrive at virtue except through knowledge of yourself, and knowledge of me, and this knowledge is more perfectly acquired in the time of temptation. It is then you know yourself to be nothing, being unable to cast off the pains and afflictions that you wish to flee....You see, then, that the Devil is my minister to torture the damned in hell and to exercise and prove virtue in the soul in this life....

Now you see, then, how great is the foolishness of men in making themselves weak, when I have made them strong, and in putting themselves into the hands of the Devil. For this reason, know that at the moment of death, they have passed their life under the lordship of the Devil – not that they were forced to do so, for they cannot be forced; they voluntarily put themselves into his hands. Arriving, then, at the point of death under this perverse lordship, they await no other judgment than that of their own conscience; and desperately, despairingly, they come to eternal damnation. [428]

Venerable Maria of Agreda

This Franciscan abbess was born in Spain in 1602. She was a mystic and author best known for writing a work in which she recorded special messages from heaven that were received during contemplation and tell the life of the Blessed Mother. The four volumes entitled *The Mystical City of God: A Divine History of the Virgin Mother of God*, overflow with intricate particulars that illustrate both interior and exterior occurrences beginning with Mary's conception and extending to Her heavenly coronation.

One particular vision focused on a scene from hell dating back to the moment that Lucifer and his minions were cast into hell. The vision begins with the defeat of the demons by the death of Jesus on the Cross. Lucifer and his followers are summoned to Calvary by Mary and forced to watch and listen as God's plan for their overthrow is discussed. Shortly thereafter, with Lucifer's head crushed by Jesus and Mary, they are cast down into hell. That is when Lucifer gathers his demons in council. This is what Blessed Maria of Agreda experienced:

The route of Lucifer and his angels from Calvary to the abyss of hell was more violent and disastrous than their first expulsion from heaven. As holy Job says (Job 10:21-22), that place is a land of darkness, covered with the shades of death, full of gloomy disorder, misery, torments, and confusion. Yet on this occasion the chaos and disorder was (sic) *increased a thousand-fold, because the damned were made to feel new horror and additional punishments at the sudden meeting of the ferocious demons in their rabid fury.*

Certainly, the devils have no power to assign the damned to a place of greater or lesser torment. All their torments are decreed by divine justice according to the measure of the offenses of each of the condemned. But besides this essential punishment, the just Judge allows them to suffer other incidental punishments from time to time according to the occasion. For their sins have left roots in the world and cause much damage to others, who are damned on their account, and the new effects still arising from former sins cause these incidental punishments in the damned.

In this way the demons devised new torments for Judas for having sold and brought about the death of Christ. They also understood then that this place of dreadful punishments, where they had thrown him...was destined for the chastisement of those who damned themselves by refusing to practice their faith in their lives and for those who purposely refuse to believe and avail themselves of the fruits of the Redemption. Against these the devils execute a more furious wrath, similar to the wrath they feel toward Jesus and Mary.

As soon as Lucifer was permitted to proceed in these matters and arise from the consternation in which he remained for some time, he set about proposing to his fellow demons, new plans because of his pride. For this purpose, he called them all together and, placing himself in an elevated position, he spoke to them:

"You, who have for so many ages followed and still follow my battle standards to carry out revenge for my wrongs, know the injury that I have now sustained at the hands of Man-God, and how for thirty-three years he has led me about in deceit, hiding his Divinity and concealing the operations of his soul, and how he has now triumphed over us by the very death that we have brought upon him.

"Before he assumed flesh, I hated him and refused to acknowledge him as being more worthy than I to be adored by the rest of creation. Although on account of this resistance I was cast out from heaven with you, and was degraded to this abominable condition so unworthy of my greatness and former beauty, I am even

more tormented to see myself thus vanquished and oppressed by this Man and by his Mother.

"From the day on which the first man was created I have sleeplessly sought to find them and destroy them. And if I could not destroy them, I at least wished to bring destruction upon all his creatures and induce them not to acknowledge him as their God, so that none of them would ever draw any benefit from his works. This has been my intent, to this all my concern and efforts were directed.

"But all in vain, since he has overcome me by His humility and poverty, crushed me by his patience, and at last has stripped me of the sovereignty of the world by his passion and frightful death. This causes me such an excruciating pain that, even if I succeeded in hurling him from the right hand of his Father, where he sits triumphant, and even if I could draw all the souls redeemed down into this hell, my wrath would not be satiated or my fury placated.

"Is it possible that the human nature, so inferior to my own, will be exalted above all the creatures? That it will be so loved and favored, as to be united to the Creator in the person of the eternal Word? That he will first make war upon me before executing this work, and afterwards overwhelm me with such humiliation?

"From the beginning I have considered this humanity to be my greatest enemy. It has always filled me with intolerable abhorrence. O men so favored and gifted by your God, whom I abhor, and so ardently loved by him! How will I hinder your good fortune? How will I bring upon you my unhappiness, since I cannot destroy the existence you have received?

"What will we now begin, O my followers? How will we restore our reign? How will we recover our power over men? How will we overcome them?

"If men from now on will no longer be so senseless and ungrateful, if they will not be worse disposed than we ourselves toward this God-Man, who has redeemed them with so much love, it is clear that all of them will eagerly follow him. None will take notice of our deceits.

"They will abhor the honors that we insidiously offer them, and they will love contempt. They will seek the mortification of the flesh, and they will discover the danger of carnal pleasure and ease. They will despise riches and treasures, and they will love the poverty so much honored by their Master.

"All that we can offer to their appetites they will abhor in imitation of their true Redeemer. In this way our reign will be destroyed, since no one will be added to our number in this place of confusion

and torments. All will reach the happiness that we have lost; all will humiliate themselves down to the dust and suffer with patience. And my wrath and haughtiness will avail me nothing.

"Ah, woe is me! What torment this mistake caused me! When I tempted him in the desert, the only result was to afford him a chance to leave the example of this victory, and by following it, men can overcome me so much more easily. My persecutions only brought out more clearly his doctrine of humility and patience. In persuading Judas to betray him, and his adversaries to subject him to the deadly torture of the Cross, I merely hastened my ruin and the salvation of men, while the doctrine I sought to blot out was only the more firmly implanted.

"How could He who is God humiliate himself to such an extent? How could he bear so much from men who are evil? How could I myself have been led to assist so much in making this salvation so full and wonderful?

"O how godlike is the power of that Man who could torment and weaken me so! And how can this Woman, his mother and my enemy, be so mighty and invincible in her opposition to me? Such power in a mere creature is a new thing, and no doubt she derived it from the divine Word, whom she clothed in human flesh.

"Through this woman the Almighty has ceaselessly waged war against me, though I have hated her in my pride from the moment I recognized her in her image or heavenly sign. But if my proud indignation is not to be relieved, I benefit nothing by my perpetual war against this Redeemer, against his mother, and against men.

"Now then, you demons who follow me, now is the time to give way to our wrath against God. Come all of you to take counsel what we are to do; for I desire to hear your opinions."

Some of the principal demons gave their answers to this dreadful proposal, encouraging Lucifer by suggesting various schemes for hindering the fruit of the Redemption among men. They all agreed that it was not possible to injure the person of Christ, to diminish the immense value of his merits, to destroy the efficacy of the Sacraments, to falsify or abolish the doctrine that Christ has preached. Yet they resolved that, in accordance with the new order of assistance and favor established by God for the salvation of men, they should now seek new ways of hindering and preventing the work of God by even greater deceits and temptations.

In reference to these plans, some of the astute and malicious demons said, "It is true that men now have at their disposal a new and very powerful doctrine and law, new and efficacious Sacraments; and in this woman, a new model and instructor of virtues, a powerful intercessor, and an advocate. Yet the natural inclinations and passions of the flesh remain just the same, and these sensual creatures who seek pleasure have not changed their nature.

"Let us then, making use of this situation with increased astuteness, foil – as far as in us lies – the effects of what this God-Man has wrought for me. Let us begin strenuous warfare against mankind by suggesting new attractions, exciting them to follow their passions in forgetfulness of all else. In this way, being taken up with these dangerous things, men will not pay attention to anything else."

Acting upon this counsel they redistributed the spheres of work among themselves, so that each squadron of demons might, with a specialized competence, tempt men to different vices. They resolved to continue to propagate idolatry in the world, so that men might not come to the knowledge of the true God and the Redemption. Wherever idolatry would fail, they concluded to establish sects and heresies, for which they would select the most perverse and depraved of the human race as leaders and teachers of error....

Lucifer showed himself content with these infernal counsels for establishing opposition to divine truth and destructive of the very foundation of man's rescue, namely, divine faith. He lavished flattering praise and high offices upon those demons who showed themselves willing and who undertook to find the blasphemous originators of those errors.

Some of the devils charged themselves with perverting the inclinations of children at their conception and birth; others, to inducing parents to be negligent in the education and instruction of their children, either through an inordinate love or aversion, and to cause a hatred of parents among the children. Some offered to create hatred between husbands and wives, to place in the way of adultery, or to think little of the faithfulness promised to their conjugal partners.

All agreed to sow among men the seeds of discord, hatred, and vengeance, proud and sensual thoughts, desire of riches or honors, by suggesting fallacious reasoning against all the virtues Christ has taught. Above all, they intended to weaken the remembrance of his passion and death, by the means of salvation, and of the eternal pains of hell. By these means the demons hoped to burden all the powers and abilities of men with concern for earthly affairs and sensual pleasures, leaving them little time for spiritual thoughts and their own salvation.

Lucifer heard these various suggestions of the demons and replied: "I am much in debt to you for your opinions. I approve of them and adopt them all. It will be easy to put them into practice with those who do not profess the law given by this Redeemer to men.

"For those who accept and embrace his laws it will be a difficult undertaking. But against this law and those who follow it, I intend to direct all my wrath and fury. I will most bitterly persecute those who hear the doctrine of this Redeemer and become his disciples.

"Against these, our most relentless battle must be waged to the end of the world. In this new Church I must strive to sow my weeds. (Matthew 14:25): the ambitions, the avarice, the sensuality, and the deadly hatreds, with all the other vices, of which I am the head. For if once these sins multiply and increase among the faithful, they will, with their accompanying malice and ingratitude, provoke God's anger, and justly deprive men of the helps of grace left to them by the merits of the Redeemer. If they strip themselves of these means of salvation, we will have assured victory over them.

"We must also exert ourselves to weaken piety and all that is spiritual and divine, so that they do not realize the power of the sacraments and receive them in mortal sin, or at least without fervor and devotion. For since these sacraments are spiritual, it is necessary to receive them with a well-disposed will in order to reap their fruits. If they despise the medicine, they will languish in their sickness and be less able to withstand our temptations.

"They will not see through our deceits. They will let the memory of their Redeemer and of the intercession of his Mother slip from their minds. In this way their foul ingratitude will make them unworthy of grace and irritate their God and Savior, so as to deprive them of his helps. In all this, I want all of you to assist me strenuously, losing no time and missing no opportunity for executing my commands."

It is not possible to rehearse all the schemes of this Dragon and his allies concocted at that time against the holy Church and her children....It is enough to state that they spent nearly a full year after the death of Christ in conferring and considering among themselves the state of the world up to that time. They discussed the changes worked by Christ our God and Master, through his death and after having manifested the light of his faith by so many miracles, blessings, and examples of holy men.

If all these labors of Our Lord had not been enough to draw all men to the way of salvation, it can be easily understood that Lucifer would have prevailed....But alas, that truths so infallible, and so much to be dreaded and avoided by men, should in our days be blotted from the minds of mortals to the irreparable danger of the whole world!

Our enemy is astute, cruel, and watchful, while we are sleepy, lukewarm, and careless! What wonder that Lucifer has entrenched himself so firmly in the world, when so many listen to him, and accept and follow his deceits; when so few resist him, and entirely forget about the eternal death that he so furiously and maliciously seeks to draw upon them!

I beg those who read this not to forget this dreadful danger. If they are not convinced of this danger through the evil condition of the world and through the evils each one experiences himself, let them at least learn of this danger by the vast and powerful remedies and helps that the Savior thought it necessary to leave behind in his Church. For he would not have provided such antidotes if our spiritual sickness and danger of eternal death were not so great and formidable.[429]

St. Bede's Depiction of the Vision of St. Drytheim

An English Benedictine monk, St. Bede lived from 673 to 735. His writings are a good demonstration of both the depth of his faith and the level of his scholarship. Like Saints Catherine of Siena and Teresa of Avila, he is a Doctor of the Church. His work, *Ecclesiastical History of the English*, includes several accounts of visions of hell. One such story is that of St. Drytheim, who in the year 696, had a near death experience that includes the following depiction of hell:

He who led me had a radiant face, and shining attire. We went in silence, as it seemed to me, toward the rising of the summer sun. And as we walked, we came to a broad and deep valley of infinite length, which lay on our left.

One side of it was terrifying with raging flames. The other was no less intolerable, because violent hail fell, and cold snows came drifting and sweeping through the whole place. Both sides were full of the souls of men, which seemed to be tossed from one side to the other as if by a violent storm. When they could no longer endure the fervent heat, the hapless souls leaped into the midst of the deadly cold and finding no rest there, they leaped back again to be burnt in the midst of the unquenchable flames.

Now a countless multitude of misshapen spirits were tormented this way both far and near, with this interchange of misery, as far as I could see, without any pause to rest. So, I began to think that this might possibly be hell, of whose intolerable torments I had often heard men talk. My guide who went before me, answered my thought, saying, "Don't think that, for this is not the hell you believe it to be."

When he had led me farther little by little, deeply dismayed by that dreadful sight, all of a sudden, I saw the place before us begin to grow dark and filled with shadows. When we entered them, the shadows gradually grew so thick that I could see nothing except the darkness and the shape and the attire of the one who led me. As we went on through the shadows in the lonely night, all of a sudden there appeared before us billows of foul flame constantly rising out of a great pit and falling back again.

When I had been led there, my guide suddenly vanished and left me alone in the midst of darkness and these fearful sights. As those same billows of fire, without pause, at one time flew up and at another fell back into the bottom of the abyss, I saw that the summits of all the flames as they ascended were full of the spirits of men. Like sparks flying upward with the smoke, they were sometimes thrown up high; and again, when the vapors of the fire fell, they dropped down into the depths below. Moreover, a stench, foul beyond compare, burst forth with the vapors and filled all those dark places.

Having stood there a long time in much dread not knowing what to do, which way to turn, or what end awaited me, all of a sudden I heard behind me the sound of a mighty and miserable lamentation, and at the same time noisy laughter, like the tumult of a rude multitude insulting captured enemies. When that noise, growing plainer, came close to me, I saw a crowd of evil spirits dragging five souls of men, wailing and shrieking, into the midst of the darkness, while they themselves exulted and laughed.

Among those human souls, I could discern, there was one shorn like a priest, one a layman, and one a woman. The evil spirits dragged them down into the midst of the burning pit. As they went down deeper, I could no longer distinguish between the lamentations of the men and the laughing of the devils, yet I still had a confused sound in my ears.

In the meantime, some of the dark spirits ascended from that flaming abyss. Running forward, they assaulted me on all sides. With their flaming eyes and the disgusting fire that they breathed forth from their mouths and nostrils, they tried to choke me. Then they threatened to lay hold on me with fiery tongs, which they had in their hands. Yet they dared not touch me in any way,

Though they tried to terrify me.

In this way I was surrounded on all sides by enemies and spirits of darkness. As I desperately looked around hoping to find some way to be saved, there appeared behind me, on the way by which I had come, a brightness like a star shining amid the darkness. Growing brighter little by little, it came rapidly toward me. When it came close, all those evil spirits who had sought to carry me away with their tongs dispersed and fled.

Now the one whose approach had sent them fleeing was the same one who had led me before. Then, turning toward the right, he began to lead me as if toward the rising of the winter sun, having soon brought me out of the darkness, led me forth into an atmosphere of clear light.

[After showing a vision of those preparing for heaven, the angel asked,] *"Do you know what all these things are that you have seen?"*

I answered no, and then he said, "That valley which you saw, terrifying with flaming fire and freezing cold, is the place where some souls are tried and punished. They delayed to confess and correct their crimes, eventually sought to repent at the point of death, and in that state went forth from the body.

"Because they, even at their death, confessed and repented, they will all be received into the kingdom of heaven on the day of judgment. But many are aided before the day of judgment, by the prayers of the living and their alms and fasting, and more especially by the celebration of Masses.

"Meanwhile, that foul flaming pit you saw is the mouth of hell. Whoever falls into it will never escape it for all eternity....

"As for you, who must now return to the body, and again live among men, if you will seek diligently to examine your actions, and preserve your manner of living and your words of righteousness and simplicity, you will, after death, have a dwelling place among these joyful hosts of blessed souls that you behold."

When he had said this to me, I hated the thought of returning to the body, being delighted with the sweetness and beauty of the place which I had seen, and with the company of those I saw in it. Nevertheless, I dared not ask my guide anything. Then suddenly I found myself, though I don't know how, alive again among men.[430]

Once fully alive and with the full memory of this near-death experience, Drytheim joined a monastery where he, living in solitude in a small cell, devoted himself freely and wholly, in service of his Creator. He lived out his life in continual prayer and penance.

Like the prophecies of the end times, there are many more stories told by saints who have seen hell and just as many who have had encounters with demons and various souls from hell. Not all of them end badly.

Saint Alphonsus Ligouri and the Vision of Blessed Richard of Saint Ann

The Italian bishop, Saint Alphonsus Ligouri, another Doctor of the Church, provides this example by recounting the vision of Blessed Richard of St. Ann, who died in 1622. In it he tells of the redemptive power of the prayers of the Rosary:

In the year 1604 there lived in a city of Flanders two young students. Instead of attending to their studies, they gave themselves up to decadence and debauchery. One night they visited the house of a prostitute. One of them, named Richard, after some time returned home. But the other remained there.

After he arrived home, Richard was undressing to go to bed when he remembered that he had not recited that day, as usual, some Hail Marys. He was oppressed with drowsiness and very weary, yet he roused himself and recited them – although without devotion, and only half awake. He then went to bed.

Having just fallen asleep, Richard heard a loud knocking at the door. But right away, before he even had time to open it, he saw before him his companion, with a hideous and ghastly appearance.

"Who are you?" he said to him.

"Don't you know me?" replied the other.

"But what has changed you so much? You look like a demon."

"Alas!" exclaimed the poor wretch. "I am damned."

"And how is this?"

"You need to know," he said, "that when I came out of that infamous house, the devil attacked me and strangled me. My body lies in the middle of the street, and my soul is in hell. You need to know as well that you would have had the same punishment as I have. But the Blessed Virgin, on account of those few Hail Marys said in her honor, has rescued you. It will be happy for you if you know how to avail yourself of this warning that the Mother of God sends you through me."

After these words he opened his cloak, showed the fire and serpents that were consuming him, and then disappeared. Then young Richard, bursting into a flood of tears, threw himself with his face on the ground to thank Mary, his deliverer. While he was turning over in his thoughts a change of life, he heard the martin bell of a neighboring Franciscan monastery.

"That's where," he exclaimed, "God calls me to do penance!"

Richard went immediately to the convent to beg the fathers to receive him. Knowing how bad his life had been, they objected. But after he had related the circumstances that had brought him there, weeping bitterly all the while, two of the fathers went out to search the street.

They actually found there the dead body of his companion, having the marks of strangulation, and black as coal. Given this circumstance, the young man was received into the monastery.

From that time on, Richard led an exemplary life. He went into India to preach the faith; from thence passed to Japan, and finally had the good fortune to receive the grace of dying a martyr for Jesus Christ, by being burned alive."[431]

Saint Peter's Apocalypse

Perhaps it would be fitting to end this chapter with a story recounted in The Apocalypse of Peter. *Saint Peter's Revelations* was not written until the middle of the second century and has within it "some of the earliest known Christian descriptions of hell outside of the New Testament."[432] Though very popular with early Christians, the text was not included in the biblical canon of the Church. Nevertheless, it is an apocryphal story worth retelling here.

I also saw another place over against that one [the place of angels] *quite squalid. It was a place of punishment, and those who were punished, and the angels who punished them, wore clothing that was dark like the air of the place.*

Some there were hanging by their tongues. These were the ones who had blasphemed the way of righteousness. Under them was laid a fire, blazing up and tormenting them.

There was also a great lake full of flaming mire, in which were certain men who had turned away from righteousness. Tormenting angels were assigned to them.

There were others as well, women who were hanged by their hair above that mire, which boiled up on them. These were the ones who had adorned themselves to engage in adultery.

The men who had joined with them in the defilement of adultery were hanging by their feet, with their heads immersed in the boiling mire. They said: "We didn't believe we would ever end up here!"

I saw the murderers and their accomplices cast into a narrow place full of evil snakes. Being stung by those serpents, they were writhing about in torment. Also covering them were worms, thick like clouds of darkness. And the souls of those who had been murdered stood and looked on the torment of their murderers and said, "O God, righteous is your judgment."

Near that place I saw another narrow place, where all the gore and filth of those in torment ran down, pooling like a lake. And there sat women up to their necks in that liquid, and over against them sat crying many children who were taken from the womb before their due time. From these children shone forth rays of fire that struck the women in the eyes. These were the accursed ones who had conceived children but obtained abortions.

Other men and women were being burned up to their middle and cast down in a dark place. There they were scourged by evil spirits, and their entrails were devoured by worms that never ceased. These were the ones who had persecuted the righteous and handed them over to death.

Near to these were women and men gnawing their lips in torment, with iron heated in the fire pressed against their eyes. They were the ones who had blasphemed and slandered the way of righteousness.

Over against these were still others, men and women gnawing their tongues with flaming fire in their mouths. These were the false witnesses.

In another place were pebbles sharper than swords or any spit, red-hot, with men and women dressed in filthy rags rolling upon them in torment. These were the ones who were rich and trusted in their riches. They had shown no pity to orphans and widows, neglecting the commandments of God.

In another great lake full of pus and blood and boiling mire stood men and women up to their knees. These were the ones who had lent money and demanded interest upon interest.

Other men and women were being cast down from the top of a great cliff to the bottom. But those tormenters assigned to them drove to go up the cliff again. From there they were cast down once more to the bottom, never resting from this torment. These were the ones who had defiled their bodies by acting as women; and the women with them were those who had lain with one another as a man lies with a woman.

Beside that cliff was a place full of blazing fire. There stood men who with their own hands made idols for themselves to worship instead of God. Beside them stood others with rods of fire, striking one another and never resting from this type of torment....

Still others were near them, men and women, burning and turning themselves over as if they were being roasted in a pan. They are the ones who had abandoned the way of God.[433]

Many of the visions of hell tell similar stories and provide eerily similar descriptions of the torments inflicted upon the unfortunate souls within its chambers. The consistency of testimony among the various witnesses to the horrors of hell should give one pause when reflecting upon the reality of the place called hell.

Part V

What Does it All Mean?

Chapter 12

Events Prelude to
the Second Coming of Christ

The Catechism of the Catholic Church teaches that, *"since the Ascension, God's plan has entered into its fulfillment. We are already at 'the last hour.' Already the final age of the world is with us, and the renewal of the world is irrevocably under way; it is even now anticipated in a certain real way, for the Church on earth is endowed already with a sanctity that is real but imperfect. Christ's kingdom already manifests its presence through the miraculous signs that attend its proclamation by the Church."*[434] That fulfillment, of course, is the Second Coming of Christ, but, Sacred Scripture explains that five things must take place prior to Jesus's triumphant return.

First, the Gospel must be preached to all Nations. This is specified in the Gospel of Matthew, which reads,

> *This Gospel of the Kingdom will be preached throughout the world as a witness to all nations, and then the end will come.*[435]

In this age of mass communication that includes television and radio, each with twenty-four-hour, around the clock programming, as well as the internet, etc., it is hard to believe that all nations have not had an opportunity to hear the Good News. In fact, the views of former Harvard Business School Professor Roy Schoeman, who was born into the Jewish faith in New York in 1951, paint an interesting picture. Schoeman has since converted to the Catholic Church, a faith decision that led him to abandon his career in the field of economics, in favor of devoting himself to the Christian mission. Schoeman teaches that this requirement, as expressed in the Gospel of Matthew, has already been fulfilled with the development of the Internet and the World Wide Web.

The **second** requirement is that of **a great apostasy**, or a falling away from the faith. This element is also found in the Gospel of Matthew and is explained further in Paul's second letter to the Thessalonians. Matthew writes:

> *And then many will be led into sin; they will betray and hate one another. Many false prophets will arise and deceive many; and because of the increase of evildoing, the love of many will grow cold. But the one who perseveres to the end will be saved.*[436]

Here, Matthew is speaking of the great apostasy of the Gentiles, a notion reinforced by St. Paul, in his second letter to the Thessalonians. In that letter Saint Paul warns:

> *Let no one deceive you in any way. For unless the apostasy comes first and the lawless one is revealed, the one doomed to perdition, who opposes and exalts himself above every so-called god and object of worship, so as to seat himself in the temple of God, claiming that he is a god....For the mystery of lawlessness is already at work. But the one who restrains is to do so only for the present, until he is removed from the scene. And then the lawless one will be revealed, whom the Lord will kill with the breath of his mouth and render powerless by the manifestation of his coming, the one whose coming springs from the power of Satan in every mighty deed and in signs and wonders that lie, and in every wicked deceit for those who are perishing because they have not accepted the love of truth so that they may be saved.*[437]

Professor Schoeman notes that this apostasy is evident in the world today, even among the Catholics who are unfaithful to the rules of the Church and don't believe in the real presence of Jesus; Body, Blood, Soul, and Divinity, in the Eucharist. Further, there are Catholics who refuse to believe in the Sacrament of Confession, who receive the Eucharist in a state of mortal sin, who repudiate devotion of the Sabbath, who support the evils of abortion and euthanasia, who engage in sex and bear children out of wedlock, and who refuse to acknowledge or accept the inviolability of the traditional family.

The **third** event that the Bible says must occur prior to the Second Coming is a **universal conversion of the Jews to Catholicism**. St. Paul describes this anticipated conversion in his letter to the Romans:

I do not want you to be unaware of this mystery, brothers, so that you will not become wise [in] *your own estimation: a hardening has come upon Israel in part, until the full number of the Gentiles comes in, and thus all Israel will be saved, as it is written: "The deliverer will come out of Zion, he will turn away godlessness from Jacob; and this is my covenant with them when I take away their sins." In respect to the gospel, they are enemies on your account; but in respect to election, they are beloved because of the patriarchs. For the gifts and the call of God are irrevocable.* [438]

This teaching is also explained in, and reinforced by, the Catholic Catechism which reads:

The glorious Messiah's coming is suspended at every moment in history until his recognition by "all Israel," for "a hardening has come upon part of Israel" in their "unbelief" toward Jesus. St. Peter says to the Jews of Jerusalem after Pentecost: "Repent therefore, and turn again, that your sins may be blotted out, that time of refreshing may come from the presence of the Lord, and that he may send the Christ appointed for you, Jesus, whom heaven must receive until the time for establishing all that God spoke by the mouth of his holy prophets from of old." St. Paul echoes him: "For if their rejection means the reconciliation of the world, what will their acceptance mean [but] *the reconciliation of the world, what will their acceptance mean but life from the dead?" The "full inclusion" of the Jews in the Messiah's salvation, in the wake of "the full number of Gentiles," will enable the People of God to achieve "the measure of the stature of the fullness of Christ," in which "God may be all in all."* [439]

In an interview on Relevant Radio, an international Catholic radio station with headquarters in Wisconsin, Professor Schoeman said he believes that we have entered the end of the age. Schoeman said he supposes that, *"Jesus is waiting for the conversion of the Jews* [His chosen people] *before He returns."* He also stated that Jews are now converting to Catholicism in unprecedented numbers, supporting his claim that we are now in the end times.

The **fourth** requirement prior to the second coming is **the return of Jerusalem to the Jews**. The Israelite history of the city dates to about 1000 BC when King David sacked Jerusalem. It then became the City of David and the capital of the United Kingdom of Israel. In July of 1099, however, Jerusalem was captured by Crusaders who took the control of it away from Israel.

Sacred Scripture, in the Gospel of Matthew, tells of Jesus's parable which indicates that Jerusalem must be returned to the Jews before the end of the age:

> *Learn a lesson from the fig tree. When its branch becomes tender and sprouts leaves, you know that summer is near. In the same way, when you see all these things, know that he is near, at those gates. Amen, I say to you, this generation will not pass away until all these things have taken place. Heaven and earth will pass away, but my words will not pass away.*[440]

Pastor Timothy Johnson of the Countryside Baptist Church in northern Parke County, Indiana, explains Scripture's use of the fig tree as follows:

> *...the fig tree as a symbolic picture of Israel. Jesus is talking about when the "fig tree" or Israel's branch is yet tender and brings forth leaves. I believe the branch being tender is the springing forth a new fig tree sapling; in other words, Israel comes to life as a new nation. It takes a little time from seeing the tree break earth until we can see leaves. "The [sprouting of] leaves" is symbolic of when Israel took control of the Holy City Jerusalem in 1967.*[441]

The earliest indication, however, that Israel would reestablish its own nation occurred on May 14, 1948. That is the date on which the British Mandate over Palestine expired. On that same day, the Jewish People's Council gathered at the Tel Aviv Museum and approved a proclamation that declared the establishment of the State of Israel.

Professor Schoeman notes that Jerusalem was in the hands of the Romans as late as the first century A.D. and governed by the Gentiles until 1967. In that year, as a result of their victory in the Six-Day War launched against Israel by the Arab world, Jerusalem was reunified under Israeli rule.

Then, on December 6, 2017, United States President Donald J. Trump formally recognized Jerusalem as the capital of Israel, stating that the American embassy would be moved from Tel Aviv to Jerusalem. Restoring Jerusalem as the capital of Israel completes the restoration of the Jewish Nation, thus fulfilling this fourth requirement.

Finally, Sacred Scripture notes that before the second coming of Christ **there will emerge an Antichrist**. The Antichrist is revealed in

Daniel's final vision in the Old Testament's Book of Daniel and seven times in the New Testament, including this most relevant passage from the Book of Revelation:

> Then I saw a beast come out of the sea with ten horns and seven heads; on its horns were ten diadems, and on its heads blasphemous name[s]. The beast I saw was like a leopard, but it had feet like a bear's, and its mouth was like the mouth of a lion. To it the dragon gave its own power and throne, along with great authority. I saw that one of its heads seemed to have been mortally wounded, but this mortal wound was healed. Fascinated, the whole world followed after the beast; they also worshiped the beast and said, "Who can compare with the beast or who can fight against it?"
>
> The beast was given a mouth, uttering proud boasts and blasphemies, and it was given authority to act for forty-two months. It opened its mouth to utter blasphemies against God, blaspheming his name and his dwelling and those who dwell in heaven. It was also allowed to wage war against the holy ones and conquer them, and it was granted authority over every tribe, people, tongue, and nation. All the inhabitants of the earth will worship it, and all whose names were not written from the foundation of the world in the book of life, which belongs to the Lamb who was slain. Whoever has ears ought to hear these words. Anyone destined for captivity goes into captivity. Anyone destined to be slain by the sword shall be slain by the sword.
>
> Then I saw another beast come up out of the earth; it had two horns like a lamb's but spoke like a dragon. It wielded all the authority of the first beast, whose mortal wound had been healed. It performed great signs, even making fire come down from heaven to earth in the sight of everyone. It deceived the inhabitants of the earth with the signs it was allowed to perform in the sight of the first beast, telling them to make an image for the beast who had been wounded by the sword and revived. It was then permitted to breathe life into the beast's image, so that the beast's image could speak and [could] have anyone who did not worship it put to death. It forced all the people, small and great, rich and poor, free and slave, to be given a stamped image on their right hands or their foreheads, so that no one could buy or sell except one who had the stamped image of the beast's name or the number that stood for its name. Wisdom is needed here; one who understands can calculate the number of the beast, for it is a number that stands for a person. His number is six hundred and sixty-six.[442]

Father Chris Alar, MIC, director of the Association of Marion Helpers at the National Shrine of Divine Mercy in Stockbridge, Massachusetts, said that *"the Antichrist is not the devil, but rather a man. Some believe that he will be a powerful Jew. He will have a deep hatred of all the saints and against our faith. He will be worse than Hitler and Napoleon."*[443] Professor Schoeman believes the Antichrist has already been born and actually identifies him as George Soros. Soros, said Schoeman, uses his immense and powerful wealth to destroy the family unit and Christianity through his propaganda.

With the five requirements enumerated in the pages of the Bible satisfied or nearing fulfillment, it would appear that the signs indicative of the end times and the advent of the second coming of Christ, as prophesied, are also at hand.

The following is a review of those signs, as foretold by Jesus and the prophets throughout Sacred Scripture. Matthew tells us that, as Jesus was sitting on the Mount of Olives, the disciples approached him privately and asked Jesus to describe the signs of the end of the age. He replied:

> *See that no one deceives you. For many will come in my name, saying, "I am the Messiah," and they will deceive many. You will hear of wars and reports of wars, see that you are not alarmed, for these things must happen, but it will not yet be the end. Nation will rise against nation, and kingdom against kingdom; there will be famines and earthquakes from place to place. All these are the beginning of the labor pains. Then they will hand you over to persecution, and they will kill you. You will be hated by all nations because of my name. And then many will be led into sin; they will betray and hate one another. Many false prophets will arise and deceive many, and because of the increase of evildoing, the love of many will grow cold. But the one who perseveres to the end will be saved. And this gospel of the kingdom will be preached throughout the world as witness to all nations, and then the end will come.*
>
> *When you see the desolating abomination spoken of through Daniel the prophet standing in the holy place* (let the reader understand), *then those in Judea must flee to the mountains, a person on the housetop must not go down to get things out of his house, a person in the field must not return to get his cloak. Woe to pregnant women and nursing mothers in those days. Pray that your flight not be in winter or on the Sabbath, for at that time there will be great tribulation, such as has not been since the beginning of the world until now, nor ever will be. And if those days had not been shortened, no one would be saved; but for the sake of the elect they will be*

shortened. If anyone says to you then, "Look, here is the Messiah!" or, "There he is!" do not believe it. False messiahs and false prophets will arise, and they will perform signs and wonders so great as to deceive, if that were possible, even the elect. Behold, I have told it to you beforehand. So if they say to you, "He is in the desert," do not go out there; if they say, "He is in the inner rooms," do not believe it. For just as lightning comes from the east and is seen as far as the west, so will the coming of the Son of Man be. Wherever the corpse is, there the vultures will gather.

Immediately after the tribulation of those days, the sun will be darkened, and the moon will not give its light, and the stars will fall from the sky, and the powers of the heavens will be shaken. And then the sign of the Son of Man will appear in heaven, and all the tribes of the earth will mourn, and they will see the Son of Man coming upon the clouds of heaven with power and great glory. And he will send out his angels with a trumpet blast, and they will gather his elect from the four winds, from one end of the heavens to the other.

Learn the lesson from the fig tree. When its branch becomes tender and sprouts leaves, you know that summer is near. In the same way, when you see all these things, know that he is near, at the gates. Amen, I say to you, this generation will not pass away until all these things have taken place. Heaven and earth will pass away, but my words will not pass away.

But of that day and hour no one knows, neither the angels of heaven, nor the Son, but the Father alone. For as it was in the days of Noah, so it will be at the coming of the Son of Man. In [those] days before the flood, they were eating and drinking, marrying and giving in marriage, up to the day that Noah entered the ark. They did not know until the flood came and carried them all away. So will it be [also] at the coming of the Son of Man. Two men will be out in the field; one will be taken, and one will be left. Two women will be grinding at the mill; one will be taken, and one will be left.

Therefore, stay awake! For you do not know on which day your Lord will come. Be sure of this: if the master of the house had known the hour of night when the thief was coming, he would have stayed awake and not let his house be broken into. So too, you also must be prepared, for at an hour you do not expect, the Son of Man will come.[444]

A very similar account of the events leading to the end of the age can be found in the Gospel of Mark Chapters 12 and 13 and in Luke Chapter 17.

If, as many have predicted, we are indeed at the end of the age, then these signs should be recognizable and evident in the world today. It should be noted that neither Jesus nor his apostles indicated that all of these things would happen everywhere in the world simultaneously, but rather only that they would happen. A growing number of people who have studied the end-times prophecies believe that they are happening now.

Chapter 13

Signs of the Times

For years, various people and groups have been proclaiming that we are in the end times. In the past twenty years alone, there have been many sensational claims that Armageddon is upon us. The Rev. Jerry Falwell, along with perhaps hundreds of others, predicted that the new millennium would be the fulfillment of the Christian prophecy of the end-times. It is hard to forget the panic that the impending Y2K brought about.

There was, of course, eighty-nine-year-old televangelist, Harold Camping, who once served as the president of the Family Radio Network. He predicted that a series of earthquakes would signal the rapture. It was to begin at 6:00 p.m. on May 21, 2011. He was so believed that many people actually quit their jobs and sat at home in fear and panic waiting for the appointed day and hour. When nothing happened, Camping moved the judgment day to October 21. When nothing happened on that day Camping grew silent and stopped making any doomsday predictions.

In August and September 2011, it was the Comet Elenin that caused fascination with end-times theorists. Internet bloggers proclaimed that the comet would create havoc on the earth and destroy the planet. When NASA pushed back against their claims, the blogosphere exploded with claims of government cover-up.

Most recently, it was the ancient Mayan calendar that caused the uproar. The Mayans, who ruled Mexico and Central America until about 900 A.D., used three different calendars. One of them ended on December 21, 2012 causing sensationalists to speculate that that would be the last day. Despite this theory having been debunked, some partied, while others planned for their own course of survival. Still others simply panicked.

It seems that every few years someone comes up with another prediction of when the end will come. Most of these have an inexplicable desire to accurately predict the exact date of the final destruction even though we have been assured by God Himself that no one but the Father knows the time and day of the Second Coming of Christ. But while speculators deliberate, Biblical scholars scour the Good Book, picking apart ancient prophecies and the very words of Jesus who foretold the exact signs that would occur when the end is near, and those prophecies have been supported by, and expanded on, by hundreds of additional prophecies over the past two thousand years.

In a broadcast on January 26, 1947, the Venerable Archbishop Fulton Sheen conveyed a prophetic sermon entitled, *Signs of Our Times*. In it he focused on the Antichrist, the apocalypse, [and] a coming chastisement, saying in part;

> *Only those who live by faith really know what is happening in the world....The battle lines are being clearly drawn and the basic issues are no longer in doubt....From now on men will divide themselves into two religions, understood again as surrender to an absolute. The conflict of the future is between an absolute who is the God-Man and an absolute which is the man-god; between the God Who became Man and the man who makes himself god; between brothers in Christ and comrades in Antichrist....*
>
> *He (the Antichrist) will come disguised as the Great Humanitarian; he will talk peace, prosperity and plenty not as means to lead us to God, but as ends in themselves....Evil catastrophe must come to reject us, to despise us, to hate us, to persecute us, and then, then we shall define our loyalties, affirm our fidelities and state on whose side we stand....Our quantity indeed will decrease, but our quality will increase. It is not for the Church that we fear, but for the world. We tremble not that God may be dethroned but that barbarism may reign....Those who have the faith had better keep in the state of grace and those who have neither had better find out what they mean, for in the coming age there will be only one way to stop your trembling knees, and that will be to get down on them and pray.[445]*

While Venerable Sheen's sermon of over seventy years ago is certainly descriptive of events of today, other Bible scholars have more recently offered explanations of the current conditions plaguing the planet. Michael Sneider is an expert on the subject of the end times and an American author who has written several books on the topic. He recognizes several current events occurring in the world that are indicative of the emergence of a great chastisement that, as prophesied by many of the great mystics, will precede the end times. The signs noted in the Bible, as well as those prophetically elucidated by so many Catholic saints and other holy people, can be clearly seen and heard today by anyone who has eyes that see and ears that hear.

Sneider points to natural disasters of all types that have occurred with regularity, and in unprecedented numbers, in the past several years. In the last two years alone news headlines have been filled with reports of vast numbers of natural and man-made disasters worldwide, some of a variety not seen in years and others of historic magnitude. These include hurricanes, tornadoes, cyclones, earthquakes, tsunamis, droughts, famines, floods, volcanic eruptions, wildfires, and plagues such as locusts, mosquitos, and novel viruses.

As of early October 2020, in the United States alone, wildfires raged out of control in California, Oregon, Alaska, Arizona, Colorado, Florida, Idaho, and Montana. Last year's wildfire in Australia was one of the worst ever recorded.

Bizarre weather patterns have been reported in many places including in California which recently experienced a single wind gust of 209 mph. In Australia in 2019 a two-month rainfall was realized in just two days, causing extraordinary and unprecedented flooding termed "biblical" by many meteorologists. Similar rain events occurred in the midwestern United States and other places as well. In May 2020, India and Bangladesh braced for the strongest storm ever recorded in the Bay of Bengal.

A massive dust cloud, perhaps the largest in fifty years, spread from the Sahara Desert across the Atlantic Ocean and into the United States in June 2020, adding to the respiratory problems already exacerbated by the Coronavirus that plagued the entire world in that year.

Earthquakes of significant magnitude have been occurring with greater frequency worldwide and in places not generally prone to tremor events, such as Ohio and Puerto Rico. Likewise, the frequency and intensity of tsunamis have grown over the past several years. There has been an increase in volcanic activity in many places, including Hawaii and Indonesia.

Earlier in 2020, an army of locusts descended upon West Africa, destroying entire farms in just seconds. At last report the swarm appeared to be heading toward China. In May, a swarm of murder hornets measuring two inches long with the ability to sting multiple times, delivering seven times more venom than a honeybee, left Asia and were found in the United States in Washington State. According to Dr. Marc Siegel, Fox News medical contributor, it is just a matter of time before they spread over the entire continent. In September 2020, large swarms of mosquitos plagued Louisiana, killing a significant number of cows, deer, horses, and other livestock there, while in Wales, dozens of octopuses washed ashore for no apparent reason.

And currently, the world is battling five different deadly viruses at the same time, including the Coronavirus, the African Swine Fever, the HINI Swine Flu, the H5N1 Bird Flu, and the H5N8 Bird Flu. In addition, the last ten years have seen world-wide wars, and racial and civil unrest unprecedented in recent history.

Biblical and post-Biblical prophets and mystics have spoken of all such events as a prelude to the great chastisement discussed in previous chapters. The Blessed Virgin Herself warned in several apparitions, in various parts of the globe, of these very things as being signs indicative of God's disappointment and anger with mankind.

The current indicators specify to many that the earth is now experiencing the smaller chastisements that were predicted as the precursor to the three days of darkness and God's great chastisement. Unlike the many failed end-times predictions of the past, the prophecies discussed in this book do not focus on trying to pinpoint the date on which Christ will come again; they simply attempt to decipher signs given by Jesus and His subsequent prophets so as to issue a warning call to conversion and repentance.

Chapter 14

Astronomical Signs

One of the elements of the prophecies of the great chastisement pertains to a comet that will collide with, or make a near pass of, the earth, causing significant destruction in its wake. Little has been said of that element of the chastisement up to this point of the book. Consequently, this chapter will look at the potential of that part of the prophecy coming to pass.

Science tells us that the universe contains hundreds of thousands of comets and, as of July 2019, more than 6,619 of these have been identified traveling within our solar system. In addition, there is a reservoir of comet-like bodies in the outer solar system estimated to be in the trillions.

It is evident that the larger cosmic bodies crashing into the Earth or a nearby planet or moon could cause disturbances in the solar system significant enough to greatly impact life on this planet. A direct crash of a comet into the earth could be sufficient to eliminate all traces of life on the planet. The Earth's atmosphere could very easily become poisoned with methane gas or other elements contained within the comet.

We now know from historical and archeological discoveries that a comet did indeed pass the Earth at the time of the Exodus, just as recorded in the Book of Exodus. The Biblical Book

> *does not speak of the comet itself, but only of what certainly appears to be its logical effects...When the tail of the Exodus comet crossed the path of the earth, a red dust, impalpable, like fine flour, began to fall. It was too fine to be seen, which is why it is not named in Exodus (7:21), but it colored everything red, and the water of the*

Egyptians was changed into "blood." The fish died and the water was poisoned by the decomposition of their flesh. It is for this reason that the Egyptians had to "scratch the Earth," that is to say, to open new wells. A similar occurrence was recorded in various parts of the world. After the fine rusty pigment fell over Egypt, there followed a coarser dust – "like ash," this is recorded in Exodus, for then it was visible. This ash irritated the skin and eyes of both men and animals. They scratched themselves and sores formed; boils appeared and changed into pustules for want of being treated. Soon, the infection spread to the whole body and death followed. After that ash-like substance came a shower of fine sand, then coarse sand, grit, gravel, small stones, large stones, and finally, boulders. The narrative of the Book of Exodus confirms this and is in turn corroborated by various documents found in Mexico, Finland, Siberia, Egypt, and India. It is therefore certain that a comet crossed the path of the earth more than three thousand years ago, causing widespread destruction. This is the kind of phenomenon (if the prophecies are accurate) which is soon to strike the earth again. And now, as it was then, this exceptional occurrence will be permitted by God as a punishment for the sins of men.[446]

Certainly, God can and has used celestial signs for his own purpose. The Star of Bethlehem that led the wise men to the baby Jesus, the eclipse at the time of Jesus's death on the cross, and the plagues brought about in the Book of Exodus as just described, are three ancient examples. More modern instances might include

...the total solar eclipse on August 21, 2017 that took place during the one hundredth anniversary of Fatima and the Revelation 12 sign that occurred. This coincided with the anniversary of the apparitions of Mary at Knock on August 21, 1879 – a silent apparition taken directly out of the book of the Apocalypse. The path of the eclipse went right through the heart of the United States as if to display the ideological division that existed in our country. Something very similar happened right before the United States Civil War and then again in 1914 right before World War I as a total solar eclipse passed over Eastern Europe, as if to announce judgment on mankind for turning its back on God. And then again on July 8, 1918 right before the Spanish Flu pandemic affected over five hundred million people worldwide.

Then you have [an] almost unbelievable celestial event that took place on September 23, 2017 – exactly thirty-three days after the

total eclipse of August 21, 2017 (Our Lady of Knock). This celestial [event] is called by many the "Revelation 12 Sign" because it is right out of the Book of the Apocalypse, Chapter 12.

The beginning of this celestial event began on November 20, 2016 (the Feast of Christ the King). It marked the end of the jubilee of Mercy. On that day, the planet Jupiter enters constellation Virgo like Christ entered the womb of Mary. Nine and one half months later, Jupiter exits "the womb of Virgo" and on that day, September 23, the sun rose and appeared behind Virgo when the moon was literally under the feet of Virgo. And above the head of Virgo was a crown of twelve stars (nine from Leo and three from the planets Mars, Venus and Mercury). We find truth in the words of Fulton Sheen, "Nothing ever happens out of Heaven except with the finesse of all details."[447]

It is possible, then, as Yves Dupont point out, that the destruction described by the prophets in the many prophecies examined in this book, could come about, not as the result of World War III, but rather as the result of a cosmic event of astronomical significance that could cause the type of calamities described in the prophecies. These include:

plagues, namely, fire in the sky, fires on earth, hail of stones, violent lightning, complete darkness, gigantic earthquakes, tidal waves, droughts, floods, air made irrespirable, tremendous hurricanes, famines, epidemics, and the presence of a comet. In other words, the prophecies list the various plagues but without giving the overall picture. In my opinion, the comet will be responsible for the other plagues in the order which I have tentatively indicated.[448]

Current science does raise the potential for astronomical events leading to an earthly disaster. In 2017, Calvin College professor Larry Molnar and his team said in a statement *"that a pair of stars on the constellation Cygnus will collide in 2022, give or take a year, creating an explosion in the night sky so bright that it will be visible to the naked eye."* They predict that the two stars will eventually *"merge and explode...at which time the star will increase its brightness ten thousandfold, becoming one of the brighter stars in the heavens for a time."[449]* This type of collision could occur at any time in any solar system and each occurrence has the potential of directly or indirectly ultimately impacting the conditions on earth.

The Hubble Telescope captured a dramatic moment recently. "In January 2018, a bright explosion of light was spotted at the outskirts of a galaxy called NGC 2525, seventy million lightyears away." The telescope was in fact filming the explosion of a star known as a Type la supernova, *"which occurs when a white dwarf star in a binary pair siphons off so much material from its companion that it becomes unstable and explodes in a supernova."*[450] Though not impacting the Earth, it clearly reveals that such celestial events do take place rather routinely and could happen within our own solar system at any time.

On June 3, 2020, Fox News reported that the National Aeronautics and Space Administration (NASA) is watching a *"massive asteroid that's coming closer to earth each day. The Space agency has an asteroid watch section of its website showing the next five approaches, which are all in the next few days."*[451] The largest of these is the size of a stadium with three others the size of a plane, and one the size of a house. While the closest approach is estimated to be 1.8 million miles away, they are getting closer with each pass and 1.8 million miles is not considered a great distance when speaking of such events.

Finally, on August 23, 2020, CNN reported that NASA's Jet Propulsion Laboratory projected that 2018VP1, a small celestial object with a diameter of six and a half feet, is expected to enter the earth's atmosphere on November 2, 2020.[452] While, because of its small size, it will not have a significant impact on the earth, it does exhibit the vulnerability of our planet when it comes to astronomical events.

In 1993, the Astronomical Society of the Pacific wrote of *"a possible collision between Earth and Comet Swift-Tuttle,"*[453] an event that could occur as early as August 14, 2126. This comet was first discovered in July 1862 by American astronomers Lewis Swift and Horace Tuttle. The comet has a highly elongated orbit with a period of about 120 years. It is twenty-six thousand meters across. A 2017 article confirms that a

> *slow-moving asteroid no larger than four hundred meters across...would be enough to cause tremendous regional devastation, destroying a city if it collided with one, causing a tsunami ten times as destructive as the one that famously hit Japan in 2011 and resulting in a crater the likes of which Earth sees perhaps just once every one hundred-thousand years. Such a strike would be ten to one hundred times more destructive than the meteor strike that created the famed Meteor Crater in the Southwestern United States. Yet if Swift-Tuttle were to strike Earth, it would release more than one billion megatons of energy: the energy equivalent to twenty-million hydrogen bombs exploding all at once. Without a doubt, the comet that gives rise to the Perseids is far and away the single most dangerous object known to humanity.*[454]

Yves Dupont describes the effects of a near pass of a comet on the Earth as it relates to the prophecies of chastisement. As the comet approaches, the climate will begin to change, causing droughts and floods. Summer will become cold as the comet's gases interfere with usual solar radiation. These conditions would worsen as the comet gets closer, leading to food shortages. Winter weather is hot because the comet is close enough to radiate its own heat. The comet's tail will cause a rain of dust and then sky fire. As the comets tail, comprised of hydrogen, mixes with the earth's oxygen, the atmosphere will ignite, causing electrical discharges between the atmosphere and the comet. The now depleted oxygen supply will be replaced by the comet's methane gas, making the air irrespirable. The Earth's surface, now dry and hot from the comet's heat, will cause fields to ignite from the falling fire stones. Forests and cities alike will flare up. Torrential rains, created by the shortage of oxygen and the combustion of the comet's hydrogen in the sky, will cause massive floods and hurricanes, brought about by the climatic changes, and the huge sky fires will spawn massive and powerful tornadoes. The thick dust and gases of the comet's tail as well as the thick layers of clouds in the sky following the combustion of the hydrogen will cause the sky to darken and blot out the sun for three days. The gravitational pull of the comet's head will cause earthquakes and tidal waves, followed by droughts, fires, and floods. The famines and injuries caused to humans will also cause widespread epidemics. In the end, the Earth, with newly enriched soil infused with nitrogen caused by the lightning strikes, will yield abundantly and the precipitation of the nitrogen will help restore the proper balance of the atmosphere after the binding of so much oxygen into water. All of this will be in place during the period of peace that is to follow.

Conclusion

Our Lady to Gisella Cardia
in the Apparitions of
Trevignano Romano, Italy

I t was in 2016 that Gisella Cardia and her husband Gianni visited the
site of the apparitions in Medjugorje, Bosnia Herzegovina. While in
the gift shop, she purchased a small statue of Our Lady. Over the
course of the next months, back in her hometown of Trevignano Romano, a small town about thirty miles outside of Rome, that statue began
to weep blood. Shortly thereafter, Cardia began receiving apparitions
from the Virgin Mary.

In this day and age, it might seem that such rumors of Marian apparitions would be a monumental event worthy of celebration by, if not
everyone, at least devout Catholics, especially in such a small town. On
the contrary, once news spread to the media, and the apparitions became
the subject of an Italian national television broadcast, Satan's minions
were fast at work. Cardia was criticized by locals and the television host.
Show panelists hit her with some heated criticism. She remained remarkably tranquil in the face of such treatment and those watching could easily notice the calm in her face.

Two books have been written about the weeping statuette, the apparitions, and Gisella's ecstatic experiences. A nihil obstat was issued by an
archbishop on the Polish translation of the second book, entitled *Cammino
con Maria (On the Way with Mary)* which describes the apparitions and the
associated messages through the end of 2018. A *nihil obstat* is a declaration
by the Catholic Church of no objection that warrants censoring of a book, to
an initiative, or to an appointment. Though a foreign nihil obstat does not

constitute in situ diocesan approval indicating that the apparitions are supernatural, it is a significant step in that direction. Further, the local bishop of Civita Castellana seems to be very supportive of Gisella by giving her access to a chapel to accommodate the plethora of pilgrims who regularly gather at Cardia's house to pray.

While waiting for final approval of the apparitions from Bishop Romano Rossi of the Diocese of Civita Castellana, Catholics have reason for optimism in the authenticity of the apparitions. That is because first, the messages that have been shared by Cardia by the Blessed Virgin are very similar to those received by other visionaries during previous apparitions of Our Lady, and this similarity is in the absence of any indication that Cardia was familiar with or aware of the existence of many of them. Second, several of the overtly prophetic messages would appear to have already been fulfilled, including the September 2019 message asking for prayers for China as the source of new airborne diseases. Finally, *"the messages have frequently been accompanied by visible phenomena, photographic evidence found in In Cammino con Maria, which cannot be the fruit of subjective imagination, notably the presence of the stigmata on Giselle's body and the appearance of crosses or religious texts in blood on Gisella's arms."*[455]

In addition to the weeping statue and the apparitions, many other mystical events have been documented. *"It also seems that Signora Gisella had seen Aramaic writings appear on the wall of her house, as on her arm, and that other inexplicable facts had occurred in the village."*[456]

Mary appears to Cardia with punctuality on the third of every month and hundreds now gather in Trevignano Romano to pray the Rosary with her. They meet in an open field atop a cliff that overlooks Lake Bracciano. A blue cross and a large, encased statue of the Virgin have been erected at the site and an array of lawn chairs and benches have been placed there to accommodate the large crowds.

Many of the messages Mary gives to Cardia while she is in ecstasy concern the coming chastisement and the variety of ways in which God will punish His people if they don't repent and turn to Him. In September 2019, for example, virtually before anyone outside of China knew of the Coronavirus, the Virgin asked Cardia to *"Pray for China, because new diseases will come from there, all ready to infect the air by unknown bacteria."*[457] Gisella recorded this message in a notebook, as she does with all the messages received from the Virgin, and later shared it with the crowd of onlookers.

Cardia also posted the message that a *"virus would arrive from China."* She, in fact, posts all the messages of Mary, right after the apparition. *"After a few months, the virus arrived,"* she said. *"It's never long before what* [Mary] *says come to pass.*"[458] That the 121-word message was posted on the date of the apparition was in fact verified by Catholic News Service.

The month prior, on August 3, shortly after three o'clock in the afternoon, Cardia knelt and looked upward as the Virgin appeared. Many in the crowd took photos and videos of the sun at that time as it moved and pulsated. At the conclusion of the ecstasy, she shared the Virgin's message with the crowd.

Cardia said that while the visions come on the third of each month, she also has locutions regularly at various times of the month. Hundreds of the messages, which Cardia claims she had been receiving directly from Mary or Jesus since April 2016, are published on the website of the Association of Our Lady of Trevignano Romano.

The following are some of the recent messages pertaining to the chastisement and the enlightenment that have been recorded in the notebook of Gisselle Cardia. A full list of all the messages of Our Lady of Trevignano Romano can be accessed at https://www.countdowntothekingdom.com/messages/:

April 3, 2020

Dear children, thank you for being here in prayer. My beloved, your prayers in union rise to heaven like the songs of angels. My cherished children, how many tears I have shed for this humanity; recall that in this period before being Crucified, my Son was humiliated, treated as a heretic and slandered, and similarly with the prophets who were persecuted in the name and for the love of Jesus. Therefore, do not be astonished if all this is happening again today with my children: such is history. I will always protect you, but remember, everything to come will be mitigated by your prayers, but cannot be cancelled, because what is written must be fulfilled. My beloved, I your Mother pray that my sons who are called to the priesthood will return to the true Faith and to the true magisterium of the Church where purification is taking place. My children, help me with this cry of pain: pray for Italy where the earth will shake fiercely. Pray for India. Now I bless you in the name of the Father, the Son and the Holy Spirit, Amen.[459]

April 21, 2020

Beloved children, thank you for being here in prayer and for having listened to my call in your hearts. My daughter, as on the first day, I once again ask you to open your doors and arms: give love, assurance and strength to the children whom I will send to you. Prepare safe refuges for the times to come; persecution is underway, always pay attention. My children, I ask you for strength and courage; pray for the dead that there are and will be, the epidemics will continue until my children see the light of God in their hearts. The cross will soon light up the sky, and it will be the final act of mercy. Soon, very soon everything will happen quickly, so much so that you will believe that you can take no more of all this pain, but entrust everything to your Savior, because he is ready to renew everything, and your life will be a receptacle of joy and love. Be not afraid, because I will be at your side and soon my Immaculate Heart will triumph with you. Your whole life will be transformed; behold, the Holy Spirit continues to act. Do not fear – strength and courage, children. Now I leave you with my Holy blessing in the name of the Father, the Son and the Holy Spirit, Amen.[460]

May 19, 2020

My children, thank you for being united in prayer and for having accepted my call in your hearts. My beloveds, evangelize and shout that Jesus is coming to save you. I am sad because you do not listen to my words and because of the pain you are causing my Son Jesus. Beloved children, do not grow weary, because now is the time to look around you to see who is in Christ and who is not; this is the moment for your speech to be either "yes, yes" or "no, no!" Be the light of the world: your light must be so strong that anyone can recognize you. Prepare safe refuges: prepare your houses as small churches, and I will be there with you. A revolt is ready, both inside and outside the Church. Now I bless you in the name of the Father, the Son and the Holy Spirit, Amen.[461]

May 30, 2020

My children, thank you for being united in prayer and for having listened to my call in your hearts. My soldiers of light, always be ready in your hearts to fight for my Son Jesus, and to be of one voice with my angels. My children, do not lose sight of prayer, because what you are experiencing is only an illusion of calm, whereas everything will suddenly fall. Remind all your brothers and sisters that the only thing that brings [you] *to heaven is the prayer of the Holy Rosary. Always remember this, children! Pray for the Church and for the consecrated, tormented by Satan, who are being led to make very painful decisions. Pray for America, because there is confusion. Now I bless you all, one by one, in the name of the Most Holy Trinity, Father, Son and Holy Spirit. Amen.*[462]

July 3rd, 2020

Dear children, thank you for being here in this blessed place and for having listened to my call in your hearts. Children, I come to you to ask you once again to convert. Children, these times of the apocalypse are times of confusion, of great sadness and tribulation, but be always united with Jesus who is joy and love – only thus can you be happy. Crosses are for everyone, but I ask you to love them with all your heart. Children, the love of God is so great, but often there is too much trusting in His mercy while forgetting His justice. I ask you the faithful and my priests to defend Jesus; do not flee in the face of difficulties. Children, a universal prayer encompassing more religions is not possible, because in this way Christianity – the sole truth – would be abolished. Please children, do not be hypocritical, but be faithful to the Lord and go forward, defending the truth. Now as your Mother I bless you in the name of the Father, the Son and the Holy Spirit. Amen.[463]

July 7, 2020

My children, thank you for being here in prayer and thank you for having listened to my call in your hearts. My little ones, it is beautiful for me to see all my children together in the prayer of the Holy Rosary; pray children, pray to Heaven, it has need of you. My children, negative influences upon the earth will cause earthquakes and these will be stronger and stronger. Pray for America: because of its perversion it will drink the bitter cup. Children, do not be afraid, I will always protect you; may your prayer for the world elite be unceasing, because they have yielded to evil and want to separate you again from each other; they want to silence you and make you slaves, but do not fear, because Jesus will soon free you from this dictatorship. Love one another, pray for Italy where earthquakes will make themselves felt, and in particular for France. Now I bless you in the name of the Father, the Son and the Holy Spirit, Amen.[464]

July 18, 2020

My children, thank you for being here in prayer and for having listened to my call in your hearts. Beloved children, thank you for making me listen to the prayers of the children who are so dear to my heart: they are innocent souls and are my children, open in their hearts. Dear children, never be afraid—even if the future will not be easy, I will protect you and give you the strength to go on in love for my Son. My daughter, you will experience the worst times that humanity has ever experienced, therefore rely on the prayer of the Holy Rosary and on the

Gospel, and nothing will ever happen to you if you believe in Jesus who is the way, the truth and the life. Pray concerning the confusion that exists within the Church and in politics. Today many graces will descend upon you. Now I leave you with the blessing of the Most Holy Trinity, Father, Son and Holy Spirit, Amen.[465]

July 21, 2020

My children, thank you for having answered my call in your hearts and for being here in prayer. Dear children, I often see you confused by the news coming from politics, the church and the world; they want to accustom you to evil as if everything were normal, but my children, I have been preparing you so much for these moments. I ask you for conversion and love for your brothers and sisters, because what will come will be much worse than what you are experiencing. Children, my children, I ask you, take the path of holiness: be flames burning where there is darkness, be light for the Church, for my Church and for your brothers and sisters as well as the world. Satan cunningly wants to seduce you with the pleasures of the world, with money and with sex; be strong, do not fall into this cunning trap, but pray, pray, pray so that your prayers would be light in the thickest darkness. Remember that this is a period of graces. Pray for China and America. Now I leave you my maternal blessing in the name of the Father, the Son and the Holy Spirit, Amen.[466]

August 4, 2020

My children, thank you for being here in prayer. My children, division is taking place, apostasy is taking place and you, too, are against one another; always have faith—it is only with faith that everything can be overcome. My children, because of its rulers, America will suffer many losses. Pray, pray for the Church, because the drums are playing a death-roll. War is very close. But do not fear, children, I am here to protect you. Now I leave you with my blessing in the name of the Father, the Son and the Holy Spirit, Amen.[467]

August 11, 2020

My children, thank you for being here in prayer. My children, this is the time of sowing: sow everywhere and speak so that your mouth proclaims the truth. Many of my sons of predilection (priests) *are even being persecuted by their fellow priests, but they should not fear. Children, do not fall into the demonic net; your persecutors are very skillful and convincing, but you should go ahead with the word of God without deviating from the truth. My children, when the Churches of the world unite with the world powers, then there will be true persecution and you will be forced to hide, because they will skillfully remove the Eucharistic Sacrifice from the Holy Mass. Children, do not fear, because your faith will make you witnesses of the Triumph of my Immaculate Heart. Now I bless you in the name of the Father, the Son and the Holy Spirit, Amen.*[468]

September 3, 2020

Beloved children, thanks for being here in prayer and thanks for having responded to my call in your hearts. My children, the Warning or Illumination will soon arrive, and I am here to ask you to make yourselves ready for this important event for humanity, when there will finally be the last opportunity to choose which side to take – that will be the moment. Preparing yourselves means making a good confession for cleansing your souls, nourishing yourselves often with the Eucharist – this will be the best way. Dear children, the Church is in the most total confusion, but I want to tell my Holy priests not to fear, because I and my Jesus, the only true Savior, will never abandon you. Children, my little ones, I am here to save you and to remind you to pray the Holy Rosary, a unique weapon against Satan. Children, you will be persecuted, there will be punching and spitting along your way, but do not fear, no one will ever be able to touch you, and whoever turns to God with great humility will be a witness to the Kingdom of Heaven and the Triumph of my Immaculate Heart. Children, always be lights burning in the world and be witnesses to my love; I am always waiting for you in this place blest by my Father. Now I bless you in the name of the Father, the Son and the Holy Spirit, Amen.[469]

September 8, 2020

Dear children, thank you for being here in prayer and for having responded to my call in your hearts. My children, I see that you fear the famine that will soon arrive, but I invite you to prepare yourselves for eternal life, because that is more important. Dear children, everything will fall, the sky will be tinged with red, the earth will shake as it has never done before. Children, it is useless thinking about a career and accumulating material goods because all this will no longer make any sense. Children, the seas and hailstones will enter into towns and destroy crops; this is a land of sin and nature is rebelling — all this will happen so that all might kneel before God, acknowledging Him as the Only God. My children, Jesus weeps because sin and abomination have entered the Church; He weeps because He loves His Church and in spite of profanation He is always there, in pain and weeping. The time is nearly over; please, children, there is no more time, convert. Look often to the heavens: at this moment my angels are fighting against the fallen angels, but pray, pray, pray, and fight on earth for the truth. Do not give in to changes because they do not come from God. Children, my remnant will have nothing to fear because my angels and archangels will protect you. Pray for America, which will soon drink the bitter cup. Now I leave you with my Holy Blessing in the name of the Father, Son and Holy Spirit, Amen.[470]

September 12, 2020

My children, thank you for being here in prayer. Dear children, now the time is truly short, but many do not realize how everything is falling down. I ask you to make more room for prayer: do not waste time on the things of the world. I can feel your hearts beating. My children, this is the time of confusion, especially of my favored sons (priests) *who unfortunately no longer know the right way to recover souls that are being lost, but I want to show you the exact way, and it is that of the Gospel, the Word of God and the Ten Commandments. Only thus will you find peace and joy in your hearts. Now Jesus will touch you one by one through the Holy blessing: Father, Son and Holy Spirit, Amen.*

September 19, 2020

My dear children, thank you for being here in prayer and for having listened to my call in your hearts. Beloved children, the battle between good and evil is underway to save my children from Satan. I am preparing your garden: come to me, clasp my hands and you will feel great peace in your hearts. Children, do not be concerned if there will be neither food nor drink: my Lord will be your restorer and you will lack nothing if only your gaze is turned to Him. Children, the financial collapse will affect everyone, especially those who doubt my words: fools are still looking to the future without thinking about prayer and eternal life. Pray, pray, pray for the Church, because it will be shaken by a strong earthquake; pray for my beloved children because they will be persecuted; be light, my children, for a world [where] *it is on the point of being extinguished. Now I bless you in the name of the Father, the Son and the Holy Spirit, Amen.[471]*

September 22, 2020

Dear Children, thank you for having responded to my call in your hearts. My children, I see that many of my children are not praying but are caught up in the things of the world; they have not yet understood that communal prayer is the greatest force against evil. My children, Rome and its Church will suffer their greatest pain for not having respected my wishes. Pray that the suffering would be lessened, as the light in their hearts has now gone out. My dearly beloved children, gloom and darkness are about to descend on the world; I ask you to help me even if everything must be fulfilled – God's justice is about to strike. I ask you once more in tears: pray, pray, pray greatly, because for those who do not believe, the suffering will be atrocious. Love God; kneel before Him who looks at you with a bleeding heart. I am concerned for priests who have chosen Satan and paganism: I ask you not to accept anything that is not God, One and Three. Now I leave you with my Maternal Blessing, in the name of the Father, Son and Holy Spirit, Amen.[472]

The Marian prophecies as reported by Giselle Cardia seem to single out certain nations which the Blessed Mother feels are ripe for chastisement and the urgency of Her most recent messages can certainly be heard. Among the nations that she warns are Italy, France, China, India, and the United States. Of these, Mary makes it clear that *"America will soon drink the bitter cup."**

It is a message She repeats several times. On July 7, 2020, Mary specifies that America needs prayers because of its perversion. Mary calls out America again on August 4, 2020 saying she *"will suffer many loses."*[473]

What are the American perversions for which this nation will drink the bitter cup and suffer many loses? For the answer, one need look no further than the current headlines. The United States has fallen into political and cultural disarray. As a result of racial tension, American cities have been turned into war zones where once peaceful protesters have harassed, attacked, and killed police officers and other military and civilian peacekeepers. In Seattle, Washington, protesters from a group calling itself Black Lives Matter (BLM) took over an entire city, commandeered a police headquarters, and burned and looted commercial storefronts all in an attempt to create the "City of Love." Quillette, an online publication providing a platform for free thought, described it this way:

* This message is repeated in Marian apparitions or locutions to Gisella Cardia at least three times; on July 7, 2020, on September 8, 2020 and on September 19, 2020.

Like other American cities over the last three weeks, Seattle saw protests rapidly become violent clashes with police. This ugliness waxed and waned for a fortnight until police withdrew from their East Precinct Building, effectively ceding the surrounding area to the protestors. Barriers were erected around it by activists who initially christened the new territory the Capitol Hill Autonomous Zone (CHAZ), and later renamed it the Capitol Hill Occupied Protest (CHOP). As their quasi-manifesto of June 9 put it, they had "liberated Free Capitol Hill in the name of the people of Seattle."[474]

State and local political leaders acquiesced to the protesters who held the city captive with armed militants for many weeks before violent crime within the precinct, now unprotected by the banished police, began to flourish. Sexual assaults and murders within the "City of Love" finally forced state and city officials to move in and retake the city.

The same group organized an assault on American history beginning with the unlawful destruction of statues and other forms of public art deemed by them to be symbols of racism and white supremacy. The assault began with attacks on the statues of Christopher Columbus, then progressed to include any public art depicting the American Civil War Confederacy. Finally, it evolved into an attack on religious statues, particularly those representing the Catholic Church.

What happened next was indicative of what some observers believe represents the actual motives of the Marxist leaders of Black Lives Matter: not the combatting of racism in America, but rather the destruction of America as we know it and the repression of religious thought in the advent of a new socialist society. The group began to promote the desecration of privately-owned religious statues on the grounds of Catholic churches and schools throughout North America.

Black Lives Matter leader Shaun King issued the following two tweets on Twitter on June 22, 2020, making clear the group's Marxist intentions:

King's first tweet reads:

Yes, I think the statues of the white European they claim is Jesus should also come down. / They are a form of white supremacy. / Always have been. / In the Bible, when the family of Jesus wanted to hide, and blend in, guess where they went? / EGYPT! / Not Denmark. / Tear them down.

King continues in a second tweet, saying:

Yes. / All murals and stained-glass windows of white Jesus, and his European mother, and their white friends should also come down. / They are a gross form of white supremacy. / Created as tools of oppression. / Racist propaganda. / They should all come down.[475]

Shortly after the tweets were published, a statue of Saint Junipero Sera was toppled and destroyed in California, while in Washington DC, calls were issued for the removal of the statue of Saint Damien of Molokai from the US Capitol, a statue that the self-avowed Democratic Socialist Congresswoman Alexandria Ocasio-Cortez of New York, said symbolized the "White Supremacist Culture."

On July 2, 2020, the New York archbishop, Cardinal Timothy Dolan, published a powerful letter decrying the destruction of statues and monuments in the United States. The letter was also printed as an op-ed in the *Wall Street Journal*. Dolan said that this unrest is *"unhelpful"* for our *"necessary common conversation on racism."* Dolan wrote:

Eliminating the monuments can lead to the virus that is historic amnesia. All of [those whose statues are being targeted for elimination] *still contributed a lot of good to our nation's progress. Defacing, tearing down, and hiding statues and portraits is today's version of puritanical book-burning. Such rash iconoclasm can lead to an historic amnesia that will eliminate something essential for our necessary common conversation on racism: the memory of flawed human beings who, while sadly and scandalously wrong on burning issues such as slavery and civil rights, were right on so many others, and need to be remembered for both. All people are imperfect and sinners. Eliminate all figures, and only Jesus and Mary would remain...God forbid we go through a cultural revolution like Mao's China did five decades ago! What a mess! What a disaster! Beware of those who want to purify memories and present a tidy – and inaccurate – history...If we only perfect saintly people of the past, I guess I'm left with only the Cross...and some people would ban that! I want to remember the good and the bad and recall with gratitude how even people of the past who had an undeniable dark side can still let light prevail and leave the world better.*[476]

Before long, Black Lives Matter protesters and sympathizers nationwide began an assault of the icons of the Church and the Church itself. A detailed timeline of the string of destruction was published in the Catholic news site, *Aleteia*. It describes the July 10, 2020 vandalism of a statue of Mary that has stood in front of a Queens, New York high school for the past 100 years then reviews seven similar crimes that took place over the course of the next week ,including this description of one of the most egregious of the crimes. That one took place

> *in Ocala, Florida, Saturday morning, July 11, parishioners were gathered for morning Mass when a minivan crashed into the front of Queen of Peace Church. A 23-year-old man allegedly got out of the car and spread gasoline around the lobby, then lit it on fire. No one was hurt, but the fire did extensive damage. Police later caught the suspect, who was charged with attempted second-degree murder and arson. According to local media, the suspect told investigators that he was recently diagnosed with a mental illness but was not taking his prescribed medication. He also reportedly told them he had problems with the Catholic Church.*[477]

Rather than report on this crime, the main-stream media ignored the sacrilegious actions. *The New York Times* chose to focus on predatory priests, whom they made the focus of two different pieces. With little attention being paid to the crimes by the mainstream media, the attacks against the Catholic Church continued, however, for the next two weeks. The Catholic News Agency provided this summary:

> *Recent weeks have seen acts of vandalism and destruction at Catholic churches across the United States, including arsons, decapitations, and graffiti. In addition to the most recent attacks, in the last two weeks statues of Christ and the Virgin Mary have been attacked in Florida, Tennessee, New York, and Colorado.*
> *Other Catholic religious statues in California, Missouri, and other places have been toppled or vandalized by protestors, including several of St. Junipero Serra.*
> *While some attacks on statues, most notably in California, have been committed in public by large groups with clear political affiliations, the perpetrators of other acts, including those against the images of the Virgin Mary and Christ, have not been identified.*[478]

In North America there have been close to a hundred attacks against statues of the Catholic Church documented on July 28, 2020 by Church-Pop, a Catholic internet service publication. This map can be accessed here: www.churchpop.com/2020/07/28/interactive-map-tracks-attacks-on-catholics-throughout-north america/?utm_campaign=ChurchPop&utm_medium=email&_hsmi=92226621&_hsenc=p2ANqtzBglkjPxKPeLo8PEyttd NLaldpWP1ZIUMxVnYiGJgRAJv0lUWnlh908ozmpBy1rwXLqWE8

CROMuQyRK49dndDMqbf8QqkZZ7KaoJZVq7PemM&utm_content=
92226621&utm_source=hs_email.

The assault on religious statues prompted the Religious Freedom Chair of the United States Conference of Bishops to call upon the United States Congress for better protection of churches and other houses of worship. The request was included in a letter to Congressional leaders. The bishops wrote, *"Our sacred spaces have been desecrated and our faithful murdered. We believe that all people ought to be free from fear while gathering for religious worship and service."*[479] The letter also quoted FBI statistics indicating that at least 1,244 hate crimes were committed against members of various Christian denominations in the year 2018 alone. FBI Director Christopher Wray told Congress in sworn testimony given on September 24, 2020, *"that houses of worship are increasingly becoming preferred targets by 'lone wolf' attackers."*[480] It should be noted that the US Bishop's letter was also signed by imams, rabbis and other Christian ministers.

There have been many other subtle and not-so-subtle recent attacks against Christianity in the United States. As of late September 2020, as part of their effort to contain the Coronavirus, the Mayor of San Francisco, California promulgated the rules for reopening places of worship. The rules were the strictest mandates for religious services in the country. Indoor services are still prohibited even six months into the shutdown. In most counties, including Santa Clara and Alameda, indoor religious gatherings are prohibited but worshippers are allowed to gather outdoors without a capacity limit.

San Francisco, however, allows only up to fifty people to gather for outdoor worship with only one person allowed inside a religious institution at any one time for individual prayer. As of October 1, 2020, the city regulations were loosened to allow for indoor services of up to a maximum of twenty-five people. But in a church like San Francisco's St. Mary's Cathedral, that equates to less than one percent of the facility's capacity, according to Archbishop Salvatore Joseph Cordileone, while restaurants can operate at twenty-five percent capacity without masks. To bring light to the injustice, he organized a gathering of several hundred Catholics for a mile-long march on City Hall called the "Free the Mass" demonstration. Once the socially distanced march reached its destination, the Archbishop conducted an outdoor worship service, one of the largest religious gatherings in the area in months. Participants remained socially distanced and donned masks.

In an op-ed written for the *Washington Post*, Cordileone said *"government officials were denying Americans right to worship and that he could no longer sit silent in the face of the unjust treatment."* He called the San Francisco restrictions insulting to the parishioners and a mockery to God.

This type of discrimination against the free practice of religion is not limited to California. Across the nation, many churches were forced to file suit to bring an end to unreasonable restrictions. The Catholic congresswoman and speaker of the United States House of Representatives said in response that Archbishop Cordileone needs to follow the science. Yet, Peter Chin-Hong, an infectious disease specialist at UC San Francisco, said he does not oppose more lenient capacity limits for indoor church services because by wearing masks and observing proper social distancing rules, the inherent risks are mitigated.

On another front, The September 6, 2020 edition of the *San Diego Union-Tribune* reported that the United States Navy announced that it was not going to renew contracts with Catholic priests in order to cut costs. The move leaves Navy bases without enough chaplains to keep services going, according to the report. The Archdiocese of the Military Services quickly called on the US Navy to reconsider its decision, saying that the savings from cancelling these contracts amounts to $250,000, approximately 0.000156% of the Navy budget. The Navy, however, was unfazed, holding fast to its position until a few days later when President Donald Trump ordered the Navy to renew the contracts.

Then, on September 18, 2020, Supreme Court Justice Ruth Bader Ginsburg succumbed to her battle with cancer. The architect of the legal fight for women's rights in the 1970s, Ginsburg subsequently served twenty-seven years on the nation's highest court, becoming its most prominent member. Within days of her passing, speculation began that Catholic Judge Amy Coney Barrett was considered a top candidate to fill the vacancy on the Supreme Court. Attacks against her Catholic faith were immediate. *Newsweek Magazine* ran a "hit piece" claiming that People of Praise, a Catholic group to which Barrett belonged, was the inspiration for *The Handmaid's Tale*, a novel by Margaret Atwood that describes a religion-based autocracy that took control of the United States, renaming it the country of Gilead. In this fictional country, women are considered sub-standard citizens who are punished if they try to escape. When the author herself denied that People of Praise inspired her fictional nation, *Newsweek* was forced to issue an immediate retraction. The criticism did not end with the retraction, however, and the attacks were increased.

Coney-Barrett, in fact, should be accustomed to her faith being routinely attacked during judicial confirmation hearings. About three years ago, when Coney-Barrett was being confirmed for a seat on the federal Court of Appeals, Senator Diane Feinstein questioned her about her Catholic faith, saying that the dogma of her faith lived loudly in her and that is a concern.

Coney-Barrett is not the only Catholic judicial nominee to be attacked on the basis of Catholicism. During the 2018 confirmation hearings of Brian Buescher's appointment to the federal court, Senators Kamala Harris and Mazie Hirono targeted Buesher's membership in the Knights of Columbus, a 137-year-old fraternal Catholic charitable organization. In the December 2018 hearings, Harris badgered Buescher, who became a member of the Knights twenty-five years earlier as a teenager, asking, *"Were you aware that the Knights of Columbus opposed a woman's right to choose when you joined the organization?"*[481] Hirono called the group *"extreme."*[482]

Miami Archbishop Thomas Wenski pushed back against the most recent attack on Coney-Barrett, noting that the United States *"Constitution specifically says there should be 'no religious test for office,'"*[483] adding that those who raise the issue *"are not honoring the principals of our Constitution and thereby contribute to undermining the rule of law in our nation."*[484] Wenski also addressed the specific issue of the use of the word "handmaid" by People of Praise, noting that the group's use of the term 'handmaiden,' was rooted in Scripture. *"The word 'Handmaiden' - 'ancilla' in Latin – has deep biblical roots and in the New Testament refers especially to Mary, the Mother of Jesus, who declares herself to be the 'handmaiden of the Lord,'"*[485] He added, *"That the novelist would 'culturally appropriate' this word to use in a distorted way to promote an ideology hostile to the Judeo-Christian patrimony of Western civilization only points to the growing biblical illiteracy of our elites and is indeed very disappointing."*[486] Wenski, it appeared, stood alone in his vocal defense of the Catholic faith.

Driving the attacks on the appointment of Catholics to the Supreme Court is the belief that Catholics will participate in an orchestrated effort to overturn Roe v. Wade, thereby pushing the decision to legalize abortion back to the states. With regard to the confirmation of Coney-Barret, Senator Dianne Feinstein didn't hide her own phobia when she noted that *"Barrett's religious views on abortion and other issues might influence her rulings on the court."* Other Democratic senators warned that Coney-Barrett's Catholic beliefs regarding issues such as abortion could influence her decision-making on the bench. Senator Mazie Hirono made that point abundantly clear during a September 30, 2020 press conference at which she said, *"the real issue [with Coney-Barrett] is whether her closely-held views can be separated from her ability to make objective, fair decisions with a lifetime appointment."* Senator Tammy Duckworth added, *"I fear that, if confirmed to the nation's highest court, Judge Barrett would be unable to resist the temptation of overturning decades of judicial precedent in an effort to force every American family to adhere to her individual moral code."*

One would think that in a country that has seemed to have lost its moral compass, the quality of morality in a candidate for the nation's highest court, or in society as a whole, would be embraced. One would be wrong.

In Westerly, Rhode Island, a sixty-three-year-old former nurse who is also blind was banned from a public park and library for two years for sharing her Christian faith. The matter is the subject of a major lawsuit which claims that she handed out religious pamphlets to patrons and would sometimes offer a copy of the *Gospel of John*. This, while hundreds of people gathered to protest in Providence, burning and looting stores and attacking unarmed bystanders, all with the support and encouragement of some sympathetic elected officials.

But the American promotion of abortion on demand, even up to the moment of delivery, is not the only issue that lends to the moral corruption of America of which Our Lady referred. There are other egregious violations of Catholic Church doctrine taking place in this nation that are also considered serious offenses against the doctrine of the Catholic Church. Euthanasia and mercy killings; the maltreatment of immigrants; the sexual abuse and cover-up within the Church itself; the dehumanization of some people within the LGBTQ community; the support for and promotion of untruths about marriage and family; the removal of God from a large segment of society including schools and government property; the assault on religious liberty; the defunding of the local police departments, a move that will lead to chaos and unacceptable lawlessness; the acceptance by many of socialism and communism as a preferred way of life, both are government formats that oppose organized religion; attempts at cloning and creating life; the harvesting of aborted fetal tissue for medical purposes; and other things considered immoral by the Catholic Church and a violation of its doctrine and Catechism. What is worse is that many of these positions are supported by increasing numbers of people who have been baptized into the Catholic faith and still consider themselves Catholic. In fact, some of these positions have been promoted and supported by Catholic bishops and priests who have written and spoken in favor of some of these atrocities against the faith. Some Catholic supporters of these antithetical positions serve at the highest levels of government within this nation.

If there are any lingering doubts about the veracity of Mary's prophetic words at Fatima regarding the apostasy infiltrating the Church at the highest levels, one need only look to the most recent outrages taking place in the Vatican and in the Diocese of New Orleans.

In Vatican City, Rome, Pope Francis fired Secretariat of State Cardinal Angelo Becciu, following the October 5, 2020 report that Becciu had *"given half a million euros to Ceilia Marogna's Slovenian company and that she had a 'great relationship of trust' with Becciu...Documents show that*

Marogna used the Vatican money to buy expensive Prada and Chanel hand-bags as well as other luxury goods,"[487] rather than on her Vatican consultancy work and her salary. Becciu was the second-ranking official, serving at the Secretariat of State from 2011 to 2018 when Pope Francis named him a cardinal and moved him to the Congregation for the Causes of Saints. That ended on September 24 when the Pope accepted Becciu's resignation as a Cardinal. He was then removed from his curial office. Becciu had previously been linked with a number of Vatican scandals that involved the misuse or misappropriation of Vatican funds.

In Louisiana, a scandal of a different type unfolded. *"On September 30, Father Travis Clark was arrested on obscenity charges when he was observed filming himself in a sexual act with two women atop the altar in his Louisiana parish."*[488] Clark was the pastor of Saints Peter and Paul Church in Pearl River, Louisiana. According to police reports and court records, a local resident called police after she peered into the church window and witnessed the thirty-seven-year-old priest engaged in sexual activity on the altar with two women later identified as Mindy Dixon (41) and Melissa Cheng (23). Dixon, a pornographic performer and dominatrix, had posted on her social media the day prior to the arrest that *"she was headed to New Orleans to 'defile a house of God' alongside another 'dominatrix,' presumably Cheng.."*[489] The altar had been outfitted with stage lighting.

Clark was ordained a priest in 2013 and was named pastor of Saints Peter and Paul Church in 2019. Recently, he was named chaplain of Pope John Paul II High School in Slidell, Louisiana. There he had replaced Father Pat Wattingy, who had been suspended from public ministry on October 1 after admitting to sexual abuse of a minor in 2018. Though the sexual abuse had been reported in February *"and the student's parents had alerted the archdiocese, Wattingy was allowed to remain in ministry at the school until the end of the academic year."* [490]

New Orleans Archbishop Gregory Aymond said in a statement released on October 9, 2020, *"the priest will never again serve in Catholic ministry. Fr. Travis Clark's obscene behavior was deplorable. His desecration of the altar in Church was demonic. I am infuriated by his actions. When the details became clear, we had the altar removed and burned. I will consecrate a new altar tomorrow."*[491]

The archbishop was not done, however. Unfortunately, Archbishop Aymond also addressed the Wattingy affair in his statement and defended the diocesan position of leaving the priest in the school until the conclusion of the academic year.

The Louisiana incidents are just the most recent examples of the great apostasy that has been prophesied and recorded throughout the pages of this book, and these are the type of things to which the Virgin

Mary spoke when She indicated God's displeasure with people of America. To be fair, America is not isolated when it comes to problems such as these. Examples of similar behavior can be found in various parts of the world and the Virgin has mentioned the other nations as well when she spoke of God's anger and the administration of His justice through chastisement.

Our Lady said at Fatima that sins of the flesh send more souls to hell than any other sin. She also said issues of marriage and the family would be a critical factor influencing God's decision to inflict a punishment. Pope Benedict XVI agrees. In a 2020 biography, the former Pontiff links same-sex marriage to the Antichrist. In the biography of the former pope, *Benedict XVI – A Life*, the ninety-three-year-old Pope Emeritus addresses these issues by making

> *a series of wide-ranging comments targeting LGBTQ people and a woman's right to choose...and complains that 'modern society' is in the middle of formulating an Antichristian creed. "One hundred years ago, everybody would have considered it to be absurd to speak of a homosexual marriage," he says in one of a series of conversations with* [author Peter] *Seewald. "Today, one is being excommunicated by society if one opposes it." Benedict believes the same is true of "abortion and to the creation of human beings in the laboratory," the latter referring to in-vitro fertilization. He proceeds to say that the "fear of this spiritual power of the Antichrist...is more than natural."[492]*

The words of Pope Benedict XVI harken back to those of Sister Lucia, the oldest of the Fatima seers who recounted the words spoken to her in Our Lady's various messages:

> *The sins of the world are very great. If men knew what eternity is, they would do everything to change their lives. Men are lost because they do not think of the death of Our Lord and do not do penance. Many marriages are not good; they do not please Our Lord, and they are not of God. The sins that lead more souls to hell are the sins of the flesh. Fashions that will greatly offend Our Lord will appear. People who serve God should not follow fashions. The Church has no fashions. Our Lord is always the same.[493]*

America has become a nation consumed with hatred and some Catholics, rather than setting an example of Christian love and acceptance, have fallen prey to the American obsession demonstrating the extent to which the prophesied apostasy has established itself. For the past fifty to seventy years, Americans, including Catholic youths, have been indoctrinated by a system intent on removing the very concept of God from the public square. It has been a subtle, incremental change of the hearts and minds of American citizens by those who, under the guise of democracy, have fallen victim to the sword of Satan. Surely, the century of evil, as described by Pope Leo XIII in 1884, is upon us. At no time in our history has the United States been at a lower point of moral decency.

The year 1958 may have been seminal in the American decline of morality. That is when Steven Engel, a Jewish New Yorker, joined with other parents to file suit against the State of New York over a state-endorsed prayer that was being recited in schools. The prayer read simply, *"Almighty God, we acknowledge our dependence upon Thee, and we beg Thy blessings upon us, our parents, our teachers, and our Country."*[494]

On June 25, 1962, the United States Supreme Court issued a decision siding with Engel and ruled that the required prayer was inconsistent with the Establishment Clause of the First Amendment of the Constitution which reads, *"Congress shall make no law respecting an establishment of religion, or prohibiting the free exercise thereof."*[495]

This decision was quickly followed by a 1963 US Supreme Court ruling that banned bible reading and overturned a state law banning the teaching of evolution, essentially meaning that the theory of evolution and not the theory of creationism must be taught in public schools.

Of course, the now controversial Roe v. Wade ruling in which the US Supreme Court affirmed the legality of a woman's right to have an abortion under Section One of the Fourteenth Amendment to the Constitution was handed down in 1973, paving the way for torture and killing of almost seventy million unborn babies since.

Following Roe v. Wade, the pace of decisions contributing to moral depravity and giving approval to the degradation of religion quickened and became less subtle with the government's acceptance and funding of art that desecrated Jesus (see photographer Andres Serrano's 1987 submission to the Southeastern Center of Contemporary Art of *Piss Christ,* which depicted a crucifix submerged in a jar of the artist's own urine - https://100photos.time.com/photos/andres-serrano-piss-christ.) and then Mary (see artist Chris Ofili's painting entitled "Holy Virgin Mary," which depicts a black Virgin Mary splattered with elephant dung and laden with pornographic pictures at an exhibition at the Brooklyn Museum of Art - https://www.khanacademy.org/humanities/global-culture/concepts-in-art-1980-to-now/ritual-spirituality-and-transcendence/a/chris-ofili-the-holy-virgin-mary.). In both cases, the government supported the right of the artist to desecrate the Christian religion in this way and even provided funding to display their art in public.

Since then a plethora of state and federal cases restricting the religious liberties of Catholics and Christians have been and continue to be handed down. Sir Edmund Burke has been credited with saying, *"The only thing necessary for the triumph of evil is for good men to do nothing."*[496] Nothing is exactly what too many Catholics in the United States have been doing to combat the many assaults against them and their Christian faith. Rather than fighting to support their religious freedom, their silent acquiescence has made them complicit in the systematic degradation of societal values. Worse, many of the morally corrupt practices pervading twenty-first century America are proactively supported by those who claim the banner of Catholicism. Their actions help fulfill the prophetic utterances identifying the great apostasy that would infect the Church.

Recently, President Donald Trump was singled out by Washington D.C. Archbishop Wilton Gregory for two appearances. In the first, Trump held a bible in front of St. John's Episcopal Church across from the White House after it had been set afire by Black Lives Matter protestors. The following day, Trump appeared at the D.C. shrine honoring Pope John Paul II, where he announced his signing of an executive order protecting religious liberty. These are two things that one might think would elicit praise from Catholics struggling to maintain their religious liberty. But rather than elevate the symbolic gestures, Archbishop Gregory slammed Trump, saying, *"I find it baffling and reprehensible that any Catholic facility would allow itself to be so egregiously misused and manipulated in a fashion that violates our religious principles, which call us to defend the rights of all people, even those with whom we might disagree..."*[497]

The Archbishop's words were used as fodder by Catholics across America, including those in the highest reaches of American government, to condemn Trump's use of the Bible as a prop. Within days, Former Apostolic Nuncio of the United Nations, Archbishop Carlo Maria Vigano, responded in an open letter to President Trump. In his three-page letter Vigano

> *warns the president of a spiritual battle he believes currently wages between good and evil in the United States. He refers to the battle as "biblical," saying he believes it is between "the children of light and the children of darkness." The retired archbishop explains these two sides as "the clear separation between the offspring of the Woman [Mary] and the offspring of the Serpent [Satan]," and that "deep state"*

groups are "waging war" against goodness. "For the first time, the United States has in you a President who courageously defends the right to life, who is not ashamed to denounce the persecution of Christians throughout the world, who speaks of Jesus Christ and the right of citizens to freedom of worship," Archbishop Vigano explains. "Your participation in the March for Life, and more recently your proclamation of the month of April as National Child Abuse Prevention Month, are actions that confirm which side you wish to fight on. And I dare to believe that both of us are on the same side in this battle, albeit with different weapons."

He also addresses what he believes is the mainstream media's attack on truth and goodness. He encourages the "children of light" to "come together and make their voices heard" through the power of prayer. "What more effective way is there to do this, Mr. President, than by prayer, asking the Lord to protect you, the United States, and all humanity from this enormous attack of the Enemy? Before the power of prayer, the deceptions of the children of darkness will collapse, their plots will be revealed, their betrayal will be shown, their frightening power will end in nothing, brought to light and exposed for what it is: an infernal deception."

The letter also follows President Trump's visit to the St. John Paul II National Shrine. The Archdiocese of Washington issued an official statement regarding the visit, calling it "baffling" and "reprehensible." However, Vigano says he believes "the attack to which you were subjected after your visit to the National Shrine of Saint John Paul II is part of the orchestrated media narrative. It is disconcerting that there are Bishops – such as those whom I recently denounced – who, by their words, prove that they are aligned on the opposing side."

However, the Archbishop believes good will ultimately defeat evil. He also ensures the President that the power of prayer will triumph over what he believes is the waging evil. He concludes with a blessing upon the president, First Lady, and the American People. "Mr. President, my prayer is constantly turned to the beloved American nation. I am praying for you and also for all those who are at your side in the government of the United States. I trust that the American people are united with me and you in prayer to Almighty God. I bless you and the First Lady, the beloved American nation, and all men and women of good will." [498]

The full letter of Archbishop Carlo Maria Vigano is available to read online.

This particular issue not only brings to light the lack of understanding of many Catholics about the importance of the current attacks on the faith as it pertains to the coming chastisement, but also highlights the great apostasy that has been prophesied by so many visionaries as a vital cause of the chastisements. Recall their prophetic words that *"bishop will rise against bishop and cardinal against cardinal,"* perhaps demonstrating just how close at hand the time of chastisement really is.

The prophecies entrusted to Gisella Cardia by the Virgin Mary have focused on the great chastisement that God has planned for a sinful humanity. Mary tells us that we can't escape the tribulation because it is promised in Divine writing. We can, however, mitigate the severity of the chastisement through prayer, sacrifice, penance, and fasting. In many ways these prophetic utterances are similar, and in some cases, identical to Marian prophecies that visionaries have provided over many centuries. But in all these messages, horrific though they may appear, is an underlying message of hope for those who heed the warning and turn back to God. Trust in Jesus will lead everyone to an inner peace in knowing that His great love will save us. Though time is quickly running out, it's not too late. Jesus told us through Saint Faustina of His great mercy. He asked her to tell everyone of His mercy as the antidote to the just punishment he will impart.

Catholics repeat again and again, *"I believe in God, the Father almighty, Creator of heaven and earth, and in Jesus Christ, His only Son, our Lord, who was conceived by the Holy Spirit, born of the Virgin Mary...."**

This Creed is recited at every Catholic Mass and every time a Catholic prays the rosary, the Chaplet of Divine Mercy and other popular prayers and devotions. The question is, if Catholics truly believe that God created everything and that Jesus, the Son of the Blessed Virgin Mary, is also the Son of God, then why would one doubt the prophetic words that Jesus and Mary provide? Is it even remotely possible that an omnipotent, omnipresent God would lie or mislead us?

Father Richard Heilman, author and founder of the Knights of Divine Mercy, an apostolate for men's faith formation, speaks to the issue of the apostasy of some Catholics and cites an example that is seen in every

* The present text of the Apostles' Creed is similar to the baptismal creed used in the church in Rome in the 3rd and 4th centuries. It reached its final form in southwestern France in the late 6th or early 7th century. It is trinitarian in structure with sections affirming belief in God the Father, God the Son, and God the Holy Spirit. The Apostles' Creed was based on Christian theological understanding of the canonical gospels, the letters of the New Testament, and to a lesser extent the Old Testament.

church today. Knowing that Jesus is present in the Eucharist, Heilman says, should cause every person to dress appropriately before entering the church to attend Mass. Yet, the actions belie the belief and many Catholics wear their worst recreational clothes to Mass, indicating that they don't really believe the doctrine. What's worse, they don't even realize they don't believe. Heilman refers to this concept as *"Stealth Arianism."[499]*

The prophetic words of Jesus and the prophets that preceded Him as told through public revelations, as well as the private revelations of those who came after Him, indicate a terrible chastisement is at hand. It will include a frightening enlightenment of the soul, a terrifying three days of darkness in which up to three quarters of the earth's population will die from unprecedented penetrating lightning and prolonged and powerful earthquakes. Some will even die of fright as the gates of hell are opened and the demons are released to freely walk the earth in search of souls to ensnare. These demons will pretend to be loved ones in search of help and will cry outside your door, begging to be allowed in. We are told, however, that if we open the door to them, go outside, or even look out a window, we will be struck dead on the spot as God does not want mankind to witness His great wrath. All unbelievers will perish as will many of the faithful, but only the faithful will live through the turbulent days. Survivors of these horrific events, we are told, will envy the dead because of the death and desolation they will find when the darkness ends. Life as we know it will have ceased. New shelter will be needed. The food that sustains us will have to be grown from the seed as nothing will remain after the darkness.

However, when it is all over, the entire world will convert to Catholicism. There will be peace and the things that were once so important to sinful people—jobs, money, travel, etc.—will no longer have significance or meaning in our lives. God tells us that for the faithful, these are days of rejoicing, as we will understand our souls and know our sins. It will be a time of great conversion and a means to salvation and for those reasons it will be a time of joy.

Catholics have been given the ultimate weapon in the fight against Satan and his temptations and distractions from all that is important. That defensive missile is the Holy Rosary given by the Blessed Virgin to Saint Dominic and Blessed Alain. At Fatima in 1917, the year of Satan's assumed commencement of his hundred-year domination granted by God in the conversation overheard by Pope Leo XIII, Mary said that praying the Rosary daily would obtain peace for the world and defeat communism. She also guaranteed that not abiding by Her request would lead to the spread of communism throughout the world. While Mary repeated this message in many of Her apparitions, She is not the only person to encourage this powerful prayer. *"St. Francis de Sales said that the greatest method of praying is to Pray the Rosary. St. Thomas Aquinas preached forty straight days in Rome, Italy, on just the Hail Mary. St. John Vianney, patron of priests, was seldom seen without a rosary in his hand. Pope Adrian VI said 'The rosary is the scourge of the devil'"*[500] while Pope Paul V called the rosary a treasure of graces. Saint Padre Pio, the stigmatist priest, said: *"The rosary is the weapon."*[501] Saint Pope John XXIII spoke thirty-eight times about Our Lady and the Rosary. He prayed fifteen decades daily. St. Louis Marie Grignion de Montfort wrote: *"The rosary is the most powerful weapon to touch the Heart of Jesus, Our Redeemer, Who so loves His Mother."*[502] The list of saints and holy people of God who proclaim the rosary the most powerful tool in the war against Satan could fill pages, but suffice it to say that there is relative unanimity in the power of this deeply contemplative Christian prayer.

The Blessed Virgin, when presenting the Rosary to St. Dominic and Blessed Alain, also spoke of fifteen promises that She would keep for anyone who prayed the Rosary daily and devoutly. Among those fifteen promises are these:

The rosary shall be a powerful armor against hell. It will destroy vice, decrease sin, and defeat heresies. *"Whoever shall recite the rosary devoutly, applying himself to the consideration of the sacred mysteries shall never be conquered by misfortune. God will not chastise him in His justice, and he shall not perish by an unprovided death; if he be just, he shall remain in the grace of God and become worthy of eternal life."*[503] Mary also promised to *"deliver from purgatory those who have been devoted to the rosary"*[504] saying, *"devotion to My rosary is a great sign of predestination."*[505]

It has been said that *"history is the story of nations following and disobeying God's laws. When people fall into error, God, in His Mercy, sends a wake-up call. The nation must then make an important decision: will it continue to sin or return to God?"*[506] Father Chris Alar, MIC, Director of the Association of Marian Helpers, believes *"the world may be so far gone that it will take a direct intervention from God to turn it around."*[507] Indeed, it does not seem that America, or many other nations of the world for that matter, are ready to repent and alter their sinful ways voluntarily. Therefore, stay awake, keep watch, stay vigilant and prepare as instructed by the prophets for that day when prayer, love, inner peace, and devotion to God will become the priority in our lives and remain such until the Second Coming of Christ on the last day.

Bibliography

Books:
A Missionary Priest with Superior's Permission, The Christian Trumpet; Previsions and Predictions About Impending General Calamities, The Universal Triumph of the Church, The Coming of Antichrist, The Last Judgement, And The End of The World: Compiled from the Writings of the Saints and Eminent Servants of God, and Other Approved Ancient and Modern Sources, London, 1875.

Ballinger, Joanne M. The Coming Three Days of Darkness: Are You Prepared? Ballinger Dev. LLC, Rancho Mirage, CA, 2015.

Caranci, Paul F. The Promise of Fatima: One Hundred Years of History, Mystery and Faith. Stillwater River Publications, Pawtucket, RI, 2017.

The Catechism of the Catholic Church, Second Edition, Revised in Accordance with the Official Latin Text Promulgated by Pope John Paul II, Paragraphs 675, 676 and 677, Libreria Editrice Vaticana, English Translation, November 2019.

Connor, Edward, Prophecy for Today: A Summary of Catholic Tradition Concerning the End-of-Time Era, Academy Library Guild, Fresno, CA 1956, reprinted by Tan Books & Publishers, Charlotte, NC, 1984.

Culleton, Rev. Gerald R., The Prophets and Our Times, Tan Books & Publishers, Charlotte, NC. 2009.

Cyr, Bruce, After The Warning To 2038, Bruce Cyr, Okotoks, Alberta, Canada, 2017.

Dos Santos, Lucia Sister, Fatima in Lucia's Own Words: Sister Lucia's Memoirs, The Ravengate Press, Cambridge, MA, 1963.

Driscoll, Craig Brother, The Coming Chastisement, Queenship Publishing Co., Santa Barbara, CA 1995.

Dupont, Yves, Catholic Prophecy: The Coming Chastisement. Tan Books and Publishers, Inc. Illinois, 1970.

Freze, Michael, S.F.O., End Times Prophecies: A Catholic Perspective, Self-Published by the Author, 2016.

Holy Bible, New International Version (NIV), Biblica, Inc., 1973.

Holy Bible, The New American Revised Edition, Oxford University Press, Oxford, New York, 2010.

James, Jerald, The Last Warnings: The Year 2017 and Thereafter, AuthorHouse, October 25, 2017.

Kowalska, Saint Maria Faustina, Divine Mercy in My Soul, The Diary of Saint Maria Faustina Kowalska, Marian Press, Stockbridge, MA 2016. Diary Entry 741.

Lord, Bob & Penny, Visions of Heaven, Hell and Purgatory, Journeys of Faith, 1996

Olmsted, Bishop Thomas J., Into the Breach. The Veritas Series: Proclaiming the Faith in the Third Millennium. Catholic Information Service, Knights of Columbus, New Haven, CT. 2015.

Petrisko, Thomas W., The Kingdom of Our Father: Who Is God The Father? Mckees Rocks, PA, 1999.

The New American Bible, The Oxford University Press, Large Print Edition, 2011.

Romero, Jesse, The Devil in the City of Angels: My Encounters with the Diabolical. TAN Books, Charlotte, NC, 2019.

Thigpen, Paul, Saints Who Saw Hell: And Other Catholic Witnesses to the Fate of the Damned, Tan Books, Charlotte, North Carolina, 2019.

Watkins, Christine, The Warning: Testimonies and Prophecies of the Illumination of Conscience. Queen of Peace Media, Sacramento, CA, 2019.

Periodicals:
The Bedford Gazette, Signs, Signs, and More Signs by Pastor Timothy Johnson, Pastor of the countryside Baptist Church in northern Parke County, IN West Penn Street, Bedford, PA. March 27, 2020.

Internet Sources:
Aradi, Zsolt, The Tears of Our lady, Trinity Communications, 2020. https://www.catholicculture.org/culture/library/view.cfm?recnum=3050.

Bailey, Sarah Pulliam and Boorstein, Michelle, I find it baffling and reprehensible': Catholic archbishop of Washington slams Trump's visit to John Paul II shrine, The Washington Post, June 2, 2020.

https://www.washingtonpost.com/religion/2020/06/02/trump-catholic-shrine-church-bible-protesters/.

Bartholomew, Courtney, Dr. M.D., The Marian Times, The Sorrowful and Immaculate Heart of Mary: The Revelations of Berthe Petit. https://www.motherofallpeoples.com/post/the-sorrowful-and-immaculate-heart-of-mary-the-revelations-of-berthe-petit.

Bemowski, Vincent T, Is Today's Church Pleasing to God and The Messages to the Churches, Catholic Messages USA.com. https://www.catholicmessagesusa.com/GREAT-CHASTISEMENT.html.

Bermowski, Vincent T, The Wrath of God in the New Testiment: Never Against His New Covenant Community, Related Media. https://bible.org/article/wrath-god-new-testament-never-against-his-new-covenant-community.

Bolin, Thomas M., Nineveh as Sin City, March 31, 2020, https://bibleodyssey.org/en/places/related-articles/nineheh-as-sin-city.

Brown, Michael, H. Mystic with Stigmata Allegedly Saw U.S. Destroyed Through Natural Disasters. Spirit Daily, https://www.spiritdaily.org/prophesyseers/res11.htm.

Bucchianeri, Elizabeth A, The Great Catholic Monarch and Angelic Pontiff Prophecies, Blog, 2019. https://greatmonarch-angelicpontiffprophecies.blogspot.com/p/st_18.html.

Bucchianeri, Elizabeth A, The Great Catholic Monarch and Angelic Pontiff Prophecies: Abbé Souffrant, Blog 2019. https://greatmonarch-angelicpontiffprophecies.blogspot.com/p/blog-page_86.html.

Bucchianeri, Elizabeth A, The Great Catholic Monarch and Angelic Pontiff Prophecies, Abbot Jacques (Joaquim) Merlin, Blog, 2019. https://greatmonarch-angelicpontiffprophecies.blogspot.com/p/blog-page_86.html.

Bucchianeri, Elizabeth A, The Great Catholic Monarch and Angelic Pontiff Prophecies, Blog, 2019. Abbot Werdin d'Otranto, https://greatmonarch-angelicpontiffprophecies.blogspot.com/p/blog-page_27.html.

Bucchianeri, Elizabeth A, The Great Catholic Monarch and Angelic Pontiff Prophecies, Blog, 2019. St. Bridget of Sweden (1303-1373), https://greatmonarch-angelicpontiffprophecies.blogspot.com/p/blog-page_6.html.

Bucchianeri, Elizabeth A, The Great Catholic Monarch and Angelic Pontiff Prophecies, Blog, 2019. Bishop Christianos Ageda, https://greatmonarch-angelicpontiffprophecies.blogspot.com/p/blog-page_20.html.

Bucchianeri, Elizabeth A, The Great Catholic Monarch and Angelic Pontiff Prophecies, Blog, 2019. St. Gaspar del Bufalo. https://greatmonarch-angelicpontiffprophecies.blogspot.com/p/blog-page_59.html.

Bucchianeri, Elizabeth A, The Great Catholic Monarch and Angelic Pontiff Prophecies, Blog 2019. St. Mariam Baouardy (1846-1878) https://greatmonarch-angelicpontiffprophecies.blogspot.com/p/st-mariam-baourardy.html.

Bucchianeri, Elizabeth A, The Great Catholic Monarch and Angelic Pontiff Prophecies: The 'Vatiguerro Prophecy of John Bassigny, Blog 2019. https://greatmonarch-angelicpontiffprophecies.blogspot.com/p/the-vatiguerro-prophecies-mid-1300s.html.

Bucchianeri, Elizabeth A, The Great Catholic Monarch and Angelic Pontiff Prophecies: Marie-Julie Jahenny, Blog 2019. https://greatmonarch-angelicpontiffprophecies.blogspot.com/p/blog-page_62.html.

Bucchianeri, Elizabeth A, The Great Catholic Monarch and Angelic Pontiff Prophecies: St. Louis-Marie de Monfort Blog 2019. https://greatmonarch-angelicpontiffprophecies.blogspot.com/p/blog-page_97.html.

Bucchianeri, Elizabeth A, The Great Catholic Monarch and Angelic Pontiff Prophecies: Cardinal Nicholas of Cusa, Blog 2019. https://greatmonarch-angelicpontiffprophecies.blogspot.com/p/blog-page_39.html.

Bucchianeri, Elizabeth A, The Great Catholic Monarch and Angelic Pontiff Prophecies: Fr. Charles Auguste Lazare Nectou. Blog 2019. https://www.facebook.com/GreatCatholicMonarchAngelicPontiffProphecies/posts/929881097376400/.

Bucchianeri, Elizabeth A, The Great Catholic Monarch and Angelic Pontiff Prophecies: St. Francis of Paola, Blog 2019. https://greatmonarch-angelicpontiffprophecies.blogspot.com/p/blog-page_55.html.

Bucchianeri, Elizabeth A, The Great Catholic Monarch and Angelic Pontiff Prophecies: St. Methodius, Blog 2019.https://greatmonarch-angelicpontiffprophecies.blogspot.com/p/st.html.

Bucchianeri, Elizabeth A, The Great Catholic Monarch and Angelic Pontiff Prophecies: Sister Jeanne de Le Royer of the Nativity (1731-1798). Blog 2019. https://catholicprophecy.org/sister-jeanne-royer/.

Bucchianeri, Elizabeth A, The Great Catholic Monarch and Angelic Pontiff Prophecies: Marcelle Lanchon (Sr. Marie France) (1891-1933) / Our Lady

Queen of France, Blog 2019. https://greatmonarch-angelicpontiffprophecies.blogspot.com/p/marcelle-lanchon-sr-marie-france-1891.html.

Bucchianeri, Elizabeth A, The Great Catholic Monarch and Angelic Pontiff Prophecies: Ven. Mary of Jesus of Agreda, Blog 2019. https://greatmonarch-angelicpontiffprophecies.blogspot.com/p/blog-page_86.html.

Bucchianeri, Elizabeth A, The Great Catholic Monarch and Angelic Pontiff Prophecies: Ida Peerdeman/The Lady of All Nations. Blog 2019. https://greatmonarch-angelicpontiffprophecies.blogspot.com/p/blog-page_79.html.

Bucchianeri, Elizabeth A, The Great Catholic Monarch and Angelic Pontiff Prophecies: Blessed Anna Maria Taigi, Blog 2019. https://greatmonarch-angelicpontiffprophecies.blogspot.com/p/blog-page_47.html.

Bucchianeri, Elizabeth A, The Great Catholic Monarch and Angelic Pontiff Prophecies: Venerable Anne Rose Josephe Du Bourg (1788-1862) Blog 2019. https://greatmonarch-angelicpontiffprophecies.blogspot.com/p/blog-page_35.html.

Bucchianeri, Elizabeth A, The Great Catholic Monarch and Angelic Pontiff Prophecies: St. Vincent Ferrer, Blog 2019. https://greatmonarch-angelicpontiffprophecies.blogspot.com/p/blog-page_12.html.

Bugnolo, Alexis Br., The Three Prophecies of John Bosco, https://franciscanarchive.org/bosco/opera/bosco.html.

Cano, Alonso, "St. Vincent Ferrer Preaching". National Catholic Register, Blogs April 5, 2019. https://www.ncregister.com/blog/joseph-pronechen/600-years-ago-the-angel-of-the-apocalypse-warned-us.

Cardinal Karol Wojtyla's homily to the 41st International Eucharistic Congress, August 1-8, at the Mass for Freedom and Justice in Veterans Stadium, Philadelphia, Pennsylvania, 1976.

Carpenter, John, Divine Mysteries and Miracles, Tilly-Sur-Seulles, France (1896-1899), December 9, 2018. http://www.divinemysteries.info/tilly-sur-seulles-france-1896-1899/.

Castellano, Daniel J., The Authentic Message of La Salette, 2007. http://www.arcaneknowledge.org/catholic/lasalette.htm.

Catholic Exchange, Today's Saint: Saint Anthony the Abbot, From the Life of Saint Anthony by Athanasius, January 17, 2020 https://catholicexchange.com/st-antony-the-abbot.

Catholic Prophecy: Abbot Joaquim Merlin, https://catholicprophecy.org/abbot-joaquim-merlin/.

Catholic Prophecy: Brother Louis Rocco, https://catholicprophecy.org/brother-louis-rocco/.

Catholic Prophecy: Liber Mirabilis, Translated by Jean de Vatiguerro, https://catholicprophecy.org/liber-mirabilis/

Catholic Prophecy: Maria Steiner, https://catholicprohecy.org/maria-steiner/.

Catholic Prophecy: Monk Adso, https://catholicprophecy.org/monk-adso/.

Catholic Prophecy: Sister Jeanne Royer, https://catholicprophecy.org/sister-jeanne-royer/.

Catholic Prophecy: St. Hilarion of Czenstochau, https://catholicprophecy.org/st-hilarion-of-czenstochau/.

Catholic Prophecy: The End Times, Queen of Peace Productions, www.SeanBloomfield.com. http://theheckhypothesis.com/pdf/COLLECTED%20CATHOLIC%20PROPHECIES.pdf.

Catholic Prophecy: The Monk of Prémol, https://catholicprophecy.org/the-monk-of-premol/.

Christianity.com Editorial Staff, Why Did God Destroy Sodom and Gomorrah? Their Story of Sin in the Bible. https://www.christianity.com/wiki/sin/why-did-god-destoy-sodom-and-gomorray-story-of-sin-in-the-bible.html.

Confraternity of St. Joan of Arc, The Coming Chastisement: Revelations to Blessed Elizabeth Canori Mora, March 2020, https://www.jehannedarc.org/mora.html. Taken from La mia vita nel cuore della Trinitŕ – Diaro della Beata Elisabetta Canori Mora, sposa e madre, (Libreria Editrice Vaticana, 1996)

ChurchPop, Editor, BLM Activist Calls for Destruction of Jesus, Mary & Saint Statues, Priest & Exorcist Respond June 23, 2020. https://churchpop.com/2020/06/23/blm-activist-calls-for-destruction-of-jesus-mary-statues-priest-exorcist-respond/?utm_campaign=ChurchPop&utm_medium=email&_hsmi=90123695&_hsenc=p2ANqtz-8idR4NB9ftdp2i27PSR1n1MlSNe8lf6BsiVCBGWzWmkNODqwTUfeKNW5lt3rn7HspN2P8HcWx5HF2SO2KcO_7t8XEUbqSQMFrmCCl9TjCGdqvP-COI&utm_content=90123695&utm_source=hs_email.

ChurchPop, Editor, Cardinal Dolan Decries Statue Destruction, Warns Against Dangerous 'Cultural Revolution," July 2, 2020. https://mail.google.com/mail/u/0/#label/Church-POP/FMfcgxwJWhsnpkLsRhPfDcFLTMkwsKsq

CNA Staff, Catholic News Agency, New Orleans Archbishop: Priest's desecration of Altar 'Demonic'. October 9, 2020, https://www.catholicnewsagency.com/news/archbishop-aymond-new-orleans-priests-desecration-of-altar-demonic-29763.

CNA Staff, Catholic News Agency, 'Security Consultant' Linked to Vatican's Becciu Scandal Arrested. October 13, 2020. https://www.catholicnewsagency.com/news/security-consultant-linked-to-vaticans-becciu-scandal-arrested-62265.

Countdown to the Kingdom Website, Apparitions in Trevignano Romano, Giselle Cardia, https://www.countdowntothekingdom.com/why-gisella-carda/#messages.

Cullerton, Fr. Gerald, The Prophets and Our Times, 1941. Extracted and reprinted In Today's Catholic World News Blog, St. Columba's Prophecy on 3 Days of Darkness (Last Days). Pages 1-2. https://www.tew-blog.com/182861438/1180765/posting/.

Dan Lynch Apostolates, Jesus King of All Nations, The Final Confrontation Between the Church and the Anti-Church, 2013. https://jkmi.worldsecuresystems.com/the-final-confrontation-between-the-church-and-the-anti-church.

Demers, Daniel, Catholic Stand.com, God's Chat with the Devil: The Vision of Pope Leo XIII. https://catholicstand.com/gods-chat-devil-popeleo/.

Di Maria, La Lucia, The Mystic Post, Weeping Statue from Medjugorje ... Italian couple receive warnings and prophecies ...June 3, 2020. (Translated from Italian). https://mysticpost.com/2020/06/weeping-statue-from-medjugorje-italian-couple-receive-warnings-and-prophecies/.

Divine Mercy Website, The Biography of Saint Maria Faustina, Marian Fathers of the Immaculate Conception of the B.V.M., 2020 https://www.thedivinemercy.org/message/stfaustina/bio.

Driskell, Robert, Sodom & Gomorrah: Bible Story with Lesson., What Christians Want to Know, December 19, 2012. https://www.whatchristianswanttoknow.com/sodom-gomorrah-bible-story-with-lesson/.

Duncan, Robert, Mary Foretold Covid-19 Pandemic, Alleged Visionary Claims. The Pilot, August 14, 2020, https://www.thebostonpilot.com/article.asp?ID=188215&utm_source=dlvr.it&utm_medium=twitter.

Eastern Bible Dictionary – Nineveh, https://www.biblestudytools.com/dictionary/nineveh.

EWTN Website, St. Anthony the Abbot. https://ewtn.com/catholicism/saints/anthony-the-abbot-473.

Explaining the Faith – Catholic View of the End Times, (Part 1 of 3). Father Chris Alar, MIC, Youtube video, 2020. https://www.youtube.com/watch?v=Jxz_14YXb-w.

Fulton Sheen Institute, Conference with Dr. Peter Howard and Fr. Richard Heilman. Presented via Zoom and broadcast via YouTube, October 7, 2020. https://www.youtube.com/watch?v=pOsp5zwzuCk&feature=youtu.be.

Garabandal Website, 2015, http://www.garabandal.ie/.

Gensens, Joseph, Return to Order, A Crisis Brings Out the Worst and the Best in People. April 4, 2020. https://www.returntoorder.org/2020/04/a-crisis-brings-out-the-worst-and-the-best-in-people/?pkg=rtoe0942.

Hadro, Matt, National Catholic Register, Miami Archbishop Wenski Blasts 'Handmaiden' Criticism of Amy Coney Barrett. October 8, 2020. https://www.ncregister.com/news/miami-archbishop-wenski-blasts-handmaiden-criticism-of-amy-coney-barrett.

Heckenkamp, Kathleen M., Our Lady of Good Success, https://www.ourladyofgoodsuccess.com/pages/history.

Holy Bible, King James Version, https://www.billkochman.com/Verse-Lists/verse030.html.

Howard, Dr. Peter, Our Times...Eclipse or Apocalypse? Fulton Sheen Institute, https://www.fultonsheen.institute/post/our-times-eclipse-or-apocalypse.

Jackson, Wayne, Ten Great Lessons from the Book of Jonah, Christian Courier, 2020. https://www.christiancourier.com/articles/66-10-great-lessons-from-the-book-of-jonah.

Kennedy, Merrit, Scientists Predict Star Collision Visible to the Naked Eye in 2022. January 9, 2017. https://www.npr.org/sections/thetwo-way/2017/01/09/509010493/scientists-predict-star-collision-visible-to-the-naked-eye-in-2022.

Kurczy, Stephen, Chinese Explorers Stand By Claim of Noah's Ark Find in Turkey. Christian Science Monitor, April 30, 2010. https://www.csmonitor.com/Science/2010/0428/Noah-s-Ark-discovered.-Again.

Lang, Nico, Ex-Pope Says Gay Marriage Will Bring About the End of the World, May 4, 2020. https://www.them.us/story/pope-benedict-says-gay-marriage-will-bring-about-the-end-of-the-world?fbclid=IwAR1lyd-LqogE1PZsPOek8fnnNgzGccv9cyexrzaAhabpr2-Mecw21BMIwQmc.

Little Pebble Official Website, Apparitions of Our Lady in Civitavecchia – 2 February 1995, Lifestyle News blog y Dr. Maike Hickson, June 2, 2020. https://littlepebble.org/2020/06/03/apparitions-of-our-lady-in-civitavecchia-2-february-1995/.

Lisi, Clemente, Catholic Churches Vandalized: Where is the National Media, Religion Unplugged, July 22, 2020. https://religionunplugged.com/news/2020/7/23/catholic-churches-vandalized-wheres-the-national-press-coverage.

McHugh, Joseph, U.S. Catholic Faith in Real Life, "What is the Prophecy of St. Malachy? Some Say Pope Francis' Election Signals the End of the World. Is It the Vision of the 12th-Century Saint, or the Work of a False Prophet?" September 2013, Vol. 78, No. 9. http://www.uscatholic.org/articles/201308/what-prophecy-st-malachy.

Monergism, The Distinction Between God's Punishment and God's Discipline. CPR Foundation, 2018. (An excerpt from Comfort for Christians, Chapter 7: Divine Chastisement. https://www.monergism.com/distinction-between-god%E2%80%99s-punishment-and-god%E2%80%99s-discipline.

My Mother Mary, We Have Been Forewarned: Catholic Prophecy on the Loss of the Holy Eucharist. Catholic Facebook Page – devoted to defending, promoting and celebrating the One, Holy, Catholic and Apostolic Church. April 7, 2020. https://www.facebook.com/CatholicTruth333/photos/catholic-prophecy-on-the-loss-of-the-holy-eucharist-we-have-been-forewarnedthe-d/808496512823052/.

Now Prophecy, Ven. Bartholomew Holzhauser Prophecy – Peter the Roman and the Great Monarch. September 13, 2015. http://nowprophecy.com/2015/09/13/ven-bartholomew-holzhauser-prophecy-peter-the-roman-and-the-great-monarch/.

One Hundred Anos Fatima, The Sorrowful and Immaculate Heart of Mary: Berthe Petit, November 14, 2017, http://confraternidadedorosario.blogspot.com/2017/11/immaculate-heart-berthe-petit.html.

O'Neill, Michael, The Miracle Hunter Website, 2015 http://www.miracle-hunter.com/marian_apparitions/approvedapparitions/bishop.html.

Prophecies of Sr. Anna-Katarina Emmerick, Excerpted from The Life of Anne Catherine Emmerich by Rev. Carl Schmoeger, C.SS.R., first published in English in 1870. http://ourlady3.tripod.com/emmerick.htm.

Richardson, Valerie, The Washington Times, Kamala Harris, Mazie Hirono Target Brian Buescher Knights of Columbus Membership. December 10, 2018 https://apnews.com/article/003d11bf795de6bcfbb5a6ada435944a.

Than, Ker, Noah's Ark Found in Turkey? National Geographic News. April 30, 2010. https://www.nationalgeographic.com/news/2010/4/100428-noahs-ark-found-in-turkey-science-religion-culture/.

The Catholic Encyclopedia: St. Caesarius of Arles, Vol. 3. Robert Appleton Company, New York, 1908. https://www.newadvent.org/cathen/03135.htm.

Prophecy in Catholic Tradition, Unveiling the Apocalypse: The Prophecies of Sr. Jeanne le Royer. July 2013, http://unveilingtheapocalypse.blogspot.com/2013/07/the-prophecies-of-sr-jeanne-le-royer.html.

Prophecy in Catholic Tradition, Unveiling the Apocalypse: Ida Peerdeman and the Prophecies of Our Lady of All Nations, March 24, 2012. http://unveilingtheapocalypse.blogspot.com/2012/03/ida-peerdeman-and-prophecies-of-our.html. Taken from "Unveiling the Apocalypse" by Emmett O'Regan.

Siegel, Ethan, The Comet That Created the Perseids Might Bring an End to Humanity, Science: Forbes Magazine, https://www.forbes.com/sites/startswithabang/2017/08/11/the-comet-that-created-the-perseids-might-bring-an-end-to-humanity/#2cca47ea2029.

Stein, Anthony, PhD, Youtube Video, Fatima Unfolding Before Our Eyes, https://www.youtube.com/watch?v=Ds2Jw1Vy-VI.

Stephens, Sally, Astronomical Society of the Pacific, A Primer on Asteroid Collisions with Earth. http://www.as.wvu.edu/~jel/skywatch/swfttle.html.

Storms, Pastor Sam, 10 Things You Should Know About Hell, Crosswalk.com, September 14, 2019. https://www.crosswalk.com/slideshows/10-things-you-should-know-about-hell.html.

Summary of End Times Events, http://www.theindivisiblelight.com/, http://nowprophecy.com/2015/09/13/ven-bartholomew-holzhauser-prophecy-peter-the-roman-and-the-great-monarch/.

Wikipedia, Berthe Petit. https://en.wikipedia.org/wiki/Berthe_Petit.

Wikepedia, Blessed Anne Catherine Emmerich, https://en.wikipedia.org/wiki/Anne_Catherine_Emmerich.

End Notes

[1] Bolin, Thomas M., Nineveh as Sin City, March 31, 2020, https://bibleodyssey.org/en/places/related-articles/nineheh-as-sin-city. Page 1.

[2] Ibid.

[3] On-line Dictionary, https://www.google.com/search?channel=cus2&client=firefox-b-1-d&q=what+is+faith.

[4] Cardinal Karol Wojtyla in a homily to the 41st International Eucharistic Congress, August 1-8, 1976, Philadelphia, Pennsylvania.

[5] Dan Lynch Apostolates, Jesus King of All Nations, The Final Confrontation Between the Church and the Anti-Church, 2013. https://jkmi.worldsecuresystems.com/the-final-confrontation-between-the-church-and-the-anti-church. Page 2.

[6] Sheen, Fulton J., as reported by Anthony Stein, PhD, in a Youtube Video entitled *Fatima Unfolding Before Our Eyes*, June 2020.
https://www.youtube.com/watch?v=Ds2Jw1Vy-VI.

[7] Olmsted, Bishop Thomas J., Into the Breach. The Veritas Series: Proclaiming the Faith in the Third Millennium. Catholic Information Service, Knights of Columbus, New Haven, CT. 2015. Page 1.

[8] Stein, Anthony, PhD, Youtube Video, Fatima Unfolding Before Our Eyes, https://www.youtube.com/watch?v=Ds2Jw1Vy-VI.

[99] The Catechism of the Catholic Church, Second Edition, Revised in Accordance with the Official Latin Text Promulgated by Pope John Paul II, Paragraphs 675, 676 and 677, Libreria Editrice Vaticana, English Translation, November 2019. Pages 176-177.

[10] O'Neill, Michael, The Miracle Hunter Website, 2015, This compendium of prophesy is taken from http://www.miraclehunter.com/marian_apparitions/messages/quito_messages.html.

[11] The New American Bible, Genesis Chapter 3, verse 16, The Oxford University Press, 2011.

[12] Ibid. Chapter 3, verses 17-19.

[13] Ibid. Chapter 3, verses 23-24.

[14] The New American Bible, Genesis Chapter 6, verses 18-22., The Oxford University Press, 2011.

[15] Ibid, Chapter 7, verses 1-5.

[16] Ibid, Chapter 8, verse 4. (Note: Ararat Mountains are located between Iran, Turkey and Armenia. The mountains contain two peaks and since 1921 have been part of Turkey. An April 28, 2010 segment of the ABC News show, Good Morning America, reported that Chinese scientific researchers are 99.9% certain that they have found Noah's Ark buried in a glacier at the top of Mt. Ararat. Carbon testing of the wood, scientists claim, dates to the time of Noah, some 4,800 years ago. See the news clip at https://www.youtube.com/watch?v=8mRQC_BY98k.)

[17] Ibid, Chapter 8, verses 13-14.

[18] Ibid, Chapter 8, verses 20-21.

[19] Than, Ker, Noah's Ark Found in Turkey? National Geographic News. April 30, 2010. https://www.nationalgeographic.com/news/2010/4/100428-noahs-ark-found-in-turkey-science-religion-culture/.

[20] Kurczy, Stephen, Chinese Explorers Stand By Claim of Noah's Ark Find in Turkey. Christian Science Monitor, April 30, 2010. https://www.csmonitor.com/Science/2010/0428/Noah-s-Ark-discovered.-Again.

[21] The New American Bible, Genesis Chapter 18, verses 23-32., The Oxford University Press, 2011.

[22] Christianity.com Editorial Staff, Why Did God Destroy Sodom and Gomorrah? Their Story of Sin in the Bible. https://www.christianity.com/wiki/sin/why-did-god-destoy-sodom-and-gomorray-story-of-sin-in-the-bible.html.

[23] (Ezekiel 16:49)

[24] Driskell, Robert, Sodom & Gomorrah: Bible Story with Lesson., What Christians Want to Know, December 19, 2012. https://www.whatchristianswanttoknow.com/sodom-gomorrah-bible-story-with-lesson/.

[25] The New American Bible, Genesis Chapter 19, verses 27-29., The Oxford University Press, 2011.

[26] Ibid. Romans I Chapter 8, verse 28.

[27] Bolin, Thomas M., Nineveh as Sin City, March 31, 2020, https://bibleodyssey.org/en/places/related-articles/nineheh-as-sin-city. Page 1.

[28] The New American Bible, Introduction to the Book of Nahum., The Oxford University Press, 2011.

[29] [29] Bolin, Thomas M., Nineveh as Sin City, March 31, 2020, https://bibleodyssey.org/en/places/related-articles/nineheh-as-sin-city. Page 1.

[30] Ibid.

[31] Holy Bible, New International Version (NIV), Jonah, Chapter 3, Verses 1-10. Biblica, Inc., 1973.

[32] Jackson, Wayne, Ten Great Lessons from the Book of Jonah, Christian Courier, 2020. https://www.christiancourier.com/articles/66-10-great-lessons-from-the-book-of-jonah.

[33] The New American Bible, Exodus, Chapter 3, Verses 1-2, The Oxford University Press, 2011.

[34] Ibid. Chapter 7, verses 16-18.

[35] Ibid. Chapter 7, verses 26-29.

[36] Ibid. Chapter 8, verse 13.

[37] Ibid. Chapter 8, verse 20.

[38] Ibid. Chapter 8, verses 27-28.

[39] Ibid. Chapter 9, verses 1-4.

[40] Ibid. Chapter 9, verse 10.

[41] Ibid. Chapter 9, verses 13 – 17.

[42] Ibid. Chapter 9, verses 23-26.

[43] Ibid. Chapter 10, verses 13-15.

[44] Ibid. Chapter 10, verse 17.

[45] Ibid. Chapter 10, verses 22-23.

[46] Ibid. Chapter 10, verse 28.

[47] Ibid. Chapter 11, verse 2.

[48] Ibid. Chapter 11, verses 4-8.

[49] Ibid. Chapter 12, verses 29-30.

[50] Ibid. Chapter 12, verse 37.

[51] Bemowski, Vincent T., Webmaster/Editor, The Wrath of God in the New Testament: Never Against His New Covenant Community. Related Media. https://bible.org/article/wrath-god-new-testament-never-against-his-new-covenant-community.

[52] Driscoll, Craig Brother, The Coming Chastisement, Queenship Publishing Co., Santa Barbara, CA 1995. Page 2.

[53] Ibid. Page 3.

[54] Driscoll. Op cit. Page 2.

[55] Bible, King James Version, Minerva Books, New York, NY. 2012. Neh 9:17, Psalms 103:8-18 and 145:8, Lam 3:22-23, Nah 1:3, Jon 4:2 and Joel 2:13 KJV. https://www.billkochman.com/VerseLists/verse030.html.

[56] The New American Bible, Acts, Chapter 5, Verses 1-11, The Oxford University Press, 2011.

[57] Ibid. Acts, Chapter 13, Verses 8-12.

[58] Bible, King James Version, Nahum 1:3, Minerva Books, New York, NY. 2012.

[59] Ibid, 2 Peter 1-22.

[60] The New American Bible, Mark, Chapter 13, Verses 1-27, The Oxford University Press, 2011. {The text that is within the brackets and in bold letters represents the descriptive language from Luke's account of the same conversation and is from the 21st Chapter.}

[61] Thigpen, Paul, Saints Who Saw Hell: And Other Catholic Witnesses to the Fate of the Damned, Tan Books, Charlotte, North Carolina, 2019. Page 2.

[62] Ibid.

[63] Dupont, Yves, Catholic Prophecy: The Coming Chastisement. Tan Books and Publishers, Inc. Illinois, 1970. Page 9.

[64] The New American Bible, 1 Corinthians 14: 1-5, The Oxford University Press, 2011.

[65] Dupont, Yves, Catholic Prophecy: The Coming Chastisement. Tan Books and Publishers, Inc. Illinois, 1970. Page 9.

[66] Dupont, Yves, Catholic Prophecy: The Coming Chastisement. Tan Books and Publishers, Inc. Illinois, 1970. Page 36.

[67] Ibid.

[68] Catholic Prophecy: St. Hilarion of Czenstochau, https://catholicprophecy.org/st-hilarion-of-czenstochau/. Pages 1-4.

[69] Bucchianeri, Elizabeth A, The Great Catholic Monarch and Angelic Pontiff Prophecies: St. Methodius, https://greatmonarch-angelicpontiffprophecies.blogspot.com/p/st.html. Page 2.

[70] Ibid.

[71] Ibid.

[72] Catholic Prophecy: The Monk of Prémol, https://catholicprophecy.org/the-monk-of-premol/. Pages 2-4.

[73] The Catholic Encyclopedia: St. Caesarius of Arles, Vol. 3. Robert Appleton Company, New York, 1908. https://www.newadvent.org/cathen/03135.htm. Page 1.

[74] Catholic Prophecy: The End Times, Queen of Peace Productions, www.SeanBloomfield.com. http://theheckhypothesis.com/pdf/COLLECTED%20CATHOLIC%20PROPHECIES.pdf. Page 58.

[75] Cullerton, Fr. Gerald, The Prophets and Our Times, 1941. Extracted and reprinted In Today's Catholic World News Blog, St. Columba's Prophecy on 3 Days of Darkness (Last Days). Pages 1-2. https://www.tewblog.com/182861438/1180765/posting/.

[76] Bucchianeri, Elizabeth A, The Great Catholic Monarch and Angelic Pontiff Prophecies, Blog, 2019. https://greatmonarch-angelicpontiffprophecies.blogspot.com/p/st_18.html. Page 2.

[77] Dupont, Yves, Catholic Prophecy: The Coming Chastisement. Tan Books and Publishers, Inc. Illinois, 1970. Page 18.

[78] Catholic Prophecy: Monk Adso, https://catholicprophecy.org/monk-adso/. Pages 1-2.

[79] Dupont, Yves, Catholic Prophecy: The Coming Chastisement. Tan Books and Publishers, Inc. Illinois, 1970. Page 18.

[80] Bucchianeri, Elizabeth A, The Great Catholic Monarch and Angelic Pontiff Prophecies, Blog, 2019. Bishop Christianos Ageda, https://greatmonarch-angelicpontiffprophecies.blogspot.com/p/blog-page_20.html. Pages 1-2.

[81] McHugh, Joseph, U.S. Catholic Faith in Real Life, "What is the Prophecy of St. Malachy? Some Say Pope Francis' Election Signals the End of the World. Is It the Vision of the 12th-Century Saint, or the Work of a False Prophet?" September 2013, Vol. 78, No. 9. http://www.uscatholic.org/articles/201308/what-prophecy-st-malachy. Page 46.

[82] Dupont, Yves, Catholic Prophecy: The Coming Chastisement. Tan Books and Publishers, Inc. Illinois, 1970. Page 15.

[83] Catholic Prophecy: St. Hildegard, https://catholicprophecy.org/st-hidegard/. Page 2.

[84] Ibid.

[85] Ibid.

[86] Ibid. Pages 2-3.

[87] Ibid. Page 3.

[88] Ibid. Pages 4-9.

[89] Bucchianeri, Elizabeth A, The Great Catholic Monarch and Angelic Pontiff Prophecies: St. Francis of Assisi (1182-1226. Blog 2019. https://greatmonarch-angelicpontiffprophecies.blogspot.com/p/st-francis-of-assisi.html.

[90] Bucchianeri, Elizabeth A, The Great Catholic Monarch and Angelic Pontiff Prophecies, Blog, 2019. Abbot Werdin d'Otranto, https://greatmonarch-angelicpontiffprophecies.blogspot.com/p/blog-page_27.html. Pages 1-4.

[91] Bucchianeri, Elizabeth A, The Great Catholic Monarch and Angelic Pontiff Prophecies, Blog, 2019. St. Bridget of Sweden (1303-1373), https://greatmonarch-angelicpontiffprophecies.blogspot.com/p/blog-page_6.html. Pages 1-3.

[92] Ibid.

[93] Ibid.

[94] Ibid.

[95] Bl. Raymond of Capua, The Life of St. Catherine of Siena: The Classic on Her Life and Accomplishments as Recorded by Her Spiritual Director, TAN Books, 2009.

[96] Bucchianeri, Elizabeth A, The Great Catholic Monarch and Angelic Pontiff Prophecies: The 'Vatiguerro Prophecy of John Bassigny, Blog 2019. https://greatmonarch-angelicpontiffprophecies.blogspot.com/p/the-vatiguerro-prophecies-mid-1300s.html. Pages 2-4.

[97] Bucchianeri, Elizabeth A, The Great Catholic Monarch and Angelic Pontiff Prophecies: St. Vincent Ferrer, Blog 2019. https://greatmonarch-angelicpontiffprophecies.blogspot.com/p/blog-page_12.html. Pages 1-3.

[98] Bucchianeri, Elizabeth A, The Great Catholic Monarch and Angelic Pontiff Prophecies: Cardinal Nicholas of Cusa, Blog 2019. https://greatmonarch-angelicpontiffprophecies.blogspot.com/p/blog-page_39.html. Pages 1-2.

[99] Bucchianeri, Elizabeth A, The Great Catholic Monarch and Angelic Pontiff Prophecies: St. Francis of Paola, Blog 2019. https://greatmonarch-angelicpontiffprophecies.blogspot.com/p/blog-page_55.html. Pages 3-7.

[100] Catholic Prophecy: Abbot Joaquim Merlin, https://catholicprophecy.org/abbot-joaquim-merlin/. Pages 1-3. Also, Dupont, Yves, Catholic Prophecy: The Coming Chastisement. Tan Books and Publishers, Inc. Illinois, 1970. Pages 26-28.

[101] Heckenkamp, Kathleen M., Our Lady of Good Success, https://www.ourladyofgoodsuccess.com/pages/history. Page 1.

[102] Ibid.

[103] Ibid.

[104] Skojec, Steve, 400 Years Ago, Our Lady Sent Us A Message From Ecuador. July 6, 2015. Page 3. https://onepeterfive.com/400-years-ago-our-lady-sent-us-a-message-from-ecuador.

[105] Skojec, Steve, OnePeterFive.com, 400 Years Ago, Our Lady Sent Us A Message From Ecuador, July 6, 2015, https://onepeterfive.com/400-years-ago-our-lady-sent-us-a-message-from-ecuador/. Pages 3-5.

[106] Ibid. Page 5.

[107] Ibid.

[108] Bucchianeri, Elizabeth A, The Great Catholic Monarch and Angelic Pontiff Prophecies: Ven. Mary of Jesus of Agreda, Blog 2019. https://greatmonarch-angelicpontiffprophecies.blogspot.com/p/blog-page_86.html. Page 2.

[109] Catholic Prophecy: The End Times, Queen of Peace Productions, www.SeanBloomfield.com. http://theheckhypothesis.com/pdf/COLLECTED%20CATHOLIC%20PROPHECIES.pdf. Page 7.

[110] Now Prophecy, Ven. Bartholomew Holzhauser Prophecy – Peter the Roman and the Great Monarch. September 13, 2015. http://nowprophecy.com/2015/09/13/ven-bartholomew-holzhauser-prophecy-peter-the-roman-and-the-great-monarch/. Pages 1-5.

[111] Wikipedia, Margaret Mary Alacoque, https://en.wikipedia.org/wiki/margaret_mary_alacoque.

[112] Catholic Prophecy: The End Times, Queen of Peace Productions, www.SeanBloomfield.com. http://theheckhypothesis.com/pdf/COLLECTED%20CATHOLIC%20PROPHECIES.pdf. Page 32.

[113] Dupont, Yves, Catholic Prophecy: The Coming Chastisement. Tan Books and Publishers, Inc. Illinois, 1970. Page 33.

[114] Bucchianeri, Elizabeth A, The Great Catholic Monarch and Angelic Pontiff Prophecies: St. Louis-Marie de Monfort
Blog 2019. https://greatmonarch-angelicpontiffprophecies.blogspot.com/p/blog-page_97.html. Page 3.

[115] Catholic Prophecy: Sister Jeanne Royer, https://catholicprophecy.org/sister-jeanne-royer/. Pages 2-3. Also, Dupont, Yves, Catholic Prophecy: The Coming Chastisement. Tan Books and Publishers, Inc. Illinois, 1970. Pages 51-60.

[116] Bucchianeri, Elizabeth A, The Great Catholic Monarch and Angelic Pontiff Prophecies: Fr. Charles Auguste Lazare Nectou. Blog 2019. https://www.facebook.com/GreatCatholicMonarchAngelicPontiffProphecies/posts/929881097376400/. Page 1.

[117] Ibid. Pages 2-5.

[118] Dupont, Yves, Catholic Prophecy: The Coming Chastisement. Tan Books and Publishers, Inc. Illinois, 1970. Pages 50-51.

[119] Ibid. Page 78.

[120] Bucchianeri, Elizabeth A, The Great Catholic Monarch and Angelic Pontiff Prophecies: Bishop George Michael Wittman, Blog 2019. Pages 1-2.

[121] Bucchianeri, Elizabeth A, The Great Catholic Monarch and Angelic Pontiff Prophecies: Blessed Anna Maria Taigi, Blog 2019. https://greatmonarch-angelicpontiffprophecies.blogspot.com/p/blog-page_47.html. Page 2.

[122] Catholic Prophecy: The End Times, Queen of Peace Productions, www.SeanBloomfield.com. http://theheckhypothesis.com/pdf/COLLECTED%20CATHOLIC%20PROPHECIES.pdf. Page 25.

[123] Confraternity of St. Joan of Arc, The Coming Chastisement: Revelations to Blessed Elizabeth Canori Mora, March 2020, https://www.jehannedarc.org/mora.html. Taken from La mia vita nel cuore della Trinitŕ – Diaro della Beata Elisabetta Canori Mora, sposa e madre, (Libreria Editrice Vaticana, 1996) pages 158-160.

[124] Ibid. From (Libreria Editrice Vaticana, 1996) pages 164.

[125] Ibid. From (Libreria Editrice Vaticana, 1996) pages 257-258.

[126] Ibid.

[127] Ibid.

[128] Ibid.

[129] The American Society for the Defense of Tradition, Family and Property, April 10, 2007. https://www.tfp.org/a-century-before-fatima-providence-announced--a-chastisement/. Page 4. Taken from the May 2002 issue of the Brazilian magazine Catolicismo.

[130] Confraternity of St. Joan of Arc, The Coming Chastisement: Revelations to Blessed Elizabeth Canori Mora, March 2020, https://www.jehannedarc.org/mora.html. Taken from La mia vita nel cuore della Trinitŕ – Diaro della Beata Elisabetta Canori Mora, sposa e madre, (Libreria Editrice Vaticana, 1996) pages 158-160.

[131] Ibid. (Libreria Editrice Vaticana, 1996) pages 158-160.

[132] Ibid..

[133] Ibid.

[134] Dupont, Yves, Catholic Prophecy: The Coming Chastisement. Tan Books and Publishers, Inc. Illinois, 1970. Page 51.

[135] Bucchianeri, Elizabeth A, The Great Catholic Monarch and Angelic Pontiff Prophecies: Abbé Souffrant, Blog 2019. https://greatmonarch-angelicpontiffprophecies.blogspot.com/p/blog-page_86.html. Page 2.

[136] Ibid. Pages 4-6.

[137] Ibid. Page 6.

[138] Ibid. Pages 6-7.

[139] Ibid. Pages 7-9.

[140] Ibid. Page 9.

[141] Wikepedia, Blessed Anne Catherine Emmerich, https://en.wikipedia.org/wiki/Anne_Catherine_Emmerich. Page 5.

[142] Prophecies of Sr. Anna-Katarina Emmerick, Excerpted from The Life of Anne Catherine Emmerich by Rev. Carl Schmoeger, C.SS.R., first published in English in 1870. http://ourlady3.tripod.com/emmerick.htm. Pages 1-4.

[143] Dupont, Yves, Catholic Prophecy: The Coming Chastisement. Tan Books and Publishers, Inc. Illinois, 1970. Page 79.

[144] Bucchianeri, Elizabeth A, The Great Catholic Monarch and Angelic Pontiff Prophecies: Sister Rosa Asdenti Di Taggia, Blog 2019. https://greatmonarch-angelicpontiffprophecies.blogspot.com/p/blog-page_47.html.

[145] Ibid.

[146] Ibid.

[147] Catholic Prophecy: Brother Louis Rocco, https://catholicprophecy.org/brother-louis-rocco/. Page 1.

[148] Connor, Edward, Prophecy for Today: A Summary of Catholic Tradition Concerning the End-of-Time Era, Academy Library Guild, Fresno, CA 1956, reprinted by Tan Books & Publishers, Charlotte, NC, 1984. Page 8.

[149] Castellano, Daniel J., The Authentic Message of La Salette, 2007. http://www.arcaneknowledge.org/catholic/lasalette.htm. Pages 2-3

[150] Ibid. Page 3

[151] Ibid. Page 4

[152] Ibid. Page 4

[153] Ibid. Page 4

[154] Aradi, Zsolt, The Tears of Our lady, Trinity Communications, 2020. https://www.catholicculture.org/culture/library/view.cfm?recnum=3050. Page 2.

[155] Castellano, Daniel J., The Authentic Message of La Salette, 2007. http://www.arcaneknowledge.org/catholic/lasalette.htm. Pages 4-5.

[156] Ibid. Pages 6-8.

[157] Bucchianeri, Elizabeth A, The Great Catholic Monarch and Angelic Pontiff Prophecies: VENERABLE ANNE ROSE JOSÈPHE DU BOURG (1788-1862) Blog 2019. https://greatmonarch-angelicpontiffprophecies.blogspot.com/p/blog-page_35.html.

[158] Ibid.

[159] Ibid.

[160] Ibid.

[161] Dupont, Yves, Catholic Prophecy: The Coming Chastisement. Tan Books and Publishers, Inc. Illinois, 1970. Page 80.

[162] Culleton, Rev. Gerald R., The Prophets and Our Times, Tan Books & Publishers, Charlotte, NC. 2009. From the Encyclical "Ineffabilis Deus" -Declaration the Dogma of the Immaculate Conception in 1854

[163] Dupont, Yves, Catholic Prophecy: The Coming Chastisement. Tan Books and Publishers, Inc. Illinois, 1970. Page 13.

[164] Catholic Prophecy: The End Times, Queen of Peace Productions, www.SeanBloomfield.com. http://theheckhypothesis.com/pdf/COLLECTED%20CATHOLIC%20PROPHECIES.pdf. Page 59.

[165] Hesemann, Michael, The Fatima Secret. Dell Publishing, NY December 2000. Page 258.
Also, Catholic Prophecy: Maria Steiner, https://catholicprohecy.org/maria-steiner/. Page 2.

[166] Connor, Edward, "Prophesy for Today: A Summary of the Catholic Tradition Concerning the End-of-Time Era. 1956, Academy Literary Guild, Fresno, CA. Reprinted in 1984 and 2010 by Tan Books & Publishers, Inc., Charlotte, NC.

[167] Carpenter, John, Divine Mysteries and Miracles, Tilly-Sur-Seulles, France (1896-1899), December 9, 2018. http://www.divinemysteries.info/tilly-sur-seulles-france-1896-1899/ Pages 1-6.

[168] Bucchianeri, Elizabeth A, The Great Catholic Monarch and Angelic Pontiff Prophecies, Blog, 2019. Marie Martel (1872 – 1913), https://greatmonarch-angelicpontiffprophecies.blogspot.com/p/blog-page_34.html Pages 1-18.

[169] Ibid.

[170] Ibid.

[171] Ibid.

[172] Ibid.

[173] Ibid.

[174] Ibid.

[175] Ibid.

[176] Ibid.

[177] Dupont, Yves, Catholic Prophecy: The Coming Chastisement. Tan Books and Publishers, Inc. Illinois, 1970. Page 77.

[178] Bugnolo, Alexis Br., The Three Prophecies of John Bosco, https://franciscan-archive.org/bosco/opera/bosco.html. Pages 3-4.

[179] Ibid.

[180] Dupont, Yves, Catholic Prophecy: The Coming Chastisement. Tan Books and Publishers, Inc. Illinois, 1970. Pages 37-38.

[181] Bucchianeri, Elizabeth A, The Great Catholic Monarch and Angelic Pontiff Prophecies: St. Mariam Baouardy (1846-1878), Blog 2019. https://greatmonarch-angelicpontiffprophecies.blogspot.com/p/st-mariam-baouardy.html. Page 2.

[182] Ibid.

[183] Ibid.

[184] Ibid.

[185] Ibid.

[186] Ibid.

[187] Ibid.

[188] Ibid. Page 3.

[189] Ibid.

[190] Ibid. Page 4.

[191] Ibid.

[192] Demers, Daniel, Catholic Stand, God's Chat with the Devil: The Vision of Pope Leo XIII, May 17, 2018, https://catholicstand.com/gods-chat-devil-popeleo/. Page 1.

[193] James, Jerald, The Last Warnings: The Year 2017 and Thereafter, AuthorHouse, October 25, 2017.

[194] Ibid.

[195] Demers, Daniel, Catholic Stand, God's Chat with the Devil: The Vision of Pope Leo XIII, May 17, 2018, https://catholicstand.com/gods-chat-devil-popeleo/. Page 2.

[196] Bucchianeri, Elizabeth A, The Great Catholic Monarch and Angelic Pontiff Prophecies: Marie-Julie Jahenny, Blog 2019. https://greatmonarch-angelicpontiffprophecies.blogspot.com/p/blog-page_62.html. Page 1.

[197] Ibid. Page 2.

[198] Ibid.

[199] Ibid. Page 3.

[200] Bucchianeri, Elizabeth A, The Great Catholic Monarch and Angelic Pontiff Prophecies: Marie-Julie Jahenny, Blog 2019. https://greatmonarch-angelicpontiffprophecies.blogspot.com/p/blog-page_62.html.

[201] Ibid.

[202] Ibid.

[203] Ibid.

[204] Ibid.

[205] Ibid.
[206] Ibid.
[207] Ibid.
[208] Ibid.
[209] Ibid.
[210] Ibid.
[211] Ibid.
[212] Ibid.
[213] Ibid.
[214] Ibid.
[215] Ibid.
[216] Ibid.
[217] Ibid.
[218] Ibid.
[219] Ibid.
[220] Ibid.
[221] Ibid.
[222] Ibid.
[223] Ibid.
[224] Ibid.
[225] Ibid.
[226] Ibid.
[227] Ibid.
[228] Ibid.
[229] Ibid.
[230] Ibid.
[231] Ibid.
[232] Ibid.
[233] Ibid.
[234] Ibid.
[235] Ibid.
[236] Ibid.
[237] Ibid.
[238] Ibid.
[239] Ibid.
[240] Ibid.
[241] Ibid.
[242] Ibid.
[243] Ibid.
[244] Ibid.
[245] Ibid.
[246] Ibid.
[247] Ibid.
[248] Ibid.
[249] Ibid.
[250] Ibid.
[251] Ibid.
[252] Ibid.

[253] Ibid.
[254] Ibid.
[255] Ibid.
[256] Ibid.
[257] Ibid.
[258] Ibid.
[259] Ibid.
[260] Ibid.
[261] Ibid.
[262] Ibid.
[263] Ibid.
[264] Ibid.
[265] Ibid.
[266] Ibid.
[267] Ibid.
[268] Ibid.
[269] Ibid.
[270] Ibid.
[271] Ibid.
[272] Ibid.
[273] Ibid.
[274] Ibid.
[275] Ibid.
[276] Ibid.
[277] Ibid.
[278] Ibid.
[279] Ibid.
[280] Ibid.
[281] Ibid.
[282] Ibid.
[283] Ibid.
[284] Ibid.
[285] Ibid.
[286] Ibid.
[287] Ibid.
[288] Ibid.
[289] Ibid.
[290] Ibid.
[291] Ibid.
[292] Ibid.
[293] Ibid.
[294] Ibid.
[295] Ibid.
[296] Ibid.
[297] Bucchianeri, Elizabeth A, The Great Catholic Monarch and Angelic Pontiff Prophecies: Marcelle Lanchon (Sr. Marie France) (1891-1933) / Our Lady Queen of France, Blog 2019. https://greatmonarch-angelicpontiffprophecies.blogspot.com/p/marcelle-

lanchon-sr-marie-france-1891.html. (Source: "Les apparitions à Versailles, Marie, Reine de France, Jésus Roi de France ", Anonyme, Edition Pierre Téqui, 2005")

[298] Ibid.

[299] Ibid.

[300] Ibid.

[301] Ibid.

[302]

[303] Ibid.

[304] Ibid.

[305] Ibid.

[306] Ibid.

[307] Ibid.

[308] Dupont, Yves, Catholic Prophecy: The Coming Chastisement. Tan Books and Publishers, Inc. Illinois, 1970. Page 72.

[309] EWTN Catholic Q&A, Benedict XVI and Something Pius X said, 4/21/2005, www.ewtn.com, 2002. https://www.ewtn.com/legacy/v/experts/showmessage_print,asp?number=436842&language=en. Page 1

[310] Ibid.

[311] Caranci, Paul F. The Promise of Fatima: One Hundred Years of History, Mystery and Faith. Stillwater River Publications, Pawtucket, RI, 2017. Page 61.

[312] Ibid. Page 69.

[313] Ibid. Page 75.

[314] Ibid.

[315] Ibid. Pages 75 - 76.

[316] Ibid. Page 95.

[317] Ibid. Page 103.

[318] Ibid. Page 113

[319] Ibid.

[320] Ibid. Pages 114-115.

[321] Dupont, Yves, Catholic Prophecy: The Coming Chastisement. Tan Books and Publishers, Inc. Illinois, 1970. Page 82.

[322] Official website of Anne de Guigné's Friends Association, An Exceptional Soul for Such a Young Child, https://www.annedeguigne.fr/en/biography/a-great-soul.html. Biographical Information, Page 1.

[323] Ibid.

[324] Ibid.

[325] Catholic Prophecy: The End Times, Queen of Peace Productions, www.SeanBloomfield.com. http://theheckhypothesis.com/pdf/COLLECTED%20CATHOLIC%20PROPHECIES.pdf. Page 31.

[326] Dupont, Yves, Catholic Prophecy: The Coming Chastisement. Tan Books and Publishers, Inc. Illinois, 1970. Page 78.

[327] Kowalska, Saint Maria Faustina, Divine Mercy in My Soul, The Diary of Saint Maria Faustina Kowalska, Marian Press, Stockbridge, MA 2016.

[328] Brown, Michael, H. Mystic with Stigmata Allegedly Saw U.S. Destroyed Through Natural Disasters. Spirit Daily, https://www.spiritdaily.org/prophesy-seers/resl1.htm. Page 2.

329 Dupont, Yves, Catholic Prophecy: The Coming Chastisement. Tan Books and Publishers, Inc. Illinois, 1970. Page 13.

330 Brown, Michael, H. Mystic with Stigmata Allegedly Saw U.S. Destroyed Through Natural Disasters. Spirit Daily, https://www.spiritdaily.org/prophesy-seers/resl1.htm. Page 2.

331 Wikipedia, Berthe Petit. https://en.wikipedia.org/wiki/Berthe_Petit. Page 1.

332 One Hundred Anos Fatima, The Sorrowful and Immaculate Heart of Mary: Berthe Petit, November 14, 2017, http://confraternidadedorosario.blogspot.com/2017/11/immaculate-heart-berthe-petit.html. Page 1.

333 Bartholomew, Courtney, Dr. M.D., The Marian Times, The Sorrowful and Immaculate Heart of Mary: The Revelations of Berthe Petit. https://www.motherofallpeoples.com/post/the-sorrowful-and-immaculate-heart-of-mary-the-revelations-of-berthe-petit. Page 3.

334 Ibid.

335 Ibid.

336 Ibid. Pages 3-4.

337 Ibid. Page 4.

338 Ibid. Page 5

339 Ibid.

340 Ibid. Page 6.

341 Ibid.

342 Ibid.

343 Ibid. Page 7. From Winston Churchill's book The Second World War.

344 One Hundred Anos Fatima, The Sorrowful and Immaculate Heart of Mary: Berthe Petit, November 14, 2017, http://confraternidadedorosario.blogspot.com/2017/11/immaculate-heart-berthe-petit.html. Page 3.

345 Ibid.

346 Ibid.

347 Ibid.

348 My Mother Mary, We Have Been Forewarned: Catholic Prophecy on the Loss of the Holy Eucharist. Catholic Facebook Page – devoted to defending, promoting and celebrating the One, Holy, Catholic and Apostolic Church. April 7, 2020. https://www.facebook.com/CatholicTruth333/photos/catholic-prophecy-on-the-loss-of-the-holy-eucharist-we-have-been-forewarnedthe-d/808496512823052/. Page 1.

349 Dupont, Yves, Catholic Prophecy: The Coming Chastisement. Tan Books and Publishers, Inc. Illinois, 1970. Page 22.

350 O'Regan, Emmett, Prophecy in Catholic Tradition, Ida Peerdeman and the Prophecies of Our Lady of All Nations, March 24, 2012. http://unveilingtheapocalypse.blogspot.com/2012/03/ida-peerdeman-and-prophecies-of-our.html. Taken from "Unveiling the Apocalypse" by Emmett O'Regan.

351 Ibid.

352 Ibid.

353 Bucchianeri, Elizabeth A, The Great Catholic Monarch and Angelic Pontiff Prophecies: Ida Peerdeman/The Lady of All Nations. Blog 2019. https://greatmonarch-angelicpontiffprophecies.blogspot.com/p/blog-page_79.html.

354 Ibid.

355 Ibid.

356 Ibid.

357 Ibid.

358 Ibid.

359 Ibid.

360 Ibid.

361 Ibid.

362 Ibid.

363 Ibid.

364 Ibid.

365 Ibid.

366 Ibid.

367 Ibid.

368 Fuentes, Fr. Augustin, Sister Lucy's Last Public Interview – 1957. https://www.traditioninaction.org/HotTopics/g23ht_Interview.html.

369 Fuentes, Fr. Augustin, Sister Lucy's Last Public Interview – 1957. https://www.traditioninaction.org/HotTopics/g23ht_Interview.html.

370 Garabandal Website, 2015, http://www.garabandal.ie/first-visit-of-angel/. Pages 1-2.

371 Garabandal Warning: Our Lady's Messages and Prophecies, Youtube documentary, 2016.

372 Ibid.

373 Garabandal Website, 2015, http://www.garabandal.ie/our-ladys-prophesies/. Pages 1-2.

374 Ibid. Pages 3-5.

375 Ibid.

376 Ibid. Page 4.

377 Ibid.

378 Ibid. Pages 4-6.

379 Ibid. Page 6.

380 Ibid.

381 Ibid. Page 7.

382 Ibid.

383 Catholic Prophecy: The End Times, Queen of Peace Productions, www.SeanBloomfield.com. http://theheckhypothesis.com/pdf/COLLECTED%20CATHOLIC%20PROPHECIES.pdf. Pages 49-50.

384 Ibid.

385 Website of the Hotel & Spa Medjugorje, Medjugorje History: The First Apparitions, 2020. https://www.medjugorjehotelspa.com/en/history-of-medjugorje-the-first-apparitions/. Page 1-2.

386 Ibid. Page 2

387 Medjugorje.com, Words From Heaven, by a Friend of Medjugorje, 11th Edition. https://www.medjugorje.com/medjugorje/the-10-secrets/overview-of-the-10-secrets.html.

388 Little Pebble Official Website, Apparitions of Our Lady in Civitavecchia – 2 February 1995, Lifestyle News blog y Dr. Maike Hickson, June 2, 2020. https://littlepebble.org/2020/06/03/apparitions-of-our-lady-in-civitavecchia-2-february-1995/. Page 2.

389 Ibid.

390 Ibid. Page 4.

391 Ibid.

[392] Ibid. Page 5.

[393] Ibid.

[394] Ibid.

[395] Ibid.

[396] Ibid.

[397] Ibid.

[398] Ibid.

[399] Ibid. Page 9.

[400] Ibid. Page 10.

[401] Thigpen, Paul, Saints Who Saw Hell: And Other Catholic Witnesses to the Fate of the Damned, Tan Books, Charlotte, North Carolina, 2019. Page xi.

[402] Ibid. Page xi.

[403] Ibid. Page xii.

[404] Ibid. Page xiii.

[405] Storms, Pastor Sam, 10 Things You Should Know About Hell, Crosswalk.com, September 14, 2019. https://www.crosswalk.com/slideshows/10-things-you-should-know-about-hell.html. Page 5.

[406] Ibid. Page 6.

[407] Thigpen, Paul, Saints Who Saw Hell: And Other Catholic Witnesses to the Fate of the Damned, Tan Books, Charlotte, North Carolina, 2019. Page xv. Also, Catechism of the Catholic Church 1864.

[408] Ibid. Page xxiv.

[409] Ibid. Page xiii.

[410] Ibid.

[411] The New American Bible, 2 Kings 23:10, Page 532; Jer. 7:31-32, Page 1291. Holy Bible, The New American Revised Large Print Edition, Oxford University Press, Oxford, New York, 2010.

[412] The New American Bible, Revelation 21:8, Page 2120. Holy Bible, The New American Revised Large Print Edition, Oxford University Press, Oxford, New York, 2010.

[413] Ibid, Matthew 25:34-40; Matthew 25:45-46. Page 1636.

[414] Ibid, Matthew 13:37-43. Page 1620.

[415] Ibid. Mark 9:42-48. Page 1695.

[416] Ibid. Revelation 20:20-21. Page 2119.

[417] Thigpen, Paul, Saints Who Saw Hell: And Other Catholic Witnesses to the Fate of the Damned, Tan Books, Charlotte, North Carolina, 2019. Page 4.

[418] Ibid. Pages 4-5. (Rom 2:6-8)

[419] Ibid. Page 5.

[420] Ibid.

[421] Ibid.

[422] Kowalska, Saint Maria Faustina, Divine Mercy in My Soul, The Diary of Saint Maria Faustina Kowalska, Marian Press, Stockbridge, MA 2016. Diary Entry 741, Pages 296-297.

[423] Dos Santos, Lucia Sister, Fatima in Lucia's Own Words: Sister Lucia's Memoirs, The Ravengate Press, Cambridge, MA, 1963. Page 104.

[424] Teresa of Avila, The Life of Teresa of Jesus: The Autobiography of Teresa of Avila, Image Books, Doubleday, Translated and edited by E. Allison Peers from the critical edition of Silverio de Santa Teresa, 2004.

425 Thigpen, Paul, Saints Who Saw Hell: And Other Catholic Witnesses to the Fate of the Damned, Tan Books, Charlotte, North Carolina, 2019. Pages 39-40.
426 Ibid. Pages 1-43.
427 Ibid. Pages 46-49.
428 Ibid. Pages 51-58.

430 Ibid. Pages 91-94.
431 Ibid. Pages 104-106.
432 Ibid. Page 109.
433 Ibid. Pages 110-112.
434 The Catechism of the Catholic Church, Second Edition, Revised in Accordance with the Official Latin Text Promulgated by Pope John Paul II, Paragraphs 675, 676 and 677, Libreria Editrice Vaticana, English Translation, November 2019. Reference 670, Page 175.
435 Holy Bible, The New American Revised Edition, Oxford University Press, Oxford, New York, 2010. Matthew 24:14. Page 1633.
436 Ibid, Matthew 24:10-13. Page 1633.
437 Ibid. 2 Thessalonians 2:4-10. Pages 2011-2012.
438 Ibid. Romans 11:25-29. Page 1895.
439 The Catechism of the Catholic Church, Second Edition, Revised in Accordance with the Official Latin Text Promulgated by Pope John Paul II, Paragraphs 675, 676 and 677, Libreria Editrice Vaticana, English Translation, November 2019. Reference 674, Page 176.
440 Holy Bible, The New American Revised Edition, Oxford University Press, Oxford, New York, 2010. Matthew 24:32-34. Page 1634.
441 Pastor Timothy Johnson, Countryside Baptist Church, The Bedford Gazette, Signs, Signs, and More Signs, March 27, 2020. Page 1.
442 Holy Bible, The New American Revised Edition, Oxford University Press, Oxford, New York, 2010. Revelation 13:1-18. Page 2113.
443 Father Chris Alar, MIC, Youtube video, Explaining the Faith – Catholic View of the End Times, (Part 1 of 3). 2020. https://www.youtube.com/watch?v=Jxz_14YXb-w.
444 Ibid. Matthew 24: 3-44. Pages 1633-1634.
445 The Virgo Sacrata, Broadcast of January 26, 1947. https://www.virgo-sacrata.com/antichrist-signs-of-our-times.html.
446 Dupont, Yves, Catholic Prophecy: The Coming Chastisement. Tan Books and Publishers, Inc. Illinois, 1970. Pages 84-85.
447 Howard, Dr. Peter, Our Times...Eclipse or Apocalypse? Fulton Sheen Institute, https://www.fultonsheen.institute/post/our-times-eclipse-or-apocalypse. Pages 1-2.
448 Dupont, Yves, Catholic Prophecy: The Coming Chastisement. Tan Books and Publishers, Inc. Illinois, 1970. Page 85.
449 Kennedy, Merrit, Scientists Predict Star Collision Visible to the Naked Eye in 2022. January 9, 2017. https://www.npr.org/sections/thetwo-way/2017/01/09/509010493/scientists-predict-star-collision-visible-to-the-naked-eye-in-2022. Pages 1-2.

450 Starr, Michelle, Sciencealert.com, Dramatic Timelapse From Hubble Shows a Star Literally Exploding in Nothingness, October 2, 2020, https://www.scienceal-ert.com/watch-hubble-s-incredible-timelapse-of-an-exploding-star?fbclid=IwAR1VerKME4Ujlp7_piVTJ1s10fMxL8qPhdd8io84SCQikikUZIbTC0XM9Ls.

451 Nexstar Media Wire, June 3, 2020, https://fox4kc.com/news/stadium-sized-aster-oid-heading-to-earth-this-week/?fbclid=IwAR0wt5MYJ9SSwTrr3qyxAAE6_9zBdEPr6Vjn9wJGwnh631Ab-VslZnEIsPnw.

452 Alonso, Melissa and Croft, Jay, CNN, Oh, Great: NASA says an Asteroid is Headed Our Way Right Before Election Day. August 23, 2020. https://www.cnn.com/2020/08/22/us/asteroid-earth-november-2020-scn-trnd/in-dex.html?fbclid=IwAR2IiMYje8ndP01ens2Hd6Kk_vyCjMt5ahrEdLg1MeeLRyaziR-ZcTVmYHRM.

453 Stephens, Sally, Astronomical Society of the Pacific, A Primer on Asteroid Collisions with Earth. http://www.as.wvu.edu/~jel/skywatch/swfttle.html. Page 1.

454 Siegel, Ethan, The Comet That Created the Perseids Might Bring an End to Human-ity, Science: Forbes Magazine, https://www.forbes.com/sites/starts-withabang/2017/08/11/the-comet-that-created-the-perseids-might-bring-an-end-to-humanity/#2cca47ea2029. Pages 6-10.

455 Countdown to the Kingdom Website, Apparitions in Trevignano Romano, Giselle Cardia, https://www.countdowntothekingdom.com/why-gisella-carda/#messages.

456 Di Maria, La Lucia, The Mystic Post, Weeping Statue from Medjugorje … Italian cou-ple receive warnings and prophecies …June 3, 2020. (Translated from Italian). https://mysticpost.com/2020/06/weeping-statue-from-medjugorje-italian-couple-re-ceive-warnings-and-prophecies/. Page 4.

457 Duncan, Robert, Mary Foretold Covid-19 Pandemic, Alleged Visionary Claims. The Pilot, August 14, 2020, https://www.thebostonpilot.com/arti-cle.asp?ID=188215&utm_source=dlvr.it&utm_medium=twitter. Page 1.

458 Ibid. Page 2.

459 Countdown to the Kingdom Website, Apparitions in Trevignano Romano, Giselle Cardia, https://www.countdowntothekingdom.com/why-gisella-carda/#messages.

460 Cardia, Giselle, The Cross Will Soon Light the Sky, Originally posted on Countdown-tothekingdom.com, April 21, 2020. http://afterthewarning.com/messages-from-heaven/giselle-cardia/2020/july/10/the-cross-will-soon-light-the-sky. Pages 1-2.

461 Ibid.

462 Ibid.

463 Ibid.

464 Ibid.

465 Ibid.

466 Ibid.

467 Ibid.

468 Ibid.

469 Ibid.

470 Ibid.

471 Ibid.

472 Catholic Prophecy/God Spy, Mysticpost.com, September 26, 2020, https://mys-ticpost.com/?s=Mary%27s+message+of+September+22%2C+2020+to+Gisella+Car-dia%27s.

[473] Ibid.

[474] Gleeson, Andrew, Seattle's Summer of Love, Quillette Magazine, June 16, 2020. https://quillette.com/2020/06/16/seattles-summer-of-love/. Page 1.

[475] Editor, ChurchPop, BLM Activist Calls for Destruction of Jesus, Mary & Saint Statues, Priest & Exorcist Respond
June 23, 2020. https://churchpop.com/2020/06/23/blm-activist-calls-for-destruction-of-jesus-mary-statues-priest-exorcist-respond/?utm_campaign=ChurchPop&utm_medium=email&_hsmi=90123695&_hsenc=p2ANqtz-8idR4NB9ftdp2i27PSR1n1MlSNe8lf6BsiVCBGWzWmkNODqwTUfeKNW5lt3rn7HspN2P8HcWx5HF2SO2KcO_7t8XEUbqSQMFrmCCl9TjCGdqvPCOl&utm_content=90123695&utm_source=hs_email.

[476] Editor, ChurchPop, Cardinal Dolan Decries Statue Destruction, Warns Against Dangerous 'Cultural Revolution," July 2, 2020. https://mail.google.com/mail/u/0/#label/ChurchPOP/FMfcgxwJWhsnpkLsRhPfDcFLTMkwsKsq.

[477] Lisi, Clemente, Catholic Churches Vandalized: Where is the National Media, Religion Unplugged, July 22, 2020. https://religionunplugged.com/news/2020/7/23/catholic-churches-vandalized-wheres-the-national-press-coverage. Page 2.

[478] Ibid. Pages 2-3.

[479] National Catholic Register, Catholic News Agency, After Wave of Church Attacks, US Bishops Call for More Security Funding, October 6, 2020. https://www.catholicnewsagency.com/news/us-bishops-call-for-more-security-funding-after-wave-of-church-attacks-39952.

[480] Ibid.

[481] Richardson, Valerie, The Washington Times, Kamala Harris, Mazie Hirono Target Brian Buescher Knights of Columbus Membership. December 10, 2018 https://apnews.com/article/003d11bf795de6bcfbb5a6ada435944a.

[482] Ibid.

[483] Hadro, Matt, National Catholic Register, Miami Archbishop Wenski Blasts 'Handmaiden' Criticism of Amy Coney Barrett. October 8, 2020. https://www.ncregister.com/news/miami-archbishop-wenski-blasts-handmaiden-criticism-of-amy-coney-barrett. Pages 1-2.

[484] Ibid.

[485] Ibid.

[486] Ibid.

[487] CNA Staff, Catholic News Agency, 'Security Consultant' Linked to Vatican's Becciu Scandal Arrested. October 13, 2020. https://www.catholicnewsagency.com/news/security-consultant-linked-to-vaticans-becciu-scandal-arrested-62265. Pages 1-2.

[488] CNA Staff, Catholic News Agency, New Orleans Archbishop: Priest's desecration of Altar 'Demonic'. October 9, 2020, https://www.catholicnewsagency.com/news/archbishop-aymond-new-orleans-priests-desecration-of-altar-demonic-29763. Page 1.

[489] Ibid.

[490] Ibid. Page 2.

[491] Ibid.

[492] Lang, Nico, Ex-Pope Says Gay Marriage Will Bring About the End of the World, May 4, 2020. https://www.them.us/story/pope-benedict-says-gay-marriage-will-bring-about-the-end-of-the-world?fbclid=IwAR1lydLqogE1PZsPOek8fnnNgzGccv9cyexrzaAhabpr-Mecw21BMIwQmc. Page 1.

[493] Bemowski, Vincent T., The Messages to the Churches, Part II of the Booklet Is To-day's (Catholic) Church Pleasing to God? And The Tribulation (Great Chastisement). https://m.catholicmessagesusa.com/GRAVE-MESSAGES.html. Page 2.

[494] Matter of Engel v. Vitale, Appellate Division of the Supreme Court of New York, Second Department, 11 A.D.2d 340 (N.Y. App. Div. 1960), https://caset-ext.com/case/matter-of-engel-v-vitale-4.

[495] Engel Et Al. v. Vitale Et Al. Issue: First Amendment – Establishment of Religion (other than pertains to parochiaid:) http://supreme-court-cases.in-sidegov.com/l/1875/Engel-Et-Al-v-Vitale-Et-Al.

[496] Quote Investigator: Tracing Quotations, https://quoteinvestiga-tor.com/2010/12/04/good-men-do/.

[497] Bailey, Sarah Pulliam and Boorstein, Michelle, I find it baffling and reprehensible': Catholic archbishop of Washington slams Trump's visit to John Paul II shrine, The Washington Post, June 2, 2020. https://www.washingtonpost.com/reli-gion/2020/06/02/trump-catholic-shrine-church-bible-protesters/.

[498] ChurchPop, Editor, Apb. Vigano Warns Pres. Trump of Spiritual Battle Waging Be-tween Good and Evil in Open Letter, June 8, 2020.

[499] Fulton Sheen Institute, Conference with Dr. Peter Howard and Fr. Richard Heilman. Presented via Zoom and broadcast via YouTube, October 7, 2020. https://www.youtube.com/watch?v=pOsp5zwzuCk&feature=youtu.be.

[500] The Original Pieta Prayer Book, Large Print Edition. Why Pray the Daily Rosary? MLOR Corp, Page 41.

[501] Ibid.

[502] Ibid.

[503] The Original Pieta Prayer Book, Large Print Edition. The Fifteen Promises of Mary to Christians Who Recite the Rosary, MLOR Corp, Page 42.

[504] Ibid.

[505] Ibid.

[506] Gensens, Joseph, Return to Order, A Crisis Brings Out the Worst and the Best in People. April 4, 2020. https://www.returntoorder.org/2020/04/a-crisis-brings-out-the-worst-and-the-best-in-people/?pkg=rtoe0942. Page 3.

[507] Alar, Father Chris, Explaining the Faith: Catholic View of End Times, Part 1 of 3, Na-tional Shrine of Divine Mercy Livestream, July 25, 2020.

About the Author

 Paul F. Caranci is a third-generation resident of North Providence and has been a student of history for many years. Paul served as Rhode Island's Deputy Secretary of State from 2007 to 2015 and was elected to the North Providence Town Council where he served from 1994 to 2010. He has a BA in political science from Providence College and is working toward an MPA from Roger Williams University.

Together with his wife Margie he founded the Municipal Heritage Group in 2009. He is an incorporating member of the Association of Rhode Island Authors (ARIA) and a member of the board of the RI Publications Society. He also served on the Board of Directors of the Heritage Harbor Museum and the Rhode Island Heritage Hall of Fame. He is past Chairman of the Diabetes Foundation of Rhode Island (formerly the American Diabetes Association, Rhode Island Affiliate) where he served on the Board for over 15 years.

During his tenure on the North Providence Town Council Paul's efforts earned him several awards. For his legislative work in the prevention of youth addiction to tobacco Paul was recognized with the James Carney Public Health Award from the RI Department of Health and an Advocacy Award from the American Cancer Society. Paul's legislation to expand health care coverage to include the equipment, supplies and education necessary for the home management of diabetes and his work toward the elimination of the pre-existing condition clause from health insurance policies written in Rhode Island were recognized with an Advocate of the Year Award from the Diabetes Foundation of RI and an Advocacy Award from the American Diabetes Association. Those new laws also made Rhode Island the first state in the nation to both eliminate the pre-existing condition clause and expand coverage for diabetes care. His efforts in exposing political corruption in his hometown earned him the Margaret Chase Smith Award for Political Courage from the National Association of Secretaries of State, the group's highest honor.

Paul is the author of eleven published books including four award winning books. *The Hanging & Redemption of John Gordon: The True Story of Rhode Island's Last Execution* (The History Press, 2013) was voted one of the top five nonfiction books of 2013 by the Providence Journal. *Scoundrels: Defining Corruption Through Tales of Political Intrigue in Rhode Island* (Stillwater River Publications, 2016) was the winner of the 2016 Dorry Award as the non-fiction book of the year. *The Promise of Fatima: One Hundred Years of History, Mystery, and Faith* (Stillwater River Publications, 2017) earned Paul a spot as a finalist in the International Book Awards, and *I Am The Immaculate Conception: The Story of Bernadette of Lourdes*, (Stillwater River Publications, 2019) landed Paul the same honor. Paul's memoir, *Wired: A Shocking True Story of Political Corruption and the FBI Informant Who Risked Everything to Expose It* (Stillwater River Publications, 2017) tells his own story of courage in the face of the political corruption that surrounded him.

Paul and his wife Margie recently celebrated their 43rd wedding anniversary. The couple have two adult children, Heather and Matthew; and four grandchildren, Matthew, Jacob, Vincent and Casey. They continue to make residence in the Town of North Providence.

Also By the Author

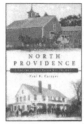

The History Press
2012

The History Press
2012
Named one of top 5
non-fiction books
of the year

Stillwater River Publications
2014

Stillwater River Publications
2014

Stillwater River Publications
2015

Stillwater River Publications
2016
Dorry Award
Non-fiction Book

Stillwater River Publications
2017

Stillwater River Publications
2017
Finalist in the 2018
International Book
Awards of the Year

Stillwater River Publications
2019
Finalist in the 2019
International Book Awards

Stillwater River Publications
2019

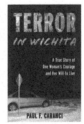

Stillwater River Publications
2020

ORDER FORM

Please use the following to order additional copies of:

1. Heavenly Portrait: The Miraculous Image of Our Lady of Guadalupe **($20.00)**
2. I Am the Immaculate Conception: The Story of St. Bernadette And Her Apparitions At Lourdes **($20.00)**
3. The Promise of Fatima: One Hundred Years of History, Mystery & Faith **($20.00)**
4. Terror in Wichita: A True Story of One Woman's Courage and Her Will to Live **($12.95)**
5. Wired: A Shocking True Story of Political Corruption and the FBI Informant Who Risked Everything to Expose It **($23.00)**
6. Scoundrels: Defining Political Corruption Through Tales of Political Intrigue in Rhode Island **($20.00)**
7. Monumental Providence: Legends of History in Sculpture, Statuary, Monuments and Memorials **($20.00)**
8. The Essential Guide to Running for Local Office **($15.00)**
9. The Hanging & Redemption of John Gordon: The True Story of Rhode Island's Last Execution **($20.00)**
10. North Providence: A History & The People Who Shaped It **($20.00)**
11. Award Winning Real Estate in a Depressed or Declining Market **($10.00)**

___ (QTY) _____(Title) X ____ (Price) = $ _____

___ (QTY) _____(Title) X ____ (Price) = $ _____

___ (QTY) _____(Title) X ____ (Price) = $ _____

___ (QTY) _____(Title) X ____ (Price) = $ _____

___ (QTY) _____(Title) X ____ (Price) = $ _____

Total for books $_____ + Postage** $_____ = **TOTAL COST** $_____

**Postage: Please add $3.00 for the first book and $1.50 for each additional book ordered.

Payment Method:

___ Personal Check Enclosed (Payable to **M. Caranci Books**)

___ Charge my Credit Card

        Name:_____ BILLING ZIP CODE:_____

        Visa____ Master Card_____

        Card Number:_____ EXP:___/__CSC (3 digit code) ____

        Signature:_____

(Order form continues on next page)

(Order form continues on next page)

Ship My Book To:

Name _____

Street _____

City_____State:_____Zip:_____

Phone _____Email:_____

Special Signing Instructions: IE To Whom do you want the book signed? Do you want me to include a message? Just sign my name? Etc.

_____

_____

MAIL YOUR COMPLETED FORM TO:

Paul F. Caranci

26 East Avenue

North Providence, RI 02911

You may also order using my Email address at municipalheritage@gmail.com

or by calling me at 401-639-4502

Please visit my Website at www.paulcaranci.com